Stories of Globalization

Stories of Globalization

Transnational Corporations,
Resistance, and the State

Alessandro Bonanno
and Douglas H. Constance

The Pennsylvania State University Press
University Park, Pennsylvania

Library of Congress Cataloging-in-Publication Data

Bonanno, Alessandro.
    Stories of globalization : transnational corporations, resistance, and the state /
Alessandro Bonanno and Douglas H. Constance.
        p.   cm. — (Rural studies series)
Includes bibliographical references and index.
Summary: "Analyses transnational corporations, groups who resist them, and the
primary context within which the relationship between transnational corporations
and their opponents unfold: the state. Argues that globalization is a contested
terrain in which the power of transnational corporations is affected by mounting
opposition and internal contradictions"—Provided by publisher.
ISBN 978-0-271-03388-4 (cloth : alk. paper)
1. International business enterprises—Case studies.
2. International economic integration—Case studies.
3. Globalization—Case studies.
I. Constance, Douglas.
II. Title.

HD2755.5.B656 2008
338.8'8—dc22
                    2008024500

The Pennsylvania State University Press is a member of the Association of American
University Presses.

It is the policy of The Pennsylvania State University Press to use acid-free paper. This
book is printed on Natures Natural, containing 50% post-consumer waste, and meets
the minimum requirements of American National Standard for Information
Sciences—Permanence of Paper for Printed Library Material, ANSI Z39.48-1992.

CONTENTS

PREFACE

This book has two objectives. The first is to present salient aspects of globalization in a way that is accessible to readers who are not necessarily familiar
with this subject. We wanted to write a book that was both scientifically
sound and also accessible to those who are not necessarily experts in globalization studies. Our decision does not imply that this manuscript cannot
appeal to more experienced scholars. We believe that the wealth of empirical
data and the analysis and narrative presented in the text offer relevant insights to those who have been following the social science debate on globalization closely. Our second objective is to provide a general view of
globalization by presenting eight specific cases—our "stories of globalization." In the social sciences, this is known as a "case-study approach."
Knowledge of a particular scientific topic is established through in-depth
analysis of one or more case studies.

In the case of globalization, most of the knowledge currently available
has been generated through the use of macroanalyses based on quantitative
aggregate data, and/or microinvestigations based on a single case study.
Generally grounded in sociohistorical frameworks, these pieces of research
have engendered a rich debate on the crisis of established socioeconomic
and cultural arrangements and the emergence of new ones. In spite of their
many positive contributions, however, these studies have not been immune
to criticism. Macroquantitative analyses have often been attacked for their
inability to analyze the social, historical, cultural, and geographical particu-
larities of globalization, and for their tendency to dissolve heterogeneous
experiences and conditions into far-reaching generalizations. Simultaneously, microanalyses have been criticized for generalizing specific cases to
other settings and to society as a whole. In effect, the most common objection to qualitative microanalyses has been to their assumed limited capacity
to extrapolate general tendencies from circumscribed observations.

While the limits of these macro- and microstudies are well known and
have been addressed through a wealth of epistemological arguments, alternative approaches have infrequently been sought. Diverging from this ten-

dency, this book employs an alternative qualitative approach that analyzes globalization through a collection of case studies. Our plan is to use these case studies to analyze selected aspects of globalization, and through them to offer pertinent generalizations. To be sure, this multiple-case-study approach has been employed in the past, but in edited books that featured contributions from a number of different authors. This book is different because it examines cases that we have researched and written ourselves; and it is the culmination of our long collaboration in the study of globalization.

This collaboration began with the study of transnational corporations' use of hypermobility to avoid local environmental and food safety laws and continued with cases that shed light on the power and limits of transnational corporations, the role and changing nature of the nation-state, the resistance of local and translocal groups to global forces, the implications of these phenomena for the future of society, and other topics debated in the globalization literature. We have focused on the agriculture and food sector, arguably one of the most globalized sectors in contemporary society. While originally designed as self-contained studies—and many of them have been published previously as journal articles[1]—these cases have been reorganized, updated, and rewritten to provide a fresh source of information qualitatively different from the simple sum of the individual research projects.

Alessandro Bonanno and Douglas H. Constance

1. Following is a list of the articles that we published as a result of the research presented in this book. By Alessandro Bonanno and Douglas H. Constance: "Corporations and the State in the Global Era: The Case of Seaboard Farms and Texas," *Rural Sociology* 71 (1) (2006): 59–84; "Corporate Strategies in the Global Era: Mega-Hog Farms in the Texas Panhandle Region," *International Journal of Sociology of Agriculture and Food* 9 (1) (2001): 5–28; "Global Agri-Food Sector and the Case of the Tuna Industry: Global Regulation and Perspectives for Development," *Journal of Developing Societies* 14 (1) (1998): 100–126. By Alessandro Bonanno, Douglas H. Constance, and Heather Lorenz: "Powers and Limits of Transnational Corporations: The Case of ADM," *Rural Sociology* 65 (3) (2000): 440–60. By Alessandro Bonanno, Douglas H. Constance, and Mary Hendrickson: "Global Agro-Food Corporations and the State: The Ferruzzi Case," *Rural Sociology* 60 (2) (1995): 274–96. By Douglas H. Constance and Alessandro Bonanno: "Regulating the Global Fisheries: The World Wildlife Fund, Unilever, and the Marine Stewardship Council," *Agriculture and Human Values* 17 (2) (2000): 125–39; "From 'Dolphin-Safe' Tuna to the Marine Stewardship Council: Eco-Coordination of the Global Fisheries," *Rural Sociology* 64 (4) (1999): 597–623. By Douglas H. Constance, Alessandro Bonanno, Caron Cates, Daniel Argo, and Mirenda Harris: "Resisting Integration in the Global Agro-food System: Corporate Chickens and Community Controversy in Texas," in *Globalisation, Localisation, and Sustainable Livelihoods,* ed. Reidar Almas and Geoffrey Lawrence (Burlington, Vt.: Ashgate Press, 2003), 103–18.

INTRODUCTION

In recent years globalization has been a buzzword and an issue that has been approached from a variety of viewpoints. Within sociology, it has attracted the attention of those interested in the development of a global culture (e.g., Featherstone 1990), the emergence of a global social integration and homogenization (e.g., Robertson 1992), the creation of greater interdependence and mutual awareness (e.g., Guillen 2001), the creation of global institutions and networks (e.g., Castells 1995; Sassen 2000), global rationalization (Ritzer 1998 and 2004), local resistance to global processes (Barber 1995), and the multifaceted, complex, and dialectical nature of global social relations (Kellner 2002). While acknowledging the significance of these aspects of globalization, we focus in this volume on another important facet of this theme: the globalization of economy and society. Like many of the works placed under the substantive category "economy and society," this book investigates issues pertaining to changes in the economy and their effects on the organization and functioning of society, and specifically on globalization's consequences for democracy.

The agrifood sector is the substantive area from which the data analyzed in this volume are derived. There are a number of reasons for this choice. First, agrifood is one of the most globalized sectors in the contemporary economy. As demonstrated by the now copious literature on commodity chains (i.e., Friedland 1991 and 1994b) and on corporate concentration (i.e., Heffernan 2000 and 1984), the production and consumption of agrifood products are a truly global affair. Second, the globalized dimension of the agrifood sector is not relevant simply in quantitative terms but represents a context in which the interlinked dimensions of globalization are clearly visible. Globalization-centered phenomena such as the emergence of global trade and financial liberalization regimes, capital-intensive technological changes and their "science"-based support, state-sponsored deregulation and re-regulation, cross-national labor flows, and a global consumption culture can be more clearly detected and analyzed in this context. And we believe that clarity is enhanced by the use of a case-study methodology that generates a rich combination of methodology and substantive area of investigation. This is a unique feature in the current scientific panorama. Indeed, the use of a methodology based on a number of case studies allows us to explore general patterns and at the same time to uncover the rich details that characterize each of the cases investigated. Finally, the study of the agrifood sector is particularly interesting because, although it is one of the most globalized sectors of the economy, its "local" importance is considered paramount for the well-being of communities in North America and other parts of the world. Arguably, the local-global link is much more visible in agrifood than in a number of other socioeconomic sectors.

From an economic and social point of view, a first step to be taken in the study of globalization is the identification of salient actors involved in the process and the sociohistorical contexts within which they operate. For this book, we selected three key protagonists of globalization: transnational corporations (TNCS), groups who resist them, and the state, which constitutes the primary mechanism through which the relationship between TNCS and their opponents unfolds. The state is typically seen in terms of its relationship with corporations and those who resist them, but also in terms of the emergence of new transnational forms of the state and alternative entities that have been taking over some of the historical roles of the state (i.e., nongovernmental organizations, or NGOs). We maintain that globalization is both a political project—a more or less orchestrated design to enhance the free mobility of capital worldwide—and a historical phenomenon characterized by the implementation of this political project and the resistance that it engenders. We further define globalization as the complex process of the transnationalization of social relations centered around the establishment of conditions that favor, and are characterized by, the growth of TNCS, free-market-oriented policies that promote their growth, and the multifaceted resistance that the expansion of TNCS generates. These events are contextualized in a sociohistorical milieu that features the development of significant new technologies, the emergence of new cultural traits, changes in political structures, systems, and equilibria that lead to the overall compression, but also the reorganization, of time and space: the world is smaller, and our everyday actions tend to be more and more affected by actors and events that are distant from us.

It is not our objective to provide an exhaustive analysis of the globalization of economy and society, but we propose to study salient actors and selected components of this extremely complex process. It is on these three broadly defined actors—TNCs, groups that resist them, and the state—that we focus our analytical attention. We also aim to present our analysis in a manner that is accessible to readers who are not necessarily familiar with the themes most often associated with globalization. This is a volume written not exclusively for experts but also for those who are interested in theoretical and empirical aspects of globalization.

Departing from views of globalization as the continuation of international relations established centuries ago—see the review of the works of authors such as Arrighi (2005 and 1998), Chase-Dunn (1998), Wallerstein (2005), and Friedland (1994b) in Chapter 1—we take the position that globalization is qualitatively different from earlier forms of world-based social relations. We distinguish between international social relations and globalization. International social relations—or relations among nations—are those centered on the evolution of the nation-state and its capacity to forge a more or less unified national identity and culture while promoting and controlling the flow of resources and processes necessary for the development of society. For the past four centuries, the creation of capitalist market economies, social classes, polities, and institutions revolved around the establishment and growth of nation-states. The development of the nation-state allowed the simultaneous existence of domestic markets and societies and relations among these nationally based markets and societies. This international system evolved through its colonial and multinational phases. The latter represented the extension of the influence of single developed nation-states over less developed and/or dependent nation-states. In relative terms and with significant contradictions, it allowed nationally based modes of regulation and control of the unwanted consequences of the expansion of capitalism (Habermas 2002; Harvey 1989).

Globalization represents a break from this long-established pattern through the creation of new flows of resources and processes that not only transcend the nation-state but reorganize the spatial and temporal dimensions of social action in ways that do not match established geosocial barriers. Peter Dicken (1998, 5) aptly states, "globalization processes are *qualitatively* different from internationalization processes. They involve not merely the geographical extension of economic activities across national boundaries but also—and more importantly—the *functional integration* of such international dispersed activities." Accordingly, globalization marks a qualitative departure from established patterns in mature capitalism. While we agree with those who stress that this qualitative global shift is grounded in past events and does not transcend capitalism as the dominant economic system worldwide, we also concur with those who emphasize that the alteration of socioeconomic arrangements created by globalization is so profound that established analytical categories have become increasingly obsolete and therefore inadequate to capture the features of current conditions (e.g., Giddens 1990, 63–65; McMichael 2002).

In particular, and following Harvey (1989), we contend that the time-space compression that characterizes globalization has reorganized the forms through which capital is accumulated, the manners through which this capital accumulation is justified to subordinate groups, and the ways in which it is resisted. This reorganization of time and space has altered the parameters that characterized the development of capitalism during most of the twentieth century and established a qualitatively different form of capitalism. Global production and consumption are now largely organized through global networks, and governance and resistance are carried out in temporal and spatial dimensions that are qualitatively different from those of only a few decades ago. In essence, we contend that established social relations have disintegrated, and that a new reintegration, connecting and reconnecting parts of society in novel temporal and spatial forms, represents a significant qualitative change from the recent past.

Our approach further identifies the origins of globalization in the crisis of Fordism, the socioeconomic form of capitalism that emerged in the early twentieth century and reached its peak in the first two decades after World War II. Fordism—like globalization—does not refer simply to a system of organization of production. Following Gramsci's classical definition, we maintain that Fordism refers to a highly rationalized form of capitalism characterized by mass production, mass consumption, and vertical integration, but also to a new culture and, equally important, new political arrangements. Because it was not simply a production system, its effects and visibility were unevenly distributed across societies and groups, and were resisted by those ruling classes whose privileges were threatened by the Fordist rationalization (Gramsci 1973, 418, 443). We also see this form of advanced capitalism as a programmed economy clearly different from the previous system based on economic individualism (ibid., 403). The previous system consisted of socioeconomic arrangements based on the concomitant existence of declining precapitalist elements and laissez-faire capitalism supported by the ideology of unchecked individualism. The crisis of this pre-Fordist phase of capitalism centered on declining rates of profit (economic crises) and subordinate classes' mounting opposition.

In the global North in the two decades after World War II, strategies of the much larger, interventionist state successfully sustained steady growth, balancing mass production and mass consumption, while private companies generated very high levels of productivity by refining widely instituted Taylorist strategies. Managers substantially enhanced their technical control by further centralizing and rationalizing the labor process. While this strategy sharpened the distinction between production workers and managerial, professional, and technical employees, the labor force was pacified by steadily increasing wages, job security, opportunity for advancement, and expanding welfare (Harvey 1989; Lipietz 1992).

This Fordist capitalism combined highly rationalized, centralized, and vertically integrated firms with nationwide unions and a substantially expanded state; it had highly specialized and mechanized production, bureaucratized firms, extensive planning, and top-to-bottom bureaucratic control. "High Fordism" is the term that defines post–World War II capitalism, or the mature, hyperrationalized type of Fordism (Antonio and Bonanno 1996). It had an elaborately segmented labor force, a very large and complex body of professional, managerial, and technical employees, and extremely sophisticated means of information, communication, transportation, and control. Despite significant differences across economic sectors and geographical regions, processes centered on high levels of state intervention, and the inclusion of labor and subordinate groups in the managing of society, characterized this period. The high Fordist state employed advanced Keynesian policies of much broader fiscal controls, socioeconomic plans regulation, and health, education, and welfare.

High Fordism enhanced the inclusion of marginalized people, raised the social wage substantially, and, in the social democracies, sharply increased labor participation. In the United States and other advanced countries, unions enrolled historically high percentages of workers, and wage/benefit packages increased sharply (Aglietta 1979; Chandler 1977; Gordon, Edwards, and Reich 1982; Habermas 2002; Harrison and Bluestone 1988; Lipietz 1987 and 1992). Overall, high Fordism coordinated mass production and mass consumption, steady accumulation, and legitimacy, and produced historically unparalleled economic growth and abundance. The tacit capital-labor accord left control over production to management, but labor's role in political discourse, policymaking, planning, and legislation increased. The middle class grew substantially and enjoyed a sharply increased standard of living. Under high Fordism, civil, political, and social rights were expanded, and regulatory legislation was increased. Equal opportunity was advanced, though the lowest strata benefited little, and sharp inequalities between the primary and secondary sectors, production workers and professional employees, and between races, ethnic groups, and genders were primary features of the Fordist pattern of rationalization and bureaucratization.[1]

Fordism reached its most advanced and efficient form from the mid-1950s to the late 1960s. But in the early 1970s the regime entered a period of crisis that exposed its most serious contradictions and eventually led to its demise (Aglietta 1979; Harvey 1989). In the advanced North, the rise of new social movements, student protest, and countercultural activities began to erode the Fordist stability. Internationally, a number of Third World–based movements challenged U.S.-led modernization projects, rejected acquiescence in Western economic interests, and demanded full integration into affluent mature capitalism. This surge resulted in further destabilization of the Fordist equilibrium. Economic downturns accelerated high Fordism's instability. Increasingly competitive international markets, increased costs of social welfare, and other factors began a new, downward phase of postwar capitalism. The oil crisis, severe recession in 1973, the end of the Bretton Woods concord, and stagflation signified a possible decomposition of U.S.-centered multinational capitalism. Harrison and Bluestone (1988) refer to this period as the beginning of the "Great U-Turn" in world capitalism: a shift to low-wage, part-time jobs and disintegration of the postwar capital-labor accord. In the late 1970s and early 1980s, Thatcherism and Reaganism marked a decisive shift to low inflation/high unemployment (and underemployment) policies (Strobel 1993; Harrison and Bluestone 1988; Bowles and Gintis 1982). The basic features of state-coordinated Fordism began to be viewed as the source of crippling *rigidities* that contributed to the growing crisis of capital accumulation. Heightened global competition and the political and economic crises mentioned above brought new strategies aimed at reducing

---

1. Fordism did not simply characterize developed countries but was employed in developing nations as well. During the post–WWII years, state intervention in the economies and societies of less advanced nations was arguably one of the most relevant developmental tools employed by local leadership and promoted by international organizations. As illustrated by Peter Evans (1995), effective state intervention determined the success or failure of development projects. While Evans imposes specific conditions on the success of state intervention—for example, state actions must be embedded in the cultural and social networks that constitute a nation—he clearly demonstrates its importance in patterns of socioeconomic growth in the second half of the twentieth century. As we argue below, globalization altered this "developmental" role of the state.

inflation by slowing growth, weakening the power of organized labor, tolerating higher unemployment, and slashing the social wage (e.g., Aglietta 1979; Gordon, Edwards, and Reich 1982; Harrison and Bluestone 1988; Lipietz 1992; Piore and Sable 1984). State interventionist policies that earlier had been envisioned as chief motor forces of postwar growth were now treated as causes of the economic contraction. Critics held that the capital-labor accord produced a crippling profit squeeze that endangered capitalism and that a substantial part of the high Fordist institutional and ideological complex ought to be dismantled (Lipietz 1992; Harvey 1989). Most important, many of the core Fordist policies that expanded opportunity and rights were made prime targets of strategies aimed at increasing the freedom of property holders at the expense of wage workers and subaltern strata and distributing wealth and power upward (Harvey 1989).

The new conditions that have emerged from the crisis of Fordism have been grouped under the concept of globalization. The globalization of economy and society entailed a number of strategies to revive capital accumulation. McMichael (2002) refers to this process as the "globalization project." From a socioeconomic view point, globalization's most decisive aspect has been increased "flexibility" on a global scale—mobile capital, free to colonize and commodify practically every sphere, has shattered relatively fixed social and temporal-spatial boundaries and has decentralized production. Production is to a much greater extent—but not exclusively—decomposed into subunits and subproduction processes, carried out by globally dispersed firms with highly divergent forms of labor, managerial, and financial organizations that may even follow traditional and local business practices and customs. More important, global companies are able to select strategies that fit their interests with an unprecedented—although not total—freedom. This freedom is the primary result of the implementation of free market policies, reduced forms of regulation, favorable economic incentives, and an overall cultural climate that welcomes corporate mobility and autonomy. Public enterprises were privatized, and the availability of vital services became increasingly associated with the capacity to pay and/or overall profitability. Nation-states and their regional counterparts—once the motor forces of the regulation and control of undesirable consequences of capitalism—actively contributed to the elimination of rules and regulations that hampered the free mobility of capital (deregulation). They effectively engineered the opening of their economies and the creation of conditions amenable to corporate interests but often averse to labor, communities, and environmental well-being (re-regulation).

These structural changes were justified by the adoption of neoliberalism as the guiding political ideology of globalization. Introduced as the necessary antidote to the agonizing Keynesianism and its ideological justification for state intervention in the economic and the social spheres, neoliberalism stressed the inevitable nature of deregulation and marketization of social relations and the overwhelming positive effects that they generate for all components of society.[2] While the virtue of the "free" functioning of the market had been proposed in the past, neoliberal theorists argued that new technological developments (i.e., computers and the Internet) and global political conditions (the end of the cold war) had created a situation in which past obstacles to the realization of "true free market and society" were eliminated and no serious alternatives to neoliberalism and corporate capitalism could be imagined (Friedman 2000; Fukuyama 1992; Smith 2007).

This globalization is not easy to map, but is not aleatory or "disorganized" (Lash and Urry 1987; Offe 1985). The new "flexible" structures serve financial rationalization, concentrating resources, bypassing obstacles, locating more efficient forms of production, hedging against possible economic shifts, and taking advantage of new financial and tax instruments. Decentralized production goes hand in hand with more highly centralized control of finance, research, and information. Globalization "economic development" and free trade policies use the state itself to enhance capital mobility, erode its own local, regional, and national regulatory instruments, and reduce labor's bargaining power and influence. Rather than the end of the nation-state, as often suggested, globalization has been characterized by strong state action in opening up domestic markets, deregulating production and consumption processes, and eroding state intervention in social services (Sassen 2000).

---

2. Charles F. Sabel and his associates (Piore and Sabel 1984; Sabel and Zeitlin 2002; Sabel 2004) stress that globalization's flexible forms of production can encourage socioeconomic development. They argue that innovations in new computer-driven machinery fit small-batch production and are affordable for small entrepreneurs. In some specific regions, such as central Italy—or "Third Italy"—the new technologies have been deployed in revived craft industries and new enterprises with relaxed workplace hierarchies, highly skilled workforces, ample opportunities for workers to become capitalists, and flexible labor processes that adjust more rapidly to changes in consumer tastes and are adept at customizing goods for niche markets. The Third Italy thesis holds that this new industrial system averted the costs and inefficiencies of managerial and union bureaucracy and provided satisfying work and good pay and benefits. It also contends that these changes built on the region's preexisting culture of cooperation, trust, and social benefits, reflected in its socialist tradition, and propelled it from being one of Italy's poorer regions to its richest. In the view of Sabel et al., "flexible specialization" breaks with Fordism's mass production and standardized mass consumption and has the potential to be applied on a much wider scale. They argue that it can forge a more democratic form of capitalism that balances individual and collective needs.

To be sure, these changes should not be interpreted as the results of the emergence of a fully globalized system in which the local territorial dimension is irrelevant (Hirst and Thompson 1996). On the contrary, globalization is a system that allows TNCs to be mobile and to take advantage of qualitatively new instruments that are employed to avoid perceived rigidities in the economy and society. Indeed, local consumption and labor markets are viewed as resources that can be included in or excluded from global circuits in accordance with corporations' needs. Simultaneously, localities are viewed as social relations that are capable of opposing, as well as favoring, TNCs' strategies. Globalization is not a globalized system; it is a system of global mobility and global actions that operates in reaction to conditions that manifest themselves in local and regional enclaves. More specifically, globalization is a project to revive capital accumulation and thereby counter many of the successes of democratic social movements that limited the ability of corporations to maintain profitable business operations.

The reversal from record postwar growth produced a pervasive sense that postwar structures of accumulation had failed and that social policy needed to be changed quickly. Globalization's efforts to reignite growth weakened or eliminated postwar mechanisms aimed at increasing equal opportunity, providing for the unemployed and needy, and blocking the colonization of valued noneconomic environments by capital. Rather than equal rights and enhanced democracy, the costs of regulation and their need to increase discipline and security are emphasized.

Despite its appeal and support, the globalization project has stimulated resistance. This has appeared in the form of organized action by established political and economic organizations such as political parties and unions. Because many of the traditional forms and actors through which resistance was carried out during the Fordist era have been weakened, however, its most salient form has been grassroots-based resistance that emerged "from below." The creation of the "antiglobalization" movement, with its multicultural and multifaceted membership and its network-based, flexible organization, symbolizes this type of resistance. The case studies presented in the following pages illustrate some instances of this type of resistance and highlight the different ways in which they originated. The common ground remains a decisive opposition to transnational designs in the context of diminishing "spaces" for substantive participation in decision-making processes. Resistance makes up the other side of the contested terrain of globalization. The strong, and often victorious, agenda of global forces and their allies is continuously contested by old and new opposition that shows resilience despite setbacks and, in some important cases, downright defeat. In other words, efforts on the part of the supporters of globalization to restructure the global political economy along neoliberal lines and thereby revive capital accumulation are consistently deemed unacceptable and illegitimate by a growing antiglobalization resistance movement.

Several additional key points should be stressed to highlight central features of globalization. First, the free mobility and global extension of capital render permeable a great number of spatial-temporal, political, and social "borders" that once constrained capital, creating new vulnerabilities for the well-being and identities of individuals and national, regional, and local communities. Despite the importance of local resources and groups, the free mobility of capital qualitatively altered established social, political, and economic relations. Many of the cases presented in the text are examples of this *hypermobility of capital* (Harvey 1989) and the power that it generates for corporate actors, but also of the resistance that it engenders. Hypermobility of capital is a concept that refers to the reduction and/or elimination of spatial and temporal barriers to the circulation and reproduction of capital. The spatial dimension of hypermobility refers to the reconfiguration of space engendered by globalization such as the decentralization of production, the creation of global commodity production and distribution chains, and the establishment of "larger" market zones—the European Union, NAFTA, Mercosur, and so on. In this case, "local" social relations are bypassed and therefore altered by new global ones. The temporal dimension refers to compression of the time necessary for the reproduction of capital. While a significant aspect of this compression of time is associated with technological advancements—for example, the development of computers that accelerate production, consumption, and transfer of resource processes—a relevant portion is social and political in nature and refers to the introduction of measures that quicken the mechanisms through which money is transformed into commodities and subsequently retransformed into money. These measures include control of labor, trade legislation, and production regulation. An important component of the hypermobility of capital is *global sourcing* (McMichael 2002). This is the enhanced ability of TNCs to search for the most convenient factors of production across the globe. Often associated with less expensive labor and natural resources, global sourcing also refers to the search for better business, political, and social climates that would place corporations at an advantage over competitors.

Second, the spatial-temporal unity of the polity and the economy that characterized the earlier phases of capitalist development has been fractured.[3] In previous phases of capitalism—from the early competitive phase to the most recent monopolistic phase—the growth of economic relations was centered on the existence of nation-states whose polities (the state) coordinated and mediated activities of economic actors. Since its inception, capitalism has mandated a political system that coordinated and assisted capital accumulation, while controlling opposition and legitimating capitalist social relations (Arrighi 1998; Habermas 2002; Holloway 1993). This aspect of capitalism allowed the emergence of earlier quasi–nation-state forms of the state, such as the city-states of Venice and Genoa, regional states like Holland, and later the establishment of nation-states such as Great Britain, France, and Spain. Under capitalism, the nation-state became the most common form of the state. With the expansion of capitalism, it evolved into the multinational form of the state, which refers to the existence of a host of nation-states that expanded their influence over a number of legally independent, but economically and politically subordinated, nation-states. Under these historical forms of the state, a spatial and temporal unity between the economy and the polity was maintained whereby the state was able to coordinate and mediate activities of economic actors who operated within its territory. These conditions also created identification between firms and nations that marked the historical expansion of capitalism in the nineteenth and twentieth centuries. Under globalization, these conditions have been altered. The nation-state's capacity to mediate between the market and society has been weakened, and the nation-state is increasingly unable to control the flow of economic resources according to the rules established through democratic processes (Habermas 2002; Harvey 1989). As indicated above, this situation should not be interpreted simply to signify that the state has been generally weakened and will disappear. It shows, conversely, that globalization has reduced the nation-state's control over its economic and noneconomic environments when these forms of control clash with corporate interests and those of the groups that support them (Sklair 2001). Simultaneously, to support capital accumulation many nation-states

---

3. Gavin Kitching (2001) makes a similar point, stressing the structural evolution of the economy. He argues that a fundamental problem of globalization is the coexistence of globalizing economic relations and older forms of political organization centered on the nation-state. Differing from what we argue in these pages, Kitching maintains that this contradiction affects primarily the sphere of money and the behavior of corporations. The lack of a global regulatory actor—that is, an actor that can perform the nation-state's regulatory role at the global level—fosters conditions that favor less scrupulous corporations. Motivated to gain short-term profits, corporations are pushed to search globally for more convenient factors of production with limited regard for the well-being of the people and environments involved.

have increased their control over a number of domestic spheres through surveillance and other forms of social control, while deliberately opening up their economies and societies to global flows (Kitching 2001; McMichael 2002; Sassen 2000). While some have interpreted these facets of globalization as necessary conditions for social and economic growth (Friedman 2000), others associate them with the shrinking of the social state and the expansion of the procapitalist state (McMichael 2002).

Third, the fracture of the spatiotemporal unity between the polity and the economy also affects the functioning of democracy. In early phases of capitalism liberal democracy emerged as one of the most relevant political expressions of national capitalism. Bourgeois ideology, centered on individual rights and freedoms, created the framework for constitutional democracy in independent nation-states (Dewey 1935/1963). Later in the Fordist phase, the struggles of political and social movements and the expansion of forces of production converged for the creation of a more inclusive and participatory form of democracy. Despite contradictions and overt abuses, democratic principles became entrenched in the cultural climate of advanced societies (Sandel 1996). The nation-state remained a class state, yet claims from subordinated classes were incorporated into the functioning of many nation-states, which allowed for the augmentation of substantive democracy (Habermas 1975). Under globalization, because the nation-state is increasingly unable to control economic and noneconomic environments, the directions that it receives from its citizens cannot be fully implemented as assumed by modern theories of democracy and as practiced in past decades. In this context, past levels of substantive democracy are eroded. The fracture of the spatiotemporal unity between the polity and the economy, therefore, signifies a crisis of political representation and substantive democracy. The nation-state is increasingly unable to represent the will of its people, and spaces for open participation in decision making are reduced.

Fourth, the crisis of the nation-state has been accompanied by the emergence of transnational state forms but also of subnational forms of the state. Because TNCs' scope of action is larger than that of the nation-state, coordination and promotion of capital accumulation must be elevated to the level of transnational state forms (e.g., Held et al. 1999; Holloway 1993; Picciotto 1991; Pitelis 1993). Institutions such as the WTO, United Nations, IMF, NAFTA, and particularly the European Union have appeared as entities whose supranational scope allows them to perform these roles. Contrary to the case of the nation-state, transnational states are mostly shielded from direct public participation in decision-making processes, which sharply diminishes their "duty" to legitimate decisions to their constituencies. Their functioning is based largely on the executive actions of elite bureaucracies with only re-mote—and in some cases nonexistent—links with the constituencies they are supposed to represent. The wto—perhaps the most important economic regulatory agency at the global level—has virtually no connection with the citizens of member countries. Even the European Union falls into this cate-gory. Despite its heralded democratic dimension and some important pro-gressive postures it has maintained in a number of situations, its legislative and executive powers are detached from its elected bodies. The net result of this situation is that transnational states can foster capital accumulation while maintaining limited concern about legitimizing it to subordinate groups. Similarly, subnational or regional state forms have emerged and have carried out some of the actions once associated with the nation-state. While regional forms of the state have been described as enhancing popular partici-pation, their ability to foster the democratization of social relations remains questionable at best.

Fifth, globalization has been seen as an American project. Advocates of globalization (such as Friedman 2000) usually see it as a natural product of diffuse, individual, rational choices, while critics argue that it is forged by U.S. economic and military power, achieved not as a result of conspiracy or direct force but rather as a consequence of the United States' "enormous structural power," which is "deeply inscribed into the nature and functioning of the present world order" (Held et al. 1999, 425). In his incisively critical *False Dawn,* Englishman and former libertarian John Gray declares that glob-alization is an "American project" fashioned with a great deal of help from the U.S. government. "Free markets are creatures of state power," he con-tends, "and persist only so long as the state is able to prevent human needs for security and the control of economic risk from finding political expres-sion" (1998, 17, 100). Scathingly rejecting claims about universal "truths" of the market, Gray argues that globalization reflects an Enlightenment ratio-nalism and universalism retrofitted to distinctly American conditions and then exported worldwide, without regard for local cultures or contexts and blind to the diversity of forms of capitalism. He holds that the practical failures of orthodox Marxism arise from similar universalizing Enlightenment tendencies (i.e., the belief that one economic model works in every setting). But he contends that globalization generates such uneven development, glaring inequalities, and intense political instability that it undermines the sociocultural foundations of its markets.

Seeing the "new world order" as an American hallucination, Gray attacks globalization's assumption that societies require only minimal state intervention. He contends that this position is a fatal error in a world where, outside the richest countries, the vast majority of people live on the margins and suffer intense socioeconomic privation and insecurity, and where rampant nationalism and religious-ethnic conflict prevail. In his view, globalization and the new communication and information technologies free markets from sociopolitical regulation, institutionally disembedding the economy, enriching elites and professional middle classes, and undercutting the prospect of freedom and well-being for the vast majority of people. He asserts that genuine "democracy and the free market are competitors rather than partners" (7, 201–2, 205, 208, 213). Gray also states sarcastically that the neoliberal creed "implies that all humans are born American, and become anything else by accident . . . [and that] American values are, or will soon be shared by all humankind." He stresses that this fervent ethnocentrism and neoliberal faith foreclose discussion of today's most pressing policy question: "how to reconcile the imperatives of deregulated markets with enduring human needs" (132).

Finally, the crisis of the nation-state and the emergence of the embryonic transnational state leave room for other alternative institutions that could perform the roles historically attributed to the state. Among these institutions, particularly relevant is the prominence that nongovernmental organizations (NGOs) have acquired in the global era. They have been in existence since the early decades of the twentieth century (Held et al. 1999; Waters 2002); but their growth is a post–World War II phenomenon, and their rapid expansion is essentially concentrated in the last two decades of the twentieth century and the first decade of the twenty-first. NGOs materialized to provide regulation and control in areas that either had been emptied by the withdrawal of the state or emerged from the evolution of globalization. In either case, their growth has been viewed in at least two opposing ways. One side views the growth of NGOs as a positive contribution to the creation of a more democratic world space (Waters 2002). In this view NGOs can bring global communities together on issues—such as human rights, the environment, and gender equality—that transcend national interests. The other side of the debate, while acknowledging the potential positive effects of the expansion of NGOs, remains critical of their ability to provide durable solutions to current global problems (Held et al. 1999). Our reading of NGOs sees them as problematic. In particular, we contend that it is important to examine the problematic nature and objectives of the groups shaping NGOs actions and the consequences of these actions in the global context.

The key organizing principle of this volume is its focus on case studies, the stories of globalization. Accordingly, our objective is to present an analysis of salient aspects of globalization through the lens of these in-depth case studies. Based on our empirical research on the globalization of agrifood sector, each case illustrates the actions of TNCs and groups that resist them and provides detailed empirical information on the ways in which these events unfolded. The agrifood sector has been the focus of our scientific investigation for more than two decades, but we have an additional reason for choosing this sector as the focus of this volume. Agrifood is among the most globalized of economic sectors, one in which not only production but also consumption, research, and marketing are globalized. In essence, agriculture and food arguably constitute one of the most appropriate substantive areas through which to investigate globalization.

The volume is divided into ten chapters. Chapter 1 presents a review of salient literature on the globalization of economy and society divided into three general theses or camps. Chapters 2 through 9 present the case studies, our stories of globalization While all of these stories speak to our tripartite focus on the power of TNCs, resistance to TNCs' actions, and the role of the state, we have grouped our stories of globalization around three foci for heuristic purposes. Chapters 2, 3, and 4 concentrate on issues pertaining to the powers of TNCs and the role of the nation-state under globalization. Chapters 5, 6, and 7 focus more closely on instances of resistance to globalization. Chapters 8 and 9 investigate the emergence of NGOs as important entities in the global era, entities that can both be agents of resistance to the globalization project and perform some of the historical functions of the state. The Conclusion offers some final remarks that reflect on the conditions of globalization in general, and on the issue of democracy in particular.

1

GLOBALIZATION OF THE ECONOMY AND SOCIETY:
SALIENT INTERPRETATIONS

The objective of this chapter is to introduce the reader to the copious literature on the globalization of economy and society. Globalization has been a
buzzword in social science circles for quite some time now. This interest
has generated a large literature that, simply because of its volume, presents
objective difficulties for anyone who wants to organize and present it in a
summary fashion. The pattern that we have selected emphasizes three general theses that are more dominant than others in the debate: the *grand
durée* thesis, the *corporate domination* thesis, and the *contradictory dimension of globalization* thesis. Accordingly, we have grouped salient contributions under these three general headings, regardless of the theoretical and
epistemological preferences of the authors. Emphasis, therefore, is placed on
the overall view of globalization, rather than on the analytical frameworks
employed to study it. Information on the latter, however, is presented in the
review of each of the theses.

The debate on the social and economic aspects of globalization has attracted the attention of contributors whose approaches cut across a number
of established intellectual spheres. First, it cuts across traditional "sociological schools." Grouping the literature according to various schools of
thought—for example, conflict theory, functionalism, and interactionism—
frequently yields the outcome that authors writing from different perspectives reach the same conclusions, while writers with the same perspective
reach divergent conclusions. Second, the debate cuts across traditional ideological lines. The classical distinction between left and right is often blurred,
which diminishes the effectiveness of organizing the literature in this way.
Third, the debate cuts across disciplinary lines, and therefore makes the
grouping of authors according to their disciplines less than useful.

Our choice stresses different readings of the three major actors explored in the book: transnational corporations, groups that resist them, and the state. We organize the literature on globalization into three groups: (a) authors who are skeptical about the analytical importance of the concept of globalization and prefer to see it as a continuation of long-established trends (grand durée); (b) those who see TNCS as the actors with the most power in terms of either shaping the behavior of other social actors or opening opportunities of development and prosperity for a significant segment of the world (corporate domination); and (c) those who see globalization as a problematic and contradictory phenomenon (contradictory dimension of globalization).

This chapter is thus divided into three sections dedicated to these three general camps. Each section opens with a brief summary of the most important characteristics of that camp and then summarizes its work. Each summary is organized around that camp's understandings of four basic aspects of the genesis and characteristics of globalization: the move toward globalization, the primary causes of this development, the role and position of TNCS, and the future outlook. Through this organization we wish to facilitate a useful comparison of the three groups and to clarify ideas that will be employed in the analysis of the case studies presented in the rest of the book.

Grand Durée

The grand durée camp consists of authors who make one or more of the following arguments about globalization: (1) globalization has existed for centuries; (2) it has not transformed the fundamental functioning of capitalism; and (3) it remains centered on the power of the nation-state. For authors who write within this paradigm, globalization affected only the "form," rather than the "substance," through which society is reproduced. For instance, Christopher Chase-Dunn (1998) illustrates the basic assumptions of the grand durée thesis through his application of the world-system perspective to the study of globalization. "Most discussions of globalization assume that, however defined, it is a fairly recent phenomenon," writes Chase-Dunn. "If we take a long-term view of the structural constants, cyclical processes, and secular trends that have operated in the Europe-centered system for several centuries we can understand that there have been no recent major transformations in the developmental logic of the world-system" (ix).

Proponents of this thesis differ, however, in several respects. First, they write from different theoretical perspectives. Accordingly, they tend to stress aspects that are typical of their school of thought. Second, while some view globalization as a contradictory process, others see it as an opportunity for nations and communities to improve their socioeconomic conditions. Third, some see TNCs as the primary actors under globalization, while others deny the existence of truly global firms. Finally, for some, globalization is the outcome of governmental forces (the United States in particular), while others see it as the result of corporate actions facilitated by technological and political changes.

This section reviews the work of Giovanni Arrighi, Paul Hirst and Grahame Thompson, William H. Friedland, and Michael Porter. With the exception of Porter, these authors write from the perspective of political economy; they center their analyses on the characteristics and evolution of capitalism. This similar theoretical posture does not prevent them from reaching different conclusions, however. For example, Arrighi's approach, grounded in world-system theory, stresses the instability of the current socioeconomic system owing to the lack of a clear world hegemonic power—the role played successfully by the United States until recently. Hirst and Thompson, by contrast, argue that the current system is governable, and they see in the triad of the United States, the European Union, and Japan the collective agent that could provide world leadership and stability. While stressing important systemic contradictions, Friedland also sees a stable socioeconomic system centered on established mechanisms of mass production reinforced by the introduction of new accumulation strategies. An important aspect of Friedland's contribution is that, while he focuses his analysis on the agrifood sector, he provides important comparisons with other global sectors, such as automotive and computers. In this respect his contribution shows (a) the global status of the agrifood sector, and (b) the common ground with which this and other major economic sectors have globalized in recent decades. Unlike the other authors included in this section, Michael Porter's work is couched in a more conventional business analytical framework. This posture allows him to view globalization in much more positive terms. Porter views TNCs' actions and the opening of markets associated with globalization as positive forces. He does concur with the other authors on the continuing importance of the nation-state and the idea that capitalism, if uncontrolled, will continue to produce social and economic instability.

Giovanni Arrighi

Giovanni Arrighi (1998) argues that globalization is nothing new. He points out that some of the heralded characteristics of globalization, such as higher rates of foreign direct investments (FDI) and international trade, and real-time forms of communication existed—albeit with differences—even before the turn of the century. The events initiated by World War I and continued after World War II changed these trends, but their reemergence toward the end of the twentieth century does not signify that they are "new." For Arrighi, it is important to examine these changes in the context of the long-term evolution of capitalism.

Change

While stressing that globalization is not new, Arrighi recognizes that the current form of globalization is characterized by an unprecedented expansion of financial capital and markets. The emergence of TNCs is the outcome of the expansion of financial markets and the enhanced global availability and mobility of capital that accompanies it. This, however, is not an indication of the crisis of the nation-state and does not support the widespread argument that enhanced global mobility of capital limits the ability of nation-states to exercise power within their territorial jurisdictions. In effect, the issue of the crisis of state powers requires important specifications. It is highly inaccurate to equate advanced and powerful nation-states such as the United States, Japan, and the major western European nations with the peripheral nation-states of Latin America and Africa. The latter, and their counterparts on other continents, never fully mastered the powers that it is said they are losing under globalization. This argument can be also extended to advanced nation-states. European nation-states, for instance, experienced a diminishing power crisis in the first part of the twentieth century, as the United States, and later the Soviet Union, began to establish world domination.

Causes

Arrighi maintains that capitalism has always been characterized by crises that displace established centers of power in favor of nascent ones. These systemic cycles of accumulation led to the current global dimension of world capitalism. In the early stages of capitalism, city-states such as Genoa and

Venice were replaced by the quasi-nation-state of Holland. Holland in turn was replaced by the British nation-state, which was subsequently superseded by the continent-wide United States. The current "globalization" is a phase of the long-term evolution of capitalism.

Transnational Corporations

The worldwide growth of TNCs allowed the United States to combat communist and nationalist threats simultaneously. The contradictory aspect of this process rests on the fact that the overseas expansion of TNCs signified that a large amount of capital did not return to the United States but remained in the emerging global financial market. Consequently, the United States became engulfed in a fiscal crisis, as pressure to address international (i.e., the Vietnam War) and domestic issues (i.e., the War on Poverty) mounted. This meant the "increase in the volume and density of the web of exchanges that linked people and territory across political jurisdictions both regionally and globally" (Arrighi 1998, 70).

Outlook

For Arrighi the interesting dimension of the current situation is that, unlike previous stages of capitalism, the displacement of the United States as the hegemonic world power has not been followed by the clear emergence of a new center of power. This signifies a realignment that sees east Asian territorial and nonterritorial organizations emerging as focal points of the new world organization of capitalism. However, the effective emergence of a new world order depends on the cooperation of a plurality of states, including the United States. In this context, Arrighi sees the relationship between TNCs and the state as one of *contradiction and complementarity*. To enhance capital accumulation, the United States was able to establish a system of administered trade liberalization that—contrary to the old British system of extraction of tributes from dependent countries—mandated multilateral trade agreements monitored by the military force of the United States. This situation fostered the rise of TNCs overseas and the growth of U.S.-based corporations' "claims on the incomes and control over the resources of foreign countries" (Arrighi 1998, 68).

Paul Hirst and Grahame Thompson

Like Arrighi, Paul Hirst and Grahame Thompson (1996) argue that globalization is not new but is a long-standing phenomenon that began during the early stages of mature capitalism. While important changes at the world level occurred in the closing decades of the twentieth century, these alterations are still part of the highly internationalized economy that characterized modern capitalism for decades. They employ this argument to question the importance of globalization and to assert that its impact on the socioeconomic organization of society is greatly exaggerated.[1]

Change

In effect, Hirst and Thompson maintain that current levels of "integration of the world economy" are not unique to contemporary society. They are only specific instances of established trends dating from the mid-twentieth century, when the conditions governing the current form of capitalism were established. For instance, they argue that today's open economy is not as open as that of the period between 1870 and 1914, the so-called *belle époque*. They contend that the opening of the economy and enhanced circulation of commodities, labor, and capital, at the world level were key features of that era of capitalism. Hirst and Thompson recognize that current world socioeconomic conditions present important differences from the past and that change has occurred as the mechanisms that guaranteed socioeconomic equilibrium in the decades following World War II have been altered.

Causes

This change was caused by a combination of events beginning in the 1970s that weakened U.S. hegemony and did not allow the United States to use its power to guarantee social stability and economic expansion. These events

1. Hirst and Thompson's position—and that of like-minded social scientists—has been criticized in a number of ways. In a balanced assessment, Mauro Guillen (2001) maintains that Hirst and Thompson contributed to the clarification of aspects of globalization that are often taken for granted. He simultaneously contends that they fail to see the new cultural and economic interconnections generated by globalization and the mutual awareness they engender. Robinson provides a stronger critique. He argues that there are quantitative and qualitative differences between globalization and previous periods of capitalist development, and in particular between globalization and the capitalism of the early twentieth century. Accordingly, it is misleading to argue that globalization is simply the continuation of trends established in the past. From a quantitative point of view, Robinson maintains that trade is much greater under globalization than in previous historical periods and that this is also the case for the scale of capital flows and the level of information and communication technology. He also stresses the differences associated with the global presence of transnational corporations and a transnational labor force. Qualitatively, Robinson emphasizes that globalization "has entailed the fragmentation and decentralization of complex production chains and the worldwide dispersal and functional integration of the different segments of these chains. . . . In this way globalization is unifying the world into a single mode of production and a single global system and bringing about the integration of different countries and regions into a new global economy" (2004, 15).

were not the result of drastic alterations of social and economic conditions, however, as some proponents of the globalization thesis argue. Rather, they were the outcome of immediate conjunctures that did not modify the basic functioning of the economy and society.

Transnational Corporations

Similarly, Hirst and Thompson maintain that true TNCs do not exist, so the purported socioeconomic changes that resulted in the creation of TNCs are unsubstantiated. Employing economic data, they argue that most corporations are still nationally based, as they are still connected to their country of origin in significant ways. They are multinational corporations that operate internationally, a situation that has not changed for most of the twentieth century. Additionally, they contend that data do not indicate the existence of trends toward the emergence of truly global corporations. In effect, their examination of FDI reveals that it is generated by companies located in North America, Europe, and Japan, and that the rest of the world is affected only marginally by these flows of economic resources.

Outlook

Departing from the arguments of others, Hirst and Thompson maintain that the contemporary world economy and society are governable. In fact, the postwar system that regulated capitalism has been displaced by a new system of regulation. This new system allows the three superpowers (United States, European Union, and Japan) to govern the world and ensure adequate levels of socioeconomic stability. This is not a global system, the authors contend. But it is an international one characterized by nationally based economic enterprises and activities that are internationally oriented. These economic activities are very much linked to nation-states and in particular to advanced societies. They conclude that this situation affects politics, as well as political action, and should be exercised primarily within the context of national political structures.

William H. Friedland

William H. Friedland's (1991, 1994a, 1994b, 1995) contribution to the debate on globalization is centered on the study of the agrifood sector. Like the other authors examined in this section, Friedland is not convinced that current changes represent a departure from established socioeconomic trends. However, also like the others, he acknowledges that the current situation presents important differences from the recent past.

Change

Friedland contends that globalization manifests itself unevenly across space. It has different consequences in different regions and across economic sectors and commodities, as not all production processes and commodities are globalized. His primary contribution to the debate is his critique of the thesis that describes the current global system in terms of the end of Fordism and the emergence of post-Fordist and/or neo-Fordist social and economic arrangements. For Friedland, authors who describe globalization in terms of post-Fordism and/or neo-Fordism make the fundamental mistake of concluding that globalization signifies the crisis of mass production and its substitution with niche/specialized markets and production processes. He acknowledges that changes at the production level have occurred and that today there is a revival of specialized production generated on a nonmass (craft) scale. But this is a phenomenon that involves only relatively small segments of society, in particular the upper and upper middle classes, while the middle and lower classes are still confined to access to mass-produced items. More important, the decentralization of production processes has been accompanied by further concentration of production control. Accordingly, the development of a new niche/specialized production system is apparent only as it conceals an actual system that still retains its mass character and remains fully controlled by large corporations. In Friedland's view, we have a system of mass production of specialized commodities that is centrally controlled by large corporations.

Causes

Mass production of specialized commodities refers to the fragmentation of once standardized mass markets into a variety of niche markets. By introducing an assortment of products to cater to new and diversified demands of global consumers, this production system responds to the crisis of homogenous mass markets. Two of the key elements of Fordism in the United States were the expansion of consumption through wage increases and assembly line–based standardized production. These two characteristics defined Henry Ford's revolutionary strategy that, once generalized, propelled mass production. Ford and like-minded entrepreneurs, politicians, and intellectuals envisioned a system whereby, through the increase of wages, mass consumption could absorb assembly line–generated mass production. Friedland emphasizes that by the early 1930s this model had reached its limits owing to *overstandardization*. It was impossible to continue to generate high consumption levels with the mass production of a limited number of items. Ford's remark that consumers could have any color of Model-T Ford, as long as it was black, suggests the essence of the problem. Alfred Sloan of General Motors addressed this impasse. Sloan recognized the importance of market niches and introduced the concept of "options." Options were variations from basic mass-produced models that consumers added in relation to their purchasing power and living standard. In other words, the introduction of options allowed a market differentiation based on class stratification that expanded and strengthened mass production and consumption.

Transnational Corporations

Over the years, this original form of "Sloanism" underwent significant changes and expanded from the automotive industry into other spheres of contemporary production, such as clothing, electronics, and food. However, Friedland argues, this situation should not be mistaken for the end of Fordism. Instead, it represents the transformation of traditional Fordism into Sloanism. This new system of mass production is controlled by large global corporations. TNCS employed legal and technical devices to fragment traditional production units. Because of their large size and related operational requirements, these units were too costly and were slow to respond to new and various market demands. Through Sloanism TNCs gained further control of the global market, and they represent the most important actors in today's global economy. TNCS exercise significant control over nation-states. While capitalist classes have always controlled the political apparatus of a country, under globalization the ability of TNCs to control the state is enhanced through the hypermobility of capital. This crisis of the nation-state is accompanied by the emergence of transnational forms of the state that are nevertheless far from replacing the nation-state under the contemporary form of capitalism.

Outlook

Friedland rejects the optimistic view of those who see in the development of craft-based production a positive alternative to dominant economic relations. He describes craft-based production as centered on small to medium-size units that are linked together horizontally. This horizontal integration refers to the nonhierarchical connection of units to form a production network. Popularized by well-studied examples in Italy—the "third Italy" model—and other parts of the world, horizontal integration has been viewed as a solution, albeit partial, to contemporary crises of capitalism. Friedland argues that because horizontal integration involves only a relatively small portion of production and because production in general is controlled by TNCs, globalization does not represent a fundamental alteration of the conditions under which capitalist production occurred. Owing to the growth and increased power of TNCs, opposition to them, while possible, has become increasingly difficult.

Michael Porter

Porter (1990, 1998) takes a much more optimistic view of globalization than the authors reviewed above. Like the others, however, he is not convinced that current socioeconomic arrangements depart significantly from those of past decades. Despite the emergence of global corporations, Porter argues that globalization has not altered the fundamental ways in which business is carried out. Accordingly, despite claims that we have a global economy and society, the nation-state remains the center of socioeconomic life, and corporations cannot successfully operate without relying on local (regional and national) resources.

Change

Change, however, has occurred, and it rests primarily in the shift from business practices based on the classical notions of comparative advantage of nations—i.e., companies take advantage of the natural resources with which a nation is endowed—to those based on the *"competitive advantage of nations."* He explains that because all TNCs can source factors of production globally and move their assembly plants to low-cost locations, the original advantage generated by these strategies has been erased. The competitive advantage now comes from local resources in the form of specialized skills, applied technologies, supporting institutions, and cooperation between companies and the nation-state that distant rivals cannot match. Competitive advantage is created and sustained through a localized process that capitalizes on differences in national values, culture, economic structures, institutions, and histories. The result is that in the era of globalization, economic geography involves a paradox. Although global technologies have increased the speed of transportation, communication, and access to global markets, locational attributes remain fundamental to competition. Countries and locales that can offer concentrations of highly specialized skills, knowledge institutions, and sophisticated customers are better off than their less innovative counterparts.

Causes

According to Porter, economic globalization is the product of corporations' expanded search for more convenient production conditions throughout the globe. Propelled by new technology and new political arrangements, global corporations are capable of acquiring production components such as labor and raw materials on a world scale and can take advantage of the availability of a number of locations offering favorable social, economic, and political conditions. As in the past, corporations need to enhance their profitability and rely on a friendly national environment to do so. This situation refers to both (1) the existence of a supportive home base, including a government that effectively assists corporations in their various endeavors, and (2) a good local business climate that provides relevant resources and good social, political, and economic conditions for their corporate use. In short, global corporations need to place their operations within a nation-state that can offer the necessary assistance and resources.

Transnational Corporations

Global corporations have been relocating their headquarters from one nation to another with increasing frequency, but they operate with more centralized control than other companies. This means that various subsidiaries are highly interdependent and may specialize in only one part of the product line. Because each subsidiary performs a specialized function in a single system, it does not necessarily need to be a profit center. As a result, enhanced production flexibility and ability to compete are achieved.

Outlook

Porter is concerned that future growth can be hampered by the introduction of policies that favor either protectionism or an uncontrolled free market. Protectionist policies stifle competition and innovation. Accordingly, the introduction of new protectionist policies will erase most of the gains generated by the opening of the economy experienced under globalization. But hampering the ability of governments to control unwanted consequences of the free market will have similarly negative effects. Indeed, Porter concludes, free market advocates ignore the vital role that governments must play in "shaping the context and institutional structure surrounding companies and in creating an environment that stimulates companies to gain competitive advantage" (1998, 184).

The Corporate Domination Thesis

The corporate domination thesis stresses the power of TNCs and their ability to affect the action of local institutions and groups. More important, exponents of this thesis view globalization as a process in which either (1) TNCs exercise significant control over national and/or local institutions such as the nation-state, or (2) the overall global flow of capital frames the actions of local actors and institutions. This perspective emphasizes the TNCs' ability to overcome nation-states' powers and transform local states into agents of transnational institutions and groups. The power of TNCs and global regulatory agencies is stressed in diverging ways. Some corporate domination scholars contend that the growth of TNCs and global organizations' powers stifles national and regional development. Others argue that these are necessary conditions for the further development of the economy and that nation-states should not counter the objectives of transnational organizations. The growth of nation-states is a key condition for the overall development of society. Authors in this camp write from diverging theoretical viewpoints. Some stress the class and/or political economy dimensions of globalization, while others center their analysis on different variables, such as structural factors (e.g., conditions necessary for profit maximization) and cultural dimensions (establishment of a good business climate). Finally, as with other debates, the diverging theoretical outlooks allow some authors to be overtly critical of globalization, while others see it as a positive force for the future of society.

This section reviews the works of Leslie Sklair, Philip McMichael, John Dunning, Kenichi Ohmae, and Alex Rubner. Sklair and McMichael write from a political economy point of view that stresses class membership, class conflict, and the problematic and unsustainable nature of current global socioeconomic arrangements. Sklair employs the class perspective more overtly and deliberately than McMichael, as his primary contribution rests on an analysis of the composition, evolution, and actions of the transnational capitalist class. This is the class that directs globalization and controls TNCs and nation-states, as well as consumption and ideology. McMichael agrees with Sklair that the globalization project is piloted by subgroups of the ruling class, including financial managers, global bureaucrats, and corporate leaders. But most of McMichael's argument is derived from the investigation of structural changes involving alterations of capital flows and markets. In addition, McMichael's analysis is centered on the study of agriculture and food. Dunning, Ohmae, and Rubner write from within a business tradition. Dunning stresses the economic and market difficulties that motivated corporations to transnationalize their operations. Along with Ohmae and Rubner, he sees globalization as a positive force for socioeconomic development. Ohmae sees the primary source of globalization in technological advancements that allow greater mobility for capital and productive resources. His central argument is that the nation-state is obsolete. Because of globalization, nation-states are incapable of regulating business activities as in the past. Accordingly, nation-states that fail to liberalize their economies and open up their territories to transnational flows of capital and resources are destined to face economic crises. Rubner proposes a pro-TNC view of globalization in which the role and actions of corporations are justified and supported. Not only are TNCs the motor forces of progress in the global era, but their stateless condition and decentralization strategies are indispensable elements for future success. Like Ohmae, Rubner warns of the negative social consequences that follow when nation-states oppose TNCs.

Leslie Sklair

Employing a class analysis, Leslie Sklair (2001) defines globalization as a process orchestrated and controlled by the transnational capitalist class, or TCC. While resistance exists and is in fact fostered by the expansion of globalization, the TCC is in firm control of today's society and economy.

Change

The major changes from previous phases of capitalism are the emergence of the TCC and TNCs. The TCC is divided into four groups: executives of TNCs (the corporate group); globalizing bureaucrats and politicians (the state group); globalizing professionals (the technical group); and merchants and the media (the consumerism group).[2] The TCC's four groups cooperate together to

---

2. Robinson proposes a very similar thesis of globalization tied to the emergence of the TCC. For Robinson, however, the TCC should include only those who own the means of production and should exclude professional and middle-class groups (2004, 36). The TCC, he maintains, is a capitalist group that controls transnational capital. Apart from this difference, the argument developed by Robinson in a number of works published in recent years (see for example 2001 and 1998) remains remarkably similar to that of Sklair. Like Sklair, Robinson writes from a Marxian point of view. However, the emergence of a transnational capitalist class is also stressed by non-Marxian theorists. A relevant example is the work of David Becker and Richard Sklar and their associates on the theory of "postimperialism" (see Becker and Sklar 1999; Becker 1999; Sklar 1999 and 1976; Myers 1999). Becker and Sklar define the current global system as postimperialist to indicate the creation of a transnational system that transcends the division of the world into nations. Accordingly, the idea that one or few nations can dominate other nations (imperialism) is obsolete. This postimperialist world is

advance the globalization project and to control the primary crises of the era: class polarization and the ecological crisis. In order to operate successfully in any given territory, TNC executives require the support of members of the other three groups. Accordingly, politicians, bureaucrats, and professionals are called into action to justify procorporate policies to their national constituencies. This is often carried out by stressing the benefits that corporate investment would generate for the nation. This is a deceptive posture, however, as TNCs are not linked, nor do they offer allegiance, to any particular nation-state. In effect, Sklair contends, to further their global profitability, TNCs seek partners from an array of national enclaves and build their global networks through the recruitment of politicians, bureaucrats, and professionals from diverse national backgrounds. This apparent inclusiveness allows TNCs to broaden their scope of action and gain support for their actions. The result is that the current form of capitalism is global. It is global also because current arrangements cannot be defined in terms of a national economy—an economy serving an exclusively sovereign national market— nor can they be defined in terms of an international economy, one in which pure national economies trade among themselves. Current conditions are based on social relations that transcend national and the international boundaries. While a global economy exists, however, it does not operate uniformly around the world, as different countries and regions experience different outcomes of the growth of TNCs and the TCC.

Causes

For Sklair, the growth of the global capitalist system is the outcome of the crisis of capital accumulation of the 1970s. Reagan's and Thatcher's neoliberal policies of the 1980s represented the proposition of a multifaceted (economic, ideological, and political) global project aimed at restarting capital accumulation, while responding to challenges coming from, and the power of, subordinate groups, particularly labor. This neoliberal proposition represented a new hegemonic strategy aimed at establishing the domination of

---

characterized by transnational class formation based on "the tendency of dominant social classes in different countries to coalesce, that is, to combine with one another in pursuit of their common interests" (1999, 3). While the emergence of a transnational working class is embryonic and facilitated by the crisis of existing labor organizations (see Myers 1999), the emerging transnational bourgeoisie is much more unified and purposeful than any other class. Sharply departing from Sklar's and Robinson's argument about the negative socioeconomic effects of the TCC, Becker and Sklar maintain that its development promotes more, rather than less, equitable development among countries because it moderates the global distribution of wealth. For a similar view about globalization's reduction of economic inequality worldwide, see Firebaugh and Goesling (2004).

the TCC. The new global system was based on the spatial and technical dispersal of the production process in a variety of discrete phases. This mobility of capital allowed TNCs to avoid production dependence on one particular factory and/or workforce and therefore to control resistance from below. Sklair notes that TNCs' actions have been "too powerful for the local organization of labor" (2001, 298). Because of TNCs' mobility, the threat of lost jobs allowed corporations to enhance control over the labor force. Workers were required to work harder and longer, and received less pay, in order to meet international competition. This "race to the bottom" turned out to be one of the most powerful strategies at the disposal of TNCs.

This system has been supported by the ideology of consumerism, an ideology of domination that equates "quality of life" and "social peace" with the "ability to consume," and defines our existence in terms of what we possess. The TCC's effort to expand the ideology of consumerism involved the development of inclusionary and good citizenship claims. Sklair maintains that the idea that globalization and localization are mutually exclusive is groundless. TNCs are not necessarily interested in destroying the local. They are interested in making profits. Accordingly, the local is used to enhance sales and promote products that, either directly or indirectly, refer to and/or find in the local a profitable market. TNCs often "localize" their operations to take on the semblance of local operations. In essence, it is more advantageous for TNCs to include than to exclude various locales and local groups in the project of mass consumption.

Transnational Corporations

TNCs are the dominant actors in the global capitalist system. The global scope of TNCs rests on three basic conditions. First, it is extremely difficult to clearly link ownership of a TNC to a specific nation-state. While it is possible to identify the national origins of management in one corporation—for instance, only a few IBM and Toyota executives are foreigners—ownership remains linked to stockholders who operate in stock markets guided by the priority of making profits. Profit making does not recognize national boundaries. Second, the fact that a company is identified with a nation does not prevent it from globalizing its operations, nor does it change its relationship with any local context within which the company operates. As Robert Reich (1991) has written, Sklair stresses that, "as far as American prosperity is concerned, Toyota plants in the USA were more American than GM plants in Japan" (Sklair 2001, 142). Third, the connection between TNCs' actions and national interests is often expressed as the globalization project advances within national territories. It is possible, therefore, clearly to distinguish TNCS from multinational corporations. Multinational corporations are companies that have strong national attachments and whose international subsidiaries are branches of the national corporation. TNCS are corporations that globalize their operations through denationalization. They have no specific attachment to their nations of origin and their global units are not extensions of the home base. In effect, the distinction between home-based and foreign operations becomes blurred to the point that is it virtually impossible to distinguish between the two. Sklair contends that as long as the world is made up of nation-states, corporations cannot operate without considering those states. There is thus no such thing as a completely stateless (purely global) corporation. The overwhelming majority of the top corporations in the world want to globalize their operations. Sklair maintains that we should talk about globalizing, rather than global, corporations; TNCS are globalizing corporations.

Because claims of social irresponsibility on the part of TNCS can threaten their market share of consumption, TNCS must promote an image that shows social responsibility—that is, good citizenship. Sklair maintains that TNCS pursue a four-component strategy of global citizenship: (1) corporate governance (TNCS must be responsible for the well-being of their employees); (2) community development (TNCS must be responsible for the well-being of the communities associated with corporate operations); (3) health and safety (they must address health and safety issues for consumers and employees; and (4) environmental concerns (they must maintain an environmentally responsible posture). The TCC thus actively promotes an ideology of *sustainable development* that reconciles TNCS' profit-making interests with social, economic, and environmental responsibility. According to this ideology, sound environmental practices and corporate interests are viewed as reconcilable. In addition, the environmental crisis is seen as a set of discrete crises that can be addressed individually. The idea that contemporary society faces a singular environmental crisis is rejected altogether. Environmental groups interested in this vision are supported by corporate actions and become part of the sustainable development hegemonic bloc. Because corporate policies have increasingly been recognized as more sensitive to the environment than they used to be, Sklair concludes that the corporate hegemonic project of sustainable development is successful in contemporary global capitalism.

Outlook

TNCS and the TCC have created a hegemonic bloc that allows them to dominate social and economic relations in the global capitalist system, but certain social groups and movements resist this hegemonic bloc by denouncing and attacking corporate practices. The process of resistance has a twofold set of implications. First, it forces TNCs, nation-states, and other institutions and organizations that support the TCC to modify their actions to meet the requests of anticorporate groups. The resistance of opposition groups has led TNCs to take some steps toward democratic governance and practices. Second, anticorporate resistance denounces the limits of the globalization project and its negative social consequences. Each corporate action, Sklair maintains, can potentially trigger opposition and the public denunciation of labor exploitation, human rights violations, and environmental degradation. The future of social relations under globalization will be determined by the outcome of the struggle between the TCC and opposition groups and movements.

Philip McMichael

McMichael (1996, 2000, 2002) sees globalization is a political project that has replaced earlier strategies of "socioeconomic development" and a process that, although dominant worldwide, excludes significant portions of the world population.

Change

McMichael focuses on structural and economic factors that generated the rise and evolution of the global system. He maintains that a fundamental aspect of the reorganization of the world order was the phenomenon of liquidization: the preference for liquid over fixed capital. Investors maneuvered to decouple liquid capital (i.e., financial assets) from productive capital (i.e., factories and production facilities) and in so doing effected the reorganization of political and economic institutions. Financial institutions' increased power translated into their ability to expand control of the servicing of debts, which in turn affected the actions of corporations and nation-states. This process was orchestrated by a global elite of financial managers assisted by global bureaucrats and corporate leaders. McMichael argues that the globalization project is the most recent attempt to stabilize capitalism. The uniqueness of globalization rests on its significant departure from older modernization strategies. The latter were based on national developmental projects aimed at replicating the experiences of advanced societies. Traditional developmental models have now been replaced by specialization strategies that trigger differentiation and integration processes in regions around the world. The globalization project also diminishes the centrality of the nation-state as the central point of governance and development. Globalization has been characterized by the emergence of institutions of global governance like the World Trade Organization (WTO). According to McMichael, this situation "not only compromises national sovereignty but also subordinates national policy to the demands of the global economy" (2002, 142–43).

Causes

This shift began in the second half of the twentieth century. McMichael shares with other proponents of the end-of-Fordism theory the belief that the 1970s represent a critical period in the reorganization of the world socio-economic order. During that decade, Third World countries accelerated processes of development in the hope of "catching up" with the developed world. Their export-oriented industrialization strategies were supported by global banks, which generated a substantial flow of unsecured loans. One of the primary outcomes was the stimulation of transnational trade and the subsequent enhancement of global economic links. The crisis of the dollar and the emergence of the "Eurodollar" undercut the Bretton Woods monetary regime and opened up a period of worldwide financial instability. These conditions fostered the further growth of global corporate activities and the creation of a new breed of global banks. In the late 1970s declining profitability in the First World and the subsequent adoption of monetarist economic policies ended the flow of loans to the Third World. Developing countries experienced severe financial crises, which motivated international financial institutions such as the IMF and World Bank to demand economic restructuring plans in the 1980s and 1990s. Developing nations were forced to restructure their social programs and to abandon projects of development centered on domestic-based economic actors. In this context, multinational institutions, the financial class, and state managers reoriented developing economies through the introduction of neoliberal policies.

Transnational Corporations

One result of the global restructuring process was the consolidation of global corporations, as the privatization of national assets and the opening of domestic markets reduced wages and weakened the powers of nation-states. TNCS seek to reduce their production costs and increase their global competitiveness by searching for more convenient conditions for production worldwide, a practice McMichael calls global sourcing. They established a global production system characterized by a network of exchanges and links that allows for the creation of global commodity chains for the production of global commodities. These exchanges and links are neither homogeneously nor symmetrically distributed across space; TNCs' global production is both unevenly distributed and unstable. However, because of TNCs' ability to move freely about the globe, these companies gained significant control of local political institutions and often transformed them into agents of transnational corporate interests. The global production system features horizontal and vertical links that allow TNCs to operate as de facto world factories. The unevenness of the process rests on the fact that financial and research centers remain firmly centered in developing countries—most notably North America, Europe, and Japan—while manufacturing is distributed around the world according to the availability of inexpensive and docile labor and favorable business climates. The *maquilladora* regions of Mexico are examples of this.

Outlook

TNCs have been able to establish a global agenda that has captured the politics of nation-states. Neoliberal agendas and their objectives of trade liberalization, free circulation of capital, deregulation, and frontal attacks on welfare and social-oriented national and regional policies characterize the actions of national governments in developed and developing countries. Despite this overall situation, the globalization project is resisted by a host of movements. Some are traditional movements, such as the labor movement; others are new social movements, such as the environmental and food safety movements; and some are local movements such as the Zapatista movement in Chiapas, Mexico. These movements constitute a resistance project that makes globalization problematic and sheds light on its genesis as a project directed by political and economic elites. Because of globalization, McMichael concludes, the concept of development is now exhausted. It viewed socioeconomic growth in national analogous terms—that is, developing countries were expected to follow the path of developed Western nations toward prosperity. While many national and international organizations still continue to act on this principle, globalization has unleashed a host of forces that have changed the terms of socioeconomic growth. These forces have brought the world to a historical juncture in which the outcome of the struggle between globalizing and resistance forces will decide the future evolution of society.

John Dunning

John Dunning (1981, 1989, 1990, 1991, 1993) defines economic globalization as the restructuring of corporate activities based on the global search for better production and business climates.

Change

This new profit-enhancing strategy departs from established ones whereby corporate decisions to invest globally (FDI) are decreasingly linked to factors such as access to raw materials and unskilled labor. It is instead increasingly determined by variables such as government regulations and the existence of a good business environment—that is, a dependable workforce, favorable tax environment, and sophisticated domestic markets. The extent to which a nation-state is able to offer advantageous conditions to TNCs determines its ability to attract corporate investments. From this point of view, globalization is characterized by the dependence of nation-states on the actions of "footloose" TNCs.

Causes

Although a relatively free market characterized the economy of the nineteenth century, and although governments became more powerful during much of the twentieth century, globalization entails TNCs' increased control over the economy and economic policy. After World War II, the United States and, later, European corporations responded to the difficulty of selling their products in foreign markets by setting up foreign producing affiliates. This type of investment accelerated until the 1970s and early 1980s, when some developing countries counteracted this practice through the expropriation of corporate assets. Simultaneously, the negative impact of the OPEC oil embargo and a move to the political left by many governments led to more state intervention. In order to overcome what they perceived as adverse conditions, TNCs established novel means to enhance profitability through a global search for convenient production sites with favorable political climates, support for deregulation, enhanced privatization of once publicly controlled enterprises and resources, opening of markets, and reduction of state intervention in the economy. This move prompted nation-states, in order to attract corporate investments, to adopt globally oriented macro-organizational strategies that shifted emphasis away from socially oriented goals—i.e., social stability, equitable socioeconomic growth, welfare spending—to profit-enhancing objectives. The allocation of FDI became increasingly linked to supportive economic policies and the "regulatory and policy instruments" employed by nation-states. This trend was a common feature of national economic policies worldwide during the final years of the twentieth century.

Transnational Corporations

Under globalization TNCs have been central players in the rapid increase in global commerce and in the implementation of policies that reduced barriers to the free circulation of capital. Mostly owing to technological advancements, TNCS are organized and operate differently from their national and multinational counterparts. In today's global economy TNCs resemble the "central nervous system" of a larger set of interdependent, but much less formally governed, activities whose purpose is to "advance the global competitive strategy of the organization" (Dunning 1993, 293). Unlike the mother-daughter relationship of earlier corporate organizational forms, the new organizational form of the global corporation is better perceived as a heterarchy rather than a hierarchy, whereby shared strategies and norms hold together a set of interdependent and geographically dispersed centers whose assets are sometimes owned but could be supplied jointly with other firms or purchased from a global network of suppliers. As a result of mergers, acquisitions, and joint ventures, TNCs' boundaries are increasingly blurred, new corporate alliances are forged, and corporate networking is overtly multifocused. Today, TNCs are orchestrators of sets of geographically dispersed but interdependent assets.

Outlook

Dunning argues that globalization is a positive force that fosters greater cooperation between TNCs and national governments. This cooperation gives both TNCs and nation-states a positive role "in facilitating and using this tried and tested mechanism to create sustainable and balanced economic development, and in a way which is both humanly acceptable, culturally sensitive and environmentally friendly" (1993, 285). Dunning sees a convergence of interests between TNCs and governments whereby the global strategies of TNCs to advance corporate profitability and growth interact positively with the strategies of national governments to promote the economic and social welfare of their citizens. He tempers his optimism with three concerns: (1) conflict and unrest due to regional tensions related to ideology and values; (2) the possible emergence of regional trade blocs and renewed protectionism; and (3) the ability and willingness of governments and TNCs to handle wisely the kind of power and freedom that the unfettered market economy offers (286). In addition, he argues that procorporate policies designed to attract FDI will diminish nation-states' desire to maintain real political sovereignty. While economic development will proceed rapidly throughout the world, and especially in Latin American and Asia, North America, Europe, and Japan will continue to dominate and largely determine the direction and pace of globalization. Technological advancements will continue to shrink both corporate and political boundaries, while at the same time forcing TNCS to seek new markets and to collaborate on cross-border value-added activities. New developments will occur in a context that is not homogenous, as differences between groups of nation-states do exist. One of the most important differences is between Western and east Asian nation-states: while the Western countries' "policies have been mainly directed at disengaging the government from the marketplace" (74), Asian governments have engaged more directly in providing the kind of business climate attractive to FDI. This trend has led to "a less adversarial and more symbiotic relationship between many governments and [corporations]—much along the style of that which has been adopted by the Japanese and Korean governments for the past two decades or more" (362).

Kenichi Ohmae

For Ohmae (1990, 1995), globalization refers to the development of a seamless economy guided by the growth of TNCS. TNCS' actions, global consumption, and the free flow of capital make nation-states, national interests, and protectionist policies obsolete and constitute obstacles to socioeconomic growth.

Change

Ohmae's primary idea is that the advancements in modern information technology have forever changed the economy. This new technology has greatly facilitated the movement of both investment and industry, as capital can be shifted instantaneously almost anywhere around the globe. In this new environment capital flows no longer need be tied to any particular physical site or movement of goods, as firms do business in many parts of the world without having to create entire business structures in each country where they have a presence. Managers have the information to direct their global economic activities in real time, can be more responsive to consumer demands, and can be much more flexible in how they organize production to meet those demands. The traditional "hurdles of cross-border participation and strategic alliance have come way down" (Ohmae 1995, 4). Business capabilities now reside in a network that can be made available virtually anywhere it is needed.

Causes

The development of the borderless global economy has been fueled by novel investment strategies carried out by TNCS. TNCS severed their objectives from national interests and directed them to serving attractive markets and taking advantage of convenient pools of resources worldwide. This posture engendered the growth of capital markets that have no geographic preference regarding lucrative business opportunities. As the percentage of money that flows across national borders is increasingly private rather than public, governments are less and less the necessary actors they were during the past two hundred years. Like capital markets, industries are also far more global and far less attached to their home countries than they were just a decade ago. Traditional government support in the form of subsidies is becoming irrelevant to business location. Global firms are moving into specific regions because that is "where their future lies," not because a host government has offered some incentive. "The uncomfortable truth is that, in terms of the global economy, nation-states have become little more than bit actors" (12). Global capital markets "dwarf the ability" of nation-states to control exchange rates and protect their currency. They have become "inescapably vulnerable" to the economic discipline of "choices made elsewhere by people and institutions over which they have no practical control" (12).

Information technologies have also allowed individual consumers to become more globally oriented. With better access to information about different lifestyles and products available around the globe, consumers are less and less likely to be conditioned to "buy American" or to respond to any other nationally oriented call for home-based consumption. Global consumers want the cheapest and highest-quality products and increasingly express this preference with their pocketbooks. By combining credit cards with the Internet, consumers can acquire products from all over the world. This progressive globalization of consumer markets has been termed the "Californianization" of taste and preference, and it is identified as the source of a new form of cross-border civilization.

Transnational Corporations.

Ohmae asserts that TNCS are dominant actors in the global economy that have cut their "home nation" attachments and operate as stateless global actors. Through their investment strategies global corporations increasingly discipline nation-states that do not adopt globally oriented economic and business policies (Ohmae 1995, 72). Accordingly, their business strategies are

centered on investing in regions that provide the most advantageous resources and conditions of production and on bypassing national regulations
and rules that hamper the maximization of production and capital accumulation. In Ohmae's view, global capital mobility makes it possible for viable
economic units to exist in any part of the world. Such ventures can obtain
resources both locally and globally and need not rely on government efforts
to attract and distribute resources. These changes make the "middleman"
function of nation-states "largely unnecessary." Because globalization
threatens the vested interests of established nation-state elites, however,
TNCS strategies are often opposed. These elites tend to pursue defensive strategies that, while responding to the demands of historically protected groups,
cause investment flows to bypass that country, hampering socioeconomic
growth. Indeed, "false kindnesses," such as welfare protection or industry
subsidies, only further diminish the future well-being of both citizens and
industries.

Outlook

Business and government organizations that fail to address this sea change
are doomed to fall behind. Socioeconomic development will be geographically concentrated in regions in which (a) nation-states will embrace globally
oriented strategies and abandon postures that protect traditional national
interest, and (b) the new natural business units, region states, are created.
Region states are the new wealth generators and the "connection" to the
global economy. Though limited in geographic size, these regions are often
huge in economic influence. Nation-states can support the development of
region states within their borders, or across neighboring borders, by embracing the concept of "special economic zones." For Ohmae, "it is from regionally
bound areas that the lion's share of future economic growth will come"
(1995, 86).

Alex Rubner

Rubner (1990) stresses the positive contributions brought about by the
growth of TNCS and the dangers that limiting their free movement can have
for society. Overall, he offers a sympathetic view of globalization and of the
behavior of, and role played by, TNCS.

Change

The primary change that took place in the late twentieth century is the
emergence of TNCS. TNCS' basic goal is to achieve profit maximization at the

global level. This task is carried out through two basic strategies. The first is efficient production; the second is penetration and control of markets. As far as the first strategy is concerned, TNCs search globally for the least expensive resources, such as labor and natural resources, favorable business climates, friendly governments, good markets, and limited competition from other TNCs. TNCs are not passive entities. They actively attempt to create the circumstances for the development of any of the conditions mentioned above. Effective production strategies are linked to the mobility of TNCs. In many instances, relatively low technology production facilities are established overseas and workers are trained relatively quickly and inexpensively. Simultaneously, the speed with which the facility is established means that it can also be liquidated on very short notice. This strategy protects TNCs from the development of less desirable or even hostile conditions in the host country. As far as the penetration and control of markets are concerned, TNCs have relatively easy access to regions protected by tariffs. The penetration of protected areas is accomplished by establishing a subsidiary in the region that is camouflaged as a local firm. This strategy is achieved by building factories with local names, purchasing a local business and maintaining the original name, creating structures where labor force and management are local, and establishing joint ventures with locally owned firms. Alfred Sloan of GM stated that the German company Opel was purchased in order to give GM a "German background instead of operating as foreigners" (Rubner 1990, 110).

Causes

In the past, Rubner argues, multinational corporations were able to count on the active assistance of nation-states. He contends that "the postulated right to invest overseas was often sustained by diplomatic pressure. The big powers intervened forcefully to protect investments owned by their nationals. If such interventions did not bear fruits, governments showed their displeasure by punishing the guilty host country" (1990, 174). This displeasure not only entailed diplomatic maneuvers but was also associated with overt or covert military actions. This is no longer the case, Rubner maintains, as "Western governments ceased to pretend that they were protecting their own TNCs" (176). A primary reason for such behavior rests on the development of anti-TNC sentiment in advanced nation-states. Accordingly, public opinion is indifferent to the treatment that TNCs receive abroad. In addition, the growth of anticorporate movements—such as the environmental and labor movements—placed public opinion in direct opposition to corporate interests. Some of the consequences of this situation are that TNCs' objectives are, now more than ever, diverging from those of nation-states, and TNCs actively operate to counter nation-states' behaviors that are damaging to their interests. This posture does not only pertain to the company itself but also to the behavior of managers.

Transnational Corporations

TNCs are "stateless supergiant corporations" organized around the concept of the maximization of profit at the global level. Accordingly, says Rubner, TNCs severed their ties with national interests and carry "a lot of flags" to accommodate their interests. Desirable factors of production and supportive business climates are the recipe for continuous economic growth. Nation-states that oppose TNCs' actions do not recognize the benefit that expanded business opportunities generate for society and will suffer negative consequences. Because of their visibility and because they obey economic laws, TNCs are attacked by a variety of sources, including unsympathetic nation-states. In order to defend themselves, they are occasionally forced to take actions that have negative social consequences in the host country. But the idea that TNCs illegally force nation-states to accommodate their interests is greatly exaggerated, according to Rubner. In effect, TNCs generate far more positive socioeconomic consequences for the communities where they operate than they do the negative consequences that are often reported in scientific and popular media.

Rudner argues that the notion of statelessness should also be applied to managers. Like the corporations they represent, managers are geocentrically oriented people who are prepared to take assignments in any location of the world at any time, regardless of their culture of origin or family obligations. Their primary objective is to place the global interests of the corporation above sectional and/or national interests. Accordingly, and regardless of their home country and personal feelings, managers cannot act patriotically, for their allegiance rests with the corporation.

To be sure, this pro-TNC argument is not solely the province of conservative thinkers like Rubner. Some "leftists" have also spoken in favor of the role of TNCs in globalization. A notable example is Gavin Kitching, who presents a "qualified defense of multinationals" (2001, 42), contending that the number of TNCs (or "supranationals," as he prefers to call them) engaged in behavior with negative social and economic consequences is greatly exaggerated and, moreover, that this behavior is the result of structural conditions that dictate how can TNCs operate. TNCs, he argues, are far better employers than many "local" companies—they provide better wages and working conditions and obey local laws—in part because they can afford to be more "generous" than local companies. The cost of labor in developing regions is so much cheaper than in developed countries that TNCs can pay wages considered high by local standards and still make a large profit. Also, because TNCs lack local political legitimacy, they need to be on their best behavior and appear model employers (43). Yet the absence of a global regulatory entity (i.e., a global state) is the most important structural reason for "negative" corporate behavior. Owing to the absence of a global regulatory entity and the consequent political instability and uncertainties, TNCs tend to prefer short-term goals (profit) over a more balanced and constructive local presence. The structural gap between a global economy and a local polity ultimately shapes the behavior of TNCs. TNCs, Kitching concludes, cannot change this situation, which can be altered only at the political level through the creation of a global political entity that could regulate the global economy.[3]

Outlook

Returning to Rubner, he argues that in the new global system the world is getting smaller. He sees geographically remote events affecting the lives of people in local communities. Rubner, however, questions the often proposed theory of the development of larger political organizations. He sees large national or supranational bodies, such as the EU, losing power as political decision making is increasingly put in the hands of smaller nation-states. Smaller nation-states will compare favorably to the larger and more powerful countries of the past, which will be affected by the "distance" between those who govern and those who are governed. Rubner predicts a crisis of large organizations at both the political and economic levels. At the economic level, TNCs that continue to adopt the strategy of economies of scale will be

---

3. While less positive about globalization than Rubner, Kitching also concludes that more globalization is actually beneficial for the world's poor and for developing regions. In this respect he joins "progressive" thinkers such as Thomas Friedman (2000) who view globalization's negative consequences as the necessary price to pay for socioeconomic growth. For Kitching, globalization's decentralization of production and hypermobility of capital create new opportunities for developing regions and workers. While jobs may be "lost" in developed regions thanks to protest by local unions and left-leaning political groups, new jobs are created in less developed regions. He contends that if one job created is equal to one job lost, the fact that jobs reappear in the less developed South is a positive sign in the struggle to reduce socioeconomic inequality worldwide. Many scholars criticize this positive view of globalization. Gereffi and his associates (Gereffi 1994; Gereffi and Korzeniewicz 1994; Gereffi, Spener, and Bair 2002), for instance, maintain that the creation of new jobs in less developed regions often does not translate into lifting workers above the subsistence level. He contends that currency instability and government attempts to maintain export competitiveness depress wages and do not eliminate the threat of plant relocation.

out-competed by those that decentralize operations. The logic of cost efficiency associated with the creation of economies of scale, he concludes, is not a viable strategy for the future.

Contradictory Dimension of Globalization Thesis

Authors included in this group view globalization as a contradictory process. While the notion of contradiction is also employed by some authors in the other two camps, a key feature of the contributions reviewed below rests on the importance that the contradictory dimension of globalization assumes in their analyses. The concept of contradiction refers to the existence of conflicting demands that create incompatible and therefore socially destabilizing outcomes. Dominant social groups' quest for continuous control of society and its components mandates the creation of conflicting demands. Attempts to address these demands generate outcomes that destabilize society and produce the prerequisites for crises but also for change. First introduced by Marx (1967) in his classical analysis of the bourgeoisie's rule of capitalist society, the concept of contradiction has been employed by contemporary social analysts to indicate the inability of ruling classes to promote sustainable change and social development. Contradictions open up spaces for resistance, which subordinate groups use to advance alternative agendas. Because the notion of contradiction is often contextualized in a political economy and/or critical theory approach, authors included in this camp concern themselves with issues of democracy, equality, and justice. The section reviews the works of the British social geographer David Harvey, the sociologists Saskia Sassen and Christos Pitelis, and the rural geographer Terry Marsden.

David Harvey

The British social geographer David Harvey (1989, 2000, 2005, 2006) defines the era of economic globalization as the change from Fordism to flexible accumulation. While he analyzes structural and economic changes associated with the emergence of globalization, he stresses that globalization is a comprehensive capitalist regime shift that involves new technologies, capital mobility, spatially reconfigured social relations, restructured organizations, but also cultural transformation.[4]

---

4. Similar points are contained in the work of Carl Boggs (2000). Boggs's central argument is that globalization signifies primarily the *corporate colonization* of the economic, political, social and cultural spheres. Dwelling on the case of the United States, he maintains that neoliberal global capitalism has translated into *antipolitics,* by which Boggs means the reduction of public spaces that allow people to participate in democratic decision making. In es-

Change

The major change of late capitalism consists of the end of Fordism and its replacement by flexible accumulation. Flexible accumulation refers to the establishment of a new system through which capitalism has been able to revitalize capital accumulation while generating compatible cultural conditions. It is characterized by an acceleration of the time, and a narrowing of the space, necessary to carry out economic activities. This time-space compression allows much enhanced mobility of capital (hypermobility of capital) and the fragmentation of industrial and social relations. Corporations move about the globe with unprecedented mobility facilitated by their new ability to decentralize and fragment production and financial operations. These changes not only restarted capital accumulation and established TNCs as the primary actors in the global society; they also altered the established balance of forces worldwide. They weakened the nation-state as they generated flows of commodities and capital that the state could not control. This situation broke the tacit alliance between "big capital" and "big nation-

---

sence, global capitalism has significantly reduced the ability of individuals and groups to participate in public life. The roots of this depoliticized society are to be found in the growth of corporate power. Since the early 1970s corporations have developed beyond their already established hegemonic status to control key spheres of human existence. By promoting neo-liberal policies, corporations have eliminated organized political opposition and stigmatized state intervention. Indeed, they equate free market mobility with freedom for the entire society. The Keynesian state and its interventionist postures are identified with oppression and ultimately lack of democracy. It follows, according to this corporate ideology, that the dismantling of the social state and its welfare programs is the necessary step to enhanced economic flexibility, which in turn generates sustained economic growth and expanded freedom. Additionally, the corporate-based stigmatization of state intervention is employed to discredit opposition theories. In this context, the end-of-ideology argument (Fukuyama 1992) (the triumph of the Western model over the Soviet system) has emerged as an accepted justification for silencing voices that criticize the market-centered paradigm. Corporate colonization of the economic and ideological spheres, Boggs maintains, is accompanied by the colonization of the cultural sphere. Here the idea of flexibility has been transported into the realm of individuality. While corporate freedom to move about the world free from state regulations is seen as a kind of freedom, the release of the individual from commitments to the public sphere is likewise liberating. Economic growth and faith in the market justify the movement toward a much more self-absorbed society. In this context, the resolution of social problems is largely shifted from the public to the private arena. Boggs uses the therapeutic revolution to argue that social problems like drug addiction are increasingly viewed as the individual's problems and should thus be addressed through such measures as "the twelve-step program," the success of which ultimately depends upon the individual's will. "The social" and "the political" are eliminated from the framework of analysis, while large-scale global issues are increasingly met with local and/or individual solutions. The corporate colonization of the state and civil society is resisted nevertheless. Boggs identifies racial, cultural, and labor-based movements, but also third-party politics, as actors who can resist corporate domination.

states" that characterized the post–World War II Fordist era, leaving the nation-state to face a much more complex and difficult set of tasks. The contradictory dimension of this situation consists of the fact that the nation-state is still needed to control the unwanted consequences of TNCs' activities. Simultaneously, however, the state must provide for its own financial means, which are guaranteed by the accumulation of capital and therefore by TNCs' investment. The state is then forced to create conditions for a "good business climate" in order to attract investments. The task of monitoring TNCs' activities and creating a "good business climate" are contradictory because nation-states do not have the instruments to effectively control global capital and commodity flows.

Causes

The structural and cultural conditions that allowed Fordism's unprecedented economic growth and social stability had been exhausted by the early 1970s. Increased international competition reduced corporate profits. Attempts to revitalize profits were frustrated by decreased productivity that displaced workers and decreased consumption. States' attempts to increase consumption through public spending triggered inflation, unemployment growth, and fiscal crisis. The failure of modernization projects to enhance the socioeconomic conditions of developing countries and the mounting demands of disenfranchised groups in developed countries added more strain to the system and put an end to the Fordist socioeconomic equilibrium. The corporate response was to overcome these Fordist "rigidities" with new flexibilities. Additionally, this rationalization dwelled on new cybernetic and information technologies that restructured work processes and firms, increased social control, raised rates of exploitation, and, through the adoption of neoliberal discourses and policies worldwide, generated a new procapital cultural climate.

Transnational Corporations

TNCs are the most important forces in the post-Fordist era. Responding to the crisis of rigidity that ended the Fordist regime of accumulation, TNCs were able to increase their flexibility of operation. According to Harvey, flexibility is meant to overcome the consequences of sclerotic mass-production systems based on high fixed capital investments, rigid labor markets, and labor allocations conditioned by strong working-class power. This process featured the emergence of decentralized forms of production and the restructuring of labor markets that weakened trade unions, working-class political parties, and welfare systems. Under post-Fordism, TNCs are able to search globally for the most convenient conditions of production, which include low costs of factors of production, favorable political and social climates, and supportive nation-states. TNCs' hypermobility threatens nation-states, which, to attract corporate investment, often tailor their economic policies to the interests of corporations. Because of their mobility, TNCs are also difficult for nation-states to control. This situation is contradictory in that it does not allow nation-states to support TNCs' actions as they did in the past. TNCs' CEOs are emerging as the most powerful component of the new ruling class.

Outlook

Harvey stresses the spatial reconfiguration of capitalism on a global basis. The current conditions of "postmodernity" are nothing more than the most recent phase of a technologically based long-term process of "time-space compression" that makes the world's farthest reaches increasingly accessible. Under capitalism, time-space compression is accelerated in great bursts following major profit squeezes and market crises, during which capitalists seek technical innovations that can accelerate capital's "turnover time" and speed the realization of profit and reinvestment. Harvey stresses the importance of capital mobility, but he addresses its significance in the context of a comprehensive vision of broader sociocultural change. He connects flexible accumulation with cultural postmodernization, attending closely to matters of representation (e.g., postmodern architecture, film, theory). The global markets that favor rootless finance capital are linked by new instant modes of communication, media, information, and transport. As a result, contemporary society is characterized by an antidemocratic and authoritarian neoliberal turn that has restored the domination of the ruling class at the expense of gains won by subordinate classes during the most of the second half of the twentieth century. This restoration of class power, Harvey concludes, is contradictory both ideologically and materially, and it is opposed by a number of groups. This is a situation that gives opposition movements opportunities to struggle for alternatives to the neoliberal, U.S.-dominated globalization.

Saskia Sassen

For Sassen (1996, 1998, 2000), globalization features the *denationalization* of socioeconomic processes, which generates a crisis of national *sovereignty*. Denationalization refers to the "offshoring" of economic activities engineered to enhance corporate profit and promoted as a tool to revitalize national economies. The crisis of sovereignty refers to the growing inability of the nation-state to control socioeconomic processes that now unfold largely outside its regulatory umbrella. The contradictory dimension of this situation rests on the fact that the nation-state's pursuit of economic well-being is carried out through processes of deregulation and liberalization that limit the nation's sovereignty. As in the case of other aspects of globalization, this process does not take place in the same way in every sector or in developed and developing regions. Globalization is not a homogenous process.

Change

In developed countries economic globalization signified the transfer of production and service facilities across national borders. This process makes it difficult for nation-states to collect taxes and enforce regulations. Simultaneously, however, the sites of corporate headquarters remain concentrated in developed countries. Accordingly, while production is decentralized, control stays in selected geographical areas. The result is that the potential for democratic decentralization of economic activities is denied for a situation in which highly integrated corporate structures concentrate profit appropriation. In developing countries denationalization consists primarily in the creation of trade and export manufacturing zones designed to attract global investments. TNCs locate facilities without being subjected to local taxes and regulations. In this case there is a de facto abatement of the jurisdiction of the nation-state, which translates into a denationalization of the area. While the circulation of commodities and the global spread of production processes proliferate, attempts to control the circulation of labor mount. Sassen contrasts the globalization of production and financial capital with the nationalization of politics—the lifting of border controls for capital and goods and the tightening of restrictions on the mobility of labor. Nation-states reassert their claims over the control of national territories. The global search for more profitable investments worldwide has created disinvestment in middle-class jobs. This situation promotes the search for profitable short-term opportunities rather than long-term socioeconomic development, which diminishes the financial capacity of nation-states to maintain entitlements at their Fordist levels. Finally, the globalization of the economy and society has eroded welfare state entitlements and citizen access to publicly funded economic and social support.

Causes

Most of the features associated with globalization are the outcome of corporate actions. TNCs responded to established forms of social and economic governance characterized by social spending and regulation deemed too high to guarantee acceptable profit levels. TNCs thus moved production offshore and concentrated finance and managerial control in selected regions of the advanced world. But globalization, in Sassen's view, cannot be attributed simply to TNCs' tendency to transnationalize production; it is the outcome of broader forces in a complex and evolving situation. In particular, attention should be paid to the fact that nation-states themselves have been promoters of processes that "opened" local economies and societies.[5] More specifically, deregulation of economic and social policies has limited the effectiveness of state-engineered forms of control. Deregulation has generated the proliferation of global financial markets, which has greatly diminished the ability of nation-states to control the economy. For instance, the emergence of foreign exchange and bond markets has reduced the capacity of central banks to regulate nations' interest rates, which are now affected more by market fluctuations than by the decisions of central banks.

Transnational Corporations

These corporations have decentralized production by dispersing production units worldwide to take advantage of favorable conditions of production. This geographical dispersal of factories is paralleled by the concentration of corporate operations. In effect, TNCs' dispersal of productive operations requires a system of coordination and control that is achieved largely through processes of concentration of central functions—i.e., planning, financial, managerial, legal, and accounting functions necessary for the operation of firms. These functions have been concentrated in developing countries. TNCs' push to globalize their operations has been a strategic move to increase profits by using advantageous conditions and factors of production and avoid stringent national and/or local regulations. While TNCs have been successful in reducing the powers of nation-states and their ability to regulate, they still need systems of coordination and regulation—for example, they still need the guarantee of property rights and contracts that allow commod-

5. This point has been stressed by a number of authors who have explored the globalization of the economy and society. Employing the case of the North American garment industry, Gereffi and his associates (Gereffi, Spener, and Bair 2002) argue that the development of global production chains has been enhanced by the "opening" of the economies of less developed regions. In the case of the garment industry, the opening of the economies of Mexico and other Central American countries, and the concomitant abandonment of "Fordist" economic measures, have facilitated the decentralization of production once carried out in the United States. The hypermobility of TNC capital, therefore, is not simply the outcome of corporate strategy but a much more complex process in which nation-states and their neoliberal principles play a significant role.

ities and assets to be moved globally. These functions were once performed by the nation-state. Today there is a tendency to transfer these organizational functions to private transnational institutions and regimes that establish new forms of regulations heavily affected by liberalist ideology.

Outlook

Globalization does not automatically mean that the nation-state is withering away. Global phenomena do manifest themselves in national territory and are mediated by national institutions and cultures. Additionally, the destabilization of sovereignty through denationalization of territories does not signal an overall inability to control global processes. Sovereignty has been decentralized and partially redistributed to other entities. Some of these entities are transnational political organizations such as the European Union, and some are international agreements and processes such as the international agreements on human rights. Others are networks of smaller geographical entities such as cities. Because flexible global flows must and do materialize at the local level, the centers where these materializations occur more frequently (i.e., the global cities) represent important new components of the global system. Owing to the fact that both supranational organizations and networks are needed for the continuous growth of capital accumulation, it is at these levels that new forms of resistance and democratization can be and ultimately are developed.

Christos Pitelis

Christos Pitelis's work (1991a, 1991b, 1993) is an example of a structuralist reading of globalization (see also Holloway 1993 and Picciotto 1991). For Pitelis the contradictory dimension of globalization rests on the inability of its primary actors to reconcile their interests. This situation concerns TNCS and nation-states whose relationship can be summarized as *"rivalry and collusion."*

Change

The decline of the United States and the concomitant growth of Europe and Japan as new world powers affected the regulation and coordination of world affairs based on a nation-state system. In the past, corporations relied on the United States to maintain global order and on nation-states' actions to support corporate interests domestically and internationally. The collapse of this old system motivated TNCS to promote the creation of transnational organizations to maintain global stability and protect them from domestic opposition and socioeconomic problems. This position contradicts some of TNCS' interests, as the decline of nation-states' powers affect TNCS' ability to control labor domestically, legitimate their presence in the national level, and better allocate factors of production. TNCS also benefited from this change, however. Pitelis argues that transnational political organizations are less affected by class struggle than national organizations are. Accordingly, they represent more desirable tools to address TNCS' needs for legitimation and coordination. At the national level, Pitelis argues, state actions that favor corporations are directly resisted by subordinate groups. The state officialdom is particularly affected by these struggles in that elected officials depend on the popular vote. Transnational political organizations are not elected by popular constituencies. Accordingly, they are less affected by class struggle than their domestic counterparts are. Therefore, by supporting the development of transnational organizations, TNCS find solutions to problems of international organization and regulation. They also find a state form (the transnational state) that is less susceptible to pressure stemming from legitimization crises. In essence, the consolidation of TNCS diminished the power of nation-states, but nation-states will persist, for TNCS need them.

Causes

For Pitelis, the origin of globalization is to be found in the crisis of corporate profit experienced from the early 1970s to the 1990s. The significant reduction in corporate profit margins and the concomitant increase in nation-states' creation of social programs and demand for corporate accountability motivated corporations to search for more profitable forms of production and reduced nation-state powers. To achieve these objectives TNCS sought to establish a system that allowed them to maneuver worldwide with enhanced flexibility, (i.e., to reduce and/or eliminate forms of political and social control over business activities) and to distance themselves from the socioeconomic commitments embedded in Fordism (most notably social stability and economic expansion that benefited lower social strata). In the new global economy, TNCS succeeded in enhancing profits by exploiting weak labor and promoting probusiness social climates worldwide.

Transnational Corporations

To achieve these objectives, TNCS avoided requests from nation-states while simultaneously demanding nation-state support. TNCS opposed nation-states' postures that required controls over production practices, use of labor and natural resources, and corporate strategies. Accordingly, one of TNCS' most important strategies in the new global economy has been to search globally for convenient factors and conditions of production worldwide. In order to benefit from favorable factors and conditions of production, however, TNCS need a national system. In order to exploit labor, for instance, TNCS need a national labor force and a national system (state) that allows the existence of weak labor pools and institutional conditions that favor their exploitation. The nation-state legitimizes TNCS' activities within its territory and allows the continuation of profitable corporate activities. While nation-states can benefit from TNCS activities,[6] TNCS' demands ultimately threaten the capacity of the state. This means that the state encounters increasing problems in its efforts to justify TNCS' activities to groups that do not benefit from them. Accordingly, state support for TNCS generates resistance, which may translate into opposition to the re-election of members of the state officialdom.[7]

Outlook

TNCS and nation-states need each other's services to prosper in the global system. This mutual dependence (collusion) is generated by opposing interests and it is ultimately contradictory. Nation-states need TNCS because they need investments to generate economic growth and progress. TNCS need nation-states to exploit labor and natural resources and to maintain probusiness climates. Simultaneously, TNCS act in ways that are not necessarily conducive to the maintenance of social, political, and economic equilibrium within a nation. Indeed, TNCS exist to make profits, not to promote social stability. This situation (rivalry) creates problems for the state, which responds by attempting to limit or control TNCS' actions. Once the state's legitimizing capacity is undermined, the potential for rivalry between nation-states and TNCS emerges, as the class nature of nation-states is exposed. The

6. Pitelis argues that nation-states that are the home bases to TNCS can benefit from their actions in several ways. First, because nation-states need TNCS to invest in their territories for the purpose of economic gain, TNCS' actions within a national territory can be directly linked to growth. Second, cheap foreign production can mean cheaper consumer goods back home. Third, depending on tax regulations and organizational forms, some overseas operations may be taxable and therefore bring tax revenue into the state. Fourth, TNCS help increase brand-name loyalty overseas, which spurs domestic exports. Finally, success in international competitiveness can provide for expanded home wages through increased export demand.

7. Pitelis stresses that TNCS' powers extend to the ideological and political arenas. Ideologically, TNCS can count on politicians who believe that prosperity depends on strong TNCS, even if this means increased costs to citizens. They also see economic prosperity as a road to re-election and therefore fervently support pro-TNC platforms. Politically this situation translates into agendas that ultimately support TNCS' interests but that are championed in terms of collective social and economic well-being.

degree of the rivalry depends on the strength of the nation-state; weaker states might face deindustrialization or be forced to introduce pro-TNC legislative measures. This situation points to the overall instability and class nature of the globalization project.

Terry Marsden

Focusing on agriculture, food, and rural development, Marsden and his associates (Marsden 2003; Marsden and Arce 1995; Marsden, Cavalcanti, and Ferreira 1996; Morgan, Marsden, and Murdoch 2006) argue that the process of globalization, while corporate dominated, is complex, contradictory, and resisted by a variety of actors. They criticize the often-cited distinction between a corporate-dominated "conventional" production and consumption system and a culturally based "alternative" system in favor of a view that stresses a much more porous and complex system of food production and consumption. The primary contradiction of the global agrifood system rests on the continuous domination of productivist postures that are ill suited to address growing demands for quality food products and environmentally sound agrifood production. While food networks have become more global, nation-states still must continue to regulate corporate activities in response to public pressure and for the good of public interests. Accordingly, state actions to satisfy its citizen-consumers often conflict with the designs of global producers and retailers whose capital accumulation activities are not necessarily linked to domestic processes that legitimize current social arrangements. As a result, a fundamental incompatibility remains between processes that enhance capital accumulation and mechanisms that promote social legitimacy. The ensuing resistance to global food networks is framed by a set of dialectically related relationships that includes processes of deregulation and re-regulation and homogenization and differentiation of consumption and production.

Causes

Marsden and his associates employ a constructionist approach to the study of globalization. While acknowledging the importance of approaches that analyze structural change, they provide a reading of global agriculture and food that incorporates social agency. In this context Marsden argues that increased world competition and difficulties in maintaining established patterns of socioeconomic development ended Keynesian production and consumption regimes. In the case of agriculture and food, Marsden stresses that slow rates of economic growth, along with the emergence of new food producers (such as the European Union), destabilized established international relations (food regimes). This situation allowed for the "deregulation" of existing (Fordist) socioeconomic systems in the North and the introduction of "structural adjustment" programs in the South. These changes paved the way for the current period of neoliberal "re-regulation" that is termed globalization. Key aspects of this new global agrifood system are the importance assumed by "after-the-farm" processes in the generation of the value of food commodities, and the unintended consequences and resistance generated at the local level. The local, therefore, remains an important social site for the definition of actions in the global arena.

Transnational Corporations

The establishment of new and global political discourses that favor neoliberal economic postures allowed the strengthening of TNCs not only at the level of production but also at levels that transcend production. Marsden sees corporate retailers as powerful new actors in the global setting. For most of the second half of the twentieth century and in the opening years of the new millennium, food consumption has been characterized by the introduction of new food items. Because of the proliferation of these food items, their value is increasingly established away from production sites and at new retail sites. Corporate retailers promote globalized consumption that creates new markets but also new forms of power and control. They define products in terms of quality and desirability (creation of value) that respond to consumers' demands but also shape and influence them. Retailers thus control the re-regulation of the quality of food items and place it in the private sphere (corporate decisions and policies) and away from the public sphere (state regulation). In addition, corporate retailers extend their control over distant actors as they impose their conditions of production on local food producers around the world. Marsden concludes that, "while [corporate retailers'] relative social and political power varies considerably across the advanced world, they have become major players in the social definition of the foods and images and identities of food. In addition, their international influence in food sourcing far outweighs their cross-national selling power" (2003, 41). The latter is increasing as the concentration of food retailers increases.

The power of transnational corporations is effectively resisted, though. Marsden and his associates stress the increased importance of the "moral economy of food," a system in which sentiments about the quality of food (i.e., its taste, preparation, health implications, etc.) take primacy over other objectives such as its cost. In the contemporary global society, consumers' preference for the moral economy of food has forced corporations to take actions that address these consumers' concerns over more strictly economically advantageous corporate strategies.

Outlook

Marsden argues that the current global conditions of food production and consumption are unsustainable. On the one hand, we have the dominant agro-industrial model of standardized food products. This system is based on deregulated markets that find their legitimacy through the implementation of hegemonic neoliberal policies. This system, however, is unable to address the mounting environmental, food security, and food safety risks that have characterized the past few decades. Alternative forms of development call for new patterns of "consumption" that see different uses of rural space, away from those of the agro-industrial productivist model. Even this post-productivist alternative is unsustainable, because it further marginalizes rural residents and producers and views nature as a consumption good to be exploited by the urban population. Unless new and more participatory uses of rural space are set in place, the current global era, Marsden concludes, will not be able to address its contradictions.

2

ENVIRONMENTALISM, INDUSTRY RESTRUCTURING, AND GLOBAL
REGULATION: THE TUNA-DOLPHIN CONTROVERSY

Tuna is the debut for a great debate between environmentalists and traders.
—Oliver Belisario, Caracas-based consultant for Venezuela's tuna industry (Brooke 1992a, 7)

The tuna-dolphin controversy covers a thirty-year struggle between environmental groups, transnational corporations (TNCs), tuna fishermen, and various nation-states and supranational organizations to define the regulations of the eastern tropical Pacific (ETP) tuna fishery. The focus of the controversy is the Marine Mammal Protection Act of 1972 (MMPA). The "dolphin-safe" label on tuna cans is an outcome of this struggle and the first ecolabel for fisheries products. This chapter traces the history of the tuna-dolphin controversy and the resulting debate over MMPA to make three analytical points regarding globalization. The first is that globalization is characterized by the power and growth of TNCs. The tuna-dolphin controversy demonstrates that tuna TNCs exercised considerable power in the industry and over the nation-state by taking advantage of the hypermobility of capital and using global sourcing. Our point, however, is that despite the power of tuna TNCs, globalization is a contested process, as resistance to TNCs emerged from various segments of the state and from social groups that operate from "below." In this case, different groups used their resources to advance competing definitions regarding the regulation of the ETP tuna-dolphin fishery. These struggles have been carried out within the nation-state, between nation-states, and increasingly under the purview of supranational trade organizations.

The second analytical point is that globalization limits the ability of the nation-state to carry out its historical roles. More specifically, globalization hinders the ability of the nation-state to mediate among relevant social

groups in order to foster accumulation of capital and simultaneously legitimize it for the rest of the population (Friedland 1991; O'Connor 1974). Capital accumulation and social legitimation are the most fundamental roles
historically played by the nation-state under capitalism (Carnoy 1984; Offe
and Ronge 1979). Fostering capital accumulation means establishing the
conditions necessary for the generation of profit within a nation-state.
Maintaining social legitimation refers to the state's role in justifying and
legitimating the processes of accumulation to the citizenry (Bonanno and
Constance 1996). In this story, the tuna fishing system—known as the
"purse-seine system"—that generated high levels of profit (accumulation)
for the tuna industry was declared illegitimate by social movement groups.

To date the U.S. government has been unable to resolve the tuna-dolphin
controversy at the national and international levels. The struggle continues
between environmentalists and free traders within the United States, as it
does between the United States and other countries, such as Mexico. Globalization also entails the emergence of supranational statelike organizations
that reproduce these state roles at the global level (Constance and Bonanno
1999b; McMichael 2002). The interventions of the Inter-American Tropical
Tuna Commission (IATTC) and the General Agreement on Tariffs and Trade/
World Trade Organization (GATT/WTO) are examples of supranational attempts
to balance capital accumulation with social legitimation via a mediating
statelike apparatus at the global level.

The third point deals with the consequences of globalization. Globalization has serious implications for the welfare of workers and other subordinate groups. As the tuna industry restructured to avoid the MMPA
regulations, thousands of tuna fisherman and processing workers on the U.S.
mainland, in Puerto Rico, and in Latin America lost their jobs. Additionally,
the early success of the environmental movement as a countervailing force
to the tuna TNCs was compromised as the environmentalist coalition split
into "mainstream" and "grassroots" segments. The mainstream groups
aligned themselves with the tuna industry, while the grassroots groups remained committed to eliminating dolphin deaths associated with tuna
fishing.

Purse-Seine Fishing: "Setting on Dolphins"

In the ETP, a stretch of ocean that reaches from Southern California to Chile
and extends about seven hundred miles west into the Pacific Ocean, dolphins

swim above schools of large yellowfin tuna. In the 1950s, with the adoption of nylon nets and hydraulic power blocs, San Diego tuna fishermen capitalized on this natural habit. When a pod of dolphins was sighted, the tuna fishermen deployed small speedboats to round up the dolphins into a tight circle. Then a medium-size boat encircled the pod with the purse-seine net and drew the net tight. The "setting on dolphins" method generated huge catches of valuable yellowfin tuna and enormous profits for the tuna industry (Tennesen 1989; Kraul 1990). Although dolphins could jump the net to safety, they did not do so. Accordingly, from the late 1950s through the late 1980s, 6 to 7 million dolphins drowned in the purse-seine nets (Brower 1989).

Public outrage over this slaughter and other marine mammal deaths brought about the passage of the Marine Mammal Protection Act of 1972. MMPA mandated that the incidence of dolphin deaths associated with tuna fishing be reduced to "insignificant levels approaching zero" (Godges 1988, 24). The American Tunaboat Association was given a two-year grace period to develop new dolphin-safe fishing techniques, but none were developed (Davis 1988). As part of MMPA, the National Marine Fisheries Service (NMFS), under the Department of Commerce, began an observer program that put observers on one-third of U.S. tuna boats to document the dolphin kills associated with tuna fishing (Holland 1991). In 1972 the U.S. tuna fleet accounted for 85 percent—368,600 of 423,678—of the dolphin kills in the ETP (Godges 1988).

Dolphin Death Quotas, Tuna Boat Reflagging, and the Foreign Fleet

By the late 1970s environmental groups perceived that little had been done to reduce the numbers of dolphin deaths associated with the practice of "setting on dolphins." Congress responded with a declining quota system that set yearly dolphin mortality rates at 78,000 in 1976 and 20,500 in 1981 (Godges 1988). During the Reagan administration the tuna industry successfully ended the managed decline in dolphin quotas, and the amendments to MMPA in 1984 extended the quota of 20,500 dolphin deaths per year indefinitely (Brower 1989; Holland 1991). Instead of abolishing the killing of dolphins associated with tuna fishing, the new quota system institutionalized the practice (Davis 1988).

To avoid the increased costs and limits on tuna fishing imposed by MMPA, between 1981 and 1987 most U.S. tuna boats reflagged under other nations

(Brower 1989; Davis 1988; Levin 1989). These limits included, among other things, a low number of dolphin kills allowed under the quota system, the presence of observers on one-third of U.S. tuna boats, and the adoption of the "Medina panel" and "backdown procedure."[1] The NMFS reported that U.S. dolphin kills declined from 268,600 in 1972 to fewer than 20,000 in 1987— mostly because the U.S. fleet shrank dramatically, from ninety-three to thirty-five boats between 1981 and 1988. Dolphin kill rates were still high in the ETP because of the rapid adoption of purse-seine technology by foreign fleets and the transfer of the U.S. fleet to foreign fleets (Levin 1989). By the late 1980s foreign fleets were responsible for the majority of the dolphin kills in the ETP—about a hundred thousand per year (*New York Times* 1989a).

In the 1970s and 1980s Mexico and some Latin American countries expanded their tuna fishing fleets and processing capacities to service the major U.S. market. The 1981–82 Mexican fleet additions were the largest in the history of the ETP. By 1987 the Mexican tuna fleet was the largest in the world (Hudgins 1987; Joseph 1986). In response to pressure from environmentalists, Congress added two amendments to MMPA in 1984 to control the foreign fleets. The amendments stated that tuna caught using purse-seine nets in the ETP could be imported to the United States only if the government of the foreign fleet could document that (1) it had implemented a dolphin-protection program "comparable" to that of the United States, and (2) the average incidental dolphin kill rate was "comparable" to that of the U.S. fleet (Trachtman 1992). Under pressure from environmental groups, Congress ordered the NMFS to close the U.S. tuna market to nations failing to meet these comparable standards (Levin 1989).

The new MMPA criteria were very problematic. By 1988 foreign tuna boats killed about four times as many dolphins as did the U.S. fleet (Audubon Society 1988). While Congress had ordered the NMFS in 1984 to ban tuna imports from "non-comparable" countries, these rules were not published until 1988 and gave countries until 1991 to achieve the comparable kill rate. In 1988 the NMFS came under strong criticism from environmentalists and Congress for delaying sanctions against foreign fleets that continued to kill dolphins at a high rate. The NMFS responded that moving any more quickly would have forced the foreign fleets to sell to other markets (Davis 1988).

In 1988 Earth Island Institute (EII), Greenpeace, the Cetacean Society, the

---

1. The "Medina panel" was a special area of finer netting near the top of the purse-seine net that reduced the frequency of dolphin beaks and flippers getting caught in the net. The "backdown procedure" was a practice whereby the tuna boat would reverse the engines and drop the back of the purse-seine net below the water line to allow the dolphins to escape.

Sierra Club, the Whale Center, and other groups pooled their resources and established the Marine Mammal Protection Act Reauthorization Coalition to push for improvements in the law and at the same time encourage boycotts (Godges 1998). The coalition filed a lawsuit in federal court in San Francisco that sought to force the Department of Commerce to honor the 1984 amendments to MMPA and to impose a ban on imports from foreign fleets. The coalition also urged major U.S. tuna industry companies Heinz (StarKist) and Ralston Purina (Chicken of the Sea) to voluntarily end tuna purchases from nations that violated U.S. laws. At the same time the National Audubon Society joined EII in a campaign to reduce annual dolphin deaths to zero (Audubon Society 1988). Early in 1988 the coalition won a court ruling that ordered the NMFS to place observers on all U.S. tuna boats to better monitor dolphin kills (Levin 1989; New York Times 1989a and 1989b).

In 1988 EII sponsored Sam LaBudde's investigative work on a Panamanian tuna boat. The video that he made was first aired in March 1988 to "horrified audiences" in the United States (Kraul 1990). LaBudde showed his video at the congressional hearings on MMPA in 1988 (Brower 1989). At those hearings several senators and congresspeople expressed displeasure with the NMFS and the Department of Commerce for their failure to implement the regulations to protect dolphins and keep "dolphin-death" tuna cans off grocery store shelves. In response to one senator's query—why had the NMFS taken four years to formulate "interim final regulations" to that end?—NMFS director Charles Fullerton replied, "It's a very delicate operation to get those regulations. We developed some over a year ago which were not acceptable to either the tuna industry or the foreign nations. So we went back to the drawing board and developed a whole new set, the ones that are now in interim phase" (Brower 1989, 35).

Tuna Industry Restructuring and Consumer Boycotts

In the 1960s and 1970s tuna companies integrated vertically through the development of long-term contracts with tuna fishermen or by owning their own boats to guarantee product for their processing plants. By the 1980s almost 70 percent of the tuna was caught, processed, traded, and distributed by ten multinational corporations with vertical integration systems (Hudgins and Fernandez 1987; Iversen 1987). In the mid-1980s the largest firms supplying the U.S. market were Heinz's StarKist, Van Camp Seafood's Chicken of the Sea (owned by Ralston Purina) and Bumble Bee (owned by Castle and

Cook). In early 1982 twenty tuna canneries operated in the United States: twelve on the mainland (most of them in California), five in Puerto Rico, two in American Samoa, and one in Hawaii (USITC 1986). By 1986 the Puerto Rican and American Samoan plants were still operating, but only one plant on the mainland was still in business. The mainland plants closed because of high labor costs, a strong U.S. dollar, rising foreign imports, and the recession of 1981 (Floyd 1987). About twenty-four hundred tuna-processing jobs were lost when Van Camp closed its San Diego plant and StarKist closed its plant in Terminal Island, California (Herrick and Koplin 1986). As mainland plants closed, capacities at the Puerto Rican and American Samoan plants increased owing to lower labor costs and tax incentives (Parks, Donley, and Herrick 1990).

Frustrated by their inability to eliminate the quota system for dolphin kills and still unhappy with lack of NMFS enforcement of the embargo, the coalition launched a consumer boycott in 1988 of the three major tuna processors in the United States. In response to the boycott and letter-writing campaign, the "Big 3" processors announced that they would no longer accept "dolphin-unsafe" tuna and turned to Asian suppliers to ensure that their tuna was not caught with purse-seine nets. They also agreed to put a "dolphin-safe" label on their products to certify their commitment (Sharecoff 1990). August Felando, president of the American Tunaboat Association, warned that the decision "would only serve to penalize the [U.S.] fishing fleet, which has improved its methods for protecting dolphins" (*Time* 1990). In the late 1980s tuna catches by the U.S. fleet dropped drastically, as did the number of U.S. tuna boats that fished the ETP (Thurston 1990; Wallace 1991).

Because of the increased cost of production associated with MMPA and the increasing necessity for U.S.-based tuna firms to source "dolphin-safe" tuna, in the 1980s these firms reversed this trend toward vertical integration, sold their tuna boats, discontinued their long-term contracts, and sourced their product on the international spot market. Almost all of the U.S. fleet moved their operations to the western tropical Pacific (WTP), where skipjack tuna and dolphin do not regularly associate. As a result of these changes the primary locus of tuna processing moved from Puerto Rico to American Samoa (Hudgins and Fernandez 1987; Parks, Donley, and Herrick 1990). Not only is American Samoa closer to the WTP, it is also outside the U.S. customs district, which means that foreign vessels can unload their catch directly into the canneries, while tuna caught by foreign vessels must be unloaded outside Puerto Rico and transhipped there for processing (Iversen 1987).

In response to high labor costs in the United States, declining tax advantages in Puerto Rico–based canneries, lower labor rates and tax advantages in American Samoa, and the consumer boycott, two of the three largest U.S.-based firms sold their tuna operations to Asian firms in the late 1980s (USITC 1992). In 1988 Ralston Purina sold its Van Camp Chicken of the Sea operations to Mantrust of Indonesia. In 1989 Pillsbury sold its Bumble Bee brand to Unicord of Thailand (Handley 1989, 108). Bumble Bee was acquired as Unicord's first step in the formation a global tuna organization (Handley 1991a). By 1990, except for StarKist's plant in Mayaguez, the Puerto Rican tuna industry was controlled by Asian firms: Unicord, Mantrust, Mitsui, and Mistubishi (Luxner 1990). From 1982 to 1992 Puerto Rico lost approximately ten thousand tuna cannery jobs as the industry relocated to the WTP (USITC 1992). Once part of the largest tuna fleet in the world, many U.S. tuna boat captains went broke, and those who remained were forced to spend $1 million or more to retrofit their purse-seiners to travel farther out into the WTP (Kraul 1990; Kronman 1991).

The Inter-American Tropical Tuna Commission

During the 1970s the Inter-American Tropical Tuna Commission (IATTC) became increasingly involved in the management of the ETP tuna-dolphin fishery. The IATTC is a nongovernmental organization (NGO) based in La Jolla, California, composed of the tuna-fishing countries that fish the ETP. The primary responsibility of the IATTC is to recommend management initiatives to maintain tuna stocks at levels that produce maximum yields on a sustained basis (Joseph and Greenough 1979). After research conducted in 1966 revealed that tuna stocks in the ETP were being depleted rapidly, an overall catch quota was adopted for yellowfin tuna within a specified area of the ETP known as the "commission's yellowfin regulatory area" (CYRA). This annual quota was established on a first come, first served basis, which favored the development of "superseiners" and resulted in the rapid reduction of the length of the CYRA fishing season (Salia and Norton 1974). In the early years the U.S. fleet took nearly 100 percent of the allowable CYRA catch. In the 1970s the IATTC initiated individual quotas to countries adjacent to the CYRA that argued they deserved special access to the tuna resources just off their coasts and that the "distant water fishing nations" (DWFN) should be restricted. DWFN nations like the United States argued that tuna are a pelagic (migratory) species and therefore were not the property of any particular nation (Joseph and Greenough 1979).

In 1976 the IATTC developed programs to maintain both tuna and dolphin populations at sustainable levels. This agenda was problematic as tuna boats reflagged under countries that did not belong to the IATTC and then fished just outside its jurisdiction. In 1980 the quota system was abandoned. In 1988 the IATTC staffed observers on the foreign tuna boats to document the dolphin kills to satisfy the MMPA amendments requiring that foreign countries prove that their dolphin kill rates were comparable to those of the U.S. fleet. The use of the backdown procedure and Medina panels were also part of this voluntary program sponsored by the IATTC. These actions rapidly reduced the numbers of dolphin deaths attributed to the foreign fleets (Tennesen 1989).

The "Dolphin-Safe" Label, Embargoes, Compromises, and GATT

Although the coalition failed to win legislation mandating a phaseout of purse-seine netting at the 1988 MMPA reauthorization hearings, the success of the consumer boycott prompted it to renew its attack. The coalition proposed the Dolphin Protection Consumer Information Act, sponsored by Representative Barbara Boxer (D-CA) and Senator Joseph Biden (D-DE), along with a hundred other sponsors. Advocates of the bill wanted tuna can product labels stating that "the tuna in this product has been captured with technologies that are known to kill dolphins" and also a label for tuna caught without the purse-seine method stating that the product was "dolphin-safe" (Salmans 1990). The proposed act was criticized by NMFS director Charles Fullerton, U.S. Tuna Foundation spokesperson David Burney, and president of the American Tunaboat Association August Felando as being unfairly harmful to the U.S. tuna industry (Vickers 1989). The Bush administration opposed the bill, saying that the "voluntary policy adopted by the canners will allow market forces to solve the problem" (Taylor 1990). The Dolphin Protection Consumer Information Act was passed in 1990, mandating standards for the labeling of tuna cans as "dolphin-safe." The act defined "dolphin-safe" as tuna that was not caught by encircling dolphins with purse-seine nets and legislated that only such tuna be labeled "dolphin-safe" and that only "dolphin-safe" tuna could be sold in the United States. It also required that the secretary of state "immediately seek, through negotiations and discussion with appropriate foreign governments, to reduce and, as soon as possible, eliminate the practice of harvesting tuna through the use of purse seine nets intentionally deployed to encircle dolphins" (National Research Council 1992, 33).

Also in 1990 the coalition brought suit in the U.S. District Court for the Northern District of California seeking to enjoin the secretary of the treasury to implement MMPA's import restrictions. The NMFS had failed to make available comparability findings on dolphin mortality necessary to implement the 1988 amendments and thus had allowed tuna imports regardless of foreign dolphin kill rates (Trachtman 1992). The failure to produce "comparability data" stemmed from a lack of consensus on how exactly to interpret MMPA's intent. The NMFS interpretation centered on maintenance of optimal sustainable populations (OSP), while the environmentalists' view focused on reducing dolphin kills to "insignificant levels approaching zero." This unresolved controversy triggered the lawsuit. Judge Theldon Henderson found in favor of the coalition and issued an embargo on all tuna not proven to be "dolphin-safe" as defined by the 1988 MMPA amendments. This embargo affected the nations of Mexico, Venezuela, Panama, Ecuador, and Vanuatu (Morain 1990). Judge Henderson said that the Bush administration was taking too long to determine whether the foreign fleets were complying with U.S. law (*New York Times* 1990). He accused the foreign nations and the U.S. government of "foot-dragging" (Morain 1990).

After losing several appeals, the Bush administration reluctantly enforced the embargo, in the face of bitter denunciations by Mexico, which saw the embargo as a ploy to protect the U.S. market share by forcing a poor, developing nation to meet unreasonably high ecological standards (Scott 1991a; Uhlig 1991). The U.S. sanctions on Mexico were an embarrassment to the Bush administration, which was trying to get congressional approval for fast-track negotiations on the North American Free Trade Agreement (NAFTA) (Scott 1991b).

After consultations with U.S. government officials failed to achieve the removal of the embargoes, Mexico filed a complaint with the General Agreements on Tariffs and Trade (GATT) charging that the U.S. law was unfair environmental trade protectionism (Trachtman 1992; Uhlig 1991). Mexico saw the U.S. law as a unilateral attempt to regulate the fishing practices of foreign fishing vessels. The GATT hearings took place while Mexico and the United States were trying to negotiate NAFTA. With NAFTA at a critical stage, the issue presented the Bush administration with a volatile trade battle at the very time that it was trying to court Mexico as a major trading partner. Mexican critics of NAFTA seized upon the dispute as an example of U.S. domination under any such pact, while U.S. environmentalists cited the behavior of the Mexican tuna fleet to emphasize the need for tough environmental scrutiny of all aspects of a free trade accord (Uhlig 1991).

The GATT panel found in favor of Mexico, stating that "a contracting party may not restrict imports of a product merely because it originates in a country with environmental policies different from its own" (*The Economist* 1991, 3). Environmental concerns about the method of production, as opposed to the product itself, are excluded from consideration under Article III of GATT (Trachtman 1992). The United States asked Mexico not to press for the enforcement of the GATT ruling and promised to try to get the U.S. law changed. In September 1991 State, Commerce, and Trade Department officials reached an understanding with Mexico over the embargo. Mexican president Salinas de Gortari, in a show of good faith, announced that Mexico would postpone the final GATT decision and pursue a bilateral solution (Scott 1991b). In exchange for the Bush administration's pledge to try to change MMPA, Mexico issued a "ten-point plan" to reduce dolphin kills (Maggs 1991).

While resource-rich developing nations saw the U.S. embargoes as "green protectionism," environmentalists feared the compromise of U.S. environmental laws in free trade pacts and opposed a new GATT agreement because they felt that GATT could override some U.S. laws barring imports that didn't comply with U.S. environmental standards (Davis 1992; Magnusson, Hong, and Oster 1992, 130). The Bush administration failed to get the U.S. laws changed.

The initial embargo had little effect at the time, as Mexican tuna accounted for only about 3 percent of U.S. imports, but in early 1992 the coalition secured a second embargo to stop tuna "laundered" through third-party countries and then reexported to the United States (Scott 1991b). In January 1992 Judge Henderson ordered the Commerce Department to ban $266 million worth of tuna imports (about half of U.S. tuna imports) from twenty countries that bought tuna from Mexico, Venezuela, and Vanuatu and then reexported it to the United States (Bradsher 1992; *New York Times* 1992b). The Bush administration tried unsuccessfully to overturn the ruling, claiming that the action went well beyond the intent of the environmental law on which it was based (Wastler 1992).

While the first embargo had only a moderate effect on the countries, the secondary embargo significantly curtailed the volume and prices of Mexican and Venezuelan exports. The price per ton of "dolphin-unsafe" tuna fell drastically in 1990 and 1991 (Ellison 1991). As a result of being closed out of the U.S. market since 1990, Venezuela's tuna fleet shrank from 118 boats in 1988 to thirty-four in 1992. In Cumana, Venezuela, sailors and canners were out of work on a massive scale (Brooke 1992a). Soon after the secondary embargo, Venezuela and Mexico, which accounted for sixty-four of the ninety-seven purse-seiners operating in the ETP, joined the IATTC and pledged significant amounts of money for dolphin-safe fishing research (Brooke 1992b).

In response to the secondary embargo, in February 1992 the European Union, along with Thailand and Venezuela, appealed to the GATT, charging the United States with unfair trade protectionism (Maggs 1991). In 1994 the GATT again ruled in their favor (Goldberg 1994; Noah 1994), stating that the United States was not entitled under GATT to use trade measures to force other countries to adopt its own domestic environmental policies (McDorman 1995). According to GATT, problems concerning the "global commons" such as the tuna-dolphin controversy should be solved through "international environmental agreements." In comments on the ruling, David Phillips of EII stated, "They are kidding themselves if they think GATT can force the US to abandon laws to protect the global environment. In the 1990s free trade and efforts to protect the environment are on a collision course" (Brooke 1992a).

The La Jolla Agreement and the International Dolphin Conservation Act of 1992

The GATT decision on the secondary embargo stated that the controversy should be resolved via an international forum. Once again, attempts to reach a compromise between the United States and the petitioning countries failed. One such attempt was the IATTC-sponsored La Jolla Agreement of 1992, which formalized the voluntary program of onboard observers and dolphin-protection techniques on all foreign tuna vessels (Scott 1998). The agreement included a seven-year program of declining annual limits of dolphin mortalities (CMC 1996; Felando 1995). Environmental groups welcomed the IATTC efforts but considered them an adequate guarantee of continued dolphin protection (Brooke 1992b).

In June 1992 Representative Gerry Studds (D-MA) introduced a bill to end the embargo on Mexico and Venezuela and place a five-year moratorium on purse-seine tuna fishing in the ETP (*New York Times* 1992a). The bill also included severe trade sanctions for nations that violated the moratorium. While Mexico and Venezuela agreed to halt dolphin killing by their tuna fleets by 1994, they also agreed to face a U.S. embargo on all seafood products except shrimp if they resumed killing dolphins (Maggs 1991). After months of negotiations, the bill achieved bipartisan support and had the backing of the environmental coalition, and had been approved by the Mexican and Venezuelan governments (Parrish 1992). The bill was passed in October as the International Dolphin Conservation Act of 1992. But because Mexico and Venezuela did not sign the moratorium agreement, the United States continued to ban the sale of all non-"dolphin-safe" tuna within its borders. The embargoes cost Mexico, Venezuela, Colombia, Costa Rica, Ecuador, and Panama more than $100 million in revenues (Nunez 1995), and Mexico lost about fifteen thousand jobs tied directly or indirectly to tuna fishing (Frazier 1996). But another compromise sponsored by the IATTC was in the works.

The Panama Declaration

In October 1995 the Panama Declaration was signed by representatives of Belize, Colombia, Costa Rica, Ecuador, France, Honduras, Mexico, Panama, Spain, the United States, Vanuatu, and Venezuela (Felando 1995). The twelve governments promised to formalize by January 1996 this binding legal instrument, which would incorporate numerous changes to the resolutions adopted by the IATTC in the voluntary La Jolla Agreement of 1992. To accomplish this task, MMPA needed to be changed in three ways (Felando 1995): (1) the existing primary and secondary embargoes needed be lifted for tuna caught in compliance with the La Jolla Agreement as modified by the Panama Declaration; (2) access to the U.S. market had to be opened to tuna from states that were members of the IATTC and from states that had initiated steps to become members; and (3) the meaning of the "dolphin-safe" label would be changed to include tuna caught in the ETP by a purse-seine vessel in a net in which no dolphin mortality occurred, as documented by observers.

Five major environmental organizations provided written support for these legislative changes. The Center for Marine Conservation, the Environmental Defense Fund, Greenpeace, the National Wildlife Federation, and the World Wildlife Fund pledged to work with foreign governments and the U.S. Congress to bring about the final ratification of the Panama Declaration (Felando 1995). The Clinton administration and prominent conservative members of Congress supported the initiative (Blum 1995; Felando 1995; Fiore 1995). The declaration was lauded as a multilateral initiative that represented the norms of the international community rather than a narrow unilateral regulation imposed by one country on others.

The Panama Declaration modified the dolphin mortality limits of the La Jolla Agreement to include a total annual mortality not to exceed five thousand dolphins. These limits would be determined by national scientific advisory committees that based their decisions on the best scientific evidence designed to maintain or restore the biomass levels of harvested and associated stocks at or above levels capable of producing maximum sustainable yields. Regarding the issue of changing the meaning of the term "dolphin-safe," the existing U.S. law stated that for tuna harvested in the ETP by a purse-seine vessel to be labeled "dolphin-safe" an observer had to certify in writing that the purse-seine net was not intentionally deployed during the entire fishing trip on or in encircling dolphins. The declaration changed the "dolphin-safe" label standard to include tuna harvested when the net was used on or to encircle dolphins if no dolphin mortality was noted by an observer (Felando 1995).

The Panama Declaration became the basis for a bill introduced in Congress by Senator Ted Stevens (R-AL), chairman of the Senate Subcommittee on Oceans and Fisheries. The Clinton administration sided with Senator Stevens, as did the five mainstream environmental organizations. Similar legislation introduced by Representatives Randy "Duke" Cunningham (R-CA) and Wayne Gilcrest (R-MD) cleared the House in May 1996 (Linden 1996; Odessey 1996). Jerry Leape of Greenpeace said that he hoped the Senate got a strong message from the House vote and encouraged Democrats in the House who voted for the bill to encourage Democrats in the Senate to vote for it as well. He also expressed gratitude for the overwhelming Republican support in the House. "While many think that the environment is just a Democratic issue," Leape said, "I think this shows that it can and should enjoy bipartisan support" (Odessey 1996). Although supporters worked to get a companion bill passed in the Senate, they were unsuccessful, owing to opponents' threat of a filibuster (Linden 1996).

Supporters of the International Dolphin Conservation Program Act (IDCPA) argued that MMPA, combined with the Dolphin Protection Consumer Information Act of 1990, was unfair to the countries that signed the Panama Declaration because their participation in the voluntary La Jolla Agreement had greatly reduced their numbers of dolphin deaths. Furthermore, if the Panama Declaration was not ratified, these countries threatened to abandon the voluntary program and start killing more dolphins again (Frazier 1996; Hebert 1997b; Palmer 1996). Proponents also argued that that the current laws were actually a major threat to the sustainability of the ETP tuna fishery because of the substantial bycatch of immature tuna and other species associated with non-purse-seine fishing methods (Frazier 1996; Young 1996). Finally, proponents stated that the Panama Declaration would enact scientifically calculated levels of protection for each dolphin species, as opposed to a system based on the banning of a particular technique (CMC 1996; EDF 1996; Greenpeace 1996; NWF 1997; Prudencio 1997). James P. Walsh, a Washington lobbyist for the tuna industry, concluded that "they catch 300,000 tons of tuna in the eastern tropical Pacific and kill 4,000 dolphins which scientists say is 'biologically insignificant.'. . . Here is a group of animals not threatened or endangered. . . . It is time for us to grow up and realize we have more or less conquered the dolphin problem" (Fiore 1995).

Opponents of the declaration organized the Dolphin-Safe Fair Trade Campaign, which included EII, the Sierra Club, the Humane Society of the United States, EarthTrust, Cetacean Society International, the ASPCA, Sea Shepherd, Defenders of Wildlife, Friends of the Earth, Fund for Animals, Ralph Nader's Public Citizen, Human Dolphin Foundation, Jacques Cousteau, Jean-Michel Cousteau, and more than seventy other environmental organizations. The campaign claimed that the complicated enforcement mechanisms included in the declaration and the possibility for corruption meant that dolphin deaths would rise again (Defenders of Wildlife 1997; EII 1995; Fiore 1995; McCarthy 1996; Palmer and Seligsohn 1996; Phinney 1995; Williamson 1996a and 1996b). Opponents cast the declaration as a free trade attempt to override democratically created laws in order to accommodate Mexico's demands that the United States observe the GATT rulings (Defenders of Wildlife 1997; Hebert 1997a). The campaign supported alternative bills proposed by Senators Barbara Boxer and Joseph Biden and Representative George Miller (D-CA) that preserved the current "dolphin-safe" label standards but also opened the U.S. market to foreign tuna caught using truly "dolphin-safe" techniques.

The coalition maintained that the proposed changes would allow tuna fishermen to chase, herd, and encircle dolphins, which is cruel and stressful, separates mothers from calves, and keeps populations from thriving (Linden 1996). Marine mammal scientists denounced the scientific assertions included in the declaration regarding the negative impacts of bycatch on tuna and other marine life populations. They argued that many stress mortalities experienced by dolphins being chased would not be observed and that the bills proposed in the House and Senate would result in the deaths of tens of thousands of additional dolphins and the deaths of untold numbers of fish, sharks, and sea turtles (Cousteau 1996; EII 1996; Hall 1996; Myrick 1996; Payne 1996).

With support from the Clinton administration, U.S. tuna companies, labor unions, and major environmental organizations, in early 1997 Representative Gilchrest (R-MD) and supporters in the House of Representatives proposed HR 408, known as the International Dolphin Conservation Program Act (Dregger 1997; McCain 1997). At the same time, Senator Stevens and cosponsors proposed the same program as S 39 in the Senate (McCain 1997). In late May the House voted to pass the act in accordance with the Panama declaration (Hebert 1997b). In July the Senate adopted an amendment to S 39 put forward by Senator Olympia Snowe (R-ME), chair of the Oceans and Fisheries Subcommittee, which changed the language in S 39 in four ways (McCain 1997). First, tuna caught in accordance with the Panama Declaration could not be labeled "dolphin-safe" if an observer saw a dolphin that had been "seriously injured" or "mortally wounded" as opposed to witnessing an actual death. Second, it authorized emergency regulations if research were to show adverse impacts on dolphin populations. Third, it mandated research on the effects of chase and encirclement fishing on dolphins. And fourth, it directed the secretary of state to take the necessary steps to create a bycatch reduction program in the ETP.

In late July both the Clinton administration and the Mexican government approved the amended version of S 39. The amended version dropped the embargo immediately but mandated up to three years of research on the effects of dolphin chasing before the label could be changed. The U.S. secretary of commerce would be in charge of this research and would make a final determination between July 2001 and December 2002 (Carter-Long 1997). On July 30 the Senate passed the amended version of the International Dolphin Conservation Program Act (Allen 1997a); on July 31 the House approved the Senate's compromise version (Reuters 1997a). The successful passage of Public Law 105–42, the International Dolphin Conservation Program Act of 1997 (IDCPA), meant that two kinds of tuna could be sold on U.S. grocery shelves: cans labeled "dolphin-safe" and cans not so labeled.

The passage of IDCPA split the environmental community. Groups like the Center for Marine Conservation, Greenpeace, the World Wildlife Fund, and the Environmental Defense Fund saw the initiative as "the beginning of a new era of greater protection and international cooperation on behalf of dolphins, other species, and the marine ecosystem." Others, including the Human Society, the Sierra Club, Defenders of Wildlife, Public Citizen, Friends of the Earth, and Earth Island Institute described it as a system whereby "Mexico and the U.S. can claim they are saving dolphins while letting the killing continue" (Knight 1998).

The 1999 Research Findings Release

In April 1999 the Commerce Department ruled that the results of research on the impact of the purse-seine method of harvesting tuna in association with dolphins used in accordance with the Panama Declaration "caused no adverse impacts on depleted dolphin populations" (Robicheaux 1999). Therefore, the "dolphin-safe" label could now be applied to tuna caught in manners consistent with the regulations established in the IDCPA. While the mainstream environmental groups lauded the decision as proper recognition that Mexico and other tuna-exporting countries had made significant progress in reducing dolphin mortalities (Kraul 2000), coalition members saw it as consumer fraud and vowed to continue to fight for the old standards that truly protect dolphins (Martin 1999). They argued that the United States was pressured into weakening the dolphin-safe tuna standards by Mexico and its tuna industry as a free trade concession (Kraul 2000; Robicheaux 1999). In July 1999 the Dolphin Safe Fair Trade Coalition filed another lawsuit, claiming that the Commerce Department's decision was "arbitrary and capricious, ignoring biological information supplied by federal researchers" (Robicheaux 1999), which showed "that despite safer fishing methods, global dolphin stocks barely grew, if at all in the 1990s" (Kraul 2000). The coalition argued that research showed that the purse-seine method of chasing and encircling dolphins causes high levels of stress and leads to high rates of calf-mother separation, which results in the deaths of the calves. As a result, the number of deaths associated with the purse-seine method is regularly underestimated (Drake 2001). Senator Boxer and Representative Miller denounced the rules as faulty science (Martin 1999). Representative Miller blamed free trade agreements (i.e., the WTO) for putting U.S. environmental laws at risk. "We don't believe people who are unaccountable to the American citizenry should be able to effectively overturn American environmental laws," said Miller's aide (Bruggers 1999).

Although the ruling allowed the meaning of the "dolphin-safe" label to change, the Big 3 tuna companies pledged to continue to "buy and sell only truly 'dolphin-safe' tuna" (Martin 1999; Robicheaux 1999). While acknowledging that he had never seen scientific studies proving the dangers of encirclement, David Burney, executive director of the U.S. Tuna Federation, said, "We don't want to be held up to the criticism of environmental groups. We'll retain our standards, and have already let the government know this." Burney added that while industry marketing studies showed that most people don't pay attention to the dolphin-safe labels, the minority who do pay attention feel "very strongly" about the issue, and he did not want to "ruffle" these consumers and environmentalists (Harper 1999).

In April 2000 Judge Henderson reinstated the ban on Mexican tuna (Kraul 2000). He ruled that the government had failed to conduct the required studies on the effects of purse-seine techniques on dolphins (Egelko 2000). In response, the Mexican tuna industry again threatened to abandon the dolphin-protective fishing measures. They pledged to "fight for looser standards on dolphin-safe labeling and called the US court's ruling a form of trade protectionism" (Quinn 2001). The U.S. State Department and the U.S. embassy in Mexico also condemned Judge Henderson's ruling, stating that the reinstated ban "threatened dolphins, rather than protected them." In Mexico, tuna boat owner Antonio Suarez's "hopes were dashed" by the reinstated ban. "We've done everything right, but we've lost hundreds of millions of dollars," Suarez said. "This is politics, a commercial problem, not about the environment" (Kraul 2000). According to Alfonso Rosignol, president of the Mexico chamber of the National Fishing Industry, the dolphin-safe program was a "prime example of how 'green standards' can become unfair trade restrictions"; the ban, he argued, had "simply served to keep the Mexican tuna out of the US, while not regulating the US industry" (*Christian Science Monitor* 1999).

In late 2000 the Justice Department and several mainstream environmental organizations appealed Judge Henderson's ruling. In July 2001 the Ninth Circuit Court of Appeals upheld the ruling, noting that the preliminary reports of the studies indicated that "stress from the fishing method was the likely reason for the continued decline in the dolphin population" and that the Commerce Department had "unreasonably delayed the stress studies" and needed "favorable results from those studies before it can legally change the label" (Egelko 2000). Reiterating concerns that the Mexican tuna industry might abandon its dolphin-protection practices, NMFS representatives announced that they were reviewing the decision and would consider appealing the ruling (Quinn 2001).

The ruling prompted Mexico's National Fishing and Aquaculture Industries Chamber (CANAINPESCA) to urge President Vicente Fox to respond "energetically" and "to look at everything that can be done at the WTO (World Trade Organization) and via diplomatic pressure" (Infolatina 2001b). The minister of economic development in the state of Baja California warned that these continued obstacles discouraged foreign fleets from protecting dolphins, as they "will try to survive by exporting to alternative markets that do not have these kinds of restrictions" (Infolatina 2001h). The chamber reported that the U.S. embargo was costing them $500 million per year and declared that they would end their participation in the La Jolla Agreement (Infolatina 2001f and 2001a).

In August 2001 the Mexican government announced that it would lodge a complaint with the WTO if the United States continued to embargo Mexican tuna. The Mexican economic minister, Ernesto Derbez, and U.S. commerce secretary Donald Evans said that the two countries would work together on a study of the "definitive" impacts of purse-seine techniques on dolphin populations that should be ready in April 2002 (Infolatina 2001e). Mexico again called for urgent talks with the United States to end the "de facto embargo" on Mexican tuna (Reuters 2001). Later in August, IATTC chairman Robin Allen urged the Mexican tuna industry to continue to participate in the programs that had reduced dolphin deaths to biologically insignificant levels (Infolatina 2001a).

While the tuna-dolphin controversy was one of the topics of the summit meeting between presidents Vicente Fox and George W. Bush in early September (Smith and Kraul 2001), because of the terrorist attacks of September 11, the talks were suspended (Infolatina 2001g). After meetings in early December (Infolatina 2001d), the Commerce Department announced that Mexican scientists would participate in the last phase of the mandated study on the impacts of purse-seine fishing on dolphin populations. CANAINPESCA praised the effort for ensuring the objectivity of the study, which would enable it to decide whether to remain in or withdraw from the dolphin conservation program (i.e., the La Jolla Agreement) (Infolatina 2001c). In March 2002 Mexico threatened trade sanctions against the United States if the NAFTA treaty was not fulfilled regarding tuna exports, sugar, and Mexican trucking (Inflolatina 2002b). Derbez announced that Mexico was again exporting tuna to the United States, mainly to ethnic markets. He noted that although the United States was not formally embargoing Mexican tuna, the major supermarkets in the United States would still buy only "dolphin-safe" tuna (Infolatina 2002h). Mexican officials expressed hope that the tuna embargo would be lifted in September or October, after the results of scientific research documenting the minimal impact of the purse-seine method on dolphin populations was released (Infolatina 2002f).

In early December EII released the results of the study conducted by the Southwest Fisheries Science Center in La Jolla, California, part of the Department of Commerce. While the Commerce Department hadn't yet made the study results public, the study lay at the heart of a trade-versus-environment battle, and EII representative Mark Palmer asserted that "the decision by the Commerce Secretary should be made in the light of day and not in secret" (Kay 2002). The study found little evidence that dolphin populations were recovering and expressed concern that the practice of chasing and encircling dolphins adversely affects the ability of these depleted stocks to recover. More specifically, based on observations from the tuna boats, the study noted that Mexican, Colombian, and Venezuelan purse-seiners had set nets around northeastern spotted dolphins and eastern spinner dolphins more than 7,600 times, chasing a total of 9.3 million dolphins, which meant "that many were counted over and over as they were repeatedly chased." A main finding of the study was that deaths of nursing calves were typically underreported by up to 15 percent; when the dead mothers were found, the calves were usually missing. The study contradicted previous claims that improvements in tuna fishing practices on the part of foreign fleets had benefited the dolphins. Commerce secretary Donald Evans had until the end of December to review all of the evidence in the study and determine whether the purse-seine fishing method was harmful to dolphins (Kay 2002).

On January 1, 2003, Evans made his ruling, and National Oceanic and Atmospheric Administration (NOAA) director Bill Hogarth issued the formal findings of the research. Hogarth reported that the current, more dolphin-friendly purse-seine fishing practices, while still accounting for about two thousand dolphin deaths per year, did not have "a 'significant' adverse impact on the animals' populations" (Nesmith 2003). Therefore, tuna caught with purse-seine nets in compliance with U.S. laws could now be imported into the United States with the "dolphin-safe" label (Deardorff 2003). Within forty-eight hours of the announcement, Mexican tuna was being shipped to the United States with the new "dolphin-safe" label (Balzar 2003). The change in the meaning of "dolphin-safe" was welcomed by Secretary of State Colin Powell, who "had eagerly advanced it" (Kay 2003; Marquis 2003a).

Environmentalists and animal rights activists assailed the announcement as a blatant contradiction of the NMFS study findings and an abdication to free trade pressures from Mexico (Deardorff 2003; Nesmith 2003). EII's David Phillips stated, "This goes against their own scientists' statements, which show chasing and encircling dolphins is not dolphin safe. It's all about trade with Mexico" (Deardorff 2003). Kitty Block, special counsel to the Humane Society of the United States, added that dolphin-deadly tuna would be sold in the United States and would "be misleadingly labeled 'dolphin-safe'" (Nesmith 2003). Mark Palmer of EII noted, "This is the poster child for the race to the bottom in global environmental standards" (Balzar 2003).

On January 2 the coalition again filed a lawsuit in federal district court in

San Francisco to halt the implementation of the new "dolphin-safe" definition and resulting tuna imports (Egelko 2003a). The suit charged that the Commerce Department had ignored its own evidence that dolphin populations had not rebounded and that severe stress on mothers and calves was associated with the use of the purse-seine technique. The coalition further asserted that the dolphin mortality documentation system could not be trusted, because fishermen pressured the observers to minimize dolphin morality reports (Kay 2003). Senator Boxer promised to challenge the decision in Congress and stated, "if I have to, I'm going to organize the kids of the United States. We did it once before. I'm not going to take this one" (Balzar 2003).

In defense of the Commerce Department's decision, the NOAA's Hogarth noted that the department "had to look at the big picture" and that it was wiser to "put some dolphins at risk" than to take the chance that Mexico and other nations would "simply drop out of the international program that is supposed to protect dolphins" (Balzar 2003). "We can assure our American consumers that they still have dolphin-safe tuna," he said, because only tuna caught without harming dolphins would be so labeled (Egelko 2003a). Also on January 2, David Burney of the U.S. Tuna Foundation reaffirmed the position that member companies would continue to sell only "dolphin-safe" tuna that was truly dolphin safe (Balzar 2003c), because "U.S. consumers and retailers do not want to buy tuna that has been caught by encircling dolphins" (Weiss 2003b). Mark Berman of EII added, "They know the B word would be back: boycott. It worked in the 1980s, when people saw how dolphins were being slaughtered for the sake of a tuna fish sandwich" (Pfister 2003).

On January 8 the coalition announced an agreement with the Bush administration to leave the stricter dolphin-safe standards in place temporarily until a hearing could be held on a preliminary injunction "that would freeze the standards indefinitely until the lawsuit went to trial" (Egelko 2003c), and that therefore they had "agreed not to seek a temporary restraining order against the government" (Marquis 2003a). Hogarth responded by affirming that the Commerce Department stood "by its original decision to change the label" but had agreed to "postpone the action to avoid the chance of a federal judge issuing a temporary restraining order" (Weiss 2003b).

Scientists Speak Out

Secretary Evans's ruling was criticized by most of the independent scientists the government had hired to review the scientific integrity of the study.

Four of five scientists expressed concerns about the conclusions reached by Secretary Evans. Dr. Robert J. Hofman, who served as scientific director of the Marine Mammal Commission for twenty-five years, called the conclusions "inconsistent." Dr. Douglas Wartzok, dean of the Graduate School at Florida International University, said the adverse effects on dolphins—including stress-related damage—were "pretty clear," adding, "I felt that the indirect effects were a significant impediment to the recovery of the populations. Obviously the secretary came to a different conclusion" (Marquis 2003a).

The day before the government agreed to put the ruling on hold in light of the coalition lawsuit, two former researchers at the Southwest Fisheries Science Center spoke to the press about how their superiors had shut down their investigations on the stress caused in dolphins by regular contact with tuna vessels, "because it clashed with the policy goals of the Clinton and Bush Administrations" (*Current Science* 2003; Marquis 2003a and 2003b). Their research indicated that the practice of chasing and encircling dolphins to catch tuna exposed dolphins to dangerous levels of stress. Dr. Albert Myrick, a wildlife biologist, said that his research indicated that the "chase and corral" technique associated with purse-seine fishing separated cows from calves and lowered pregnancy rates. After seven years of researching this topic, he was told to abandon his research in 1995, during the time that Mexico was heavily lobbying the United States to weaken its dolphin-safe rules (*Current Science* 2003, 12; Marquis 2003b).

Dr. Sarka Southern, a biophysical chemist, was hired by the Southwest Fisheries Science Center in 1998 to develop a method for measuring stress in skin samples of dolphins (Marquis 2003b). In her study of 868 dolphins Dr. Southern "found the highest levels of stress among dolphins chased most often by tuna fishing boats" (*Current Science* 2003, 12). Her project was cancelled in early 2001, shortly after her boss told her not to publicize her results. "He came to my office," Dr. Southern said, "and said that I have to understand that there's science and there's politics, and the politics dictates what sort of science can be used" (Marquis 2003b). Officials at the Southwest Fisheries Science Center denied that the research results had been suppressed and cited funding constraints and peer review problems as the reasons why the projects were terminated (*Current Science* 2003; Marquis 2003b). Senator Boxer said she would call for congressional hearings to determine whether the Bush administration was suppressing evidence and running roughshod over the scientific evidence (Marquis 2003b).

In April, Judge Theldon Henderson of San Francisco issued a preliminary injunction, stopping the change in the meaning of the "dolphin-safe" label.

Judge Henderson wrote that "the decision to change the dolphin-safe definition appears to have been influenced more by international trade policies than scientific evidence" (Weiss 2003a). Furthermore, he ruled that the environmentalists had "shown they were likely to prove that Evans' finding was 'contrary to the best available scientific evidence'" (Egelko 2003b). Judge Henderson felt that the main reason that dolphin numbers had not recovered was the repeated netting that stressed mothers and calves but escaped the notice of the onboard observers. He further noted that the government had not completed all the research required by the 1997 law and cited the declarations of research scientists that NOAA officials had interfered with their research. Judge Henderson ruled that these allegations, combined with Secretary Powell's letters urging Secretary Evans to adopt the new meaning of "dolphin-safe," were sufficient "to raise a serious question as to the integrity of the decision-making process" (Egleko 2003b).

The letters that Powell wrote Evans in early December 2002 emphasized the international importance of the issue. Powell said that Evans's tuna-dolphin study ruling would affect the State Department's role in an agreement among the European Union and fourteen other nations that had reduced dolphin deaths through voluntary changes in tuna practices (the La Jolla Agreement) (Egelko 2003b). Judge Henderson concluded that while Evans had "wisely refrained" from mentioning trade policy as a justification for the new label standards, there was "little doubt" that he faced pressure from Secretary Powell to liberalize the "dolphin-safe" rule (Weiss 2003b). Speaking for Earth Island Institute, attorney Joshua R. Floum commented, "It's a violation of truth in labeling to change the meaning of the labels that say it is dolphin-safe when it isn't. It's Orwellian" (Weiss 2003a).

The Mexican Ministry of Finance announced that it would appeal the judge's decision (Pfister 2003). In defense of the change in the meaning of the dolphin-safe label, Mario Aguilar, the Washington-based representative of Mexico's fishing commission, charged that U.S. environmental extremists had "hijacked" the debate. "These are not a charismatic species," said Aguilar. "It's very touching to say baby dolphins are being hurt using the large nets" (Pfister 2003).

Globalization critics called the new rulings a "pre-emptive strike to head off a Mexican appeal to the WTO demanding access to U.S. grocery stores." Under NAFTA Mexico would enjoy a mere 5 percent tariff on tuna imports, as compared to the 25 percent rate that applies to Thailand, the main source of tuna U.S. imports today. "This is the big deal, the 'smoking-dolphin,'" said Lori Wallach, director of Public Citizen's Global Trade Watch. "It is a smoking-gun example of how [the wto] can and does undermine key environmental, consumer and health laws. The last thing any administration wants is a wto decision that forces them to implement policy" (Pfister 2003).

Analysis and Discussion

We focus on three interrelated points in the analysis. The first is that while TNCs emerge as powerful actors that impose limits on the nation-state, globalization as a whole is a contested process in which no one group or entity is able to implement its agenda in full. Pro-environmental legislation in the form of MMPA was created and partially implemented. The environmentalists employed a mixture of legislation, lawsuits, and consumer boycotts to advance their agenda. Tuna TNCs' attempts, supported by the U.S. executive branch (Department of Commerce/NMFS), stalled MMPA but fell short of their proposed objectives to reopen the ETP tuna-dolphin fishery to purse-seine fishing. The tuna industry supported attempts to resolve the controversy through bilateral negotiations with Mexico, but these failed. The industry also supported multilateral agreements such as the IATTC-sponsored La Jolla Agreement and Panama Declaration, but even with the support of President Clinton and both houses of Congress these initiatives were challenged in the courts. Although the Panama Declaration promised to regulate the ETP tuna-dolphin fishery based on scientific research, the Big 3 tuna TNCs restated their commitment to the traditional definition of dolphin-safe tuna to avoid consumer boycotts they had faced in the past. The controversy over the scientific studies on the effects of chasing dolphins in pursuit of tuna further highlights the contested nature of tuna-dolphin case.

While the conditions of globalizations are contested, TNCs emerge as powerful actors that limit nation-states' actions. The limits of the nation-state are grounded in TNCs' hypermobility and the practice of global sourcing (Constance and Heffernan 1991; Friedmann and McMichael 1989; Harvey 1989; Sanderson 1985). In response to growing competition from Latin America, U.S. tuna-processing plants with high labor costs were closed in California and relocated to Puerto Rico to take advantage of lower wages and tax incentives. As MMPA regulations were more strictly enforced, tuna TNCs deintegrated their company tuna boats and sourced their tuna on the international spot market. Then the tuna boats reflagged under foreign fleets while still using the purse-seine nets in the ETP, thereby evading U.S. laws. When this action was countered with the 1984 and 1988 MMPA amendments, the tuna industry shifted its focus from the ETP to the WTP, where dolphin and tuna don't associate. The relocation to American Samoa took advantage of low wages and special customs considerations. During this time, two of the top three U.S. tuna TNCs sold their operations to Asia-based firms. When Unicord of Thailand purchased Bumble Bee, it gained direct access to the U.S. market through its processing plant in Puerto Rico. As part of the restructuring, the majority of the tuna-processing factories in Puerto Rico became owned by Asian firms linked to U.S. markets through American Samoa and Puerto Rico.[2]

The second point is that under globalization the ability of nation-states to manage social and economic relations is weakened by TNCs. To foster social development, nation-states must provide for capital accumulation and societal legitimation. Governments must provide a stable business climate that attracts capital investment, creates jobs, and generates taxes to support government functions. But if the business climate is too lenient, citizens may find the accumulation strategies unacceptable, resulting in a legitimation crisis for the nation-state. At this time social movements may rise up to try to change the law and/or regulations. If the business climate is too strict, then TNCs move their capital and go elsewhere for better production conditions. The globalization of economy and society complicates the ability of nation-states to balance capital accumulation with social legitimation and mediate conflicts between competing classes or parts of classes. The adoption of the purse-seine fishing system of setting on dolphins provided huge profits for the tuna industry but led to environmental protests that called the practice into question. For thirty years the state tried to resolve this conflict, as environmentalists and free traders fought in the U.S. Congress, courts, and international organizations over the regulation of the ETP tuna-dolphin fishery and the meaning of the "dolphin-safe" label. The environ-

2. It can be argued that the actions of the Mexican state in favor of its workers and the relocation of the tuna TNCs are an indication of the strength of that nation-state vis-à-vis the power of transnational corporations. This would suggest that the Mexican state was able to undermine the actions of pro-environmental groups in favor of local economic interests. While this objection stresses the point that globalization is a contested terrain, it does not take into account the contradictory position that less developed nation-states have assumed under globalization. Pressed to adopt measures that foster socioeconomic growth, less developed nation-states often support TNCs' relocation into their territories. But these measures do not generate the expected results and in fact contribute to the further exploitation of the human and natural resources of the region. The case of Mexico and the *maquiladoras* factories is arguably the best-known of these cases. In this instance, the Mexican state seemingly acted in protection of Mexican tuna workers and boats, yet in fact it supported the designs of TNCs and their fight against U.S. pro-environment forces.

mentalist coalition used its allies in the judicial and legislative branches of the U.S. government, while the free traders used their allies in executive branch and supranational organizations such as the IATTC and the GATT/WTO. The state apparatus as a whole was increasingly unable to fulfill its role of mediator between various social groups. The threat of enforcement of the GATT/WTO rulings calls into question the durability of MMPA in the short run and the ability of the United States to defend democracy in the long run.

Furthermore, state actions in response to the demands of social groups are problematic when lodged in a transnational arena. The bypassing of state action through tuna boats' reflagging and industry relocation demonstrated the state's diminished ability to perform its historical roles. The state is increasingly unable to regulate TNCs' actions (enforce compliance with MMPA), enhance TNCs interests (defeat pro-environmental groups), or respond to demands stemming from other social groups, such as environmentalists (implementation of MMPA). Also problematic are attempts to extend state regulation of economic activities at the international level. The various compromises reached by the United States, Venezuela, and Mexico were designed to respond to the global hypermobility of TNCs (i.e., the move to Asia) and to foster legitimizing and accumulative actions at the domestic level (respond to environmentalists' demands in the United States and to the loss of employment and economic opportunities in the United States, Venezuela, and Mexico). These territorially limited accords do not match TNCs' geographical sphere of action. More specifically, TNCs escaped the pro-environmental MMPA regulations by going global, something that nation-states, obviously, cannot do.

The case also demonstrates the difficulties related to supranational forms of socioeconomic regulation. The failed accords among the United States, Venezuela, Mexico, and other governments in the form of the Panama Declaration, the various appeals to GATT/WTO, and domestic attempts to implement policy are cases in point. James Joseph of the IATTC commented on the difficulty of successfully regulating activity in a global fishery where the "free-rider" tuna boats of nonparticipating countries fish just outside the regulated fishery. The GATT stated its preference for international accords to resolve disputes about global commons such as the ETP tuna-dolphin fishery. The case illustrates the increasing importance of NGOs such as the IATTC and supranational organizations such as the GATT/WTO in providing global forms of governance that mediate the conflicts between economic development and societal legitimation in the global era (McMichael 2002). The tuna-dolphin case also provides valuable information on how developing countries might use the WTO to challenge what they perceive as unfair "green protectionism" by developed countries. It is fair to conclude that the regulatory situation at the global level is extremely unsettled and is characterized by a combination of old forms of regulation and emerging new ones. Traditional forms of regulation include the mediation and organizational roles, both domestic and international, of nation-states. New forms of regulation are embodied in the increasingly important role performed by transnational organizations such as the IATTC and the GATT/WTO as they attempt to emulate the state functions of accumulation, legitimation, and mediation in an emerging system of global governance.

The third point to be made is that, while TNCs actions are resisted, sometimes powerfully, the overall well-being of workers and environmentalists and the environment itself are threatened by globalization. The transnational move of the tuna industry had important repercussions in terms of employment and overall economic well-being of fishing communities. Although the introduction of the purse-seine technology in the ETP expanded employment and economic opportunities in the United States, the passage and contested implementation of MMPA fostered the shift of tuna industry operations to low-wage regions of Latin America. This corporate move generated employment growth in those regions and economic decline among tuna fishing communities in the United States. Later, the secondary embargoes on Latin American producers, combined with a consumer boycott that affected the Big 3 tuna processors, stimulated the industry's move to Asia, curtailing employment and economic growth in Latin American fishing areas. Thousands of tuna-processing jobs were lost on the U.S. mainland, in Puerto Rico, and in Latin America as a result of the restructuring.

Although environmentalists fought for legislation that would "reduce incidental dolphin deaths to insignificant levels approaching zero," tuna industry advocates countered with a quota system based on scientific fisheries management that allowed an "acceptable" number of 20,500 dolphin deaths per year. During the development of the Panama Declaration, the environmental coalition that secured MMPA split into two camps: the "mainstream" and the "grassroots." The mainstream group aligned itself with the free trade agenda of scientific management of the ETP tuna-dolphin fishery, while the grassroots coalition remained committed to the original intent of MMPA: no dolphin chasing and encirclement. Even with mainstream environmental support, to get the Panama Declaration provisions through the U.S. Congress an amendment had to be added that promised that the meaning of the "dolphin-safe" label would not be changed without definitive research on the impacts of purse-seine fishing on depleted dolphin populations. The research findings did not meet the goals of the tuna industry, finding that depleted populations had not rebounded because the continued use of the chase and corral method separated mothers from calves and caused mortalities. The State Department's pressure on the Commerce Department to make a favorable ruling captures the impact of politics and economics on science. It is worth noting that the Commerce Department backed off its favorable ruling the day after the dolphin scientists announced that their research had been suppressed in the name of politics.

These analytical points speak directly to the literature summarized in Chapter 1. The events of the case presented in this story support the view that globalization has not transcended capitalism. In effect, globalization is not only based on the accumulation of capital, it is also designed to bypass conditions that might thwart or retard the reproduction of capital. In this respect the events illustrated in this chapter support the point made by the "grand durée" school. Similarly, the ability of TNCs to bypass state regulations and control opposition, while diminishing the analytical value of the assertion that the nation-state still retains important powers (a point also made by authors in the grand durée camp) illustrates the clout of TNCs under globalization—as authors of the "corporate domination" school have observed. Finally, the fact that TNCs' actions are resisted and that no specific actor is in full control of the current situation supports the argument of the "contradictory dimension of globalization" group of writers. According to these authors, globalization engenders resistance, but it also worsens the conditions of subordinate groups.

3

TRANSNATIONAL CORPORATIONS AND THEIR POWER OVER THE STATE: THE CASE OF FERRUZZI

In June 1992, San Diego recorded an unusually high presence of Italian tourists. They were there in support of the Italian boat *Il Moro di Venezia* (The Moor of Venice), which had reached the finals of the prestigious America's Cup. The *Moro* was sponsored by the TNC Ferruzzi, one of the world's largest agrochemical corporations at the time. This boat and her presence in the international regatta were the work of Raul Gardini, a self-made millionaire of humble peasant origins and now Ferruzzi's CEO. His love for boating was well known, but the *Moro* was also part of his broader design to project an image of Ferruzzi comparable to its status as a global corporation. The *Moro* displayed on her side the symbol of the Montedison Corporation, a large petrochemical group recently acquired by the Ferruzzi conglomerate. Italian tourists in San Diego, and millions of Italians who followed the America's Cup regatta through intercontinental Italian TV broadcasts, had a sense that Ferruzzi's takeover of Montedison had catapulted the company into a primary role in the global arena. Little did they realize that this new phase would mark the beginning of the end for Ferruzzi.

As with the tuna-dolphin controversy addressed in Chapter 2, we look at the story of Ferruzzi to illustrate the relationship between TNCs and nation-states. The case of Ferruzzi confirms that TNCs use hypermobility of capital to increase their profits and avoid state regulation—and also that resistance to TNCs makes globalization a contested terrain. As in Chapter 2 and the chapters that follow, the case of Ferruzzi confirms that the relationship between TNCs and the state is characterized in part by contradictions internal to both, contradictions that limit their powers. The importance of this story of globalization rests also on the fact that Ferruzzi is one of those TNCs that use their ability to avoid national regulations to carry out illegal operations. Before the now infamous cases of Enron and WorldCom, Ferruzzi was the first TNC to be indicted for, and eventually found guilty of, a global corporate crime. Using original, unfiltered information on the growth and collapse of this agrifood and agrochemical TNC, this chapter takes a close look at the ways in which Ferruzzi operated in the global system.

Created by Serafino Ferruzzi in 1948 as a small agricultural trade company specializing in wheat, Ferruzzi became a corporate giant with interests in several countries and a number of economic sectors, among them chemicals, retail, cement and concrete, agrifood, and finance. Normally the study of TNCs is based on data collected by public or private agencies, made available by TNCs themselves, and/or derived from observations of the consequences of corporate actions. These data are easily controlled by corporations. Data protected by corporate supervision are seldom if ever made available to researchers. Fortunately, we are not hampered by these problems in our investigation of Ferruzzi. An unprecedented episode in recent Italian history known as "Clean Hands" generated deep legal scrutiny of corporate actions and resulted in numerous indictments and trials of important companies in Italy.[1] Ferruzzi's legal problems, its indictment for a number of criminal violations, and its eventual collapse generated a wealth of information previously denied to the public. In a way that is rare in the corporate world, the most intimate secrets of the workings of a corporation were uncovered and made public through media coverage of the criminal trial of Ferruzzi officials. The story of Ferruzzi can be viewed as a valuable predecessor to the corporate misconduct of firms such as Enron, WorldCom, Tyco, and others.

The Origins of the Case

Gardini, Ferruzzi, and the Chemical Sector

The story begins with Ferruzzi's takeover of Montedison. Media accounts portrayed Gardini's motivation for this nearly $2 billion acquisition as an attempt to overcome his inferiority complex with respect to the local business establishment by becoming the richest man in Italy (Andreoli 1994b; Kramer 1994). Despite his business success, in Milan, the capital of Italian business,

---

1. In the early 1990s Italy was shaken by the uncovering of a network of corruption schemes linking politicians to business leaders. Led by a group of prosecutors, the police and legal actions that generated the uncovering and dismantling of this network became known as "Clean Hands."

Gardini was still considered an outsider and was kept out of the tight inner circle of Italian entrepreneurs. He was a "Romagnolo" (an "exaggerated Italian" of impulsive behavior from the state of Romagna) (Kramer 1994, 72). Gardini felt that he could shed this provincial and unsophisticated image by conquering the prestigious chemical sector. The acquisition of Montedison and subsequent business ventures made Ferruzzi one of the major chemical companies in the world, prompting Gardini to declare triumphantly, "I am the chemical sector" (Andreoli 1994b; Kramer 1994).

There were reasons, beyond Gardini's personal agenda, for Ferruzzi to acquire Montedison. In light of the emerging limits of its traditional agrifood and cement sectors, Ferruzzi officials viewed the rapidly expanding chemical sector as a promising alternative industrial strategy. Furthermore, Montedison was not just in the chemical sector; its large retail chains, insurance and financial operations, household product plants, and media holdings were compatible with the diversification strategies of Ferruzzi management (Bianco 1988). Montedison was only its first investment in the chemical sector. The joint venture between Ferruzzi and ENI, the Italian energy giant, created the short-lived Enimont Corporation, whose birth and demise are at the center of this case.

ENI and the Socialist Party Leadership

ENI (Ente Nazionale Idrocarburi, or National Hydrocarbons Agency) was one of the largest state-owned corporations created in Italy during Mussolini's fascist regime. Because of the lack of capital and entrepreneurship after World War II, direct state intervention in the economy was continued as a strategy to stimulate growth (Graziani 1979). While these state-owned corporations contributed to the reconstruction of the economy, they also became important political tools for access to economic power. Members of the political establishment used these corporations for personal and party gains (Andreoli 1994b, 22–23). This was the case with ENI, a corporation of 124,000 employees with subsidiaries in the chemical, manufacturing, distribution, marketing, and fertilizer sectors.

Although the Christian Democratic Party (CD) had ruled Italy since the end of the war, in the 1980s it experienced a loss of electoral support owing to the growing power of minor parties of the center and right. To counter this trend, the Socialist Party (PSI) became the CD's necessary ally in governing cabinet coalitions. In exchange for its cooperation, PSI's leader, Bettino Craxi, demanded privileges from the ruling CD, including more control over state intervention in the economy. The PSI became a powerful political party, and Craxi became the first socialist prime minister of Italy. With the CD leaders Giulio Andreotti and Arnaldo Forlani, Craxi formed a tacit triumvirate with de facto control over Italian political and economic affairs (Andreoli 1994b; Stille 1996).

The PSI's growing power was based in part on the control of some of the large state-owned corporations, of which ENI was the most important. In early 1989 Craxi appointed Gabriele Cagliari as ENI's CEO. Cagliari had developed a close relationship with PSI's vice secretary, Claudio Martelli, and thereby gained Craxi's trust. Cagliari was aware that his appointment was the result more of his political allegiance to PSI and Craxi than of his managerial skills. After taking office, Cagliari promptly notified Craxi of his intention to contribute generously to the party finances and to reward party members with key jobs at ENI. In May 1989 Cagliari met with Craxi's staff person Bartolomeo de Toma and told de Toma of his intention to make a cash contribution to the PSI (de Toma 1993). A legal contribution to the PSI required that Cagliari contact the PSI financial office and the proper Italian authorities. Cagliari, however, followed the informal, yet more powerful, rules dominant in Italy at the time. According to these unwritten rules, his tribute to Craxi had to be made in unrecorded and therefore nontaxable payments. Similarly, during the first six months of his administration, Cagliari staffed managerial and public relations positions with individuals who were linked closely to both Martelli and Craxi.

The Enimont Joint Venture

The System of Bribes and the Joint Venture Plan

Gardini knew that his plans to expand into the chemical sector via the ENI joint venture would be difficult to achieve. ENI was controlled by the PSI and was therefore focused more on political than on economic plans. A direct confrontation with ENI for control of the chemical sector would be very costly, with no guarantee of success. Gardini knew that the joint venture required the assent of the political establishment, which had to be secured through the payment of kickbacks, an unspoken expectation in Italian managerial and political circles (Pergolini 1993). As Craxi put it, "In Italy, the system of financing parties involves irregularities and illegalities, which I believe have been around since the founding of the republic" (1993, 50).

During the "Clean Hands" legal proceedings, former Ferruzzi and Montedison CEO (1991–93) Carlo Sama reported that Gardini had a number of meetings with high-level Italian cabinet officials and with leaders of the CD and PSI. By providing kickbacks, Gardini was able to receive assurances from then prime minister Ciriaco De Mita (CD) that his party and the Italian government would not oppose the deal (Moody 1993; Zurlo 1994). PSI support was gained through direct cash payments made to Martelli (Sama 1993).

The joint venture agreement between ENI and Montedison specified that each corporation would control 40 percent of the new company, Enimont, with the remaining 20 percent traded on the stock market. According to the agreement, both corporations' stock had to have the same market price. But because Montedison stock had a much lower value than ENI's, it had to be revalued to match the ENI stock (Colaprico and Rossi 1993). This revaluation involved a capital gain, which was taxable under Italian law. The tax was about $600 million, a sum that Ferruzzi executives decided they should not pay. It was speculated that Gardini and his staff felt that the money should be used for commercial and noncommercial activities. The latter included support for the lavish lifestyle of the Ferruzzi family and Gardini himself, a lifestyle that required a flow of resources larger than the family business could provide (Kramer 1994).

Ferruzzi planned to resolve the issue by getting legislation passed that would exempt Montedison from paying the tax. To accomplish this, Ferruzzi committed $1 million for direct payments to political organizations and politicians (Consarino 1993). According to Sama and other members of Ferruzzi's establishment, the company made payments for the introduction and passage of a special bill to a number of politicians across the Italian political spectrum (Colaprico 1994b).

The Defiscalization Bill and the Opposition

As a result of Ferruzzi's efforts, in December 1988 the Italian administration introduced the so-called defiscalization bill to exempt Montedison from paying the tax. The bill was rejected by the lower chamber of the Italian Parliament. Under Italian law, however, the government can create "law by decrees" without Parliament's approval. These decrees must be ratified by Parliament within sixty days. Using this procedure, the Italian government transformed the defiscalization bill into an act that became effective in May 1989 but was again rejected by Parliament in July. After more pressure from Gardini and his associates, the governing coalition parties proposed a new version of the bill in September. After a two-week debate, Parliament rejected the proposed legislation, primarily because of the opposition of the Italian Communist Party (PCI), which mobilized to defeat the bill. Additional votes against the bill came from the right-wing conservative party the National Alliance (AN). The AN argued that "this is a bill made for one specific person. It has a first and last name, a place and date of birth, and a place of residence" (Colaprico and Rossi 1993, 4). The PCI shared this position.

Pressured by Gardini, the government proposal a new bill in the fall of 1989 that would have reduced the tax by 50 percent; this bill was discussed in both December 1989 and January 1990. On both occasions, however, PCI representatives adopted filibustering techniques that led to the withdrawal of the measure. Furthermore, in March 1990 the PCI proposed the creation of a parliamentary commission to investigate the Enimont affair. This commission was never established (Colaprico and Rossi 1993).

The Creation and Crisis of Enimont: The Montedison-ENI Controversy

Industrial Strategies

From the outset, ENI and Ferruzzi management disagreed on the business strategy for the joint venture; this disagreement can be explained by the public and private natures of these two corporations. Gardini proposed a restructuring strategy that would reduce the size of Enimont in terms of both plants and employees (Garofano 1993; Kramer 1994; Sama 1993). ENI preferred to keep the plants as part of the structure of Enimont. Gardini argued that Italy lacked a competitive advantage in refining raw materials and should focus on producing value-added commodities (Peruzzi 1994, 25). Ultimately, his industrial policy proposal for Enimont was centered on the production of advanced plastics developed by Montedison's research department.

Gardini was also concerned about the location of some of the Enimont plants. He felt that the chemical complex located in Marghera, an industrial area near Venice, should be closed because the high pollution levels and the historical value of the area, and its economic importance in terms of tourism, demanded significant restructuring and maintenance costs. The strategically valuable polyolefine plants should be relocated to offshore platforms. In southern Italy he focused on the two industrial complexes near Crotone and Gela. Created as part of a government strategy to generate economic growth and alleviate rampant unemployment, these complexes were used by politicians to control social tensions, maintain political consensus, and gain economic advantages for themselves and their clients. A client-centered rather than an economic form of rationality guided the purpose of these complexes

(Peruzzi 1994, 25). Viewing this approach as a waste of resources, Gardini called for the relocation and restructuring of these plants, the reduction of employment, and the elimination of unnecessary and politically generated expenses. News concerning the possible closing of plants prompted union and left-wing strikes and demonstrations (Peruzzi 1994).

While Ferruzzi and Gardini focused on economic efficiency, ENI's leaders gave priority to the political role played by the corporation within the Italian system (Grotti 1994). ENI's political focus centered on the legitimating role that state-directed industrialization played in the post–World War II era and the client-centered power engendered by state intervention in southern Italy. These plants performed a valuable legitimating role in the less developed regions by providing jobs and suppressing potential social instability. PSI's linkages with labor unions and its ideological commitment to the working class produced an industrial policy focused on employment and regional socioeconomic growth. In essence, PSI's control of ENI meant that it could not disregard the historical commitment to working-class issues (Peruzzi 1994).

PSI was also involved deeply in client-centered practices. The reproduction of political power through electoral support often translated into the creation of clienteles maintained through the distribution of favors. ENI's plants represented centers of power for the distribution of jobs, subcontracts, and franchises that benefited the local population economically. Gardini knew that ENI could not escape its client-centered heritage, so he found ways to take advantage of the situation by forcing ENI to contribute the best plants to Enimont. In return, Ferruzzi kept its best companies under the Montedison umbrella while contributing its most outdated plants to Enimont. Ferruzzi was aware that unprofitable companies and related jobs were often rescued by the state (Kramer 1994).

ENI's disagreement with Gardini's restructuring proposal could not be made public in terms of the defense of client-oriented business and party power. ENI officially took a position that rejected Ferruzzi's posture as technically unsound and cast Gardini as lacking knowledge of the chemical sector. Gardini countered that ENI executives were corrupt managers who used their companies as a source of illegal personal gain. In his words, these managers were nothing more than "a bunch of thieves who wanted to keep stealing. . . . They didn't want to change their attitude and did what they do best" (Peruzzi 1994, 30). Gardini also charged ENI with managerial ineffectiveness regarding its inability to conduct a joint venture with a private company properly. In addition, Gardini chastised the Italian government for its inability to finalize the defiscalization bill, despite its promises to do so.

Efforts by members of the Italian political establishment and the business community were unsuccessful; the contrasting positions could not be reconciled (Guatelli 1994). From Ferruzzi's perspective, the execution of business activities in the global era required a high degree of flexibility that the slow-moving, obsolete, and distorted system of state-owned corporations did not permit. ENI could not abandon its legitimating and client-centered approach, which generated social stability, political favors, and personal gains. The result was a stalemate over the control of Enimont.

The Struggle for Control of Enimont: Ferruzzi's Takeover Attempt and ENI's Response

To resolve the stalemate, Gardini and the Ferruzzi leadership sought to take full control of Enimont by circumventing the formal rules of ownership. They mobilized a number of members of the international financial community close to Gardini and asked them to buy a majority of the remaining 20 percent of Enimont in the stock market. Gardini's friend, French banker Jean Marc Vernes—a key player in Ferruzzi's takeover of the French-based agri-food corporation Beghin Say—used Ferruzzi funds to buy a little more than 2 percent of the outstanding stock. A number of other friends bought a total of 8 percent of the stock. With 10 percent of the outstanding shares bought by Ferruzzi allies, in March 1990 seven of the twelve seats on the Enimont board of directors were Ferruzzi appointees (Kramer 1994, 76). Ferruzzi had control of Enimont.

Gardini's victory was short lived. ENI mounted a counterattack orchestrated by Pompeo Locatelli that challenged the legality of the acquisition of the Enimont stock. ENI requested that an injunction be used by the court of Milan, the site of the Italian stock exchange, to suspend the trading of Enimont shares and place all ENI stock in receivership. ENI maintained that Ferruzzi's extra stock was acquired in violation of the agreement between the founding companies. To carry out its plan, ENI needed the assistance of the political apparatus and a complacent judge who would issue the injunction against Ferruzzi. For ENI the stakes were too high to rely on the judgment of an impartial court and face a possible negative verdict (Andreoli 1994b, 98). ENI officials identified Vincenzo Palladino, senior vice president of Banca Commerciale Italiana, the major commercial bank in Italy, as their political ally. Palladino was very close to the PSI leadership and a personal friend of Craxi. Palladino not only found an accommodating senior judge in the Milan court system, Diego Curtó, but convinced Curtó to nominate him as the custodian of the confiscated stock. This move gave Palladino direct control over the stock and provided ENI with the means to prohibit Ferruzzi from regaining control of Enimont. In the end, Palladino paid Curtó a relatively modest $250,000 bribe. He demanded for himself an $11 million fee paid equally by ENI and Montedison (Riva 1993). Ferruzzi's leadership realized that it was important to pay Palladino to minimize negative consequences and maintain friendly terms with the stock's caretaker. However, it negotiated a much reduced $2.5 million fee (Andreoli 1994b, 99). In November 1990 Gardini realized that the battle for control of Enimont was lost forever.

The Sale of Enimont

According to Gardini and his associates (Andreoli 1994b, 98–104; Peruzzi 1994, 25–26), Ferruzzi did not break the law when it had third parties acquire Enimont stock on its behalf. Angered by the loss of Enimont, Gardini devised a new strategy to recoup the damages and generate significant gains for the company, the Ferruzzi family, but also ENI and some politicians. His plan was to revalue the stock in question in a way that would generate substantial profits. Because the Enimont stock had been taken off the market, any trading of this stock would have to be based on the establishment of a political or nonmarket price. If an inflated price could be established, those who cooperated in the scheme could obtain lucrative gains from the sale of the stock. The financing of the operation would come from public coffers. Politicians and ENI officials, in other words, would be asked to be accomplices of Ferruzzi in preparing the conditions for the inflated sale of the Enimont stock. However, the initial bribe would come from Ferruzzi in the form of about $94 million to politicians and ENI officials (Kramer 1994).

In November 1990 Gardini gained the approval of the political apparatus. Important political leaders were paid to cooperate, among them Craxi, former Christian Democratic prime minister Arnaldo Forlani, ministers, and leaders of each of the five parties forming the government coalition. ENI officials agreed after bribes were paid to CEO Cagliari ($2.6 million) and other members of the company (Zurlo 1994, 27). The government-appointed committee created to establish the market value of the Enimont stock hired the financial organization Morgan Stanley to evaluate the stock price. Morgan Stanley had to rely on ENI's, as well as Ferruzzi officials', information, which systematically distorted the actual value of Enimont. As the conspirators had hoped, Morgan Stanley set the value of the Enimont stock at $2.5 billion, at least one billion more than fair market value. Following Morgan Stanley's recommendation, the government-appointed committee ratified the proposed price on November 21.

Ferruzzi made $1.5 billion from the deal (Kramer 1994). Cagliari reinforced his control of Enimont and, according to the sworn testimony of ENI's Locatelli ($1.2 million bribe), some of his bribe money was to be used for future bribes to political leaders to secure Cagliari's renewed appointment as CEO of ENI. Craxi was paid $12.5 million, while Forlani received $5.8 million. The ministers also received substantial bribes. The losers in this deal were the Italian taxpayers, who paid the bill for the public acquisition of Enimont. The estimated cost of the Enimont fraud to Italian citizens of all ages was about $250 each. But this estimate includes only the costs of the purchase of the Enimont stock and does not take into consideration the other costs that Ferruzzi passed on to the public. For example, when Enimont was created, Montedison contributed obsolete plants that required more than $5 million of upgrading; Enimont plants recorded a deficit for every year of their existence, totaling more than $4 million, and the ecological damage caused by these chemical plants was estimated at $1.5 million (Novelli 1994).

The Berlini System

Estimates of the bribes paid by the Ferruzzi Corporation in the Enimont case ranged from $94 million (Cowell 1993) to $140 million (Kramer 1994). How did Ferruzzi mobilize these funds? Was there an illegal bookkeeping system that allowed the corporation to generate this money? Indeed, Ferruzzi used a sophisticated system of double-entry bookkeeping dating back to the days of Serafino Ferruzzi, the founder of the company. This system is commonly known as the Berlini system, after the financier Pino Berlini, who was in charge of managing it for Serafino, and later for Gardini and Sama. This system evolved in a global arena, taking full advantage of the new fiscal conditions associated with globalization.

Serafino Ferruzzi created a financial company in Switzerland and put Berlini in charge of it. Taking advantage of Switzerland's favorable banking laws, the company operated in secrecy in order to subtract significant sums of money from taxes and the Italian legal and fiscal systems (Raggi 1994). It was a system in which company funds were channeled into family control without satisfying legal and managerial requirements. Ferruzzi used this money for bribery, but also for personal use. False billing allowed him to free this cash for export. During the years of Serafino's chairmanship, money was smuggled out of Italy through the exchange of briefcases full of cash at the border (Pergolini and Tortorella 1994b). It is estimated that by the time of his death, $250 million had been transferred abroad (Tamburini 1994a).

Serafino Ferruzzi probably had a safety net for his family and associates in mind. He was not one of the aggressive capitalists of the new global era (Kramer 1994). Things changed when Gardini took over the corporation. He used the Berlini system to pay for his intricate network of bribes and also to support his lifestyle and personal interests, including his passion for sailing. Through the Berlini system, a sizable amount of money was mobilized and used for years, undetected by authorities.

The Functioning of the Berlini System

The system took full advantage of the proliferation of fiscal safe havens around the world. These countries' fiscal systems are characterized by (1) the virtual absence of taxation of profits, (2) laws guaranteeing high levels of secrecy of bank operations, and (3) very flexible legislation regarding the creation and actions of companies (Pergolini and Tortorella 1994b). Countries such as the Bahamas, Hong Kong, the Cayman Islands, as well as Liechtenstein, Monaco, and Switzerland, all qualify as fiscal safe havens. In the emerging global system, financial safe havens have become important elements for the transnationalization of capital (Raggi 1994).

The ease with which companies can be created and the size of the Ferruzzi Corporation are keys to understanding the functioning of the Berlini system. First, companies would be created in fiscal safe havens. Then, through false billings, Ferruzzi enterprises became indebted to the newly created offshore companies. Once funds were transferred offshore, they entered the "hot money" system and were virtually untraceable, as they changed type and place of use with extreme rapidity, often many times within a twenty-four-hour period (Pergoloni and Tortorella 1994a). In most cases, false billing involved the siphoning of funds from the most productive enterprises of Ferruzzi, such as Montedison and the agricultural corporations Eridania and Beghin Say. In some cases false billing was paralleled by false operations on exchange rates involving transactions between companies located in different countries. Because of Ferruzzi's extensive holdings, Berlini could operate from his headquarters in Switzerland in stock markets around the world. Directed by Gardini and other Ferruzzi officials, he used privileged information concerning Ferruzzi subsidiaries to buy and sell sure winners. The Berlini system was fueled by an insider-trading scheme engineered by the very corporation whose company's stock was the object of trade (Tamburini 1994a).

The Use of the Money

For years the Berlini system created substantial sources of undetected funds. By Berlini's own admission, by the end of 1988 the system was working at full steam and the "books" showed a surplus of $190 million (Raggi 1994). He also pointed out, however, that by June 1991 the system had a $270 million debt. One of the reasons for such a drastic financial change was speculated to be the $205 million loss linked to the failed attempt to fix the soybean futures market at the Chicago Board of Trade (CBOT) in 1989 (Modolo 1994b). In 1989 Ferruzzi bought the major U.S. soybean firm Central Soya and immediately began going "long" in the soybean market, buying up futures contracts on the CBOT (Rerrick 1993). While Ferruzzi argued that it had legitimate needs for the soybeans, other major agribusiness corporations, such as Cargill, convinced the CBOT that Ferruzzi was trying to corner the market (Guebert 2002). In July 1989 the CBOT forced Ferruzzi to liquidate its position and filed a lawsuit against Ferruzzi and its subsidiary Central Soya, charging them with trying to corner the market. Without admitting guilt, Ferruzzi agreed to pay the CBOT $2 million in fines and $1 million in court expenses to settle the suit (Szala 1992).

However, Berlini reported that Gardini recovered the majority of lost funds through financial deals with other subsidiaries (Raggi 1994). According to Clean Hands prosecutor Francesco Mauro Iacoviello, the Berlini system funds were used for various bribing schemes and to finance the expenses of the family (Tamburini 1994c). While Gardini combined his interest in the expansion of the corporation with the financing of his expensive hobbies, the family "was not interested in financial statements. The family was interested in skimming whatever it could from Ferfin's[2] companies before those companies went under" (Kramer 1994, 73).

The Other Side of the Berlini System

The creation of untraceable funds is the first step in a system of bribes. The second step is a process that delivers them without detection by authorities. In the Enimont affair, Ferruzzi used two distinct methods of bribery. The first was briefcases full of cash delivered by highly paid intermediaries and high-ranking Ferruzzi officials (Colaprico 1994a). The second involved the

---

2. Ferfin was Ferruzzi's financial holding company.

transfer of funds through financial institutions located in fiscal safe havens. Politicians from all over the Italian political spectrum used the first method. Members of the government coalition (CD and PSI) and opposition parties benefited from Ferruzzi's illegal donations (Ravelli 1994b, 6).

The second method is quite similar to the Berlini system. In the Enimont affair, it was used mostly by financiers linked to the PSI and to its former leader, Bettino Craxi. Financial experts used their financial institutions to transfer bribe money to politicians. For example, Sergio Cusani, a Ferruzzi financial consultant, created Merchant International Holding, with headquarters in Luxembourg, in 1988. Industrialists in search of favors received false bills from Merchant. Then they deposited the payments in one of Merchant's foreign accounts, such as the National Bank of Luxembourg or the Union Swiss Bank, the most powerful of the Swiss banks (Pergolini and Tortorella 1994a). Once in these accounts, the bribes were transformed into "hot money" and their final destinations were virtually untraceable (Modolo 1994a).

The Clean Hands investigation of the Enimont affair also revealed the involvement of the Vatican bank Istituto per le Opere Religiose (Institute for Religious Works) or IOR. In late 1990 Sama formed a foundation under the auspices of the IOR with funds he received from Gardini (Sama 1993). Although Sama said that the objective of the foundation was charity, according to Italian authorities it was a money-laundering shell. A portion of the bribes that Ferruzzi paid for the defiscalization of Enimont was paid in treasury bonds (TBS). According to court records, "about 600 million dollars in treasury bonds were laundered through the bank of the Holy See. These TBS were transformed into dollars, Swiss francs, and other currencies and were subsequently routed outside Italy through at least 12 operations on foreign accounts" (Martini 1994, 14). Sama reported in sworn court testimony that IOR charged $6 million to handle the entire operation. The Vatican has always denied these allegations, but it refused requests from Italian authorities to investigate IOR budgets.

Ferruzzi's Internal Conflict: A New Crisis

Several members of the Ferruzzi family and several top executives were not satisfied with Gardini's handling of the Enimont affair. In particular, Sama believed that he was a better manager than Gardini and wanted a bigger role in the corporation. The family tensions erupted when Gardini and Sama quarreled during the family Christmas celebration in 1990. After this epi-sode, Gardini decided that to increase his control of the corporation he needed to reduce the power of the Ferruzzi family members who controlled the corporation. His elaborate plan was to resign from the corporation, trans-fer the shares belonging to Serafino Ferruzzi's children (Arurto, Idina, Franca, and Alessandra) to their children, install his own son, Ivan Gardini (then twenty-one years old), as chairman of the company, and gain the proxy vote for each of the Ferruzzi grandchildren, who as minors could not vote. The family, with the exception of Gardini's wife, Idina,[3] rejected the proposal. In July 1991 they offered Gardini, his wife, and his children $380 million to leave the corporation permanently. Gardini was forced to accept the offer, and with this money he formed a new corporation, Gardini, Inc., which he directed until his death in 1993. The Ferruzzi family gave Carlo Sama full power to direct the corporation in June 1992. The final stage of this family conflict was the legal suit the Ferruzzi family filed against the Gardini family—that is, against all of Raul's heirs, including his wife, Idina Ferruzzi.

Gardini's problems with the Ferruzzi family were exacerbated by the ac-tions of his financial consultant, Sergio Cusani. Gardini hired Cusani to ar-range and deliver the bribes. Cusani sided with the Ferruzzi family in the conflict and never completed the bribery jobs Gardini assigned him. He took $38 million of the Enimont bribe money and hid it in a secret offshore bank account. He failed to give politicians all of the money promised to them and never told the rest of the Ferruzzi family (Colaprico 1994c). Because Cusani never told Gardini all of the details regarding the bribes, Gardini could not cooperate fully with Clean Hands investigators and was arrested (Ravelli 1994a).

Ferruzzi's Legitimation Strategy in the Aftermath of Enimont

Ferruzzi's image was tarnished within the business community and the coun-try by the family quarrels and business problems related to Enimont and the Chicago Board of Trade episode (Pergolini 1994). The new CEO, Carlo Sama, set out to restore the credibility of Ferruzzi and reorganize the corporation. The strategy to accomplish these goals included manipulated media cam-paigns and electoral bribes.

---

3. Idina was the daughter of the company founder Serafino Ferruzzi. She married Raul Gardini in 1955.

Dirty Pens

Sama and his staff implemented the so-called family project to improve Ferruzzi's image by bribing well-known figures in the financial media. Clean Hands testimony revealed that three prominent financial journalists were paid a total of $760,000 to comment favorably on the corporation's latest business activities (Leone 1994). Sama testified that columnists from the influential newspapers *La Repubblica*, *La Stampa*, and *Il Sole 24 Ore* received cash payments from Ferruzzi. *La Repubblica* was the major Italian daily paper and had ties to socialists and a center-left readership. *La Stampa* was owned by FIAT and appealed largely to a politically centrist probusiness readership. *Il Sole 24 Ore* was strictly a business newspaper modeled after the *Wall Street Journal*, with editorials that expressed a relatively conservative, neoliberal posture that was often critical of the nation's left and pro-labor programs. Because of the concurrent operation of Clean Hands, the bribing of newspaper reporters was dubbed Penne Sporche (Dirty Pens).

Sama's plan was to cover a wide spectrum of national public opinion and thereby provide Ferruzzi with the necessary credibility to undertake the restructuring project. The Dirty Pens journalists all denied wrongdoing and took voluntary leaves of absence from their jobs during the criminal investigation. They also received full support from the industry, whose unions organized a four-day strike to protest "a deliberate attack on the freedom of press" (Leone 1994). Sama's testimony was corroborated by Cusani, who indicated that he personally delivered bribes to the journalists (Andreoli 1994b, 66–67). Despite these assertions, the Italian court found insufficient evidence to try the journalists.

Ferruzzi's Bribes, Political Parties, and Elections

During the 1992 national elections, Sama implemented the plan to bribe political parties and leaders to gain support for Ferruzzi. While the private financing of political parties and campaigns is legal in Italy, recipients of donations must register each contribution with the Ministry of the Interior, which then reports the information to the public. Contributors who wish to remain anonymous resort to illegal donations. In addition, unrecorded donations allow corrupt politicians to pocket the contributions.

The governing coalition parties PSI and CD were the primary targets of the bribes. According to testimony given during the criminal investigations, Bettino Craxi knowingly received bribes on twenty different occasions (Fazzo 1994). Tried "in absentia," Craxi was found guilty and sentenced to eight years in jail. He escaped arrest by fleeing to Tunisia, where, despite numerous extradition attempts, he remained in asylum until his death in 1996. Other prominent Socialist Party members, among them former PSI vice secretary and former minister of justice Claudio Martelli and former foreign minister Gianni De Michelis, also admitted receiving bribes.

The former administrative head of the CD, Senator Severino Citaristi, testified that over the years he had received $100 million in illegal payments to the party. He stated that such payments were authorized by party officials and were a common solution to the lack of funds experienced by a large political party. Italian authorities charged Citaristi with receiving $20 million from Montedison and ENI in connection with the Enimont affair. Citaristi met Ferruzzi's Sama and ENI's Cragnotti in his office and at restaurants and bars, where the bribes were exchanged (Zurlo 1994, 28). Furthermore, Citaristi admitted that the CD needed an annual budget of more than $14 million, a very difficult sum to obtain through legal means (Andreoli 1994a, 11).

The CD's officials were not just passive recipients of voluntary donations from Ferruzzi. It was customary in Italy for governing parties and politicians to request kickbacks in business deals. This practice, as we have seen, applied to the Enimont case and was clearly highlighted by one of Cagliari's statements: "when it was time to sell the Enimont stocks, it was the then Minister of Industry Franco Piga who asked me to get in touch with Montedison's chairperson Giuseppe Garofano. One of the objectives of the meeting was to study the sale of the stocks. The other was to inform Garofano of the amount of payment that CD wanted to receive in return for its patronage of the deal" (Andreoli 1994b, 33). Similarly, former Italian budget minister Paolo Cirino Pomicino admitted that he illegally accepted money from Ferruzzi to finance his 1992 general election campaign (Pomicino 1993). Beyond the focus of the governing coalition, Ferruzzi also provided bribes to opposition groups such as the PCI and the populist-federalist Northern League (Consarino 1994; Ravelli 1994b).

The Final Act

The Reorganization of the Corporation and Mediobanca

Maneuvers to reestablish credibility were paralleled by efforts to reorganize Ferruzzi. Sama was concerned with the company's deficit, the constant need to finance bribes, and the family's lifestyle. To address these problems, he and his associates requested the assistance of Mediobanca, formerly a fully public and now a privately owned merchant bank specializing in the financial assistance to corporations (Pergolini 1994). In post–World War II Italy, Mediobanca played a fundamental role in providing capital to major industrial groups and fostering significant economic growth in Italy. For many years Mediobanca had been guided by its president, Enrico Cuccia, who managed the bank with a unique personal style that emphasized sound managerial skills, loyalty, and inner-circle membership (Beria di Argentine and Mucchetti 1994; Oldani 1994). Cuccia's inner circle was made up of representatives of Italy's industrial elite and was out of reach to newcomers like Ferruzzi. Moreover, Cuccia had a conservative attitude and opposed entrepreneurs who asserted independence from the business elites (Beria di Argentine and Mucchetti 1994). While some interpreted this attitude as a sign of financial wisdom, others viewed it as a naked display of power (Pergolini 1994).

When Ferruzzi purchased Montedison, Cuccia supported the acquisition because he did not like Montedison's director, Mario Schimberni. Schimberni had often challenged Cuccia and had claimed autonomy from the country's business elite (Tamburini 1994b). The "honeymoon" between Gardini and Cuccia was short lived, for Cuccia realized that Gardini's management style was even less respectful than Schimberni's. More important, Cuccia never approved of Ferruzzi's full control of Montedision (Tamburini 1994b). Gardini's criticism of the political establishment's behavior in the Enimont case and his attempt to control the Enimont joint venture turned Cuccia against him.

Despite all of this, Sama felt that he needed Mediobanca's help in the Ferruzzi reorganization. Sama's plan included the involvement of the U.S. financial institution Goldman Sachs and a merger between Ferruzzi and Gardini's new company, Gardini, Inc. Minor financial partners, such as Gardini's associate Sergio Cragnotti, would also contribute to the operation. This plan, however, never materialized. According to Sama, this was the outcome of Mediobanca's deliberate attempt to destroy Ferruzzi. Sama argued that Mediobanca robbed the Ferruzzi family and effectively "brought the company down" when it called in a number of loans taken out by Ferruzzi. Sama maintained that Mediobanca's attempt to gain control of Ferruzzi was carried out in agreement with the Italian economic establishment, which used Ferruzzi as a scapegoat for the wave of scandals that were engulfing the sector. In fact, Sama indicated that the decision to call in Ferruzzi's loans was made in private meetings attended by the CEOs of top corporations in the country, Cuccia's inner circle. After Mediobanca's action, the Ferruzzi family lost control of the various segments of the Ferruzzi Corporation, which eventually were taken over by a consortium of banks (Tamburini 1994c). While the Ferruzzi family lost control of the corporation, the Ferruzzi Corporation survived the scandal and continued operations.

Neither Gardini nor Mediobanca nor Goldman Sachs agreed with Sama's version of events. According to Gardini's lawyer, Sama proposed a deal to save Ferruzzi that required that Gardini and Cragnotti buy portions of Ferfin. Sama and the Ferruzzi family would relinquish control of the corporation to Gardini, while retaining 30 percent of the company's shares. After meetings with Banca Commerciale Italiana to discuss the offer, Gardini expressed his intention to reject Sama's proposal (Pergolini 1994). According to Mediobanca, Ferruzzi's financial situation was so serious that any restructuring attempt would require a radical and sophisticated intervention that only a bank of Mediobanca's stature could provide. More important, the repercussions of a possible Ferruzzi bankruptcy would have negative repercussions for creditor institutions, numerous corporations, and workers in Italy and elsewhere. Mediobanca stated that it was only when it learned of the Berlini system, and the history of illegal budgetary practices, that it withdrew from the rescue plan. The position of Goldman Sachs was similar to that of Mediobanca. The bank's representative in Italy indicated that its rescue plan was based on the budgets officially disclosed by Ferruzzi. Goldman Sachs asserted that once it became aware of the illegal Berlini system of generating money for bribes, it terminated the restructuring plan (Beria di Argentine and Mucchetti 1994).

The Italian authorities associated with the Clean Hands investigation questioned just how much Goldman Sachs and Mediobanca knew about Ferruzzi's budget. Prosecutors argued that officials at Mediobanca, and perhaps also at Goldman Sachs, were aware of the Berlini system and Ferruzzi's financial maneuvers before these were made public. Additionally, Mediobanca planned to assist Ferruzzi despite its awareness of the false budgets. In this view, Mediobanca's withdrawal of support was based on its participation in a scheme to make Ferruzzi the scapegoat for the troubles of the entire business community. Faced with a wave of legal probes due to Clean Hands, the business community identified Ferruzzi as the "sacrificial lamb" so as to regain credibility and legitimize its position in the new social climate. Indeed, the fact that Ferruzzi was a new and rapidly growing corporation experiencing leadership problems made it a perfect candidate for the role. This explanation supported Sama's version of events and implied the existence of a conflict among the major actors operating in the corporate sector. Despite further investigations, Mediobanca was never brought to trial, and formal charges against it were dismissed (Pergolini 1994).

The various accounts of the story agree that Mediobanca was willing to prepare a rescue plan for Ferruzzi. Mediobanca requested full disclosure of Ferruzzi's budgets and the appointment of Guido Rossi—a manager trusted by the bank—as the new CEO of Montedison and Ferfin. In May 1993 Ferruzzi's board of directors approved the company's budget and sent it to Mediobanca, but this budget did not disclose the transfer of funds to the Berlini system. After reviewing the budget, Rossi made its illegal activities public. At this point Mediobanca halted its cooperation with Ferruzzi, and criminal charges were issued against Ferruzzi. The Clean Hands prosecutors' point was that Mediobanca knew that the budget delivered to them was doctored and disclosed this only when it was convenient or inevitable. The state of affairs emerged as prosecutors continued their investigation of the company and Ferruzzi officials began cooperating with authorities (Andreoli 1994b).

After the criminal allegations were made public, ENI's Cagliari was detained on charges concerning Enimont and other cases. Cagliari felt betrayed by the system. In his view, illegal behavior by corporate managers was business as usual, and the rules had suddenly been changed (Andreoli 1994b, 24–25). He lashed out at prosecutors who could not understand that if managers were to conduct business, they had to remove obstacles that prevented them from reaching their legitimate goals. Bribes were nothing more than user fees that a voracious political class demanded from the entrepreneurial world. Cagliari was denied bail and remained in prison, where he underwent daily interrogations. On July 20, 1993, frustrated by his plight and unable to comprehend the rationale behind the accusations against him, Cagliari put a plastic bag over his head and committed suicide.

Gardini was also busy defending himself against mounting accusations. He agreed with Cagliari that the corrupt political system was to blame for Ferruzzi's illegal actions (Peruzzi 1994). According to his wife, Idina, Gardini was not the reckless manager that Clean Hands prosecutors described. He was a capable manager who made Ferruzzi into a leading world corporation, who brought jobs and prosperity to thousand of households around the globe, and who fought for the introduction in Europe of alternative and environmentally sound energy sources such as ethanol (Guatelli 1994). He wanted to cooperate with the Enimont investigation and was prepared to disclose information about the bribes paid in the case (Lantos 1995). But he lacked access to the information that could exonerate him, which was in the hands of his associates (Cusani). Regardless of the accuracy of Idina's version of the events, Gardini, like Cagliari, could not face the humiliation of a criminal investigation and the stigma associated with it.

On July 22, 1993, only two days after Cagliari's suicide, Gardini spent the day with his lawyers preparing a defense against the accusations contained in the warrant for his arrest. The following morning Gardini appeared ready to face the questioning of prosecutors and his inevitable arrest. He had an early breakfast served by his old butler, Brunetti. But instead of getting dressed to go to court, he opened one of his desk drawers and took out a Walther 7.65 millimeter pistol, which he kept there in case of an emergency. Then he wrote a note listing the names of his wife and children and ended with a lone "grazie." A shot followed, and when Brunetti entered the room, he discovered Gardini's lifeless body on the floor.

Analysis and Discussion

The objective of this chapter was to explore further the relationship between TNCs and the nation-state. The Ferruzzi case supports the argument made in Chapter 2 that globalization is a contested process in which TNCs have a complex and contradictory set of relations with nation-states. The power of TNCs influences the actions of nation-states, but national governments also oppose certain kinds of TNC actions; globalization is contested terrain. As we argued in the previous chapter, this conclusion is compatible with "contradictory dimension of globalization" camp.

The Ferruzzi case confirms that TNCs are powerful actors and can thus often bypass national laws. Essentially, their power derives from their ability to operate globally through the hypermobility of capital, which favors the transnationalization of corporate operations. Ferruzzi implemented a number of strategies to which segments of the state fell prey. For example, Ferruzzi was able to enlist key political actors to assist Montedison's joint venture with ENI, and despite disagreements with the public sector (ENI), Ferruzzi officials were able to control the price of Enimont stock and its sale. Moreover, the transnational character of Ferruzzi allowed for the creation of new strategies. The generation of funds for bribes depended heavily on global insider trading, the use of "hot money," and the creation and functioning of the Berlini system. However, as we concluded in Chapter 2, TNCs' power over the nation-state is only partial, in that the state has its own powers, which it can use to oppose TNCs. In this case, prosecutors' investigations and the PCI's opposition to defiscalization legislation show that the

Italian state did not relinquish its powers vis-à-vis Ferruzzi. On the contrary, anticorruption investigations indicate that the state had considerable power that it could bring to bear against transnational actors. Taken independently, the actions of Ferruzzi and the Italian government can be seen to support the position of the "corporate domination" group and the "grand durée" group, respectively. Our point is that, taken in their totality, these events illustrate the complex relationship between TNCs and the nation-state and the contested nature of globalization.

The Ferruzzi case further reveals that TNCs have internal contradictions that weaken their position vis-à-vis their opponents. More specifically, it indicates that TNC strategies are the outcome of complex forms of negotiation and often create conflict among their leading members. The management of the Ferruzzi Corporation was characterized by internal disagreements, attempts and counterattempts to gain control of the corporation, open hostility, and even deception. Obviously this situation affected the direction of Ferruzzi's industrial policy. But it also affected the manner in which the corporation related to the public sphere. Ferruzzi family members themselves have cited Gardini's fall as something that weakened the company's position. Indeed, Sama's restructuring program involved the return of Gardini as the head of the company, in spite of the animosity between the two sides of the family. Internal conflict is particularly significant here because it took place in the context of a family-owned TNC. Clearly, family ownership does not make a corporation immune to the kind of conflict generally considered more typical of other forms of corporate management.

Similar observations can be made about the state's role in this case, especially about the conflict between different branches of the state. The Italian judiciary has been a powerful factor in the demise of the political class that has governed Italy for decades: parties that have led the governing coalition since the end of World War II have been dissolved or reduced to nominal representation in Parliament. The executive branch and segments of the legislative branch that supported the executive attempted to halt the action of the judicial branch. More significantly, new legislation has attempted to reduce the independence of the judiciary. Former prime minister Bettino Craxi introduced such legislation as early as 1983 (Andreoli 1994a). Moreover, a significant portion of the political apparatus was involved in discrediting the actions of prosecutors on the grounds that they were "abusing" the powers assigned them by the constitution.

4

CORPORATE POWER AND THE FREE GLOBAL MARKET:
THE LYSINE PRICE-FIXING CASE OF ADM

Through the previous two stories of globalization, we established that the dominant power of TNCs is opposed by state action and weakened by internal contradictions. In this chapter we continue to probe the power of TNCs under globalization by analyzing their ability to affect the functioning of the market. More specifically, we attempt to shed some light on the often mentioned ability of TNCs to organize global production in ways that affect the market and avoid the regulatory actions of nation-states. The free market is perhaps the most recognized symbol of globalization. It constitutes the centerpiece of neoliberal theory and is employed in a variety of other analytical approaches that focus on global social relations. Promoters of the neoliberal position see the free market as the foundation of the most desirable form of political and social relations. They contend that the growth and free mobility of capital and commodities, and the concomitant reduction of state intervention, are fundamental conditions for social and human development. Neoliberalism has been formulated in slightly different terms during the past few decades. In the now classic 1960s formulation of neoliberalism, Milton Friedman maintains that market relations take primacy over other spheres of human activity. Accordingly, social well-being is subordinate to economic freedom; it is "an end in itself" and the most basic condition for the development of society (1962/1982, 8–9; 1977, 10–11). "The kind of economic organization that provides economic freedom directly, namely, competitive capitalism, also promotes political freedom" (1962/1982, 9). In Friedman's view, the primacy of economic freedom makes laissez-faire economic systems superior to those that involve state intervention in the economy. Friedman sees poverty and marginalization as unalterable natural conditions that arise from aggregated inherited differences in individual cognitive skills or in individual character and morality. Moreover, he holds that the elimination of special protections and programs for racial and ethnic minorities and women would make for a more just society (ibid., 108–18). He further argues that the increased flexibility and tax savings that result from the dismantling of state intervention revive opportunity for all and provide solutions to mounting social problems.

This original, radical form of neoliberalism has been followed by newer versions, which were employed at the end of the Soviet era to legitimize market-centered society. Francis Fukuyama's "end of history" thesis is arguably the most popular and widely known instance. Fukuyama proclaimed that a new age of unchallenged neoliberal global democracy had arisen from the ashes of the defeated Soviet system. Indeed, for Fukuyama, the failed Soviet experience, postwar, state-based liberalism, and these systems' misguided search for economic egalitarianism and social engineering proved that "free-market democracy" was the *only* option for any nation aspiring to socioeconomic progress and prosperity. He speculated that we might now be "at a point where we cannot imagine a world substantially different from our own, in which there is no apparent or obvious way in which the future will represent a fundamental improvement over our current order" (1992, 51). Fukuyama revived triumphal postwar ideas of progressive modernization and the end of ideology, but his free markets and formal equality-based democracy differ significantly from the emphasis on social justice and the welfare state articulated by Talcott Parsons (1971).

Thomas L. Friedman's *Lexus and the Olive Tree* is perhaps the newest and the most comprehensive contemporary expression of the optimistic neoliberal view of globalization. Friedman contends that an integrated, cosmopolitan global system, composed of global free markets, new technologies and organizations, and rational investors, has replaced the "divided," "frozen," "Cold War System." This new system, he contends, represents a global revolution. The democratization of technology, finance, and information has created a "fast world," a nonhierarchical, open, dynamic "web" with the "internet as its backbone" (2000, 8–9, 44–72, 200). Emphasizing that modernization is driven by global free markets and investor choices, Friedman argues that the "electronic herd" of e-trading individual investors and multinational companies stimulates the economy so effectively that all nations aspiring to be modern must move toward the American model. Refusal to don the "golden straightjacket" (i.e., neoliberal globalization) condemns a nation to marginality (ibid., 104–11). Friedman's argument rests on two critical presuppositions: first, free markets work efficiently, enrich the majority, and open the way for rational choices that advance economic growth and globalization; second, global free markets need U.S. military power and intervention to stem brushfire wars and terrorism and to ensure property rights and social stability. Distancing himself from radical neoliberal positions, however, he supports the nation's social safety net, its multicultural character, and its international role in global organizations such as the UN, NATO, WTO, and IMF.

As indicated above, critics of neoliberalism argue that for most of the twentieth century the growth of capitalism has been regulated by a strong intervening state (e.g., Carnoy 1984; Harvey 1989 and 2005; Spybey 1996). Despite differences between core and dependent states and differences in regional economic policies, state activities have been able to foster the growth of capital accumulation while legitimizing its actions with segments of society that did not benefit directly from these actions (e.g., Giddens 1994; Gordon et al. 1982; O'Connor 1986; Offe 1985; Poulantzas 1978). These critics further argue that the growth of TNCs has altered the ability of nation-states to organize and coordinate social and economic activities. Because of the emergence of TNCs, the nation-state has been transformed into an instrument of transnational capital and is therefore unable to regulate capitalism (e.g., Akard 1992; Antonio and Bonanno 1996; Constance and Heffernan 1991; Ross and Trachte 1990; Sassen 1996; Yergin and Stanislaw 1998). As we have seen in the preceding chapters, this point is illustrated by these stories of globalization.

The case studied in this chapter revolves around a price-fixing scandal involving the food-processing giant Archer Daniels Midland (ADM) and Asian-based corporations. It involves five global food and feed TNCs: the U.S.-based ADM, two Japan-based companies, Kyowa Hakko and Ajinomoto, and two Korea-based companies, Sewon (and its subsidiary Sewon America) and Cheil Jedang, Ltd. (Kneene 1998). For the purpose of this analysis, we focus on the three major corporate actors involved: ADM, Ajinomoto, and Kyowa Hakko. The two Japan-based TNCs also have headquarters in the United States, where they operate under different names (Heartland 1998). The price-fixing scheme was investigated in three product lines: lysine, a feed additive that promotes the growth of lean muscle; high-fructose corn syrup, a sweetener used in soft drinks and other foods and beverages; and citric acid, a common food flavoring (Henkoff 1995a). For heuristic purposes only, this chapter concentrates on the case of lysine.

Lysine is an amino acid that is one of most widely used feed supplements worldwide. Lysine has no substitutes, but soybean meal contains small amounts of it. Because corn-based feed is relatively low in amino acids, it became commercially and nutritionally desirable to supplement some livestock feeds with lysine. Lysine supplements allow the increased use of much less expensive feed ingredients for the production of high-quality lean meat (Heartland 1998). In the 1960s, Asian biotechnology firms discovered a fermentation process that converts dextrose into lysine (L-Lysine) at a much lower cost than conventional methods. By the 1980s they were importing large quantities of dextrose from U.S. wet corn millers and exporting high-priced lysine back into the United States (Connor 1998). The commercialization of L-Lysine rapidly augmented the availability of lysine as a livestock feed supplement (Heartland 1998).

A Short Summary of ADM and Its Competitors' Backgrounds

In the 1990s ADM was one of the leading food processors in the United States and the world (Sorkins 1997); it remains so today (ADM 2006). ADM is in the business of procuring, transporting, storing, processing, and selling agricultural commodities and related products. Some of its major divisions are corn processing, bioproducts, oils, produce, and grains, while its products include vegetable and seed oils, hydroponically grown vegetables, flavoring agents, sweeteners, animal feed, amino acids, and several other commodities. Growth in the 1990s included the strengthening of its oilseed sector through the acquisition of a number of companies, including Master Mix, a subsidiary of Central Soya, which in turn was part of the Ferruzzi group. With processing plants and sales offices on four continents and in forty-three countries, ADM is one of the largest TNCs in the agrifood sector (Sorkins 1997; EverGreen 1997; Heffernan 1999b). ADM's self-description as the "premier food supplier" in the world and the "supermarket to the world" (*Agbiz Tiller* 1997) capture ADM's status as a TNC. ADM's success is largely credited to CEO Dwayne Andreas, who converted a soybean-milling company into a diversified transnational powerhouse with more than $12 billion in annual sales (*Frontline* 1997).

ADM's main competitors in the lysine business are the Japan-based TNCs Kyowa Hakko and Ajinomoto. Kyowa Hakko, and its U.S.-based subsidiary Biokyowa, were the first companies to make lysine using the fermentation process (Henkoff 1996). Kyowa Hakko is a major manufacturer of pharmaceuticals, liquor, food, and chemical products, and one of the largest makers of amino acids worldwide (Japan Economic Institute 1991). Ajinomoto is the leading supplier of technical assistance for using feed-grade amino acids. Ajinomoto established its U.S. subsidiary, Heartland, in 1984 and opened its main lysine plant in Iowa in 1986 (Heartland 1998).

The Global Lysine Price-Fixing Scandal

In the late 1980s, Ajinomoto, Kyowa Hakko, and Sewon were exporting about $30 million worth of lysine per year to the United States. This Asia-sourced lysine product sold for much less than the lysine made by U.S. organic chemical companies. ADM soon discovered why these Asian biotechnology firms were buying such large quantities of dextrose from the United States; dextrose was the raw ingredient used for lysine fermentation (Connor 1998). In 1989 ADM committed $150 million to building the world's largest lysine plant. It hired thirty-two-year-old Mark Whitacre to head the new bioproducts division and establish ADM's first lysine production division. ADM leadership was particularly interested in Whitacre's performance because the lysine division was identified as a strategically important sector owing to the expected opportunity to operate in the rapidly growing animal feed market with a very cost-effective product. With his energy and drive, Whitacre took charge of the division and quickly gained favor with CEO Dwayne Andreas (Henkoff 1995c).

The new lysine plant opened in February 1991. The first objective was to establish ADM as a major player in the lysine market by offering prices below those of competitors. The plan worked, and ADM captured about 50 percent of the U.S. market (Connor 1998). However, it also created a lysine glut that dropped the price severely and brought about a "price war." Phase two of ADM's strategy was to make the division profitable. This was not easy, because the company was losing about $2 million a month owing to a combination of declining prices and production problems. ADM officials believed that a fermenter was contaminated with a type of bacteria that did not produce lysine (Henkoff 1995c). Despite this difficult beginning, Andreas continued to think highly of Whitacre and promoted him to vice president of the bioproducts division.

In February 1992 the situation began to change for Whitacre. The lysine division was still losing several million dollars per month. Andreas brought in the president of ADM's corn-processing division, Terry Wilson, a business veteran with significant managerial experience, to mentor Whitacre on the basic business practices at ADM, including the art of price-fixing. Despite its illegal nature, Whitacre quickly learned that price-fixing was a condoned practice at ADM. Uncomfortable with this business philosophy, Whitacre considered quitting but decided to stick with ADM and try to "fix" the company from the inside (Henkoff 1995c).

In June 1992 lysine prices were at an all-time low as the marketplace absorbed "the full impact of ADM's entry" (Shon 1992). ADM decided that action was needed to stabilize the lysine market and make lysine profitable. Whitacre and Wilson took the first step toward the creation of a price-fixing strategy and met with Ajinomoto and Kyowa Hakko representatives in Tokyo, where Wilson proposed forming an amino acids association (Connor 1998; Henkoff 1995c). Ajinomoto's first response was skeptical (Henkoff 1995c). The persistently weak market motivated ADM to renew its attempts to reach an agreement with its competitors. Later in June, executives for Ajinomoto, Kyowa Hakko, and ADM met at the Nikkei Hotel in Mexico City, the first of many meetings of the "lysine association." At that time the three companies (and later other Korean companies mentioned above) discussed "raising prices, allocating production, and setting sales shares across several regions of the world" (Connor 1998, 15). Wilson illustrated the principal profitability problem in the lysine market—production capacity was 20 percent higher than demand. "Well, gentlemen," he told his colleagues, "there's $200 million that we're giving to our customers. In other words, the customer is benefiting, not the people who spent hundreds of millions of dollars building these plants" (Henkoff 1995c, 54–55). He then emphasized the importance of cooperation among producers as part of ADM's philosophy. ADM's business philosophy was first presented at this meeting: "The competitor is our friend, and the customer is our enemy" (Henkoff 1995c, 55; Krebs 2002; Rao and Kano 1996).

In September 1992 the first two lysine industry summit meetings were held in Decatur, Illinois. In October a meeting was held in California to discuss worldwide sales volumes; this was followed by a second summit attended by the six major lysine producers in Hawaii (Greenwald 1996). The result of this and other meetings was that sales quotas and target prices were established for each lysine producer and each region of the world (Bahner 1995). Following this accord, prices rebounded and ADM enjoyed record exports of lysine (Cintron 1993a).

Price-fixing was a common practice at ADM and was not confined to top executives; neither was it a matter of particular concern among ADM mid- and upper-level managers. Upon returning from Mexico City, Whitacre noted that "several people from Terry [Wilson]'s corn-processing division came up to me and said kind of half jokingly, 'oh, you and Terry have been at one of [those] price-fixing meetings'" (Henkoff 1995c, 55). These company executives knew that Wilson's technical expertise was in corn processing, not lysine, and they had some knowledge of his past involvement with price-fixing.

In the summer of 1992 representatives of Ajinomoto and Kyowa Hakko came on separate occasions to see ADM's huge lysine facility in Decatur, Illinois (Cintron 1993b). Although things seemed to be progressing well with this new "partnership," Michael Andreas, son of Dwayne and an ADM executive vice president, and Whitacre had reservations about trusting the Japanese completely, as ADM suspected sabotage in the contamination problem in the fermenter (Henkoff 1995c). Indeed, the history of these Japanese companies supported their suspicion. Ajinomoto was of particular concern. In 1969 Kyowa Hakko charged Ajinomoto with stealing bacteria that Kyowa Hakko had discovered and that could be used to make lysine through fermentation. A Japanese court found Ajinomoto guilty of patent infringement, sentenced the company, and prohibited Ajinomoto from using the same bacteria to produce lysine. Twenty years later ADM suspected Ajinomoto of "bribing an ADM factory worker to spike the dextrose soup" (Henkoff 1996, 116).

In September 1992, with the contamination issue still unresolved, Dwayne Andreas called a friend in the CIA for help. The plan was to simulate an act of sabotage in which the CIA would pay an engineer from Ajinomoto to obtain "the magic bullet technology but really to smoke him out about the suspected sabotage" (Henkoff 1995b, 116). In the end, Andreas asked the FBI to initiate a formal investigation of the espionage matter. The FBI designed a sting operation that involved a $3 million payment to an Ajinomoto representative in return for an act of industrial sabotage. As part of this operation, FBI agent Bryan Shepard installed a listening device on one of Whitacre's phones to monitor conversations with potential Ajinomoto contacts. The FBI investigation concluded that there was no evidence of sabotage (Henkoff 1996).

Because of ADM's price-fixing negotiations with Ajinomoto and Kyowa Hakko, the FBI presence at ADM worried Michael Andreas. Knowing that Whitacre would be questioned, Michael instructed him to conceal any information related to the price-fixing agreement. When interviewed by the FBI, Whitacre followed orders. In order to avoid surprises, however, Andreas asked one of Wilson's associates to sit in on Whitacre's interview (Henkoff 1995c). Shortly after delivering his original statement to the FBI, Whitacre decided to expose ADM's price-fixing practices. In November 1992, when FBI agent Shepard came to install the phone tap for the sting operation, Whitacre told him of the price-fixing operations. Whitacre was prompted by his concern that the FBI might also be tapping his other phone line, the one he used for price-fixing discussions with the Japanese officials. Within weeks of confessing to Agent Shepard, Whitacre "had signed a cooperation agreement officially designating him an undercover agent" (Henkoff 1997, 85). Agent Shepard asked Whitacre to carry a concealed listening device to listen in on conversations between "senior executives at ADM and top officials of some of its leading competitors" (Henkoff 1995b, 110).

According to Whitacre, he was pulled much further into the scandal than he had originally intended. At the outset, he simply wanted to stop ADM's unethical business practices from within the company. After his original involvement with the FBI, Whitacre grew increasingly uncomfortable with his informant role and wished to terminate his cooperation, but the FBI informed him that unless he continued to cooperate, he would be implicated with the rest of the conspirators (Henkoff 1995b). Whitacre ended up providing hundreds of audio tapes and numerous videos to the FBI (Connor 1998).

In June 1995 a federal grand jury in Chicago secured "subpoenas for all information on price-fixing by ADM and its co-conspirators" (Connor 1998, 15). On June 27 FBI agents raided ADM's headquarters and seized relevant documents that revealed the 1992–95 sales targets and actual sales by all the members of the "lysine association." In the following three months ADM's stock fell 24 percent (about $2.4 billion in market value). At the 1995 stockholders meeting, Dwayne Andreas did not allow discussion of the price-fixing charges.

Before the raid, the FBI advised Whitacre to find a lawyer not linked to ADM. Whitacre did not heed this advice, and two days later ADM found out that Whitacre was an FBI informant. ADM fired Whitacre in August. His dismissal was based not on his role in the price-fixing operation but on his alleged embezzlement of $2.5 million from the company (Henkoff 1995c). Whitacre acknowledged that he had received payments but denied he had embezzled anything, stating that this money was a bonus that top ADM executives received regularly (Henkoff 1995a).

The Outcomes of the Scandal

ADM accused Whitacre of embezzlement and sued for more than $30 million. The company's claim was based on the amount allegedly embezzled plus Whi-

tacre's salary during his time as an FBI informant. Whitacre lashed back at
ADM by releasing an affidavit accusing ADM of knowingly selling tainted cattle
feed (Associated Press 1996). ADM's move against Whitacre was characterized
as its "latest salvo" aimed at "attacking his credibility" (Kelley 1996).

By February 1996 at least eighty-five lawsuits had been filed against ADM,
"fourteen by lysine buyers and many others by stockholders claiming mismanagement" (Connor 1998, 15). There were at least five civil cases for conspiring to fix prices; three of these were class-action suits and two were
allegations by the U.S. Justice Department. In addition, a group of Missouri
cattle ranchers filed suit against the company for selling contaminated feed
that allegedly killed their livestock (*Agbiz Tiller* 1996). Regarding the class-
action suits, the U.S. District Court of the Northern District of Illinois ruled
that ADM and its co-conspirators had engaged in a conspiracy to suppress
competition by fixing the price and allocating the sales volumes of lysine to
customers in and outside the United States. These practices violated the
Sherman Anti-Trust Act, which prohibits unreasonable restraint of interstate
trade and commerce. Some of the actions of which ADM was accused were said
to substantially affect interstate trade and commerce. These included (1)
meeting to discuss amounts of lysine sold worldwide; (2) agreeing to charge
prices at certain levels and otherwise to increase and maintain prices of
lysine sold in the United States and elsewhere; (3) announcing prices agreed
upon; and (4) meeting to monitor and enforce adherence to the agreed-upon
prices and sales volumes.

Another class-action suit for price-fixing was filed against ADM by several
farmers' organizations (Kinsella 1996). In response to this lawsuit, "without
admitting any wrongdoing, the Illinois company agreed to pay $25 mil-
lion—a surprisingly little sum—to settle on behalf of the some 600 lysine
customers" (Henkoff 1996, 113). Ajinomoto and Kyowa Hakko also agreed to
pay a total of $20 million to settle their portion of the suit (Greenwald 1996).

During this time the antitrust division of the Justice Department conducted "a major criminal investigation into whether ADM and other agricultural companies conspired to fix prices of food and feed additives" (Henkoff
1995a, 35). By the spring of 1996 the Justice Department had not yet filed
any indictments and its case was beginning to falter. Although it targeted
Michael Andreas and Terry Wilson, not a single ADM officer offered any cor-
roborating evidence. The Asian TNCs also refused to cooperate. Furthermore,
Whitacre's credibility was damaged as a result of his admission that he had
taken millions of dollars from ADM (Connor 1998).

While the various ADM cases were being deliberated, cases involving its

Asian competitors were also under way. In August 1996, in a serious setback for ADM, the three Asian co-defendants admitted their guilt and "copped a plea" with the U.S. Justice Department in exchange for leniency. Three of their executives admitted to personal guilt and agreed to testify against ADM (Connor 1998). In September the Asian TNCs and three of their executives were ordered to pay more than $20 million in fines for conspiring to raise world prices for lysine (Cintron 1996).

"Now isolated, ADM's lawyers began to negotiate in earnest with the Department of Justice" (Connor 1998, 16). In October ADM pled guilty to two counts of collusion to set prices on citric acid and lysine and agreed to pay $100 million in penalties: $70 million in the lysine case and $30 million for other violations (Bilchik 1996). ADM also agreed to cooperate fully with the Justice Department regarding the prosecution of Michael Andreas and Terry Wilson. As a result of this arrangement, there were several changes in the composition of ADM's board of directors: Michael Andreas was placed on administrative leave, Terry Wilson resigned, and Dwayne Andreas stepped down as CEO (though he kept his title of chairman) (Connor 1998). According to agribusiness observer Al Krebs, despite being the largest fine in history levied against an American corporation for antitrust violations, $100 million was an extremely small amount compared to the enormous profits that ADM reaped from fixing world prices (*Agbiz Tiller* 1996).

By November 1996 all of the U.S. criminal investigations of ADM had been resolved, and the company had agreed to pay $190 million in fines and civil settlements (proceedings were still in progress against individuals) (*Agbiz Tiller* 1996). ADM gained immunity, however, from charges of price-fixing in the sale of high-fructose corn syrup (Associated Press 1996). Furthermore, as part of the agreement, the details of the case were closed to public scrutiny (Kneene 1998). This "plea agreement" resulted from talks between the Justice Department and a special committee of ADM board members appointed to supervise ADM's response to the investigation (Associated Press 1996). In addition, a "compliance agreement in lieu of debarment" was negotiated that allowed ADM to continue to do business with the USDA even though it was a convicted criminal (Krebs 2001b). Justice Department representatives said that ADM's substantial cooperation in the investigation facilitated the resolution of the plea and compliance agreements (*Agbiz Tiller* 1996; Krebs 2001b).

In December 1996 a federal grand jury indicted Mark Whitacre, Michael Andreas, Terry Wilson, and Kazutoshi Yamada, managing director of Ajinomoto, on charges of conspiring to fix worldwide prices for lysine (Fox News 1996). In response to allegations and requests by ADM, Whitacre was charged with forty-five counts of wire fraud, money laundering, conspiracy, obstruction of justice, filing false income tax returns, and transportation of stolen property across state lines. After Whitacre pled innocent to the charges, his lawyer commented that the "bonus plan" had been an ADM practice for twenty years and that this was a sad ending, in that Whitacre had voluntarily tried to help the FBI expose illegal activity. Prosecutors argued that the payments violated Whitacre's immunity agreement with the Justice Department (Henkoff 1996). Feeling betrayed and penalized by those he had helped, Whitacre announced that he would no longer cooperate with the government authorities and accused the FBI of ordering him to destroy tapes that did not support their case. Based on the indictment of Whitacre and Whitacre's allegations against the FBI, lawyers for Andreas and Wilson asked the district judge to throw out much of the government's evidence because Whitacre had obviously "gone bad for the government" and because these extraordinary actions suggested "a case in disarray" (Edwards 1996).

In October 1997 Whitacre changed his plea to guilty (Reuters 1997b). In March 1998 he was sentenced to nine years in prison and ordered to repay more than $11 million to ADM (Minich 1998). The sentencing had to be postponed because Whitacre attempted suicide just hours before his court appearance (*Decatur Herald and Review* 1998). Between the indictments and the sentencing Whitacre was diagnosed as suffering from a bipolar personality disorder. According to Whitacre, "For what I did for them—I risked my life, my family, my career and everything—they should have given me immunity on everything. And to indict me on price-fixing, that just doesn't make sense" (Henkoff 1996, 91).

In September 1998 a federal jury in Chicago convicted Michael Andreas, Terry Wilson, and Mark Whitacre for conspiring to fix lysine prices, a crime that carries a maximum sentence of three years in prison and a fine of up to $350,000. Whitacre, who had attempted suicide several times since his indictment, was imprisoned in North Carolina and did not appear in court to hear the verdict (*Houston Chronicle* 1998). Although government prosecutors asked for the maximum penalties for the defendants, in July 1999 Andreas and Wilson were each sentenced to two years in prison and ordered to pay a $350,000 fine for their price-fixing activities. Mark Whitacre was sentenced to another two and a half years in prison on these charges (Robinson 1999).

In 1998 and 2000 the price-fixing fines were expanded to Canada and Europe (Krebs 2000). As the result of an investigation by the Canadian Bureau of Competition, in 1998 ADM paid a fine of $10.83 million for price-fixing on the Canadian market. In 2000, following an investigation that began in

1997, the European Union imposed fines on the members of the lysine price-fixing cartel: ADM ($45 million), Ajinomoto ($26.9 million), Kyowa Hakko Kogyo ($12.5 million), Cheil Jedang, Ltd. ($11.6 million), and Sewon Corp. ($8.5 million). The EU investigation determined that the cartel fixed sales quotas worldwide in general, and for the EU market in particular, and exchanged quota-fixing information during the early 1990s. ADM commented that the "size of the fine wouldn't have a material impact on its earnings." With the addition of these fines, the total legal costs for the price-fixing scandal, including criminal fines, civil settlements, and lawyer bills, came to more than $250 million (Krebs 2000).

While applauding the EU actions to punish ADM and the cartel for price-fixing, Nicholas E. Hollis, president of the Agribusiness Council, commented that "fining predators" like ADM was not enough to discourage their illegal behavior. He noted that the Department of Justice was "practically allowing ADM to walk with a fine, and permitting the company to maintain its business with the government, in spite of felony convictions" (Krebs 2000). Hollis implied that the light sentence might be related to the fact that ADM "was and is" one of the largest campaign contributors to both the Republican and Democratic Parties.

Debarment, Campaign Contributions, and Corporate Welfare

In 2000 the publication of *Rats in the Grain: The Dirty Tricks and Trails of Archer Daniels Midland, the Supermarket to the World,* by James Lieber, brought the issue of the compliance agreement in lieu of debarment into public view. The USDA was criticized for not debarring ADM in light of its history of criminal conduct (Krebs 2001b). Critics charged that by failing to debar ADM, the USDA had effectively forced the American taxpayers to pay $80 million of the $100 million fine imposed for price-fixing. The USDA responded that the compliance agreement was facilitated by ADM's "substantial assistance" in cooperating with the Justice Department in the original plea agreement, was made as part of the overall effort to ensure a high degree of integrity in future business dealings, and was in the best interest of the United States. Critics challenged the USDA's position, noting that ADM did not deserve the compliance agreement given its history of criminal activity over the past four decades and its numerous fines in both the United States and other countries. In other words, the compliance agreement was emphatically not in the best interest of the United States or American taxpayers. Furthermore, critics noted that the indictment and subsequent suspension from government contracting of the three ADM executives amounted to little more than "window dressing" that made for "great publicity with no de facto penalty" (Krebs 2001b). Whitacre was fired and went to prison. The other two executives were given legal representation by prominent law firms by ADM and either retired or took a leave of absence from the company, effectively negating the impact of their suspension from government contracting.

The announcement in February 2001 that former secretary of agriculture Dan Glickman had accepted a position at the law firm of Akin, Gump, Strauss, Hauer and Feld added some fuel to the debarment controversy (Krebs 2001a). Glickman had been secretary of agriculture during the price-fixing episode. In taking the new position, Glickman expressed his admiration for the firm's senior partner, Strauss, a longtime personal friend of former ADM CEO Dwayne Andreas. Indeed, Akin, Gump had represented ADM in its negotiations with the USDA regarding the debarment issue. Hollis, of the Agribusiness Council, remarked that although it was common for companies entering guilty pleas in federal criminal cases to be automatically disbarred from conducting government business for a period of time, it appeared that "a shrouded deal was struck between USDA and Akin, Gump (representing ADM), which enabled the price fixing company to maintain its lucrative federal contracts and subsidies" (Krebs 2001a). Hollis noted that the fact that the USDA and the Justice Department "professed different stories" regarding the compliance negotiations cast further doubt on the integrity of the process. While Justice Department representatives stated that they were not aware of the terms of the compliance agreement when the plea agreement was finalized, a USDA spokesperson asserted that the Justice Department was in fact aware of the compliance agreement (Krebs 2001a).

Even before the guilty verdicts and legal agreements related to the price-fixing scandal became public knowledge, ADM was in the news regarding its substantial political contributions and public subsidies, known by critics as "corporate welfare." A Cato Institute study on corporate welfare reported that ADM "has been one of the most prominent recipients of corporate welfare in recent U.S. history. ADM and its chairman Dwayne Andreas have lavishly fertilized both political parties with millions of dollars in handouts and in return have reaped billion-dollar windfalls from taxpayers and consumers" (Bovard 1995). The Center for Responsive Politics provides evidence in support of this claim. It reports that from 1990 through 2006 ADM contributed more than $7.85 million to both Republicans ($4.45 million) and Democrats ($3.4 million) in the form of political action committee (PAC) and individual contributions to federal candidates, as well as PAC, individual, and soft-money donations to political parties (CRP 2007). The CATO Institute study maintained that through federal protection of the sugar industry, ethanol subsidies, subsidized grain exports, and other programs, ADM had cost both the American economy and American taxpayers billions of dollars in higher prices and higher taxes since 1980. For example, every $1 of profit ADM earned on high-fructose corn syrup cost consumers $10, while every $1 of profit on ethanol cost taxpayers $20. The report concluded that more than 40 percent of ADM's annual profits came from heavily subsidized or protected products (Bovard 1995). Over the decades ADM has been the recipient of state and federal corn and ethanol subsidies totaling billions of dollars (Lilley 2006).

In 2002, in response to the rising level of negative publicity linked to both the price-fixing scandals[1] and the corporate welfare accusations, ADM launched its "The ADM Way" code-of-conduct campaign to assure both suppliers and customers that its business was being conducted with the utmost integrity (Krebs 2002). More recently, the boom in government subsidies for ethanol production has again thrust ADM into the public light thanks to its dominant position in that industry. Industry critics state that "ADM has skillfully and quietly created a niche for itself with the US political economy," whereby it buys 12 percent of the nation's corn crop at "heavily subsidized" prices and converts it into high-fructose corn syrup and ethanol—two "products that owe their markets completely to government intervention" (Philpott 2005). Indeed, ADM financed the lobbying effort that created the protectionist sugar quota system in 1982 that still is in effect today. Similarly, thanks to ADM CEO Dwayne Andreas's efforts in the 1970s and 1980s to push the idea of transforming corn into fuel, ethanol subsidies have received, and continue to receive, strong support from key senators and congressmen (Barrionuevo 2006; Philpott 2005). Most recently, U.S. energy secretary Samuel W. Bodman visited ADM's headquarters in Decatur to highlight ADM's role in President Bush's "biofuels initiative." Secretary Bodman posed for pictures with then ADM chair, CEO, and president G. Allen Andreas and announced $160 million in Department of Energy subsidies for expanded ethanol production. "It's been some 30 years since we got a call from the White House asking for the agricultural industry, ADM in particular, to take

---

1. In 2000, the same year that Lieber's book *Rats in the Grain* was published, Kurt Eichenwald's *The Informant: A True Story* was released. This book is a quasi-fictional account of the ADM price-fixing scandal focusing on a character based on Mark Whitacre.

a serious look at the possibilities of building facilities to produce alternative sources of energy for our fuel supply in the United States," said Allen. "We are delighted to participate in any way that we can in the president's programs" (Lilley 2006).

Critics of the ethanol initiative note that ethanol is not energy efficient, that it takes more energy to make ethanol than it produces, and that the negative environmental consequences of ethanol production add to its shortcomings (Barrionuevo 2006; Lilley 2006). They note that ADM is "by far the biggest beneficiary" of the $2 billion yearly ethanol subsidies through the fifty-one-cent-per-gallon tax credit given to ethanol refiners and blenders. An industry analyst reported that ADM is estimated to earn $1.3 billion from ethanol in fiscal 2007, up from $556 million in 2006 (Barrionuevo 2006). In a report entitled *Agricultural Restructuring and Concentration in the United States: Who Wins, Who Loses?* the Food First Institute concluded that the "direction of U.S. agricultural policy is being set not by the needs of farming communities, nor by the needs of the majority of U.S. citizens, but by the political influence of a handful of powerful corporate interests" (Memarsadeghi and Patel 2003, 2).

Analysis and Discussion

The case of ADM highlights one specific aspect of the power of TNCs under globalization: their ability to control the market. Contrary to accounts that describe the current global market as one that "approaches perfect free market conditions" (Friedman 2000), the events described above show that TNCs organize and control global markets to their advantage. ADM's "corporate culture" supported collusion with business rivals that translated into the control of lysine prices and quantity worldwide that damaged consumers while generating large profits for the corporation. Simultaneously, the events of the case confirm an analytical point illustrated in the previous chapters: TNCs can bypass requirements imposed by national governments that do not benefit them and can consequently limit state powers. This is exemplified by ADM's adopting unfair price practices and bypassing long-established U.S. antitrust legislation.

It is true that ADM's illegal actions were discovered and that the company was eventually indicted and convicted, which suggests that nation-states can exercise some control over TNCs. Ultimately, however, this corporation came away from this lucrative illegal enterprise with minimum damage. The relative leniency with which the U.S. court system treated ADM far exceeds in relevance the fact that this company was punished; and it supports claims that the powers of TNCs are significant enough to affect the functioning of specific branches of the nation-state such as the judiciary. The $100 million fine—although the largest to date in U.S. history—was small compared to the corporate assets and profits of ADM. Furthermore, while Whitacre was ordered to pay back several million dollars to ADM and was sentenced to a total of more than ten years in prison, Andreas and Wilson received only two-year prison terms and were fined only $350,000. ADM did get caught, but it was able to shift much of the blame for the price-fixing onto Whitacre— and it made more money during the price-fixing episode than it had to pay in fines and remains a dominant global TNC today. In addition, the "penalties" imposed overseas point to the lenient treatment given to ADM. As illustrated above, they were considered insufficient to "discourage illegal behavior" or affect the company's profits in any significant way. The guilty verdict, more- over, did not change ADM's ability to enjoy state-sponsored business (i.e., contracts from the USDA) or to benefit from "corporate welfare."

The ADM price-fixing case supports the basic tenet of the "corporate domi- nation thesis" school that TNCs control both nation-states and the market. In particular, this case study supports McMichael's point that, under globaliza- tion, the nation-state is now often an agent of global corporate interests. It also supports Leslie Sklair's argument for the existence of a transnational capitalist class that includes members of the corporate elite but also mem- bers of national governments who actively work to ensure TNCs' dominance. Sklair maintains that some state officials have shifted their allegiance from national to transnational interests. One last observation on the control of the market has been made by scholars such as Thomas Friedman (2000) and Francis Fukuyama (1992), who hold that the global free market generates the best possible form of democracy. While large corporations exercised overt power over the state and other social actors in the past, neoliberal and pro- globalization theorists argue that the claim about the ability of large corpo- rations to move beyond the democratically established limits of legal and ethical behavior has been greatly exaggerated in the global era. The details of this story of globalization indicate not only that the free market fails to mitigate the power of corporations but that the market's supposed benefit to democracy is a sham. If the creation and maintenance of substantive de- mocracy is a key social goal, it is far from guaranteed by the functioning of the global free market. Writers like Friedman and Fukuyama fail to address the power of TNCs to control market outcomes. As classical proponents of laissez-faire economics like Adam Smith and John Stuart Mill, and critics of the self-regulating market theory like Karl Polanyi, argue, the market can function well only if the rules that govern all aspects of society are made independently of the market itself.

Our analysis of the cases discussed in the previous two chapters pointed out that TNCs' powers under globalization are opposed by the actions of the nation-state and that globalization is a contested terrain. The events illustrated in this chapter allow us to add that TNCs' powers come with internal contradictions. Three points support this conclusion.

The first refers to ADM's lack of trust in its corporate partners. Despite orchestrating the price-fixing accord with Kyowa Hakko and Ajinomoto, ADM officials remained suspicious of their partners and displayed little confidence in their ability to maintain a friendly relationship. Indeed, ADM officials feared sabotage of their lysine production process. This lack of trust affected the internal organization of ADM as well, as Whitacre distanced himself from, and eventually forcefully opposed, ADM's corporate culture. Whitacre's actions support the claim that individuals are able to make sense of their everyday existence in ways that escape the logic of larger social and economic organizations. Whitacre's rejection of and struggle against ADM's corporate culture reflects the fragmented dimension of TNCs' actions and their limits in establishing homogenous behavior within their internal system. Despite their undeniable power, TNCs cannot always exercise full control over the thinking and conduct of their employees. This vulnerability, as we see in the case of ADM, can be used against them.

The importance of trust in socioeconomic relations has always been acknowledged. Classical thinkers such as Durkheim (1984), Marx (1973, 1967, 1963), and Polanyi (1975) have shown that contractual relationships and economic exchange must be built upon a substructure of social connections that must be strengthened, expanded, and made more conscious in order to combat capitalism's instrumental features and centrifugal types of fragmentation. The market cannot regulate itself unless it operates within limits shaped by broader social ties, needs, memories, and trust.

Historically, the consolidation of an interventionist nation-state supported the establishment of regulatory frameworks that enhanced business confidence (Danley 1994; Lipietz 1992). The state functioned as the guarantor of good business climates and created mechanisms that strengthened trust among economic actors (Bonanno and Constance 1996). TNCs' bypassing of the state altered this arrangement, for it weakened the state's capacity to mediate between competing economic agents. In a situation in which TNCs have trouble achieving a reasonable level of trust, their power to coordinate economic activities becomes a liability (Harvey 2005). The "contradictory dimension of globalization" school of thought stresses this point. More specifically, and to varying degrees, members of this group stress that the actions of TNCs—while aimed at addressing some of the limits imposed by strong state intervention—generate new problems that TNCs themselves are not currently equipped to address. This makes TNCs' actions problematic and limits their power.

The second point is that although TNCs attempt to bypass government laws and regulations, they still need state assistance. This is exemplified by ADM's criticism of the FBI for its handling of the case at the same time that the company asked law enforcement agencies to monitor its overseas competitors. In modern society, the state has been able to assist corporations in the pursuit of their interests. In return, the state has required that those corporations acknowledge the legitimacy of the state's power to maintain social stability and to identify and censure illegitimate corporate conduct. Stable and peaceful social relations have always been a necessary precondition of economic growth (Carnoy 1984; Offe 1985; O'Connor 1986 and 1974). The events of the ADM price-fixing case point to the difficulties TNCs have with this role of the state and to the contradiction that they are at once dependent on and resistant to some level of state power and control. As TNCs attempt to free themselves from state control, they also weaken the ability of the nation-state to maintain social control. Indeed, TNCs defend their autonomy by attempting to undermine the investigative authority of the state, while at the same time they demand protection from the illegal or illegitimate activities of their global economic competitors.

Finally, as demonstrated in the previous two chapters as well, the state can successfully—albeit partially—oppose TNCs' actions. In the case of ADM, the U.S. government was eventually able to assert some control over the company's illegal activities, and to penalize the company accordingly. Not only were the FBI and the Justice Department able to defend U.S. laws, but Mark Whitacre was able to use his agency to challenge the illegal business practices of ADM and bring those practices to light. That Whitacre's opposition was only partially successful is shown by the relative leniency with which ADM was eventually sanctioned.

5

GLOBALIZATION AND RESISTANCE FROM BELOW:
INDUSTRIAL CHICKEN PRODUCTION IN SOUTHEAST TEXAS

In the previous chapters we established that opposition to corporate actions can come from the state. Although they are often controlled by TNCs, various segments of the state have been able to contest corporate designs. Governments are not the only source of resistance to TNCs, however. In this and the following two chapters we investigate resistance "from below," that is, resistance generated by local social groups in response to the presence and consequences of corporate operations.

This chapter tells the story of how corporate actions designed to foster capital accumulation created a crisis of legitimacy that prompted resistance at the local level. The TNC we look at in the following pages—Sanderson Farms—claimed that its actions benefited a region in economic decline and were justified by the alleged social and economic good of an unfettered free market. Sanderson Farms thus presented itself as a socially responsible company and its profit-making interests as compatible with the social, economic, and environmental sustainability of local communities. Its actions did not match its claims, however, but to the contrary had negative consequences for local communities and gave rise to vigorous local resistance; local opponents charged Sanderson Farms with environmental degradation and community disruption. The case of Sanderson Farms is a good example of the community resistance that can arise when the government lacks the capacity to mediate between contrasting interests.

In 1995, as part of its expansion strategy, Sanderson Farms, Inc., a Mississippi-based poultry corporation, took advantage of substantial incentives offered by Brazos County and the town of Bryan, Texas, and announced that it would build a new vertically integrated broiler chicken operation in the area. The lax environmental regulations in Texas, the fact that there were no "planning and zoning" regulations in rural areas, and the proximity of Bryan to large metropolitan consumer markets in Dallas/Fort Worth, Houston, Austin, and San Antonio made this area of Texas a very attractive site in which to expand operations. Soon after the poultry growout barns were built, local residents began to express concerns about the negative impact of the chicken barns on their quality of life, specifically about odor, flies, water contamination from manure, property devaluation, and community divisions over these issues. They formed a variety of organizations to advance these concerns and lobbied the appropriate government officials. Some of their initiatives were successful; others were not. We proceed with an overview of the industrialization and globalization of the broiler industry so as to provide context for the events of this case.

The Industrialization and Globalization of the Broiler Industry

The broiler industry was the first livestock commodity sector to industrialize. The broiler model is characterized by vertical integration of the various factors of production under the control of agribusiness corporations and the corresponding growth in these firms' market power through mergers and acquisitions, which have led to high levels of economic concentration. The organizational structure of the broiler industry in the United States has often been described as a model for agricultural methods of the future (Breimyer 1965; Heffernan 1984; Marion and Arthur 1973; Marion 1986; Morrison 1998; Reimund, Martin, and Moore 1981; Rogers 1963; Stull, Broadway, and Griffith 1995; Thu and Durrenberger 1998; Tobin and Arthur 1964; Vogeler 1981).

Prior to World War II, broiler production was a residual activity associated with egg production. On most farms, both eggs and broilers were part of a household-based subsistence strategy controlled by women (Fink 1986; Sachs 1983). Broilers were the male offspring (called cockerels) of laying hens that could be consumed as food by the family and/or exchanged or sold for nonfarm-produced goods and services. A major advantage of broilers was that little capital was required to produce them. Almost any building could be converted to a "chicken house" by adding a roosting area and nesting boxes. During the warm months chickens roamed freely around the farmstead during the day, where they scavenged most of the food they required. Often the poultry operation provided weekly or biweekly income through egg sales, which helped pay for the farm family's basic day-to-day needs. Because poultry required few purchased inputs and had a short production time, it was a relatively inexpensive addition to a farm enterprise (Heffernan 1984; Mann and Dickenson 1978).

History gives credit to Cecile Steele of Ocean View, Delaware, for raising and selling the first commercial flock of broilers. Though Steele was an egg producer, in 1923 there was a mistake in her order and five hundred chicks were delivered instead of the usual fifty. When her brood of chicks reached two pounds, she sold them to a local buyer for sixty-two cents a pound. News of this profitable business spread, and by 1925 some fifty thousand broilers were being raised in the area (Gordy 1974).

Broiler processing also started in the Delaware, Maryland, and Virginia area. In 1937 Hendrich Poultry (a subsidiary of Swift and Co.) converted an old tomato cannery into the first broiler-processing plant. As the local fishing economy declined, many other canneries were converted and local growers built more chicken houses. By the mid-1940s the plants were processing almost three hundred thousand birds per day. In 1930 C. S. Platt of the New Jersey Experiment Station observed that the broiler industry lent itself "rather easily to factory methods of production" (Gordy 1974, 418, 384).

In these early days, the broiler business was an uncoordinated system of independent "mom-and-pop" feed mills, slaughter plants, and family farms. Most rural communities had several hatcheries and feed stores where chicks and feed could be bought. Farmers usually had access to many firms from which to purchase their inputs and to which to sell their broilers and/or eggs. The industry not only provided an income source for farm families, it also provided jobs for thousands of people in numerous rural communities across the country (Heffernan 1984; Marion and Arthur 1973; Tobin and Arthur 1964).

Until after World War II, the region of Delaware, Maryland, and Virginia was the leading broiler production area in the United States. After the war, both the location and the structure of the broiler industry shifted (Martin and Zering 1997). The industry relocated, primarily to the South, to avoid entrenched independent broiler producers in the Delaware, Maryland, and Virginia peninsula area and union representation in the processing plants. By moving to the South the industry obtained low-cost labor in the form of African American women. The industry also took advantage of desperate southern farm families who were suffering from the cotton blight (Breimyer 1965; Reimund, Martin, and Moore 1981; Martin and Zering 1997).

Through the late 1940s the South experienced chronically depressed farming conditions due to boll weevil outbreaks and cotton crop failures. Many farmers saw contract production as similar to sharecropping and readily accepted broiler production as an amendment to their traditional operations (Martin and Zering 1997; Skully 1998). Underemployed farm labor, a favorable climate, lower wages and less unionization, and the stabilization of feed prices contributed to the increasing advantage of the South (Breimyer 1965; Easterling, Braschler, and Kuehn 1985; Reimund, Martin, and Moore 1981). These factors made the South an attractive region for the development of a new broiler production system based on an industrial model. Although broilers continued to be raised throughout the country, by the 1950s almost half of all broilers produced in the United States were raised in the South. By the early 1970s the South accounted for about 90 percent of total broiler output (Lasley 1983; Reimund, Martin, and Moore 1981). The South still accounts for about 75 percent of broiler production (USDA/NASS 2002).

After World War II, publicly funded research at land grant universities focused on developing vaccines and using antibiotics that would allow large numbers of birds to be raised in crowded quarters in confinement. New methods included confinement housing, genetic manipulation that would produce faster-growing, meatier birds, feed rations for faster weight gain, and mechanized feeding and watering, which reduced labor. All of these technologies reduced the risks of raising and processing broilers. Much of the uncertainty due to nature was eliminated as raising broilers moved from the barnyard to the factory. At the same time, new technologies in chicken processing, such as the automated rubber-fingered feather plucker, made processing less labor intensive. These developments combined to make it possible to raise larger numbers of uniform broilers in shorter amounts of time (Heffernan 1984 and 1972; Reimund, Martin, and Moore 1981).

Because of these technological advancements and the resulting reduction of risk, organizational changes in the broiler industry accompanied the geographic shift to the South. The percentage of farms raising more than a hundred thousand birds rose rapidly from zero in 1954 to about 30 percent in 1974 (Reimund, Martin, and Moore 1981). By 1960, 98.4 percent of broilers were raised either on contract or in company-owned facilities (Marion 1986). By the mid-1990s nearly 100 percent of production came from farms raising more than a hundred thousand birds per year (Welsh 1996), with about 90 percent of production organized on formal contracts with integrators (Welsh 1997). Similarly, the development of mechanized killing and processing lines followed models established by industrial factories.

The most important factor in broiler industrialization was the organizational innovation of vertical integration. As the risk was reduced in the broiler business, agribusiness firms invested and began to coordinate all aspects of the broiler enterprise through vertical integration. During the 1950s and 1960s feed mills bought processing plants and contracted with area farmers to raise broilers for a certain amount per pound. Companies like Ralston Purina, Cargill, Tyson, and Wayne Feeds (a division of Continental Grain) integrated the feeding, raising, slaughter, processing, distribution, and sale of broilers under one system of management (Heffernan 1984). Vertical integration rationalized the broiler industry by bringing all aspects of the production chain under the control of the integrating firm (Reimund, Martin, and Moore 1981). By the 1980s the integrating firms had developed the process even further by gaining access to retail markets through joint ventures with fast food retail chains (Brooks 1980).

Central to this system was the adoption of the production contract as the formal link between the broiler grower and the processing firm. Broilers were first raised by independent growers who paid cash for the chicks and feed and then sold the mature birds on the open market. As the flocks became larger, the local feed dealer rapidly became the major source of credit for inputs and had "first call" on the profits (Gordy 1974). By the 1950s these informal contractual agreements became formalized, as the growers became increasingly dependent on the feed dealers for inputs. This process of vertical integration moved broiler production from a farm sideline to a highly developed agribusiness (Lasley 1983).

Under a broiler production contract, the integrating firm (contractor) provides day-old chicks, feed rations, veterinary services, and management oversight to the farmer (contractee). The contractee is responsible for supplying the land, growout buildings, utilities, labor, and manure management. Growers usually mortgage their land to build the specialized growout buildings, which cost about $100,000 apiece; the mortgage is typically for a period of ten to twenty years. Integrating firms prefer to have more than one building per farm to reduce the transportation costs of delivering the feed and picking up the broilers for processing. The broiler growout building is so highly specialized that it can seldom be used profitably for anything but broiler production (Heffernan 1984). Without production contracts "and the opportunities they afforded for coordinating the several stages of the sub-sector, it is doubtful the new entrants, primarily feed manufacturers and dealers, would have considered broiler production very attractive" (Reimund, Martin, and Moore 1981, 8).

As suppliers of the chicks and feed, as well as processors and distributors, were combined into single integrated firms, the ownership of the birds during the production process shifted from the farmer to the integrating firm (contractor). In this system the farmer became a contractee and relinquished all major decision-making responsibilities. The main job of the contractee is to make sure that the automated feeding, watering, and climate devices work properly. Other jobs include removing dead birds and watching out for outbreaks of disease. Contractees are offered incentives for high feed-conversion ratios and low numbers of dead birds. Although contractees provide capital for the buildings, the buildings have to be built to company specifications. The length of the contract varies but historically has been based on a "batch-by-batch" system. In other words, there is no formal long-term contract between the contractor and the contractee. Because the integrating firm owns the birds and provides the feed, it decides when the birds will be delivered and picked up, and what they are fed (Heffernan 1972 and 1984).

The contract poultry grower becomes a semiautonomous employee who still holds title to his land but has otherwise lost control over decision making and the labor process (Mooney 1983). Heffernan (1984) adds that because of the high cost and narrow purpose of the poultry barns, poultry producers are less secure than other contract producers, such as vegetable growers. Furthermore, as the broiler industry was consolidated into fewer firms, growers became locked into one integrator, with no option to raise birds for another firm if they lost their contract. Other researchers have discussed the market power that integrators have over contract producers (see Brandow 1969; Wellford 1972). In his study of contract growers, Roy (1972) concluded that while there are advantages and disadvantages to the arrangements, contract farmers are in a position similar to that of sharecroppers. Vogeler (1991) states that the contract grower has a transitional status between a family farmer and an agricultural worker. Davis (1980) refers to contract growers as a "propertied laborers." Breimyer (1965) calls them "serfs on the land."

Mirroring the trend toward vertical integration, economic concentration increased steadily. In 1960 the nineteen largest broiler-processing firms accounted for about 30 percent of production; in 1975 the top eight firms controlled 30 percent; and in 1988 the four largest firms accounted for about half of total broiler production (Heffernan 2000; Reimund, Martin, and Moore 1981). During the 1980s and 1990s the rate of mergers and acquisitions increased rapidly in the food industries, with the result that many broiler firms became consolidated under larger agrifood corporations. For example, Tyson Foods, the largest broiler producer and processor in the world, has dominant holdings in beef and pork through its subsidiary IBP. Several other researchers have documented the oligopolistic market structure of the broiler industry (Breimyer 1965; Heffernan 1984; Marion and Arthur 1973; Rogers 1963; Tobin and Arthur 1964; Wellford 1972).

As economic concentration increased at the national level, U.S.-based poultry firms were expanding operations globally (Heffernan 1990) on the basis of the concept of global sourcing (Constance and Heffernan 1991; Heffernan and Constance 1994; McMichael 2000). In 1987, for example, Tyson Foods formed a joint venture called CITRA with C. Itoh of Japan and Trasgo of Mexico to raise, process, and market poultry products. As part of this arrangement, Tyson employed a "dual labor process," removing the breast meat in Arkansas for the U.S. fast food industry, then shipping the leg quarters to Mexico to be deboned by hand at much lower labor costs. The marinated meat was shipped to Japan as "Yakatori Sticks," a fast food item. C. Itoh sourced technology and product in the United States and the low-cost labor in Mexico to service its Asian markets. Similarly, in 1989 Cargill, Inc., entered into a joint venture with Nippon Meat Packers to established Sun Valley Thailand. This operation linked U.S.-based technology and organizational structure to a "new agricultural country" with low-cost feed and labor and profitable consumer markets in Japan and other countries. Cargill provided the "turnkey" vertically integrated broiler operation, Thailand provided the low-cost broiler production platform, and Nippon Meat Packers provided access to markets (Constance and Heffernan 1991).

Many of the major broiler operations are subsidiaries of agribusiness TNCs sourcing the most advantageous factors of production at the global level (Constance and Heffernan 1991; Heffernan 2000; Heffernan and Constance 1994; see also Friedmann and McMichael 1989). These agribusiness TNCs integrated their feed operations with poultry businesses. In the early 1990s, for example, U.S.-based firms such as Tyson had operations in Mexico and Canada; Conagra was in Puerto Rico, Portugal, Spain, and the Soviet Union; and Cargill was in Argentina, England, Brazil, and Thailand. Japan-based firms such as Mitsui and Co., C. Itoh, Mitsubishi, Ajinomoto, and Nippon Meat Packers had operations in Malaysia, Mexico, Brazil, and Thailand. Finally, the Italy-based TNC Ferruzzi (see Chapter 3) had feed operations in support of poultry and hog businesses in France, the Netherlands, Taiwan, Portugal, Puerto Rico, Thailand, Yugoslavia, the Soviet Union, Hungary, Poland, and China. In the late 1980s Ferruzzi bought the major U.S. feed business Central

Soya and thereby gained direct access to the United States in terms of both production and marketing. By the early 1990s the dominant agribusiness TNCs had created a global poultry agrifood complex that linked the most favorable areas of production to profitable consumer markets (Constance and Heffernan 1991). Two examples of this system are Tyson Foods and Pilgrim's Pride.

Tyson Foods is headquartered in Springdale, Arkansas, and in 2003 was the largest processor and marketer of chicken and red meat in the world, with $24.5 billion in sales. It was the second-largest food company in the Fortune 500 (Tyson Foods, Inc. 2004–5). Tyson Foods began in the 1930s, as John Tyson sold truckloads of chickens raised in Arkansas to markets in St. Louis, Kansas City, and Chicago. John Tyson incorporated in 1947 as Tyson Feed and Hatchery. After buying its first processing plant in 1958, the name was changed to Tyson Foods, Inc., in 1963. In the following years the company grew rapidly through a series of acquisitions, including the broiler division of Wilson Foods in 1978, Valmac Industries in 1984, Lane Processing in 1986, Holly Farms in 1989, and Hudson Foods (then the sixth-largest in the United States) in 1998. In 2001 it bought IBP, the world's largest beef and pork processor. By 2003 Tyson had 120,000 employees in three hundred facilities and offices in twenty-seven states and twenty-two countries. It processed 40 million broilers a week, 198,000 cattle a week, and 344,000 hogs a week in 120 processing plants. Tyson had 7,600 contract poultry growers and owned 110,000 sows (ibid.). Tyson's corporate philosophy is "segment, concentrate, and dominate." A statement on its Web site reads, "We anticipate consumer demand, segment a market, concentrate production and marketing, and, subsequently, dominate that segment."

Tyson International was created in 1987 and by 2003 had joint-venture beef operations in China, Ireland, and Russia and chicken joint-venture operations in Argentina, Brazil, China, Denmark, Indonesia, Japan, Korea, Malaysia, Panama, the Philippines, Spain, the United Kingdom, and Venezuela. In 2003 Tyson was the number one supplier of cowhide to Japan for the auto industry and to Italy for the shoe industry. In 1994 the company expanded its operations in Mexico when it acquired majority control of Trasgo de Mexico and became Tyson de Mexico. By 2003 Tyson had bought out 95 percent of the remaining interest in Trasgo de Mexico and had also bought a nearby fully integrated broiler operation. In 2003 Tyson de Mexico was the largest producer of value-added chicken for both retail and food service in Mexico and was expanding into other areas of Latin America. In 2001 Tyson International expanded its operations with Alimentos Procesados Melo, S.A., in Panama City, Panama, to provide a wide range of chicken products for the food service and retail markets in Panama and neighboring South and Central America. In 2001 Tyson International also entered into a joint venture with Chinese partner Zhucheng Da Long Enterprises to own and operate a chicken-processing plant in Shangdong Province, China. The plant produces chicken leg meat products to be marketed in Japan, other countries in the Pacific Rim, and the Middle East (Tyson Foods, Inc. 2004–5, 2005a, and 2005b). According to Greg Huett, president of Tyson International, "These efforts move us quickly forward along our strategy of producing quality products for our worldwide customers from cost effective global locations" (Tyson Foods, Inc. 2005b).

Pilgrim's Pride, Inc., is headquartered in Pittsburg, Texas, and in 2004 was the second-largest poultry producer in the United States, with $5 billion in sales (Pilgrim's Pride, Inc. 2005a). Aubrey Pilgrim started Pilgrim's Pride as a feed store in 1946 and was soon joined in partnership by his brother, Bo Pilgrim. The brothers started their broiler business by giving away a hundred baby chicks with each feed bag purchased. Then they sold baby chicks to farmers who brought the chickens back to them to sell. As demand for the chickens grew in the 1950s, individual growers in the region started building chicken houses to raise crops of three thousand broilers for the Pilgrim brothers to sell. As demand continued to grow, the brothers bought their first hatchery and began paying growers to raise chicks for them on contract. In 1958 they became investors in a new processing plant and in 1966 bought controlling interest in the plant. Over the next several years plants were added across east Texas. With the acquisition of ConAgra's chicken division in 2003 (then the second-largest in the United States), the company doubled its size and became the undisputed second-largest poultry processor in the country. Pilgrim's Pride is also the second-largest broiler company in Mexico and the largest in Puerto Rico (Pilgrim's Pride, Inc. 2005a and 2005b).

In 2004 Pilgrim's Pride employed forty thousand people in the United States, Mexico, and Puerto Rico. It owns and operates twenty-six chicken-processing plants (twenty-two in the United States, three in Mexico, and one in Puerto Rico), eight chicken prepared-food plants, two turkey-processing plants, one turkey further-processing plant, and feed mills, hatcheries, and approximately four thousand growout facilities to supply these plants. It has major facilities in Alabama, Arkansas, Georgia, Kentucky, Louisiana, North Carolina, Pennsylvania, Tennessee, Texas, Virginia, West Virginia, Mexico, and Puerto Rico and other facilities in Arizona, California, Iowa, Mississippi, Utah, and Wisconsin. The company processes about 30 million birds a week for a total of more than 6 billion pounds a year. Pilgrim's Pride operates seventeen distribution centers in the United States and thirteen in Mexico. It entered the Mexican market in 1995 with the purchase of five Mexican broiler companies in the state of Queretaro (Pilgrim's Pride, Inc. 2005c). The plants in Mexico are strategically located to serve 75 percent of all Mexican consumers. The company exports commodity chicken and turkey products to more than seventy countries, including Japan, China, and Russia, and supplies significant product to U.S. chain restaurants overseas (Pilgrim's Pride, Inc. 2005a).

Sanderson Farms Comes to Texas: Global Sourcing and Economic Incentives

Sanderson Farms began in 1947 as a farm supply business in Laurel, Mississippi. In the 1950s the company added breeder hen production, a small hatchery, and broiler growout in both contract and company-owned facilities. The business was incorporated in 1955 as Sanderson Brothers Farms, Inc. In 1961 full integration was reached when the merger with Miss Goldy, Inc., included a broiler-processing plant (Sanderson Farms 1999b). Through continued mergers, acquisitions, and expansions in Mississippi and Louisiana, Sanderson Farms was the thirteenth-largest broiler company in the United States by 1995, with $393 million in sales (*Feedstuffs* 1995; WATT PoultryUSA 2001).

In early 1995 Sanderson Farms announced the end of the first phase of its expansion program. Phase one had increased its production 114 percent from 1991. The second phase of expansion began in 1995 (Smith 1995). By 2000 Sanderson Farms was slaughtering an average of 5 million broilers per week and had grown to the seventh-largest poultry firm in the United States. It employed 8,147 people in its five integrated poultry complexes in Mississippi, Louisiana, and Texas. At that time the company's broilers were raised on contract with 495 farmers in 2,075 houses with a capacity of 5.2 million placements per week. Sanderson Farms marketed more than five hundred different products and shipped to every state in the United States and many foreign countries. In fiscal year 1999–2000 exports accounted for about 7 percent of the total sales of $603 million (Sanderson Farms 1999a; WATT PoultryUSA 2001). By 2005 Sanderson Farms was the fifth-largest poultry company in the United States, with more than $1 billion in sales (Sanderson Farms 2005).

In early 1995 Sanderson Farms announced that it was evaluating sites in Texas for its next phase of growth. CEO Joe Sanderson Jr. said that the new complex would require a total investment of $68 million for the new feed mill, hatchery, and poultry-processing plant, plus another $56 million from the contract growers for pullet and broiler housing and growout equipment. Sanderson stated, "Texas offers a unique opportunity for the next phase of growth for Sanderson Farms" (Brown 1995b, 9).

City officials of Bryan, Texas, met to consider a request from the Bryan–College Station Economic Development Corporation (EDC) to offer incentives to attract a new Sanderson Farms poultry-processing plant to the area (Howell 1995b). After Bryan–College Station officials visited a Sanderson Farms processing plant in Mississippi, they commented that they were impressed with the company and its operations. John Anderson, president of the EDC, stated, "It would distress me if it went somewhere else. It's something that would be good for the community" (Howell 1995a). In an effort to attract the Sanderson plant to the area, the Bryan City Council decided not to annex the area of the proposed plant for fifteen years, a decision that would allow the plant to remain in Brazos County (Whitley 1995). Soon thereafter, the Brazos County commissioners granted a ten-year tax abatement for Sanderson Farms. In defending the announcement, Commissioner Gary Norton stated, "In today's way of doing business, if you don't play the corporate game you lose out" (Lambert 1995). County judge Al Jones said that the court would continue to offer whatever incentives it could in order to compete with other areas. "As long as there are entities competing for new business, Brazos County must be a participant in offering abatements and incentives," said Jones (ibid.).

In May 1995 Sanderson Farms announced that it would build its new processing plant in Brazos County and its new feed mill in adjacent Robertson County (Brown 1995a). The new complex would process 1.2 million broilers per week and add 29 percent to production capacity. CEO Sanderson cited market accessibility to the 14 million people living within two hundred miles of Bryan–College Station as the most important factor in the decision to locate in Brazos County. Other criteria were local economic conditions and probusiness attitude, the residents' reception to the company, and available resources, such as utilities, potable water, and labor. According to Sanderson, the new complex would be designed to provide "maximum marketing flexibility" through the production and processing of branded products, as well as value-added products, for both retail and food service market segments (Logan 1995). At full staff, the operation would employ fourteen hundred workers, making it the largest nongovernmental employer in the county (Taylor 1997).

Sanderson Farms was promised more than $600,000 by local government, in addition to city and county tax abatements. It was also given 11.62 acres in the Bryan Business Park for its hatchery site. While some consumer and environmental activists opposed the location of the plant and the incentives Sanderson was given to locate in Brazos County, supporters predicted that the city's investment of time and money would pay off. Opponents argued that poultry litter contains arsenic that would contaminate local soil and water. They also raised the issue of the inevitable stench and the influx of workers to fill low-wage poultry-processing jobs, which would strain the community's social service resources (Taylor 1997).

The Sanderson Farms hatchery opened in late 1996, followed by the feed mill and the processing plant in early 1997. After opening a second process-ing line at the same location in mid-1997, the plant reached its full first-shift capacity of 650,000 birds per week. With double shifts operating on both lines, the plant has the capacity to process 1.2 million birds per week. At full operation, the complex supports about eighty-five independent con-tract producers operating forty-eight breeder houses, twenty-four pullet houses, and 320 broiler houses. The Texas complex provides Sanderson Farms access to the large and growing Texas market as well as markets in the South-west and on the West Coast (Sanderson Farms 1999b). Bob Billingsley, the company's director of development, said that the entire Brazos Valley com-munity would benefit. "We feel it is our role as good corporate citizens to be a vital part of the community," he said. Texas's commissioner of agriculture at the time, Rick Perry (now governor of Texas), commented, "One of the very wise things Sanderson Farms did was work closely with the community leaders before settling on Bryan–College Station. It will pay huge dividends for them" (Krinsky 1998). In its 1999 annual report Sanderson Farms stated that "one tradition that has been adhered to through the years, regardless of location, is a mutually beneficial relationship between Sanderson and the communities in which we work" (Sanderson Farms 1999a, 11).

The Leon Country Environmental Group: Legitimacy Crises and Resistance from Below

While the Sanderson processing plant is located in the Brazos County Indus-trial Park, the growout barns are spread throughout nearby Leon, Madison,

Grimes, and Robertson counties. Broiler growout barns are typically forty feet wide by five hundred feet long and house about thirty thousand broilers. Each barn costs about $125,000, with four to twenty-six barns per site. The average operation of eight barns requires a $1 million investment. The contractor arranges for the contractee to secure building loans. The contractee mortgages its land to borrow money to construct the growout barns. The contractor is responsible for delivering the day-old baby chicks to the contractee, providing the feed and veterinary services, and picking up the birds for processing forty days later. The contractee is responsible for housing costs, water, electricity, and labor (including picking up and incinerating the "deads," monitoring the watering and feed devices, and litter disposal). The contractee is paid by the amount of weight the birds gain, a factor that is greatly affected by the number of birds still alive at the end of the growing cycle.

Some of the first barns to go up were near Normangee and Flynn in Leon County. In the spring of 1998, according to Tom Abernathy, one of the first residents to protest the poultry operation, "twelve to fifteen couples joined together to discuss the problems of the influx of chicken barns in the area." Abernathy lives near Flynn and had already seen six broiler houses erected "in [his] backyard." The main concern of the group was to determine how many chicken houses were going up in the area, for they were already having problems with odor, flies, and respiratory ailments. At their first meeting they decided to call themselves the Normangee Group. Officers were elected, and each family contributed $100 to cover mailings, newsletters, and similar expenses (Abernathy 2000).

In June 1998 the Normangee Group retained a lawyer in an effort to stop the construction of some of the proposed chicken barns. The attorney sent a formal letter to the contractee stating that his clients were concerned about the possible negative effects of the broiler barns on their lives and demanding that the contractee "cease and desist all plans" to build the broiler barns. The letter cited the foul odor that would drift across the neighbors' property on a daily basis, a dramatic increase in the fly population due to the increase in chicken litter, dust from the feed and litter being blown on the neighbors' residences, and the noise pollution of cackling chickens, alarm bells, and whistles installed in the poultry houses. The consequences of these effects, the letter concluded, "will be that my clients will have to suffer substantial physical discomfort, annoyance and inconvenience in using their own homes, and the market value of their home and property will be diminished significantly" (Bennett 1998b). Furthermore, the lawyer alleged, the neighbors' health would be put at risk as a result of long-term exposure to the barns. In response, a Sanderson Farms lawyer contacted the Normangee Group lawyer and informed him that the contractees were moving forward with construction and that "Sanderson Farms would provide legal defense for this particular grower and anyone else who is sued for constructing houses" (Bennett 1998a).

In July a representative of the Normangee Group wrote a letter to state senator Steve Ogden complaining about the odors of the chicken houses in Leon County and requesting an investigation. Ogden's office turned the issue over to the Texas Natural Resource Conservation Commission (TNRCC). A TNRCC representative was sent to Leon County to investigate the alleged odors and concluded that the growers were in compliance with the environmental regulations according to Texas standards. The representative added, however, "herein lies the challenge. The current odor regulations in Texas are subjective—no benchmark exists by which to measure the severity of or harm created by a particular odor . . . any new regulation must balance the legitimate and competing interest of two groups: private property owners and private citizens" (Ogden 1998).

The Normangee Group held regular meetings, started a newsletter, and grew in number. The group decided that in order to include everyone in the Leon County area they would change the name to the Leon County Environmental Group (LCEG). New officers were elected, and members wrote letters to regional and national news programs and placed ads in local newspapers (LCEG 1998a). In the meantime their attorney reported back to the group regarding the proposed lawsuit. Because of the unknown costs associated with a protracted lawsuit in which Sanderson Farms would provide legal support for its contractees, as well as the uncertainty of the outcome, the LCEG reluctantly decided to not pursue the lawsuit (LCEG 1998b). The LCEG renewed its letter-writing campaign to state political representatives, but all of the letters were forwarded to the TNRCC. The TNRCC responded to each letter and suggested that the group contact the Texas Department of Health about fly infestation and local authorities regarding noise-related issues (Saitas 1998).

In late September a "poultry summit" was held in Leon County to address the concerns of the LCEG. It was attended by state senator Steve Ogden, county commissioners, county judges, local growers, representatives of the state representative's office, Sanderson Farms, the Texas State Soil and Water Conservation Board, the U.S. Natural Resource Conservation Service, the Texas Poultry Federation, and the TNRCC, along with local and regional news media. Issues discussed were the odor, flies, noise, declining property values, stockpiling of manure, and the response time for complaints about these issues. Nothing was resolved, however, and Senator Ogden closed the summit by suggesting potential solutions, such as limiting the number of houses within an area and having one agency monitor all the problems (*Normangee [TX] Star* 1998; Johnson 1998).

Texas for Responsible Poultry Production: Engaging the State

By early January 1999 LCEG meetings had grown to include people from Madison and Grimes counties as well, who were increasingly concerned about the risks associated with poultry production in their communities. The LCEG decided that in order to be inclusive and represent all Texans, it would change its name to Texans for Responsible Poultry Production (TRPP) (Abernathy 2000). Each county would be represented as a chapter of TRPP. Andre Dean, a member of the Madison County chapter, said he had heard rumors that a chicken farm was coming to his neighborhood. According to Dean:

> We had heard of a bad situation with chicken farms in Leon County and some of us went to their meeting in December 1998. That was the spark to get going or we would suffer their fate of twelve to twenty-four chicken houses within one mile of this little community of twelve homes near Jewett that was under a nasty cloud of stench and flies, and valid concerns for the future of massive buildup of chicken manure with the real health concerns for our future. Concerns were stench, fly infestations, health concerns, lack of any enforceable controls or constraints by any government agency, inability of private citizens to sue for redress by state law, protecting all agricultural projects from lawsuits after their first year of operation, manure runoff, and loss of enjoyment of our own property as a violation of our Fifth and Fourteenth Amendment rights to property. (Dean 2000)

Along with the name change, TRPP set new goals directed at changing the legislation governing poultry operations—for example, removing the AFO/CAFO distinctions for poultry producers. In Texas, broiler operations were considered animal-feeding operations (AFOS) because of their dry manure system and were not subject to the stricter regulations associated with confined animal-feeding operations (CAFOS), which have liquid manure systems and are subject to stronger waste management regulations (LCEG 1999).

After several trips to the state legislature to express their concerns, TRPP members decided to draft their own legislation—the Enjoyment of Private Property Bill. They sent a draft of the bill to Senator Ogden and asked him to recommend improvements. The primary elements of the bill were (1) that the nuisance protection of poultry growers be remanded, (2) that nuisance be defined by law, (3) that an "odor tolerance zone" be established, (4) that mandatory setbacks from neighboring properties be created, and (5) that an administrative process be required for licensing of the broiler barns. They also asked Senator Ogden to sponsor the bill (TRPP 1999a).

In April 1999 Senator Ogden and other state legislators added a rider to the appropriations bill calling for $100,000 in funding to conduct a statewide assessment of poultry operations. The rider provided funding for research to be done by the TNRCC and Texas A&M University on minimizing odor emissions and arsenic contamination from poultry facilities and on determining the best method of corrective action when nuisance odors are confirmed. TRPP expressed the hope that this rider might help the growers, Sanderson Farms, and the neighbors come to a "workable solution to what is considered a serious threat to the enjoyment of life and property—some of our most fundamental rights under the constitution" (TRPP 1999b, 1). In May the Enjoyment of Private Property Bill, along with more than a thousand citizens' signatures, was hand-delivered to two state senators and five representatives. Although it was lauded by the legislators as an example of democracy in action, the bill was not introduced in that legislative session because there was insufficient time to mobilize the necessary support. Senator Ogden assured TRPP members that the utmost attention would be given to the matter of poultry operations and that the rider study would look at all sides of the issue (TRPP 1999b).

Citizens Against Poultry Pollution: Expanding the Social Movement Base

At their first meeting of 2000, TRPP asked political candidates to attend a meeting and discuss their positions on the growth of the poultry industry in the region. Most candidates said they were not aware of the extent of the growth of the industry in the "out counties" and expressed their "concern about the proximity of the chicken houses to populated areas and about property devaluation" (TRPP 2000, 1). At this meeting TRPP elected an executive board that included one representative each from Leon, Madison, Robertson, and Grimes counties and one from the north Texas chapter and the east Texas chapter. The chairpersons of each group were to meet each month and report to their respective groups. The entire group met every three months. TRPP also decided to change its name once again, this time to Citizens Against Poultry Pollution (CAPP), so as to remedy potential confusion about the nature of the group (some people felt that TRPP suggested that the group was in favor of poultry production) (TRPP 2000). The CAPP members renewed their commitment to using the legislative process to change state laws related to the regulation of the poultry industry and the protection of their private property rights (CAPP 2000a).

In the summer of 2000 the results of the TNRCC and Texas A&M University research funded by the rider were announced, much to CAPP's disappointment. In CAPP's view the study report was only an extensive review of the literature and lacked a substantive research dimension (CAPP 2000b). CAPP argued that while the TNRCC had done some air testing at one site in Madison County, the testing was useless because there were no chickens at the facility when the testing was conducted (CAPP 2000c).

In early 2001, as a result of the increased controversy over the possible negative water quality impacts of the growth of large-scale poultry operations, the Texas legislature passed legislation that requires that each person who owns or operates a poultry facility design, submit, and implement a water quality management plan (WQMP) to protect the natural resources of the state of Texas (Telicon 2001). CAPP welcomed this legislation but felt that it did not go far enough, as it did not address other important issues such as air quality and property values (Hagerbaumer 2001). The group continued to meet and draw public attention to these issues until 2005, when lack of success and leadership burnout brought an end to CAPP's activities (Hagerbaumer 2007).

Analysis and Discussion

This chapter documents an episode of local resistance to the hypermobility of capital and global sourcing. The economic development strategies of Sanderson Farms and local political and economic elites met with local resistance in the form of social movement groups that challenged a private enterprise as destructive to their quality of life. As illustrated in Chapter 1, supporters of the globalization project promise renewed economic development through the deregulation of restrictive government policies and the implementation of re-regulation projects based on the free market. Pro-globalization policies governing socioeconomic development allegedly enhance the free mobility of capital and diminish the means through which communities and governments can control undesirable consequences of capitalism.

For the past two decades, the improvement of the socioeconomic conditions of Texans has been promoted through free market–oriented policies, deregulation, and the fostering of a pro–free market cultural climate (Bonanno and Constance 2000; Constance and Bonanno 1999a). It is no coincidence that in the past three local elections, key state posts were won by Republican candidates who supported the free market and opposed its regulation—a position that they claimed would bring socioeconomic improvement for all. The Texas governor's office has advertised the fact that Texas "is wide open for business" and that if corporations don't like high taxes, they "should come to Texas" (State of Texas, Office of the Governor 2004). Joe Sanderson Jr., the CEO of Sanderson Farms, acknowledged that Texas offered "a unique opportunity," hence the company's decision to launch its second phase of expansion there. In this respect Sanderson Farms followed a common practice of global TNCs—global sourcing.

The events of the case reveal the problematic nature of this project. Sanderson Farms benefited from the probusiness climate of the region, the strategic location of its production facilities, and the human and natural resources available. Brazos County is a rural area that has experienced a steady decline in traditional agricultural operations (mostly cattle ranching), is located near a very large metropolitan area (Houston) that is a gateway to even larger markets, and has no regulation concerning the location of intensive poultry production facilities. Within the framework of capital hypermobility and global sourcing, Brazos and counties like it had clear advantages over competing areas. Furthermore, local political and economic elites supported the Sanderson Farms initiative. They viewed the poultry industry as an opportunity to bring economic viability to a depressed region, and they offered economic incentives accordingly. "If you don't play the corporate game" of offering incentives, they noted, "you lose out." Corporate claims of soliciting community involvement notwithstanding, the invitation to participate in Sanderson Farms' expansion in Texas was extended discreetly, planning was confined to the poultry-processing plant in Bryant, and only a few people in the four-county area knew of the new initiative before the barns were actually erected.

The Sanderson Farms project operated well in terms of generating profit for the corporation, but it showed its limits in terms of the consequences to the communities involved, a point documented by other studies of globalization that include all the camps discussed in Chapter 1 (see Friedland 1995; Marsden 2003; McMichael 2002). In their writings on agriculture and food, scholars such as Friedland, McMichael, and Marsden maintain that globalization is more often than not a phenomenon that increases socioeconomic inequality and hampers community development.

Although Sanderson Farms professed its dedication to social responsibility and "working with the community" so that all would benefit, it did not in fact contemplate real community involvement, and although it received the cooperation of upper-class Texas, it did not really make an effort to consult with local residents or seek substantive community participation. Following the rhetoric of globalization and the so-called free market, Sanderson Farms operated as if business expansion would automatically translate into community well-being. In fact, however, corporate expansion proceeded without any real community benefit and with substantial detriment to the community. This has become a typical outcome of global economic projects.

The divorce of economic expansion from community socioeconomic well-being, and the absence of mechanisms to address problems associated with the economic expansion of TNCs, served in this case as in others to radicalize community response to corporate penetration. The extent of the local response is arguably the most surprising aspect of this case, for it represents a departure from early readings of global sourcing. Scholars have tended in the past to see corporate hypermobility and local underdevelopment as factors that either suppressed resistance (McMichael 1996) or left room for only low-level community resistance (Arce 1997). In the case of Sanderson Farms in Texas, the chasm between the company's claims of community benefits and the reality of community degradation led to local resistance. While environmental degradation was a primary factor, it was the issue of property that catalyzed this resistance. The inability of Sanderson Farms to address concerns about the loss of property value in any real way triggered the widest opposition. Within three years the resistance group grew from twelve families into a statewide organization with an active legislative agenda and political strategy. Traditionally, issues of corporate legitimacy have been addressed through the intervention of the state (Offe 1996). In the context of globalization, however, state powers have either been greatly reduced or have accommodated capital mobility and been unwilling or unable to offer effective mediation. The Texas government's intervention was tilted heavily toward the protection of corporate interests. The state's assistance to Sanderson Farms, its lack of support for the regulation of animal-feeding operations, and the inadequacy of its research into these and other issues reveal the limits of local state agencies in mediating conflicting demands. The opening of local communities to economic globalization has not been accompanied by institutions capable of buffering the unwanted consequences of the growth of capitalism and controlling its most powerful actors. This situation can engender fierce resistance to the corporate globalization project.

To be sure, these points have been made in the globalization literature we surveyed in Chapter 1. The "corporate domination" camp has stressed both the limited ability of the state to control corporations and the state's subordination to them (McMichael 2002; Sklair 2001). This camp might emphasize the state's attempt to counter TRPP's attempt at democratic intervention (via the Enjoyment of Private Property Bill with the impact study that promised to look at all sides of the issue) as a prime example of how the state tries to deflect the challenges of resistance groups and protect the interests of transnational corporations. At the same time, those who write within the "contradictory dimension of globalization" approach stress the dearth of public institutions that can adequately perform the historical roles of the state (Sassen 2000; Pitelis 1993).

6

TNCS' COLONIZATION OF THE LOCAL AND RESISTANCE:
MEGA HOG FARMS IN THE TEXAS PANHANDLE

We have established in the previous chapters that globalization is a contested terrain in which TNCs are opposed by local groups and segments of the state and also affected by their own internal contradictions. In this chapter we illustrate corporate actions that allow TNCs effectively to control the state and justify their actions to shareholders. Like Sanderson Farms, the TNCs discussed in this chapter—Seaboard Farms and other hog companies—took advantage of their hypermobility and successfully adopted global sourcing strategies. But unlike Sanderson Farms, they were able to employ sophisticated and fruitful techniques that allowed them to control the political apparatus and legitimize their actions. In spite of their effectiveness, however, these strategies met with local resistance that also achieved some important results.

This story of globalization looks at the expansion of large hog production facilities in the Texas Panhandle region. This region also includes the Oklahoma panhandle and southwest Kansas, an area well suited to hog production because of its dry climate, sparse population, access to feed supplies, and availability of water from the Ogallala aquifer. While the case is centered on Seaboard Farms, other hog TNCs, such as Texas Farm and Smithfield Foods, are also integral parts of this story. We document the state-supported growth of confined animal feeding operations (CAFOs) in hog production and the concomitant emergence of resistance at the local and state levels. Resistance in Texas forced Seaboard to look elsewhere for locations in which to expand. Yet resistance emerged quickly in these areas as well. Texas eventually resurfaced as the most attractive location, for it offered a sympathetic regulation system and extremely cooperative public officials and local leaders.

The Industrialization and Global Expansion of the Hog Industry

In recent years the hog industry has been industrialized and integrated into the global agrifood system (Constance, Kleiner, and Rikoon 2003; Freese 1999a; Heffernan 1999a; Rhodes 1995; Welsh 1996). Fueled by growing global demand and the need to generate a standardized product, this trend is characterized by the decline of family farms and the strengthening of a system based on corporate-controlled CAFOS. CAFOS can produce thousands of standardized hogs in relatively small geographic areas (Drabenstott 1998; Rhodes 1995; Welsh 1996). Some rural people see CAFO hog production as a desirable form of socioeconomic development that can provide needed jobs. Others view hog CAFOS as an undesirable model of development in which the negative impacts, such as loss of family farms, odor problems, poor water quality, health concerns, depressed property values, and community disruption far outweigh any benefits (Constance, Kleiner, and Rikoon 2003; Heffernan 1999b; Schiffman 1998; Thu 1996b).

Fueled by market liberalization policies and expanding world demand, the top ten U.S. pork corporations increased production from 20 million pigs in 1994 to 23 million in 1995. By 1997 the U.S. pork industry was a $30 billion-a-year business. The twelve largest hog producers owned about 20 percent of the sows in the country, and their market share was increasing (Bryce 1997). By 2002 pork exports had risen for eleven straight years to 8.21 percent of total production. The top three buyers—Japan, Mexico, and Canada—bought 79 percent of the pork; Japan alone bought 48 percent (Vansickle 2003). In 2002 the National Pork Producers Council led a coalition of eighty U.S. agricultural organizations in securing trade promotion authority from the U.S. Congress that allowed it to take part in WTO agricultural negotiations to reduce trade barriers to pork exports (NPPC 2003).

At the same time that the hog industry was expanding to service growing global markets, mergers and acquisitions and vertical integration allowed fewer large corporations to become dominant (Bryce 1997; Heffernan 1999b; Hendrickson and Heffernan 2002). Seaboard, Inc., and Continental Grain are major agrifood TNCS. Nippon Meat Packers is the largest meat processor in Japan. Smithfield Foods is the largest hog producer and processor in the world. Tyson Foods, the largest chicken producer and processor in the world, now owns IBP's pork and beef divisions (Heffernan 1999b). All of these firms have been very active in Texas.

In response to the increased regulations that resulted from environmental contamination and community disruption, the CAFO-based hog industry has migrated west from North Carolina and nearby areas to the Midwest and the Southwest, and is now concentrated in Texas, Oklahoma, and Kansas (Bryce 1997; Curry1998c). The hog industry was lured to the Texas Panhandle region by a dry climate, sparse population, and "political leaders eager for a boost in economic development." As Texas state representative David Swinford (R-Dumas) observed, "There has been a steady decline in the employment of people in oil and gas production, as well as other non-agriculture jobs. However, turning our water into grain and our grain into meats seems to be what we do best. Our cattle industry started in the early 1960s and has grown each year. We are at the beginning level in terms of pork production when compared to the beef industry" (Curry 1998c).

Seaboard Farms Moves to Oklahoma: Global Sourcing and Economic Incentives

In 1992 Seaboard Farms announced that it would build a new pork-processing facility in the Panhandle town of Guymon, Oklahoma. Seaboard Farms, Inc., is a division of Seaboard Corporation, based in Merriam, Kansas, a diversified transnational agribusiness and transportation company engaged primarily in pork processing and cargo shipping domestically, and commodity merchandising, flour and feed milling, sugar production, and electric power generation globally. In 2003 Seaboard Corporation had five thousand U.S. and five thousand international employees with annual net sales of $1.8 billion (Seaboard Corporation 2003a). According to Seaboard, the total control of production, from genetic engineering through processing, has enabled the firm to increase its market share in the United States quickly and to become a leading exporter of pork to Japan, Mexico, and other global markets (Seaboard Corporation 2003b).

Seaboard Farms entered the pork business in 1990 when it bought the old Wilson Foods plant in Albert Lea, Minnesota (Barlett and Steele 1998). Before Seaboard arrived, the city of Albert Lea ($3.4 million), the state of Minnesota ($5.1 million), and the federal government ($25.5 million) had subsidized the building and operation of the plant and later provided further subsidies to entice Seaboard into operating the plant. Even as Seaboard announced that it would build a new hog-processing facility in Guymon, it promised to keep the Albert Lea plant open. Although the city continued to provide more than $13 million in additional subsidies, Seaboard closed the plant in 1994. To attract Seaboard to Guymon, the city, county, and state put together an initial $21 million package of incentives. The nonunion immigrant labor and probusiness corporate farming laws in Oklahoma also made Guymon attractive. The state of Oklahoma funded road and bridge work and also paid $1.79 million of Seaboard's $2.78 million in county taxes for fiscal years 1996–97 and 1997–98 (ibid.). Overall, Oklahoma taxpayers provided about $60 million in subsidies for Seaboard's Guymon location (KCSA 2000).

The Incident at Palo Duro Feedyard and the F/R Cattle Co. Lawsuit

In May 1993 a plume of airborne cattle manure extended over three miles from the Palo Duro Feedyard across David Bergin's ranch. Bergin's son went into respiratory arrest and was rushed by helicopter to a hospital. In response to a complaint from Bergin, Texas Natural Resources Conservation Commission (TNRCC) investigator Kathy Palmer inspected the Palo Duro facility in July 1994 and reported that the "dust being carried outside the feedlot was adequate to interfere with the normal usage and enjoyment of the property to the north, including [Bergin's] house." The dust could potentially cause adverse physiological discomfort to persons of ordinary sensitivity, she concluded, and people with acute health conditions could be affected more severely. Soon thereafter, Rick Costa, the TNRCC air quality manager in Amarillo, visited the same feedlot and noticed the dust problem, but his "supervisors in Austin would not allow him to cite Palo Duro for creating a nuisance because he had no proof that homes in the area were affected" (Morris 1997). After Bergin and his family abandoned the ranch temporarily and moved to a nearby town, he told a newspaper reporter, "To me, there's a reason those regulations are in existence. When you can pretty much ignore them and do what you want, that's really disappointing" (Morris 1997).

In response to TNRCC's failure to cite Palo Duro, Debra Barber, air program director for TNRCC's field operations division, explained that the agency's ability to cite CAFOs for nuisance odors had been impaired by a 1993 Texas Supreme Court ruling. In 1993 F/R Cattle Co. contested a citation from the Texas Air Control Board (TNRCC's predecessor), claiming that the odors emanating from the feedlot were part of a "natural process" and were therefore exempt from Texas Clean Air Act regulations. While both the lower court and the appeals court ruled against F/R Cattle, the Texas Supreme Court ruled in favor of the company. As a result, Barber informed the TNRCC regional offices that all CAFO odor citations were to be sent first to a review committee that would ascertain whether there was evidence of flagrantly bad management practices and/or extremely intense impact. During the following three and a half years TNRCC issued only four nuisance odor citations to CAFOS, none resulting in a fine. When asked about the Palo Duro situation, Barber told a reporter, "We did not confirm a nuisance situation there" (Morris 1997).

The Rewriting of the CAFO Regulations in Texas

In December 1993 state senator Teel Bivins met with five men who had a strong interest in Texas's nuisance odor rule, three from TNRCC and two from the Texas Cattle Feeders Association, an organization that the senator had once directed. The feedlot representatives were there to protest TNRCC's persistent citing of cattle feedlots. In 1994 Senator Bivins drafted a proposal to simplify Texas's CAFO permit process that included the elimination of the public hearing process for CAFO locations. In a letter to TNRCC the senator stated, "The perception throughout the United States is that the regulatory environment in Texas is burdensome and creates disincentives for [CAFOS] to locate in Texas." In 1995 the TNRCC incorporated Bivins's suggestions into new CAFO permit rules. According to a newspaper report, the new CAFO permit process "broke a regulatory logjam enabling pork producers to quickly establish themselves in virgin territory" (Morris 1997). By 1999 Seaboard Farms and four other major hog companies had significantly expanded their operations in the Texas Panhandle region (Ledbetter 1997d; Lee 1999).

The Great Hog Expansion in the Texas Panhandle:
Economic Accumulation

Seaboard's decision to locate its new processing plant in Guymon, combined with the deregulation of the nuisance and CAFO regulations in Texas, allowed for the rapid expansion of the hog industry in the Texas Panhandle region (Ledbetter 1997b). By 1997 the major hog production firms had permits to raise more than 2 million hogs in the region (Ledbetter 1997a). In 1997 Murphy Family Farms was the largest hog producer in the United States, with more than 275,000 sows in North Carolina, Missouri, Iowa, Oklahoma, Kansas, and Illinois (Roth 1997). The same year, Murphy Family Farms was bought by Smithfield Foods, the largest vertically integrated pork producer in the United States, with 675,000 sows. In 1999 Smithfield Foods was the largest pork producer and processor in the world, with operations in the

United States, France, Canada, Mexico, Brazil, and Poland (Freese 1999a; Miller 2000; Smithfield 1999–2000).

Premium Standard Farms (PSF) was the first major hog corporation to arrive in the Texas Panhandle outside Dalhart (Lee 1999). PSF began as a junk-bond-funded vertically integrated pork production system in Missouri in the late 1980s. But by the mid-1990s its markets included the European Union, Japan, and other parts of Asia (Marbery 1994a). In 1998 Continental Grain bought majority interest in PSF (Jereski and Smith 1996; Stroud 1998). As part of the ContiGroup, Continental Grain had extensive agriculture-related activities globally, including the largest animal feed and poultry company in China, substantial animal feed, poultry, and flour-milling operations in Ecuador, the Caribbean, Paraguay, Venezuela, Peru, and Haiti, and substantial feed and poultry investments in Europe (ContiGroup 1998). In 1998 Continental Grain was the world's largest cattle feeder, third-largest fully integrated hog producer, sixth-largest integrated poultry company, and an important player in the global animal feed and nutrition business. PSF/Continental was the second-largest hog producer in the United States, with 162,000 sows (Freese 1998).

During the time of the expansion in Texas Panhandle region, Seaboard moved from the eighth-largest to the third-largest hog TNC in the United States; Continental Grain/PSF moved from thirteenth to second place with the PSF acquisition; Smithfield Foods moved from fourth to first place with its Murphy Family Farms and Carroll Food acquisitions; Spanish-owned Vall, Inc., moved from forty-fourth to twenty-fifth place; and Texas Farm, a wholly owned subsidiary of Nippon Meat Packers, moved to twentieth-largest hog operation (Freese 1998 and 1999b). For Panhandle communities like Perryton, Texas, which had suffered from the oil bust, Texas Farm became the largest employer. Lieutenant Governor Rick Perry (formerly Texas's agricultural commissioner and now governor of the state) hailed the farms as a great example of economic development. "Frankly," he said, "nobody has shown me a compelling reason not to be for it" (Lee 1999).

Texas Farm and ACCORD: Global Sourcing and Organized Resistance

As a part of the state policy to attract business aggressively, Texas economic development officials recruited Nippon Meat Packers to create a pork production platform to raise hogs in Texas and export pork back to Japan. Seiji Yamaguchi, the director and general manager of Texas Farm, said that the

company located in Ochiltree County because of the "region's history in animal agriculture" and its "excellent resources of people, land and grain"
(Curry 1998c). Nippon Meat Packers, as noted above, is the largest meat-
processing firm in Japan and one of Japan's largest food companies, with
120 consolidated subsidiaries, ninety-four in Japan and twenty-six abroad
(Wright Analysis 2000).

The state of Texas and Ochiltree County provided fiscal incentives—
including large tax exemptions and the building of infrastructure—to attract
Texas Farm to the Panhandle area (Ledbetter 1997b and 1997e; Lee 1999).
The former director of the Perryton Economic Development Corporation,
Myron McCartor, stated that he had "no qualms" about helping lure Texas
Farm to Ochiltree County. The county tax based had declined $400 million
since the oil bust (Curry 1998c). Within a few years Texas Farm's $200 million
investment made Ochiltree the fourth-largest pork-producing county in the
United States (Bryce 1997).

The state leaders' idea that CAFOS represented a solid community development strategy was not shared by all local residents. As CAFO numbers increased, some residents who lived near the Texas Farm facilities formed a
group called Active Citizens Concerned over Resources Development (ACCORD)
to address the negative impacts of CAFO development (Lee 1999; Morris 1997);
by early 1998 the group had grown to 155 members (Lee 1998). "There's no
way to describe the odor," said Barbara Phillipp, who lives on a farm about
half a mile from a Texas Farm barn. "You live here, have a good life, and then
this thing comes in. It turns your life totally upside down" (Morris 1997).
Other ACCORD members talked about ailments ranging from burning eyes to
nosebleeds. Others expressed concerns about the negative impact of CAFOS on
water quality and quantity. Under the current Texas laws ACCORD members
are "stuck with the stench"; they cannot sue Texas Farm for being a public
nuisance because CAFOS are exempt from nuisance laws and state regulations
do not allow public hearings that might challenge the permit process (Bryce
1997).

In response to these charges, Texas Farm stated that it had selected the
Texas Panhandle because it was sound environmentally and had a long, successful history of large cattle feedlots. The company stressed that its lagoons
surpassed federal and state standards and that it intended to bring "new
life" to the declining local economy (Morris 1997). Calling the odor problem
"challenging," Texas Farm representative Don Clift claimed that Texas Farm
had located its barns as far from residences as possible and continually evaluated its state-of-the-art waste-treatment systems (Lee 1998). Dean Paul, a

local man who expanded his operations, dismissed the critics as "radicals" who "need a cause," claiming that his permits had all the required safeguards for odor and spillage. "We don't need a watchdog group to oversee our operations. The TNRCC's got that completely covered," he said (Morris 1997).

According to community organizer Jean Gramstorff, ACCORD's original plan was to demand public hearings on every operation, but in June 1995 the permit rules changed. The new rules stated that permits could be challenged only on technical merit, not merely because a barn might stink. According to Brad Jones, TNRCC's regional manager in Amarillo, "We don't do property value. We don't do truck traffic." He said he sympathized with ACCORD but added, "I guess they don't know how unempowered environmental agencies have become. We're frustrated as well." TNRCC chairman Barry McBee stated, "If you compare what Texas requires with what other stares require, we are as stringent, if not more stringent. What we require in Texas is protective of the environment and the people around these facilities" (Morris 1997).

The ACCORD Lawsuit: Re-regulation and Corporate and State Responses

Some Ochiltree County residents felt that successful lobbying by powerful agribusiness interests was the real reason for the rule changes. Senator Bivins and two of the three TNRCC commissioners had close ties to agriculture. Commissioner McBee was deputy commissioner of the Texas Department of Agriculture, and Commissioner Baker had been director of the Texas Farm Bureau and other agricultural organizations. Similarly, the TNRCC's Agriculture Advisory Committee was dominated by large-scale agricultural interests (Morris 1997).

ACCORD hired Austin attorney Stuart Henry and sued the TNRCC, claiming that the rule changes deprived property owners of their fundamental right to a hearing prior to the permitting of a feedlot (Lee 1998; Morris 1997). ACCORD maintained that the CAFO odors wafted into their homes and threatened their quality of life, and they attributed the Panhandle hog boom solely to Senator Bivins. "Basically, Senator Bivins has written off the citizens of Ochiltree County. He doesn't care that those folks up there are being stunk out of their houses," said Henry. Bivins replied that CAFOs should not be outlawed just because some neighbors found them offensive (Morris 1997).

In November 1997 district judge Margaret Cooper in Austin notified parties in the ACCORD versus TNRCC lawsuit that she believed that the fifty-six CAFO permits approved by TNRCC under subchapter K since 1995 were invalid (Ledbetter 1997c; Lee 1998). Judge Cooper ruled that the TNRCC had failed to show "reasoned justification" for eliminating public hearings (Lee 1998). Subchapter K permits were those issued after the TNRCC changed its permit regulations and eliminated the public hearing process for neighbors of cattle feedlots or hog farms; under subchapter B permits, neighbors were allowed such hearings (Ledbetter 1997c).

Industry representatives argued that the new regulations were more stringent than ever, while doing away with frivolous complaints and speeding up the process (Lee 1998). Ben Weinheimer of the Texas Cattle Feeders Association maintained that "Subchapter K is a very stringent set of rules that puts the burden on the applicant to show the facility to be protective of the environment. Judge Cooper's ruling is based on a legal technicality and not on the technical provisions of Subchapter K." Don Clift of Texas Farm said that Judge Cooper's ruling was strictly procedural and had nothing to do with protecting the environment. Rejecting these claims, ACCORD stressed that hog farms without valid permits should be shut down (Ledbetter 1997c).

In response to the ruling, TNRCC and Texas Farm filed motions requesting that Judge Cooper allow TNRCC to correct the "reasoned justification problem" and readopt the rules. The Texas Cattle Feeders Association, Texas Pork Producers Association, Texas Poultry Federation, Texas Association of Dairymen, and the former Associated Milk Producers, Inc., filed a motion in support of TNRCC and Texas Farm. These industry representatives claimed that the blocked permits affected operations worth $2.3 billion and twenty-four hundred jobs; they believed that the ruling could be accommodated by incorporating new language in the rules. ACCORD disagreed (Lee 1998).

Although the ruling focused on a technical legal point, some felt that it might have a broader meaning and curtail the recent expansion of the hog industry. While Texas had been viewed as the next frontier for giant hog farms, there was concern that the ruling could deflate that perception by prompting a reexamination of the regulations. According to John McGlone, professor of animal science and director of the Pork Industry Institute at Texas Tech University, "It has already had an effect. Companies are doing site selection—they're just doing it in other states." Plans for expansion were disrupted. Don Clift of Texas Farm noted that the ruling had "given pause" to the parent company, Nippon Meat Packers, and that construction on "major additions is on hold" (Lee 1998).

The CAFO Tour and Public Hearing in Ochiltree County: Legitimation Tactics

In April 1998 the Perryton Chamber of Commerce sponsored a CAFO tour of Ochiltree County, followed by a public hearing. On the tour were state representatives Warren Chisum (R-Pampa), David Swinford (R-Amarillo), five members of the House Environmental Regulation Committee, which Chisum chairs, and several CAFO industry officials and interested citizens. The official purpose of the tour and meeting was to study the "cumulative effects of numerous CAFOs in a concentrated geographic area and to determine whether environmental protections are adequate." The tour stopped at two Texas Farm facilities near Perryton, where tour members got no closer than the county road, from which no animals or waste lagoons were visible. The group also stopped at a lagoon and some feed mills under construction, where industry representatives explained their dedication to environmental protection and detailed efforts to control dust and minimize odors (Brown 1998). Representative John Hirschi (D-Wichita Falls) commented that the group had "learned that there is a lot of support for it because of its economic benefits" but that the mail was running nine to one against hogs. Hirschi was concerned that the tour organizers did not show "us anything they did not want us to see"; "the whole time we were there we never saw a pig" (Curry 1998a).

Visitors signing in at the public meeting were greeted with banners for ProAg (Plains Residents Organization for Ag Growth), a newly formed organization that local attorney and ProAg president Bob Lemons reported had fifteen hundred members in Kansas, Oklahoma, and Texas. ProAg formed in early 1998 to combat opposition to corporate hog farms that had emerged in several states "targeted by the industry for development." The House Environmental Regulation Committee, along with Senators Swinford and Bivins, heard the testimony of twenty-nine people. Swinford began by praising the economic benefits of pork production and the slaughter facilities he promised would follow. He cited the hog expansion around Guymon, Oklahoma, after Seaboard Farms located there, adding that an $8 million investment by the City of Guymon had resulted in five thousand new jobs, residential property value increases of up to 30 percent, and 140 new businesses in five years (Brown 1998). Swinford admitted that Guymon was also experiencing housing shortages, a surging crime rate, school crowding, and odor problems, but he argued that those were "more social problems than pork problems." He shrugged off complaints about noxious odors coming from the hog farms, saying, "Once you get a mile away, you can't hardly smell them" (Brown 1998).

Challenging Senator Swinford's definition of the situation, Vancy Elliott testified that the third-generation farm she lived on had four hundred thousand hogs nearby. "Our roots run deep," said Elliott. "We care about our community and our environment. I live by hogs 24 hours a day, and have not found one Seaboard or Hitch official that lives by them" (Brown 1998). Elliott noted that neighbors of hog farms suffered health problems such as nausea, headaches, and sinus congestion, and that their quality of life and property values had declined. She reported other negative effects such as increased gang activity in the schools, increased demand on welfare programs, and elevated crime rates (Brown 1998).

Dr. John McGlone of Texas Tech University testified that the hog industry would double in size in the next five years. "We can shrink—and eventually die—or grow. The pig industry has provided a vehicle for communities to grow [and] to preserve a way of life." He recommended the maintenance of Texas's environmental law and adoption of the latest CAFO technologies. McGlone also suggested that the state legislature make penalties for false charges against CAFOS equal to the penalties for violations by CAFOS. Furthermore, he argued, along with physical setbacks there should be "philosophical setbacks," or what he referred to as "pig enterprise zones," which would buffer the industry from "agricultural terrorism" and "corporate sabotage." McGlone concluded by saying that it was possible to produce pigs in confinement in ways that does not harm the environment (Brown 1998; Curry 1998c).

Senator Chisum asked Dr. John Sweeten, director of the Texas Agricultural Experiment Station in Amarillo, to provide a scientific review. A committee member asked Dr. Sweeten whether hydrogen sulfide (H_2S) monitoring could provide greater accuracy in monitoring odor levels. "We are gearing up for that," Sweeten replied. "But it is not our job to go around the countryside and monitor odors. It is our job to conduct replication studies." Doug Ricketts, a member of Citizens for Natural Resource Policy, referred to studies that showed the adverse effects of exposure to H_2S fumes and pointed out that the technology needed for monitoring H_2S was already available in the gas industry. Donnie Dendy, president of ACCORD, testified that his group had conducted an H_2S study and found measurable levels of contaminants as far as six miles from the Texas Farm facilities. Larry Swink, a resident of Ochiltree County, testified that Texas Farm had obtained a permit for a 76,000-hog facility half a mile from his water well. "It is the equivalent of all the sewage in Amarillo dumped in open pits," said Swink. Jeanne Gramstorff of ACCORD asked the committee why open cesspools of hog waste were legal if such systems for human waste were banned (Brown 1998). "My number one concern is the water, and second would be the air and soil," she said. "I feel very protective of the Ogallala Aquifer because we've only got one of them" (Curry 1998c).

Perryton mayor David Hale testified that given the rapid increase in hogs in the area, he wanted changes in the procedures for permitting and monitoring CAFOs so as to protect the environment, especially the Ogallala aquifer. The mayor of Higgins, Hilton Menser, testified that pork production would reverse the declining job situation in his community. Tim Cooper, senior vice president of the First Bank of the Southwest, testified to the beneficial effects on what was a rapidly declining tax base in the county. Bob Lemon, president of ProAg, testified that there had not been a single documented incidence of CAFO pollution in Texas, Kansas, or Oklahoma getting into the aquifer. Don Clift of Texas Farm testified that not only did the pork industry provide stable jobs, a good working environment, and good benefits, but that (then) Governor George W. Bush and Agricultural Commissioner Rick Perry had assisted in recruiting the corporate hog industry to Texas (Brown 1998).

After attending the public meeting, Sandra Drake of Ochiltree County criticized the position of the tour sponsors, which she found biased in favor of the hog industry. Drake charged that the tour and public hearing had been poorly publicized and that the news articles announcing the tour made no mention of public participation. If it had truly been a neutral and objective tour, she asked, then why had it not stopped at the homes of residents living near the existing CAFOs (Drake 1998). In a letter to the editor of an Amarillo newspaper, Kay Cartwright charged that the tour was "carefully orchestrated by the Chamber of Commerce and the hog CAFOs" (Cartwright 1999).

Seaboard Farms and Keyes, Oklahoma: Negotiating Economic Development

In late December 1997 Seaboard Farms announced that it was negotiating with officials of Cimarron County, Oklahoma, to build hog production facilities to house four hundred thousand hogs on eight thousand acres on fourteen contiguous sections of land (Ledbetter 1997b). If the deal was finalized, the eight-thousand-acre farm would be the biggest contiguous farm in the state. Seaboard would locate a feed mill in Keyes and would help Keyes get its elementary school reopened (Ledbetter 1997d). Mark Campbell of Seaboard Farms said that the operation would add $50 million to the tax rolls and have an annual payroll of $2.5 million. "The Keyes school district was in trouble," said Campbell. "We agreed to give them some up-front money ($125,000) so they could reopen their elementary school," which had been closed after asbestos removal (*Dallas Morning News* 1997). Commissioner Williams commented that Keyes was most interested in the feed mill that would supply the hog barns. According to Williams, "We want to give this county an option to vote" (Ledbetter 1997d).

Beyond the $125,000 contribution for the school, the proposal approved by Cimarron County commissioners included agreements for Seaboard to (1) limit the number of hog-finishing buildings in the county, (2) limit the location of the farms within a five-mile radius of currently owned property and outside a five-mile radius of any town in the county, (3) make a $2,500 donation to the school district for each new student directly related to Seaboard employment for the first two years, and (4) provide its own water supply and wastewater treatment (Ledbetter 1997d). In return, the city and county would "not take any action to restrict Seaboard's ability to acquire land for the construction of the farms"; this last part of the agreement "would not apply to any further construction than the original plan" (Ledbetter 1997b).

Some residents were not happy with the deal. Carla Smalts, a Keyes resident and head of the protest group Safe Oklahoma Resource Development (SORD), said the agreement was signed with the commissioners before most people knew what was going on. Jarrod Stewart, a fifth-generation farmer, said that Seaboard's site near his land planned to put between 300,000 and 350,000 hogs on 6,000 acres with 300 to 350 houses (Ledbetter 1997d). Steward noted that the Seaboard Farms officials "did their homework well" and quickly determined that an offer to fix the school would win over the town leaders (*Dallas Morning News* 1997). Stewart expressed concern that the number of hogs would cause an environmental problem because the location was on extremely sandy soil near the Cimarron River. "My opposition is on the environmental soundness of the industry and with Seaboard personally. They've broken a lot of promises they've made in the past to communities," said Stewart (Ledbetter 1997d).

Kenneth Maness, Cimarron County commissioner, maintained that in general people didn't want the hogs but that this could not stop people from selling their land to Seaboard. Commissioner Williams stated, "I have mixed feelings about it. I represent the community and the community of Keyes is in support of the feedmill." The county commissioners and city officials refused a Seaboard request to grant tax abatements. Williams commented, "We won't be a part of any bonds. We learned our lesson from Guymon's experience." According to Williams, "There's two sides to this story. The human interest part is this town is dying, and the people see this as the only way to get our grade school back open" (Ledbetter 1997d). The arrangement between Keyes and Seaboard was not completed because of a hog moratorium passed in the Oklahoma legislature in 1998.

Stricter CAFO Regulations in Panhandle Region States: Legitimation Crises and Re-regulation

As more information on the effects of CAFOs became available, several states and counties in the Panhandle region began rewriting corporate farming laws to further regulate the industry. By late 1997 eighteen of the twenty counties in Kansas that had held referenda on whether to allow large hogs farms had voted no, among them Seward County, where Seaboard hoped to expand (Bryce 1997). By 1999 Colorado required covers on waste lagoons (Lee 1999). In early 1998 the Oklahoma legislature created a one-year moratorium on future hog and poultry operations (Talley 1998). Seaboard criticized the moratorium and said it was looking at optional sites in other states. Sponsors of the bill said they were "trying to do what's responsible for Oklahoma" and "get a handle on these issues before we go forward with further expansion" (*Amarillo Globe-News* 1998a). During the same time period, Seaboard agreed to pay an $88,200 fine imposed by the state of Oklahoma for improperly disposing of its dead hogs (*Amarillo Globe-News* 1998b). Oklahoma went on to pass some of the strictest rules in the nation, whereby new large hog CAFOs had to be at least two miles from a residence (Derichsweiler 1998; Lee 1999). "It's much, much too restricting," said Seaboard CEO Rick Hoffman. "I think ultimately Oklahoma is not going to be an attractive place for swine production" (Talley 1998).

The Search for Seaboard's "Second Hog Pyramid": Global Sourcing and Local Resistance

Seaboard Farms invested $550 million in the Panhandle region of Kansas, Oklahoma, and Texas to develop its "first hog pyramid" of growout buildings, breeding facilities, a feed mill, and a processing plant around Guymon. In early 1998 it started searching for the site of its "second pyramid" (Lee 1999). In February three Texas Panhandle cities (Dumas, Hereford, and Pampas) and two Kansas cities (Garden City and Great Bend) were under consideration for the location of the processing plant. In March Seaboard announced that it would build its new plant in Great Bend. Expressing his disappointment, the mayor of Hereford commented, "I guess one of the reasons they selected Great Bend was the uproar over the CAFO regulations" in Texas. A board member of the Dumas Economic Development Corporation stated, "When the judge downstate sided with the environmentalists, it pretty much throttled hog operations. I think it redirected live production to other areas" (Storm 1998).

In April there was a backlash against Seaboard in Great Bend, when four city council members who supported Seaboard were "handily defeated by write-in candidates" (McLean 1998). The newly elected city council refused to allow Seaboard to connect to its sewage plant (Davis 2001b). The action of the city council members raised fears that several Republican lawmakers statewide could be vulnerable in the November elections (McLean 1998). Even with the setback in Great Bend, in August 1999 Seaboard proceeded with plans to expand in Kansas and applied for hog production permits in four western Kansas counties—Wallace, Wichita, Scott, and Kearny. The Kearny County Alliance hired an engineer and attorney to fight Seaboard, and Wallace County commissioners placed a one-year moratorium on all new construction in rural areas until the county wrote zoning codes. The moratorium was patterned after the one adopted in Stevens County when Seaboard was expanding there (*Amarillo Globe-News* 1999).

In February 2000 Seaboard agreed to pay fines of $30,250 involving spills and the lack of equipment used to contain odors at its Dorman Sow Farm in Beaver County, Oklahoma. Critics noted that they "found it pathetic and ironic" that Seaboard had been fined for not having the odor abatement system but was still allowed to operate. In responding to the critics, the attorney for the Agricultural Department's water quality division said there had been a misunderstanding. While the agency had said that the system should be installed and working properly, Seaboard understood that it was to be phased into operation (*Amarillo Globe-News* 2000). In June the Sierra Club filed a federal lawsuit against Seaboard, alleging twelve violations of the federal Clean Water Act at the Dorman site. The chairman of the Oklahoma chapter of the Sierra Club said Seaboard had "repeatedly polluted Oklahoman's waterways" and violated federal law (Jenkins 2000). Because the fines assessed by the state were "woefully inadequate," the Sierra Club was going to a "higher authority" (George 2000).

Rising opposition to the plant in Great Bend and the decreased availability of hogs in central Kansas owing to local opposition forced Seaboard to abandon its plans to expand in Kansas (*St. Joseph (MO) Morning Sun* 2000b; WWIM 2000). In February 2000 Seaboard announced that it was now considering St. Joseph, Missouri, as the site for its second processing plant (*St. Joseph (MO) Morning Sun* 2000b). As news of the plan spread, some businesspeople expressed concerns that the labor market was already tight and that Seaboard might attract employees away from their companies. Other citizens feared an influx of immigrant workers and increased demands on social services (*St. Joseph (MO) Morning Sun* 2000a). The group Citizens Opposing Seaboard formed and the St. Joseph City Council soon passed a resolution against the company (Davis 2001d; Taylor 2001).

As opposition to the plant grew in St. Joseph, Seaboard evaluated a location across the state line in the Doniphan County town of Elwood, Kansas. In August 2000 it bought land for a new plant there (*St. Joseph (MO) Morning Sun* 2000c; WWIM 2000). Seaboard quickly ran into opposition in the Elwood area as well. The first tension arose between the Doniphan County Zoning Board and the City of Elwood (Davis 2001c). The zoning board voted twice to deny the company the zoning change needed to build the plant, but the city council had the final word and voted in favor of the change. The pattern repeated itself regarding a "conditional use permit" for Seaboard's rendering plant; the zoning board again voted against the permit and sent the decision back to the city council. During this time Concerned Citizens of Doniphan County formed and filed a lawsuit against Elwood for granting Seaboard the annexation and the rezoning "in a closed door session to try to keep the public from knowing about the proposed project" (Davis 2001e). Finally, other cities and counties in the area began developing various restrictions and zoning alterations to prevent the development of the hog farms that would service the Elwood plant.

In March 2001 Seaboard announced that its plans to build in Elwood had been "terminated" because of downturn in the U.S. stock market and the slowdown of exports to Asia (Davis 2001d). That the Kansas Department of Health and Environment had informed Seaboard that there were problems with its air permit was at least a contributing factor. While Elwood city officials expressed regrets about losing the economic development opportunities, opponents of Seaboard were elated. Seaboard CEO Rick Hoffman said it was not the opposition but rather the lagging economy that had forced the decision (Davis 2001b).

New CAFO Regulations for Texas: Re-regulation and EPA Harmonization

In February 1998 the TNRCC proposed revisions to the Texas CAFO regulations to address the concerns raised by Judge Cooper's ruling. Depending on the type of operation, some CAFO applicants would have to go through the public hearing process as demanded by the ACCORD lawsuit, but others would not. TNRCC Chairman McBee urged quick adoption of the revisions because, as he put it, "we've got an industry that's at a complete standstill now" (Robbins 1998a). During the public hearings on the revisions, ACCORD and other groups expressed concerns about the safety of the Ogallala aquifer, as well as other quality-of-life issues (Robbins 1998d). These groups were especially worried about the permits that did not require a notice or public hearing (Morris 1997). Industry representatives urged the TNRCC to base the new rules on the best available science and sound engineering, while critics asked them to write them as they'd want them if they lived next to a facility (Robbins 1998c).

The TNRCC announced in August that it had approved the proposed revisions, but the new rules were put on hold while the group negotiated for authority from the U.S. Environmental Protection Agency to administer the federal water quality permitting program (Robbins 1998e). In September the EPA granted TNRCC authority to implement a "Texas version" of the Clean Water Act's national pollution discharge elimination system (Robbins 1998b). Under the Texas version, CAFOS could apply for one permit to meet both state and federal regulations. CAFOS could obtain a "permit by rule" that avoided notices and public hearings if the company agreed to go through a standardized process to meet certain criteria. A public comment period allowed citizens to challenge the permits, and the TNRCC evaluated the challenges based primarily on technical merit. The new permits also required a "nutrient utilization plan" to manage the waste being applied to the land, but the permits did "not regulate land application of manure by third-party capacity" (Ledbetter 1999). The TNRCC commissioner commented, "That industry is important to Texas. We cannot go completely out of whack in relation to other states or they'll go to other states—or even other countries." ACCORD's attorney, Stuart Henry, criticized the regulations. "The word's gotten out around the country that if you want to create a nuisance and get away with it, come to Texas," he said (Lee 1999).

Seaboard Heads Back to Texas: Global Sourcing and Local Resistance

Because of resistance to its plans in Kansas and Missouri, in December 2001 Seaboard turned its attention back to Texas. It applied for a permit on the Moore and Hutchinson county line near Dumas, a site it had investigated in 1998. A Seaboard spokesman commented that "pork-processing in Texas looks extremely attractive compared to one in Oklahoma" (Storm 2001). In response, the Panhandle Alliance formed in Moore County in 2001 and quickly mounted an information campaign to educate citizens about the hazards of CAFO-based hog production (Panhandle Alliance 2001a). The coordinator of the Oklahoma Family Farm Alliance provided some advice to the Panhandle Alliance and other residents of Moore County and Dumas. She asserted that the hog industry could be a plus to the area but that citizens "must act now" or regret it later. "Is Seaboard headed your direction because the company loves your rural landscape and wants to see towns prosper?" she asked. "Frankly, it sees you as a pushover. Texas law is weak in protection of the environment and the rights of rural citizens. More populist states, such as Oklahoma, allow legal hearings on almost every permit. Texas does not. Oklahoma passed laws and established agency rules restricting the swine industry. Not Texas" (Hatfield 2001).

She encouraged Dumas to "realize their leverage" and force Seaboard to be a "good corporate citizen." By now Seaboard had been trying to locate the second processing plant for four years. It was "rebuffed by Kansas, slapped by Oklahoma, banned in Nebraska, cold-shouldered in Missouri and Colorado," a local newspaper reported, so the "last thing they want to do is start all over again." Seaboard should pay good wages instead of requiring public subsidies, she advised, and should shoulder the social costs instead of asking for tax abatements. County commissioners and other officials should use their powers to enact ordinances to protect the quality of life of their constituents; Seaboard would abide by these if it truly wanted to be a "good corporate citizen." She concluded that "any public official who is not willing to negotiate the best deal for Dumas should be evicted immediately" (Hatfield 2001).

Early in 2002, in response to a petition drive against the plant, the Dumas

Economic Development Corporation (DEDC) held a public meeting to discuss the situation. DEDC's executive director noted that after Seaboard contacted the DEDC, the office had only done its job in providing informational support and conducting an impact study on the proposed processing plant. The director stated that if Seaboard did locate near Dumas, the DEDC would make $400,000 available to cover infrastructure costs and encourage the building of low- to moderate-cost housing and $40,000 for parks and other amenities. "The $440,000 was the amount defined by the study as the net tax gain if the project was to be located in Dumas," he said (Storm 2002a).

In mid-January the Dumas City Council held a meeting to discuss the possibility of selling water to Seaboard for the processing plant (Storm 2002c). The city manager reported that it would cost about $3.6 million to bring the 770,000 million gallons of water per year to the plant and that "Seaboard would pay for it." According to a Seaboard spokesperson, "As far as the plant goes, the locations we are looking at continue to flip-flop. We are actively looking at two or three sites, and Moore County is one of those sites" (Storm 2002c). The following week the city council voted 5–0 to sell the water to Seaboard (Storm 2002b). At the "overflow meeting," agency officials reported that although there was adequate water for the plant, the council would have to plan to acquire more water rights because conservative estimates suggested that Dumas had only thirty-one years' worth of water supply remaining at current usage rates. The board president of the DEDC, also a local banker, spoke of how Moore County's agricultural and petrochemical industries were in decline. "In a community, you can't hold still; you grow or die," he said. "We don't get to pick and choose. This is an opportunity that came to us" (Storm 2002b). Critics of the plan pointed to a county newspaper poll showing that 82 percent of local residents opposed the new plant.

Soon after the Moore County Commission voted to provide revenue bonds to build a sewage-treatment plant if the processing plant located in the area (Storm 2002d), Seaboard announced that Moore County would be the location for its new plant. The mayor of Dumas said, "Dumas and Moore County are pleased with Seaboard Farms' decision to locate in our area. This project will provide a tremendous amount of economic stimulus to our community" (Storm 2002f). A Seaboard spokesperson commented that the entire project would involve about $350 million in investments, including several area sites to raise hogs for slaughter. Upon hearing the news, a Dumas resident who had spearheaded the effort to oppose the plant said angrily, "It's been a set-up deal, is all I can say. In my opinion, this was a done deal before the public ever knew about it. I'm disappointed that the public was left out of the process" (Storm 2002f). After the announcement, Seaboard filed several permit applications for the processing plant near Dumas and for production facilities to produce about 1.5 million hogs in the Sherman/Moore County area (Storm 2002f and 2002g).

As Seaboard filed the permit applications, the Palo Duro River Authority board of directors sent a letter to the TNRCC expressing concern about the proliferation of hog CAFOS in its watershed area (Storm 2002h) and asking the agency to examine the issue more thoroughly. At the same time the Panhandle Alliance held an educational meeting in Amarillo that featured a number of area speakers with expertise on water issues from organizations such as the Panhandle Groundwater Conservation District, the Canadian River Municipal Water Authority, City of Amarillo Utilities, and the Promised Land Network (Panhandle Alliance 2001b). Speakers noted that the Ogallala aquifer was the only source of water in the area and one of the most valuable assets of the land. One attendee concluded, "I believe elected officials have sold out to agribusiness" (Burleson 2002).

On June 27 the advisor to the Pampa chapter of ACCORD sent a letter to Governor Rick Perry that expressed ACCORD's deep concern regarding the contamination of the Ogallala aquifer by hog waste and the large quantity of water needed to supply the established and proposed hog farms in the Panhandle region. He doubted whether the TNRCC had considered the cumulative impact that 4 million more hogs would have on the area, adding, "This area has become first choice of the pig industry, because other states have been forced to severely restrict and regulate pig factories for environmental reasons. Yet Texas still permits the open-pit waste lagoons, which are the most economical for pig producers, but pose the most danger to the environment." In concluding, he requested that Governor Perry rectify the TNRCC's failure to protect the natural resources of Texas "before it is too late" (Haydon 2002a). In his response, Governor Perry expressed his conviction that the TNRCC would care for the state's natural resources properly. He stated that he "had no authority over the agency's registration or permitting process" but did "believe that affected Texans should have a fair opportunity to have their views considered as part of the permitting process" (Perry 2002).

National Pig Development and Pampa: Global Sourcing and Blocked Resistance

In July 2001 the director of the Pampa Economic Development Corporation, Susan Tripplehorn, announced that National Pig Development (NPD), a wholly owned subsidiary of Smithfield Foods, planned to build an $18 million genetic research facility eleven miles east of Pampa in Gray County. The facility would employ forty-five people and produce up to fifty thousand hogs per year. A public meeting was held the following week at which NPD representatives and county officials addressed questions about the facility; roughly 160 people attended. After the meeting, a local chapter of ACCORD was formed in an attempt to keep the CAFO from locating in the area. Many residents were concerned about the rapid expansion of hogs in the Texas Panhandle area. By 2002 the Texas Panhandle contained 85 percent of the state's 920,000 hogs, up from 8 percent in 1990 (Blaney 2002; Young 2002a and 2002b).

In early December 2002 NPD applied to the TNRCC for the necessary permit. Under the new Texas CAFO laws residents had one month to submit written comments on the CAFO to the TNRCC. Because residents of the area expressed numerous concerns about the operation, state representative Warren Chisum (R-Pampa) requested that the TNRCC and NPD hold a public meeting to field questions. At this meeting, held in early January, about forty-five residents presented verbal comments both for and against the facility (Young 2002b). Owing to the very large volume of "written comments" submitted in opposition to the facility, by April TNRCC had still not ruled on the permit. On June 4 TNRCC executive director Jeffrey Saitas signed the registration application. "It's a beautiful day in Pampa, Texas," said NPD general manager John Carter. "I had a lot of confidence that TNRCC would approve the application. I knew the merits of it would stand up well. They are very professional, and Texas should be proud of this department." Jean Pieper-Voshell, media representative for the TNRCC, said that people who objected to the decision had twenty-five days to file a motion to overturn TNRCC's ruling (Young 2002a).

On June 27 an advisor to ACCORD's Pampa chapter, Dr. Louis Haydon, sent a letter of appeal and copies of the four separate motions to overturn the TRNCC decision on NPD to Governor Perry (Haydon 2002a). ACCORD had sent the original motions to the TNRCC. The copies bore the signatures of about 350 citizens of the area. Dr. Haydon expressed ACCORD's deep concern regarding the contamination of the Ogallala aquifer by hog waste and the large quantity of water needed for such a facility. He questioned whether the TNRCC had considered the cumulative impact that 4 million more hogs would have on the Panhandle area.

By early July TNRCC has received almost a thousand letters protesting the approval of the NPD permit and requesting that Jeff Saitas overturn his decision. TNRCC had also received several "motions to overturn" in opposition to the facility. "Motions to overturn" are requests for TNRCC to review the executive director's approval of the registration and must explain why the decision should be reviewed (Norton 2002; Young 2002c). In August the TNRCC general counsel declined to place the motions to overturn the NDP application on the TNRCC commissioner's agenda, thus ending the appeals process to TNRCC (Storm 2002h).

A few months after the ruling approving the NPD operation, Dr. Haydon sent a letter to the editor of a local newspaper highlighting the expected consequences of the location of Smithfield's NPD operation near Pampas, including Smithfield's recent acquisition of the operations of Vall, Inc. Haydon noted that Smithfield Foods, the largest pork producer and processor in the world, owned Circle Four Farms in Beaver and Iron counties, Utah. Circle Four had recently been fined $45,000 for water contamination episodes from the use of the open-pit hog waste lagoons. Smithfield had also been fined more than $15 million for polluting streams and bays in the eastern and southern United States, and the state of North Carolina had recently ordered it to pay $65 million over the next two decades to eliminate open lagoons (Haydon 2002b and 2002c). Dr. Haydon quoted agricultural economist Bill Weida concerning the Circle Four Farms situation and the implications for Texas. Weida noted that "Smithfield is looking for someplace else where they can pollute with impunity and without local government resistance—and that place is Texas." Haydon continued:

> If you wonder what this all has to do with Texas, it is just this: If people in these counties in Utah cannot tolerate the impact of the open-air waste pits on their lives and environment, and the government of North Carolina has also expressed its outrage by imposing fines, penalties and restrictions, how then can the people of the Panhandle of Texas be expected to accept this industry passively and without question in view of the fact that Smithfield (parent company of National Pig Development USA) is starting to dig the pits, even as I write, for a pig factory to house 50,000 animals, just east of Pampa, and will utilize 46 acres of exactly the same open waste pits which are at issue here, and in use in all pig factories in Texas. Sad to say, Texas has become the location of choice for the hog industry because its lax laws permit such abuse. (Haydon 2002c)

Analysis and Discussion

While other stories of globalization have shown that TNCs' actions are opposed by segments of the state, this case demonstrates the ability of TNCs to affect state actions and use state support to achieve their objectives. It also underscores that TNCs accompany their attempt to control the state apparatus with legitimation strategies that are aimed at justifying their economic behavior to stakeholders. This story of globalization provides some examples of these strategies. It also confirms that, in spite of these legitimation strategies, resistance can be successful.

The Direct Control of the Polity

The CAFO industry was able to control environment regulation processes and state environmental agencies in Texas. Threatened by anticorporate activism, CAFO corporations worked to weaken the content of environmental legislation and to diminish the sanctioning power of state agencies. Paralleling arguments proposed by members of the corporate domination camp described in Chapter 1, in which corporate actors control the polity, these corporations were able to mobilize support from key members of the state political apparatus. Taking the position that the TNRCC's policy of "nuisance citations" for CAFOs and "public hearings" regarding CAFO siting was overbearing and ultimately counterproductive to the well-being of Texas agriculture, the agricultural industry secured procorporate reform of the CAFO legislation that depoliticized the issue through the elimination of public hearings, the restriction of complains to technical merit, and the creation of alternative permits. Despite opposition, pro-CAFO groups were able to neutralize the use of the TNRCC as a venue for anticorporate resistance. Similarly, when the state of Texas secured Clean Water Act jurisdiction from the EPA, another avenue of dissent was closed. These changes deprived local residents of the capacity to question corporate policies and practices and voice their dissent; the possibility of engaging in substantive democracy was eliminated. As will be discussed below, TNCs' ability to control the state apparatus was locally bound, for it pertained to the case of Texas alone. In other locations, both state institutions and social movements successfully opposed corporate designs.

Legitimation Strategies

CAFO TNCs worked to project an image that would justify their objectives to groups that would not benefit from them. The case reveals three types of these strategies. First, the Keyes, Oklahoma, episode provides an example of the legitimation of corporate agendas through the exploitation of local economic problems to silence opposition. In this case, Seaboard intervened with a donation to the public school district and with other commercial concessions, which were described as "good-faith efforts" to restore community well-being. In return, the company secured the community's commitment not to oppose corporate plans. More important, through a relatively small donation Seaboard was able to force community residents to renounce their basic rights of free speech and freedom of dissent. Several other events in the case show how TNCs and their supporters used economic development issues to counter opposition. They stressed that environmental legislation in Texas was burdensome for economic development and that in order to bring "new life" to the declining local economy and to "preserve a way of life," it was of paramount importance to reform this legislation. Similarly, the CAFO TNCs argued that failure to do so would only hasten job decline and diminish the rapidly shrinking tax base further.

Second, TNCs fought off opposition by presenting themselves as responsible stewards of the environment. They argued that their operations conformed to existing rules and regulations that protected both the environment and the people who lived near the hog facilities. Furthermore, they supported the argument that modern technology enabled them to raise hogs in ways that did not "harm the environment" or produce an unacceptable level of odor. And they stressed their willingness to address environmental contamination in the event that it should occur.

The third type of strategy was to downplay the legitimacy of the court ruling against CAFOs. The companies depicted the court's rejection of the new permit rules as based on a legal technicality rather than on real environmental shortcomings. Industry representatives argued that the new regulations were more stringent than ever before and also did away with frivolous complaints. Similarly, the proposal to change the public hearing rule in the CAFO permit process was based on the argument that pollution claims against CAFOs pertained to environmental issues and not to pertinent technical factors. On this basis they argued that hearings became unnecessary and that citations against CAFOs could be carried out only on grounds of technical merit.

Challenging the Globalization Project

While the hog TNCs and their supporters were successful in keeping Texas "open for business," anti-CAFO activists were also successful in halting the expansion of the industry in surrounding states. Similarly, while the state of Texas aligned with the CAFOs and secured Texas as the "next frontier" for hog TNCs, surrounding states tightened their corporate farming laws to limit CAFO development and counter global sourcing strategies. Citizens of Great Bend, Kansas, Seaboard's first choice for its second hog pyramid, voted out the city councilors who supported Seaboard and then denied Seaboard access to the city's water treatment. Counties all across Kansas voted in new zoning regulations to limit hog expansion. Sponsors of the hog moratorium in Oklahoma stated that they were "trying to do what's responsible for Oklahoma." The Oklahoma Family Farm Alliance representative urged the citizens of Dumas, Texas, to stand strong against Seaboard because it was desperate to locate its second hog pyramid there now that it had been "rebuffed by Kansas, slapped by Oklahoma, banned in Nebraska, cold-shouldered in Missouri and Colorado." Even though ACCORD failed in the long run in Texas, groups like the Oklahoma Family Farm Alliance, Citizens Opposing Seaboard in St. Joseph, Missouri, and Concerned Citizens of Doniphan County, Kansas, mobilized to resist what they saw as an illegitimate form of economic development.

Two points can be made here. The first concerns the different results of resistance in the Midwest and Texas. We contend that, while specific local issues motivated these state-based outcomes, the presence of a "populist" ideology made resistance in the Midwest different from resistance in Texas. The story presented in this chapter clearly indicates that the opposition that developed in St. Joseph, Missouri, was qualitatively different from that which emerged in other midwestern states. In St. Joseph, anti-CAFO sentiments were driven by xenophobic fears linked to concerns about the job market. Local leaders and residents feared that the influx of immigrants to the area would negatively affect already unstable socioeconomic conditions. This conservative "tribal" posture was not a significant factor in the other midwestern states. Here, opposition rested on negative views about big corporations and anti-elite sentiment. Both views are typical of populist ideologies (Brass 2000; Conovan 1981). As far as opposition to large corporations is concerned, the difference between the Midwest and Texas rests primarily on the fact that in Texas it was confined to militantly anti-CAFO organizations, while in the Midwest it received broader popular support. Local elections were affected by the belief that these large CAFO corporations were attempting to locate in these areas only to take advantage of local resources, with little consideration for the needs and wishes of local residents (Hatfield 2001). Similarly, voters opposed the support of local political elites for corporate expansion plans, a dynamic that was not in play in Texas. In Texas, leaders who supported the expansion of CAFOS have retained their political clout and enjoyed continuing electoral success (Storm 2002f).

The second point is that all these events lend support to the "contradictory dimensions of globalization" thesis. Although TNCs do exhibit significant powers in support of their accumulation strategies, there are opportunities for resistance. TNCs can exert substantial influence on the state apparatus to support their agendas, but the state can also be enlisted by subordinate groups to counter corporate actions. The expansion of the CAFO-based hog industry in the Texas Panhandle region is a good illustration of how corporate interests can use the state to limit citizens' access to democratic decision making. The elimination of the public hearing process regarding CAFO permits is a classic example. But the case also shows that citizens in other locales successfully mobilized and challenged the power of the TNCs. This story of globalization demonstrates that the globalization of economy and society is a contested terrain in which the accumulation strategies of global corporations meet organized resistance from social movement groups.

7

OLD AND NEW SOCIAL MOVEMENTS IN THE GLOBAL ERA:
THE CASE OF MAXXAM AND THE HEADWATERS FOREST REDWOODS

We made the point in the Introduction that the instruments and strategies of resistance are different under globalization from those employed under Fordism. Fordism recognized and codified forms of resistance by acknowledging the social importance of labor movements and their strategies of struggle. These actors and their forms of resistance had a major impact on the laws governing the democratic countries of the world. Indeed, labor unions and their right to protest poor pay and working conditions were often identified with democracy and freedom (Habermas 2002; Harvey 1989). Under high Fordism, the power of labor movements was a condition of the "capital-labor accord" and earned these movements a seat at the negotiation table with the interests of capital. Their power was also one of the sources of Fordism's "rigidities" and one of the targets of attack for the powers that promoted globalization (Antonio and Bonanno 1996; Boggs 2000; Goldfield 1987; Harvey 2005 and 1989; Lipietz 1992; Regini 1992; Western 1995). At the outset of the twenty-first century, global economic restructuring, and its attendant neoliberal political change, greatly reduced labor's political strength and sociocultural influence. Critics and supporters alike now consider the labor movement unable to effectively oppose global corporate expansion and political dominance (e.g., Bauman 1998; Beck 1997; Goldfield 1987; Nissen 2002).

Many observers believe that new social movements have begun to fill the void left by the demise of labor unions (Axford 1995; Beck 1995; Faber 1998b; Melucci 1996; Offe 1987). The environmental movement in particular has been identified as a source of renewed hope for the possibility of new, more equitable and sustainable social relations (Bellamy Foster 1993; Buttel 1996 and 1994; Gordon 1998). The environmental movement's challenges to traditional projects of socioeconomic development, modernization theories, modern science and technology, and its support for local groups, local knowledge, and diversity, have increased social and cultural sensitivity to a range of issues. Through its emphasis on individual emancipation, quality of life, and identity, the environmental movement has created a fresh version of radical democracy that decisively breaks with traditional interest group politics (e.g., Beck 1997 and 1995; Buttel 1994; Dreiling 1998; Melucci 1996; Obach 1999; Schnaiberg 1980).

In the stories of globalization illustrated in the preceding two chapters, global capital expansion was met with opposition from below. While environmental concerns played a significant role in both cases, the opposition was local and the strategies regional. This chapter looks at broader forms of anti-globalization that involve organized movements. In particular, it explores the question of whether resistance to global corporate clout is possible through an alliance between the labor and environmental movements. In some instances—as in the case of the tuna-dolphin controversy—the relationship between these two movements varies from ambiguous to adversarial. In others, labor organizations are conspicuously absent. It is instructive, therefore, to explore a case of global capitalism in which the relationship between the labor and environmental movements occupies center stage. Despite their different trajectories, labor and environmentalism are two of the most powerful movements in the world; united, they have the potential to become a strong progressive alliance in the corporate-dominated global system (Boggs 1986; Dreiling 1998; Nissen 2002; Siegmann 1986). Or, as Brian Obach has written, "the dynamics of alignment or conflict between these movements present a theoretically interesting and practically important case of examination. . . . The practical importance lies in the fact that organized labor and the environmental movement represent two of the most powerful social movement sectors in the United States. Their collaboration or conflict is of great significance to the general direction of social and political change, and a united labor-environmental alliance could present a strong force in favor of a just and ecologically sustainable economy" (1999, 46). Carl Boggs echoes this position, arguing that "the key to any future social transformation . . . depends upon the extent to which a sustained connection between new social movements and working-class struggles—between community and workplace, universal goals and specific material demands—can be theoretically and politically established" (1986, 20).

This chapter examines the case of the Headwaters Forest, an old-growth redwood forest in northern California that comprises a unique and fragile ecosystem. Owned by a large corporation, Maxxam, Headwaters Forest has been the subject of intensive logging by one of Maxxam's subsidiaries, Pacific Lumber. Pressured by mounting protest from environmental groups, local and federal authorities intervened to force Maxxam to halt its exploitation of the forest. Originally the proposal called for the cancellation of Maxxam's debts, incurred as a result of its involvement in the 1980s bankruptcy of a Texas savings and loan company (s&l), in return for the corporation's forfeiting its Headwaters property. The agreement that emerged after a lengthy dispute, however, was significantly different. It contemplated the direct purchase of the land by state and federal agencies, while Maxxam would be allowed to continue the exploitation of timber resources, albeit at a reduced rate. This agreement angered environmentalists and loggers alike, but it was well received by Maxxam and celebrated by state and federal authorities as a victory for environmentalism.

Our choice of this case was motivated primarily by the fact that the timber industry has been one of the most difficult arenas for the development of an alliance between environmentalists and labor. This industry has historically been the target of strong environmental protests, to which timber companies have responded by threatening to fire workers who refused to oppose environmentalists' goals. A common result has been conflict between labor and environmentalists in the form of accusations, distrust, and often overt violence (Bevington 1998; Dumont 1996; Faber 1998a; Levenstein and Wooding 1998; Ramos 1995; Wayburn 1978).

Logging and Saving the Forest

Logging has been one of the primary economic activities in the Pacific Northwest for more than a century. Indeed, Pacific Lumber has been in operation in northern California since 1869, and since the 1930s has owned approximately two hundred thousand acres of land there. Under the control of the Murphy family from 1930 to 1986, Pacific Lumber was a model of responsible timber production. The company "engaged in long-term, sustainable, community-oriented logging. The volume of trees cut never exceeded the volume grown. This insured future jobs, and avoided the boom-and-bust cycles endured by the rest of the lumber industry" (Miller 1998). In 1986 Maxxam, a Houston-based corporation, bought out Pacific Lumber and set the company on a new path.

Maxxam is owned by Charles Hurwitz, a Houston businessman, who in

1985 also controlled United Savings Association of Texas (USAT). He purchased USAT in 1982 with a "handful of trusted friends" and then used this S&L to finance more than $700 million in junk bonds, which he used to purchase Pacific Lumber. In order to pay off the junk bond debt, Maxxam proceeded to more than double Pacific Lumber's logging of virgin old-growth redwood stands, severely endangering the unique and fragile ecosystem of Headwaters Forest (World Stewardship Institute 1997). In the process, local communities like Scotia, California, became sites of unprecedented social struggle (Gumbel 1998; Mendes 1989).

Workers' Opposition to Maxxam

While some employees heralded the increased economic activity that would be brought by Maxxam/Pacific Lumber, others raised serious doubts from the beginning. Although Pacific Lumber was never unionized, workers spoke out against what they deemed an undesirable situation. Shortly after Maxxam's takeover of Pacific Lumber, more than three hundred employees signed a petition protesting the effects they anticipated increased logging would have on the stability of their community. On November 17, 1985, the *Eureka Times Standard* ran an ad accompanying the signed petition in which employees expressed doubt that "a company of real estate investors from the east coast [sic] can manage resources such as ours with the consideration that has been shown all these years by the Murphy Family" (Fritz 1985). The petition was part of a failed attempt to purchase the company from Maxxam through a formal employee stock-option plan (Bari 1989).

Pacific Lumber employees saw Maxxam as just another large outside corporation looking to make a fast buck. For decades large timber companies had moved into the area, taken what they could from the forest, and left. According to Dave Chism, a longtime employee of the timber industry, these companies had "had their way for one hundred years. They've cut. They've run. A worker is no more than a piece of equipment to them and when they don't have anything more for them to do, just get rid of them. Timber operations such as Maxxam's Pacific Lumber provoked fears of economic hardship for local communities. Clear-cutting not only quickens the pace at which the forest disappears, it is one of the least labor-intensive methods of logging. "We're basically becoming aware that we are going to be a very small, probably highly automated workforce here," said Chism. "The vast amount of profit won't be dumped back into the community. There will be very few people; it won't be very labor intensive at all" (Chism and Cramer 1997). The end result would be less money in the community, along with growing unemployment and environmental degradation. As uneasiness among employees spread, opposition from regional environmental organizations grew as well.

The Environmentalists' Struggle

In 1987 environmental activists in the northern California communities of Garberville, Carlotta, Redway, Arcata, and Loleta took notice of the rapidly increasing logging traffic and began hiking into hidden groves of redwoods and giving each section a name (Kay 1995; Earth First! 1997). Enraged by what they saw as the looting of a thousand-year-old forest for the purpose of meeting monthly interest payments, activists began to challenge Maxxam's claim to legitimate business practices, contesting them in the courts and resisting them in the forest.

The Environmental Protection Information Center (EPIC), in conjunction with Earth First! and other local and national groups, filed the first lawsuit against Maxxam in May 1987. Its aim was to stop Pacific Lumber from logging under what the plaintiffs called illegitimate timber harvest plans (THPS). A Humboldt County judge ruled that "the California Department of Forestry had not only rubber-stamped the THPS, but had intimidated the Department of Fish and Game and the Regional Water Quality Control Board staff from making any comments critical of THPS" (EPIC 1998).

In response to another EPIC lawsuit, filed in September 1992, a Humboldt County judge granted a fifteen-day restraining order on a 237-acre THP in a section of Headwaters known as Owl Creek. While still negotiating the lawsuit with state officials and the U.S. Fish and Wildlife Service, Pacific Lumber sent loggers into Owl Creek on Thanksgiving weekend while the courts were closed (Skow 1994).

This episode confirmed to Earth First! and other environmental groups participating in the struggle that Maxxam's Pacific Lumber had little respect for the court's actions and, simultaneously, that despite their rhetoric local authorities had little interest in environmental protection. Consequently, they decided to supplement their legal actions with a civil disobedience campaign in the hope of forcing Maxxam to cease its dangerous industrial strategies. Their civil disobedience on and near Pacific Lumber property outside Scotia had some success, but their disruption of logging activities was felt primarily by workers. "A blow against PL," a local logger said, "is a blow against our own livelihood" (Miller 1998). Another observer added that "if a road blockade by Earth First! prevents a logger from working more than 30 hours in a week, then 30 hour pay is all the logger gets" (Gumbel 1998). It became obvious to both environmentalists and labor leaders that without careful planning, the negative economic impact on loggers, and the cultural differences between loggers and environmental activists, could turn a potential anticorporate alliance into a divisive feud that could only help Maxxam (Bevington 1998; Hill 2000; Dumont 1996; Satterfield 1996).

While some important differences between loggers and environmentalists remained, it was clear to most of them that Maxxam was encouraging the internal conflict. Some local residents acknowledged that local law enforcement had historically intimidated outside forces on behalf of the timber industry (Chism and Cramer 1997), and at least part of the bad blood between loggers and environmentalists stemmed from police involvement at protests. At the request of Pacific Lumber, the Humboldt County Sheriff's Department had provided crowd control for most of the protests, and the result, all too often, was increased agitation. Beginning with Redwood Summer,[1] confrontations between environmentalists and law enforcement worsened, peaking in 1996 with the arrest of a thousand people at an Earth First! protest (Weinberg 1997).

Local law enforcement used force against environmentalists again in late 1996, when Humboldt County sheriff deputies used pepper spray on nonviolent protestors on two occasions. The incidents took place on September 25 at Pacific Lumber's Scotia headquarters and on October 16 at the Eureka offices of Republican representative Frank Riggs (Weinberg 1997). In both cases the protestors walked in peacefully, locked themselves together, and refused to leave the property. While the popular press condemned the use of pepper spray in these incidents, Representative Riggs himself was quoted as saying, "I think under the circumstances, this was probably an appropriate use of force, as opposed to the laying on of hands or some other technique" (Reed 1997).

Debt for Nature

As workers' and environmentalists' protest mounted, federal and state government officials displayed an unusually sensitive attitude toward saving the

---

1. This was a protest in 1996 organized by various environmental organizations that called for the continuous presence of demonstrators in the region and their engagement in a number of protests against Pacific Lumber.

Headwaters Forest. In particular, members of the Clinton administration and California state legislators supported a grassroots proposal known as the "debt-for-nature" swap. Many people held Maxxam responsible for the 1988 collapse of the USAT. And many thought the corporation should swap enough of its Pacific Lumber holdings to pay back the public for bailing out the S&L. Charles Hurwitz, CEO of Maxxam and then de facto controller of USAT, used the S&L to "free up its federally insured deposits to fund Maxxam's hostile takeover of Pacific Lumber" (Seidenstein 1996).[2]

The first group to urge the FDIC to take action against Maxxam was Earth First! It proposed that 57,000 to 76,000 acres of Pacific Lumber's redwoods be accepted as payment for some of the $1.6 billion it cost to bail out USAT (Seidenstein 1996). The forest saved through the swap would have been placed in public hands for long-term protection. After Earth First! made its proposal, other groups (Greenpeace, the Sierra Club, the Legal Defense Fund, the Environmental Protection Information Center, and several other smaller organizations) joined in. The environmentalists' point was clear: why should the taxpayers pay Maxxam for the forest when the corporation already owed the public for S&L debt? As Earth First! member Naomi Wagner put it, "why should he [Maxxam's CEO Charles Hurwitz] get one more penny, let alone one more tree . . . why is the government rewarding and encouraging such sociopathic greed?" (Wagner 1997).

Along with environmentalists, labor groups also supported the debt-for-nature swap. Members of the California Department of Forestry Firefighters IAFF Local 2881 were extremely vocal about what they saw as "an egregious offense against one of California's most unique natural resources." In addition to actively supporting the debt-for-nature proposal, Local 2881 urged other local unions holding Maxxam stock to divest. One group to do just that was the California State Teachers Retirement System, which sold its Maxxam stock in late summer of 1997. Approximately twenty local labor groups pressured the California Public Employees Retirement System, a major Maxxam shareholder, to use its power to force the company into a debt-for-nature swap (Allshouse 1997).

In late October 1997 two Western Council of Industrial Workers (WCIW) locals in California passed resolutions against Maxxam. According to the *Union Register,* Local 3074 in Chester and Local 2749 in Camino decided that "union pension funds should not continue to support a company that is so

---

2. Maxxam did not use the assets of USAT directly for the purchase of Pacific Lumber, but it encouraged the notorious Drexel Burnham Lambert, Inc., to provide financing in exchange for USAT's purchase of high-risk junk bonds (World Stewardship Institute 1997, 1).

disastrous to workers." Their resolutions called for "the FDIC to enter into discussions with the company to transfer ownership of certain old growth forests to the federal government to satisfy the debt related to the failed savings and loan" (*Portland* [Oregon] *Union Register* 1997).

In February 1999 the United Steelworkers of America (USWA) joined the opposition to Maxxam's business operations. Environmentalists and steelworkers gathered in Houston, Texas, to protest the company's labor and logging practices. The steelworkers were employees of Kaiser Aluminum (owned by Maxxam) who were on strike after negotiations between management and union workers had failed to produce a new contract. In a personal communication, Bill Harman, a USWA representative, said that Maxxam had undermined union power through, among other things, "outsourcing for Kaiser jobs and cutting seniority privileges" (Harman 1999). Harman indicated that the union was very interested in strengthening its cooperation with the environmentalists. Echoing other labor voices, the USWA joined in supporting a suit against Maxxam for its involvement in the collapse of USAT (Nissimov 1999).

The Federal and State Governments Challenge Maxxam

In August 1995 the FDIC had filed suit against Maxxam in U.S. district court in Houston seeking $250 million in restitution for USAT's failure. The suit alleged: "By keeping USAT open and free from regulatory intervention, Hurwitz was able to continue reciprocal business arrangements with Drexel to forestall regulatory intervention. Hurwitz and his colleagues covered up the true state of the Association by a pattern of deceptive financial reporting and balance sheet manipulation" (World Stewardship Institute 1997).

Almost four months later the Office of Thrift Supervision (OTS) increased pressure on Maxxam for a debt-for-nature swap by filing a suit similar to, but separate from, the FDIC suit. The OTS charged that Maxxam had turned a traditional home mortgage lender into a "vehicle for speculative, highly leveraged, high risk investments" (Seidenstein 1996), thereby facilitating the S&L's collapse.

Maxxam responded to the FDIC and OTS lawsuits with its own counterclaims. The corporation denied the charges brought by both agencies, maintaining that "Maxxam controlled less than a quarter of the S&L's parent, United Financial Group, and is not responsible for the decisions that ultimately brought down the S&L" (Kay 1995). Maxxam also counteracted by using Pacific Lumber, backed by the California timber industry, to lobby Congress to pass the pro-logging, pro-jobs Headwaters Forest Act, HR 2866 (Kay 1995).

FDIC official Ricki Tigert-Helfer conceded early on that "the [FDIC] lawsuit cannot compel Maxxam, Pacific Lumber, or their boards of directors to consider a debt for nature swap since they might decide to use other assets to satisfy their liability" (Seidenstein 1996). The FDIC also ran into considerable problems over its actions surrounding the lawsuit. An internal FDIC document made public in 1998 showed that the lawsuit was filed "despite their own assessment that it was highly unlikely the agency could win the case." The document also revealed that FDIC officials had targeted people close to Maxxam and had "attempted to hide the fact that it was secretly financing another agency's investigation and prosecution of Hurwitz." Maxxam's lawyer claimed that the FDIC had succumbed to pressure from the White House, Congress, and environmentalists to pursue the lawsuit despite the lack of evidence. Exploiting widespread sentiment against government intervention, Maxxam's ultimate position was that "the Headwaters Forest will not be traded for a debt that does not exist, nor will it be a pawn in any abuse of governmental power" (Sablatura 1998).

As the FDIC suit stalled in the face of corporate resistance, the OTS continued to pursue its case. In March 1999 an official of the J. Paul Getty Trust stepped forward to pay $1 million to settle charges associated with the 1988 failure of USAT (Pulliam 1997). Although Maxxam was associated with the Getty official, the company was not part of the agreement to settle, and federal regulators therefore continued to pursue charges. After a year of fancy maneuvering, however, it became clear that Maxxam's legal team had been able to defeat the federal government's debt-for-nature swap.

Given the political visibility of the issue, the admitted pro-environmental stance of influential members of the Clinton administration and the California political establishment, and, most important, general public support, federal and state officials next pursued an alternative strategy. Significantly, though, in doing so, these officials abandoned their original position that Maxxam ought to surrender the land in reparation for past unethical actions. They agreed on Maxxam's basic argument: that the Headwaters Forest was this corporation's exclusive property and that therefore alterations to current land use should be pursued in a market-based (i.e., commodified) framework. Accordingly, federal and state officials initiated actions to purchase the Headwaters Forest with public money.

Who Will Save the Redwoods?

Support for the purchase of the Headwaters Forest was not unanimous among members of Congress and the California political establishment—nor, more significantly, did environmentalists and labor agree that this was the best course. The environmentalist-labor coalition proposed two alternatives to what they saw as paying Maxxam for its questionable business practices. Prominent environmental activist Judi Bari was put in charge of a congressional committee to write a worker's clause for the Headwaters acquisition bill. Bari "convened a group of displaced and currently employed loggers and millworkers from Maxxam, Simpson [a local timber company] and PL [Pacific Lumber], who met with a small group of hand-picked Earth First!ers." Loggers and environmentalists assisted in developing a proposal based on the argument that "the employees of Pacific Lumber are not responsible for the crimes of Maxxam, and they should not have to bear the brunt of them. Displaced workers are entitled to a severance package that gives them an opportunity for equivalent pay to those lost through the creation of the Headwaters Forest Redwood Complex. This plan calls for providing those jobs in restoration work, as part of a forest rehabilitation plan for the devastated lands surrounding the Headwaters Forest ancient groves" (Bari 1995).

The proposal addressed the number of jobs to be created, a voluntary option plan for employees (which included a severance package for displaced workers who wished to opt out of the timber job market), and planning for land management. A total of forty-four thousand acres would be protected under Bari's proposal, including six fragmented groves of old-growth forest connected by damaged cutover lands. Five thousand acres would remain undisturbed, but thirty-nine thousand acres would be rehabilitated, "and providing for stream protection, wildlife corridors, and other ecological considerations, the cutover lands could be gradually brought back into saw log production" (Bari 1995).

The second proposal was called the Headwaters Forest Stewardship Plan and was sponsored by the Trees Foundation. The issues of jobs and community stability were at the core of this proposal as well. "The Headwaters Forest Stewardship Plan is a vision for the permanent protection of the Headwaters Forest and the workers who depend on it for their livelihood," read the Trees Foundation proposal. "This ecologically-based forest land management plan emphasized the principles of conservation biology, ecosystem restoration, and responsible forestry. The primary objective of the Headwaters Forest Stewardship Plan (HFSP) was to maintain and/or restore the levels of biodiversity at Headwaters, while providing stable, honorable employment" (Trees Foundation 1997).

Unlike the Bari plan, the HFSP attempted to avoid the issues of property ownership or acquisition. According to the proposal, "Headwaters Forest could theoretically be owned by Pacific Lumber, or a community-based not-for-profit corporation, and be managed according to the conservation biology principles and forestry prescriptions presented within the Stewardship Plan." Under the HFSP, approximately sixty thousand acres would be preserved. Six different types of areas would be designed for management, according to the condition and restoration needs of those areas. The HFSP also planned for the return of pre-Maxxam production levels, which historically had been perceived as conducive to forest and community health. Loggers and environmentalists would both have a hand in the proposal; "the stewardship model asks that a broad cross-section of the community become independent and responsible resource managers, discussing long-range goals and plans" (Trees Foundation 1997).

While both of these plans were realistic proposals to save the Headwaters Forest and maintain stable communities, neither was backed by the federal government in its negotiations with Maxxam. Instead the "deal" the government made with Maxxam, as it came to be known, was the result of the company's political and economic clout rather than a response to community pressure.

The "Deal" to Save Headwaters

Representative Dan Hamburg introduced the Headwaters Forest Act, HR 2866, in the House of Representatives in 1994 (Bari 1995). The House version, which would save forty-four thousand acres in exchange for other publicly owned timber reserves, "authorized the US Forest Service to begin negotiating with Pacific Lumber and other landowners of Headwaters to attach the forest to the Six Rivers National Forest" (Seidenstein 1996). Environmentalists felt that the segment of the forest to be protected was too small and that Maxxam's unethical actions should be grounds for stripping it of the land without the use of any public funds. An editorial in the *Coastal Post* (1996) echoed the sentiments of a majority of environmentalists and workers: "The federal deal to save the Headwaters Grove is a step in the right direction, but it's not enough. Actions to save this forest won't end until all six groves and buffer zones, totaling 60,000 acres, have been protected, and

Charles Hurwitz is prosecuted for his part in the Savings and Loan scandal of the 1980's."

The bill passed the House but stalled in the Senate, where it became mired in a debate over what became known as the Riggs rider (introduced by Representative Frank Riggs). The rider exempted Pacific Lumber from the provisions of the Endangered Species Act, allowed it to "log forever in its forests, including other old growth redwood stands," and granted it "unused government land" (Kay 1995). More than a dozen environmental organizations, including the Sierra Club, EPIC, and Earth First! opposed the bill, calling it "a slick move to hold the Headwaters Forest hostage in an attempt to open logging old growth on public lands" (ibid.). Faced with such strong opposition, the rider was not passed. Acting on behalf of the timber industry, Riggs tried again by introducing a bill that would have opened Headwaters to logging if negotiations between the Forest Service and landowners fell through within an eighteen-month period (Seidenstein 1996). This bill also encountered strong opposition and was defeated in the House. The initial debates over HR 2866 set the tone for what would become a lengthy negotiation. Maxxam's control of key segments of the political establishment was contested by the unity and mobilization of environmentalists and labor.

In late 1996 federal and state negotiators began to offer Hurwitz various surplus assets in exchange for Headwaters. The federal government's portion of the plan was $250 million in cash, while California state officials offered Maxxam $130 million in property. Included were California's Central Valley oil and gas fields, San Francisco's Transbay Terminal, and more than twenty thousand acres of timberland. Maxxam rejected the offer, insisting that California's part of the exchange, $130 million, be paid in cash (Barnum 1997; Kay 1997).

By 1997 the proposed deal involved paying Maxxam $380 million in exchange for seventy-five hundred acres of the Headwaters Forest. Additionally, all parties had to agree upon a habitat conservation plan (HCP) (a long-term blueprint for protecting endangered species on private property) submitted by Pacific Lumber to manage the remaining twenty thousand acres of Pacific Lumber–owned forest surrounding the Headwaters grove. As long as the landowner sets aside property and manages land to protect endangered species, the HCP provides an exemption from the Endangered Species Act. An HCP had been drafted by late 1997, but the issue proved to be extremely divisive.

Douglas Wheeler, California's resource secretary, hailed the plan as an unprecedented effort toward forest conservation that would stand up to public scrutiny. Before the plan was made public, however, environmental groups expressed serious doubt about Pacific Lumber's ability to "protect" the forest. Among their concerns were Pacific Lumber's intention to log four other stands of ancient redwoods not included in the deal and the inability of an HCP to adequately protect endangered species (Barnum 1997). The Environmental Protection Information Center called the HCP a "license to kill" and charged Maxxam with "taking advantage of the government's fear of addressing the issue of private property and public trust issues" (Frost 1998). The Sierra Club also took issue with the HCP, claiming that "the enforcement record of the state and federal agencies ranges from incompetent to complicity." Echoing other environmental organizations, the Sierra Club argued that HCPS "serve to immunize loggers, miners, and the like against the Endangered Species Act" (Skow 1998).

By September 1998 Governor Pete Wilson had signed a bill that would secure California's portion of the money needed to go forward with the deal. While the controversy over the HCP still raged, Wilson and Senator Diane Feinstein heralded the action as a step toward victory. Save the Redwoods League (the only environmental organization present at the signing ceremony) also praised the bill, holding that "the only way to save the trees is to buy them" (Clifford 1999).

With the money for the purchase guaranteed, the final draft of the agreement hinged on the review of a combined federal environmental impact statement and state environmental impact report, which represented a large-scale assessment of the environmental impact of the proposed HCP. According to Mike Spear, California/Nevada operations manager for the U.S. Fish and Wildlife Service, these studies were carried out in conjunction with Pacific Lumber to ensure the protection of the ancient forest (Industry Group 99 1998). Copies of these documents were made available over the Internet for public comment from October 2 to November 16, 1998. The Fish and Wildlife Service and the California Environmental Resources Evaluation System also held four hearings to provide the public an opportunity to comment on the proposal.

Five days before the November 16 deadline for public comment, California state forestry officials suspended Pacific Lumber's license to log. The suspension was the result of more than a hundred citations, over the course of two years, for "willful violations of state forestry regulations and gross negligence" (Morain and Vanzi 1998). Pacific Lumber's logging license had also been suspended in 1997, but California state forestry officials had issued the company a provisional license. The California Department of Forestry, which had issued citations against Pacific Lumber, allowed the company to continue logging on a conditional basis (AP Online 1998a). These developments only served to strengthen claims made by opponents of the "deal." Meanwhile, state and federal negotiators continued to work with Maxxam on drafting a final agreement as the battle over the fate of the forest intensified.

In January 1999 the federal government broke with precedent and took control of drafting the controversial habitat conservation plan that lay at the heart of the Headwaters deal. Normally the timber company is responsible for drafting the HCP, which is then submitted to government agencies for approval. In an attempt to expedite the process, however, Pacific Lumber agreed to place the HCP in the hands of the National Marine Fisheries Service, the Fish and Wildlife Service, and other federal agencies authorized to sign off on the deal (Howard 1999). According to the new arrangements, Pacific Lumber was to have the opportunity to decide whether the government's plan was acceptable. On March 2, 1999, a little more than a month later, the Headwaters agreement was signed, and the Headwaters Forest officially became public property.

We Saved the Forest!

When the Headwaters Forest Act was introduced in Congress in 1994, it proposed to shield forty-four thousand acres of ancient redwoods. Under the final agreement, the federal government and the state of California purchased the seventy-five-thousand-acre Headwaters Forest for $480 million. In addition, the official habitat conservation plan proposed to protect twelve smaller groves of ancient redwoods comprising eight thousand acres. The plan also identified the Bureau of Land Management, a bureau within the Department of the Interior, and the state of California as co-managers of the Headwaters Forest. Those who had drafted the deal celebrated the long-awaited occasion, while those who opposed it responded with anger and anxiety.

Senator Diane Feinstein, who played a key role throughout the negotiations, rejoiced that "we could preserve this priceless resource through an environmentally and economically sound plan" (Capitol Hill Press 1999). President Clinton echoed her remarks, proclaiming that "this ancient forest, and the web of life it sustains, are now saved for all times." Secretary of the Interior Bruce Babbitt called the agreement "a wonderful gift to the people of this nation and to future generations." Babbitt especially praised the HCP, which he said was "good for everybody," adding that "it allows the company to meet its economic goals, and it will protect the species we need to protect under the Endangered Species Act" (US Newswire 1999b).

Pacific Lumber representatives also praised the deal. John Campbell, president of Pacific Lumber, proclaimed, "we were able to preserve the Headwaters and at the same time give the company the stability it needs to remain a vital part of the North Coast economy" (Clifford 1999). As part of a small group of environmental organizations that supported the deal, both the Wilderness Society and the office of California's secretary of resources also approved of the final draft of the Headwaters agreement.

The critics also had plenty to say about the government buyout of Headwaters Forest. In addition to their long-standing distrust of the HCP and their frustration over what they saw as an inadequate amount of acreage preserved, many environmentalists expressed scorn for Maxxam's last-minute maneuver. Eight days before the deal was signed, Maxxam had rejected the government's offer, claiming that it would not enable the company to harvest enough timber to remain economically profitable. Caving in to Maxxam, federal officials sent two letters to the corporation explaining that the original timber production estimates done by the California Department of Forestry were low. Maxxam was also assured that other areas initially off limits would be subject to change after further analysis (Clifford 1999).

These developments further frustrated environmentalists and labor. Both the Sierra Club and EPIC raised concerns over loopholes they felt were built into the plan. EPIC even vowed to use legal means to challenge these loopholes if necessary (ibid.). One month after the deal was finalized, the United Steelworkers of America joined the opposition to the agreement. The USWA filed a lawsuit against the California Department of Forestry and Fire Protection for its approval of a portion of the agreement that covered Pacific Lumber's future sustainable timber production. The union felt that the plan "authorizes unsustainably high harvests of old growth timber and fails to consider the long-range economic impacts of these unsustainably high harvests" (PR Newswire 1999).

In an attempt to elucidate the "critical" importance of the issue for both labor and environmentalists, but also to demonstrate the "existence of a common consciousness" between labor and the environmental movement, Don Kegley of the USWA said, "Forests are the source of our building materials, our paper, our furniture, our firewood—they are also our source of water, our fish, our climactic stability, and our clean air. Without the forest, our culture will crumble and worse, our planet will die. And there are no jobs on a dead planet" (PR Newswire 1998).

The Final Act

In early 2007 Pacific Lumber filed for bankruptcy, explaining that California's regional water boards had imposed too many restrictions on its logging operations. Regional water boards were not originally included in the Headwaters agreement, but they claimed that they could impose new requirements on Pacific Lumber in the event that its actions did additional damage to the environment. Regional water boards maintained that Pacific Lumber logging was still polluting streams and rivers in Humboldt County. Pacific Lumber reacted by filing for bankruptcy and later by initiating the sale of its operations. The company claimed that the water board restrictions significantly reduced its profitability and created an unfavorable business climate. An editorial in the *Houston Chronicle* commented that while "Hurwitz has been right . . . [one] can be right and still lose," the implication being that the environmental movement had gone too far with its demands and had finally, in effect, driven Maxxam out of business. It also contended that with Pacific Lumber's departure, other companies would be reluctant to conduct business in the area. Any timber company that was as environmentally friendly as the critics wanted would never be able to make a profit, the newspaper contended. The environmentalists had hounded Pacific Lumber—and by implication any other logging operation—out of the region, and were thus responsible for hurting the area's workers. Environmentalists, for their part, maintained consistently that Pacific Lumber had never been seriously interested in the substance of the Headwaters agreement and that its primary objective had always been the economic exploitation of the forest, without regard for the ecological costs. The epilogue to the case seems to have proved them right.

Analysis and Discussion

The events of this case cast serious doubt on the argument that a progressive alliance between labor and the environmental movement is almost impossible. Both radical and moderate segments of the environmental movement and of labor unions united in opposing the deal that ended the Headwaters

Forest dispute. This opposition was grounded on these two movements' common concerns about the importance of preserving the forest, their condemnation of the limited scope of the accord, and their agreement about the significant advantages Maxxam reaped from the deal.

Environmentalists and loggers managed to work together for a common goal in spite of their cultural differences—and despite a slowdown in the timber industry that might have been expected to thwart their alliance. Even so, Maxxam was able to exploit friction between the two camps with some success, lending credence to the view that a lasting partnership between labor and environmental activists will be difficult to achieve, and that powerful corporations will always attempt to divide and conquer social movements that threaten their profits. This conclusion supports the "contradictory dimension of globalization" thesis.

Grassroots militants like Judi Bari and union organizers established a dialogue between loggers and environmentalists that fostered a common understanding and shared purpose. The alliance was based on an opposition to the "commodification of nature" that both sides shared and that helped unify them by reminding them of their common anticorporate roots. In their opposition to the "deal," large segments of labor and the environmental movement rejected the idea that environment can or should be protected by market mechanisms (commodification). While the government, at both the national and the state level, opted in effect to pay Maxxam off, labor and environmentalists pursued a more ethical approach.

The labor-environmental coalition took the position that Maxxam was ethically responsible for the injuries created by its reckless exploitation of nature. Both labor and environmental activists could agree that Maxxam's unscrupulous pursuit of profit had hurt the public good. Why should such a company be effectively rewarded with a buyout funded by taxpayer dollars? This anticorporate stance was grounded in the shared understanding that sustainable economic development and a sustainable ecosystem must go hand in hand. Unlike cases in which workers defend the interests of their corporate employers out of fear of losing their jobs, the loggers in this case recognized the long-term damage that Maxxam's industrial policy had done, and would continue to do, to their economic well-being and job security.

Despite some internal dissent, this shared point of view extended not only to the leadership of the two movements but also to their rank-and-file members. This was a departure from the norm in the logging industry, where labor-environmental alliances have traditionally been difficult and often limited to leaders (Dumont 1996; Gray 1998; Wayburn 1978). The broad support of an anticorporate posture in this case supports those who argue that the success of such an alliance depends on the participation of the rank and file.

Nevertheless, the labor-environmentalist alliance forged in the Headwaters Forest case was only partially successful. The shared goals of enhancing protection of the forest, achieving economic and ecological sustainability, and stopping Maxxam's destructive policies were less than fully realized. This is in part a consequence of the divisions and differences within and between the two movements, but it is also of the result of Maxxam's power and the absence of a correspondingly powerful environmental ethic among the general public. Maxxam not only gained economically, it was also able to set the ideological terms for the resolution of the case. Economically, Maxxam was rewarded well above its original investment and merits. It was paid to limit its exploitation of natural resources to levels that still allowed it to make a lucrative profit. Faced with the threat of being held accountable for previous financial and ecological wrongdoing, Maxxam managed to win a hefty public payment and largely to dictate the terms of the habitat conservation plan for the area. When forced to comply with the substantive core of the agreement and respect the environment, Pacific Lumber simply packed up and left. Although this was a partial victory for environmentalists whose primary goal was to stop ecological pillage and degradation, it was small consolation to the workers who lost their jobs.

Ideologically, while the Clinton administration celebrated the outcome as a victory for environmental protection, the terms in which the case was resolved ran counter to the views of the majority of environmental and labor groups. Indeed, the final version of the "deal" supported Maxxam's ideological framework, based as it was on the assumption that environmental protection should be addressed through market mechanisms, in a context in which the laws of private property are paramount. The economically less onerous "debt-for-nature" proposal was eventually abandoned by national and state officials, additional proof of Maxxam's superior power. In the struggle to define the ideological context within which the case was to be interpreted and adjudicated, Maxxam clearly had the upper hand.

Maxxam's corporate viewpoint clearly shaped the hegemonic discourse of the case. Maxxam's participation in the protection of the redwood forest had to be placed in a commodified context in which the forfeiting—albeit partial—of logging activities was compensated in ways commensurate with the economic values of private property and business. That U.S. and California taxpayers bore the costs of Maxxam's exploitation of the forest was viewed as politically acceptable and socially legitimate. It was "a success for everyone," as various members of the Clinton administration, including the president himself, and Congress put it forcefully and unequivocally. The case of Maxxam and Headwaters Forest also reveals the weak environmental position of the Clinton administration. Governing from the center, Clinton's "New Democrats" followed a political agenda that abandoned the more liberal objectives that constituted the traditional political agenda of that party.[3] While the move to the center gave the Democrats control of Congress and the White House for most of the 1990s, it also created a political arena receptive to corporate interests. It is not accidental, therefore, that Maxxam's view of environmentalism and that of the Clinton administration and leading Democrats coincided.[4]

The Clinton administration's acceptance of the terms of the debate set by Maxxam is one further indication of the problematic status of democracy in a globalized economy. That unions and environmentalists can fight a common battle suggests that democratic channels from below are open and allow subordinate voices to be heard. At the same time, however, the consensus viewpoint of companies like Maxxam and neoliberal democratic governments like Clinton's underscore the fact that in a global "regime," those in power tend to see commodified social relations as desirable. This, of course, makes challenges to globalization (and the political structures that support it) that much more difficult to mount and sustain.

3. New Democrats argued that their party's losses resulted from its "too liberal" stands on welfare, taxes, economic development, crime, foreign policy, and culture and the consequent narrowing of its political base to left-leaning white intellectuals and racial and ethnic minorities. New Democrats supported expanding economic growth rather than redistributing wealth, cutting crime rather than encouraging permissiveness, strengthening families rather than cultivating welfare dependency, embracing shared cultural values rather than difference, and advocating global free markets and democracy rather than accepting socialism and dictatorship. They aimed to shed the liberal label but held that they did not accept supply-side economics, cultural conservatism, or nationalism and that they still supported social justice, inclusion, and multilateralism. Bill Clinton's victory over George H. W. Bush was a triumph for the New Democrats' "third-way" strategy (i.e., abandoning New Deal politics but stopping short of Republican conservatism).

4. The Clinton administration's and local and national politicians' support for the deal also suggests that Maxxam was able to extend its hegemony over the state. While the state initially backed the "debt-for-nature" proposal, it was unable to legally outmaneuver Maxxam and consequently abandoned the project. Simultaneously, state officials formally proclaimed their commitment to the protection of the environment but substantively backed away from environmentalists and labor. Largely motivated by the corporate environmentalism that marked the Clinton administration, this outcome can be read as evidence in favor of those who question the ability of the state to take a substantive pro-environment and pro-labor position. Furthermore, this state posture undermines calls for the creation of state-based programs to aid loggers who lost their jobs because of the implementation of environmentalist policies.

8

NGOS UNDER GLOBALIZATION: THE MARINE STEWARDSHIP COUNCIL

These last years of the century are giving birth to a new alliance: a type of ruthless, unsentimental, large-scale action which entirely bypasses governments. After years of mutual suspicion and tension, the environmentalists and the industrialists, the sandals and the suits, are working things out together.
—*Times* (London) columnist (*Samudra* 1996a, 16)

The hypermobility and global sourcing methods of TNCs, along with their adoption of neoliberal postures, have limited the ability of national governments to regulate and control social and economic issues in the way they did during the Fordist era. The vacuum created by this withdrawal of the state has been partially filled by nongovernment organizations, or NGOs. As indicated in the Introduction, supporters view NGOs as entities that can provide regulation and control in areas that either have experienced the withdrawal of the state or require additional forms of intervention. They see the establishment of NGOs as a positive contribution to the creation of more democratic institutions and social relations. Critics stress that NGOs lack the democratic features of governments and in some cases have actually accelerated the withdrawal of the state. In their view, NGOs do not necessarily represent all stakeholders, something that is possible in public institutions. In addition, NGOs tend to be elitist rather than democratic, and they give TNCs a particularly relevant role in how they actually function. In some cases TNCs co-opt opposition groups—for example, environmental organizations—establishing a "green" image for themselves and thus doing their best to legitimize corporate agendas (Buttel 1992; Harvey 2005). The events illustrated in Chapter 2, and in particular the role of the IATTC in coalition with "mainstream environmental organizations," supports this observation.

This chapter addresses the establishment of an NGO, the Marine Stewardship Council (MSC), that was created to certify that the commercial exploitation of marine fish stocks was ecologically sound. The MSC was the product of collaboration between an agrifood TNC, Unilever, and one of the world's largest environmental organizations, the World Wildlife Fund for Nature (WWF). Initiated by Unilever, the purpose of this collaboration was to create an international organization that, through a formal certification process, would guarantee that Unilever fish commodities, and fish products sold through other venues, were produced following sound environmental practices. Motivated by consumer concerns and the reward of reduced government oversight, Unilever proposed a certification model that would appease critics and satisfy consumers. While broad segments of the business community and environmental organizations praised the initiative, others protested the MSC. This resistance made Unilever's commitment to buy only MSC-certified products by 2005 difficult to fulfill and stresses the contested nature of this initiative.

The Historical Development of the Marine Stewardship Council

We are currently experiencing the greatest extinction of plants and animals since the Ice Age; forests are disappearing, fish stocks are plummeting, and evidence of global warming grows daily. These problems are man-made and therefore it is time for everyone, including corporations, to reverse this tide of destruction.
—Jim Leape, World Wildlife Fund senior vice president (PR Newswire 1998)

Fishing has been called the last buffalo hunt. People realize there is trouble in the oceans. They want to know what they can do.
—Mercedes Lee (Boer 2001)

In 1997 the United Nations Food and Agricultural Organization (FAO) reported that more than 70 percent of the world's commercially important marine fish stocks were overexploited, fully exploited, depleted, or recovering from overexploitation (FAO 1997). By 1992 the FAO had already recorded sixteen major fishery species whose global catch had declined by more than 50 percent over the preceding three decades (Mulvaney 1998). Most fisheries analysts agree that something has to be done to ensure that future consumers will have access to sustainable commercial fish populations. Similarly, most seafood organizations concur that the problem can be blamed in large part on industrial fishing fleets that use thirty- and forty-mile-long drift nets and longlines that kill large numbers of "bycatch" fish and seabirds (Prewitt 1999). Such fishing practices kill and waste an average of 27 million tons of fish, sea birds, sea turtles, marine mammals, and other ocean life annually— fully a third of the global catch (*Samudra* 1996c).

A Greenpeace report entitled *Assessment of the World's Fishing Fleet, 1991–1997* found that during that period 1,654 new vessels were added to the global industrial fishing fleet, increasing its fishing capacity by more than 20 percent (Walz 1998). Overfishing has led to catastrophic declines in fisheries that have sustained coastal communities for generations. These trends have severe negative consequences for hundreds of thousands of jobs in industrialized countries, and for entire communities in the developing world that face economic and social collapse (WWF 1996b). According to the World Wildlife Fund, "to reverse this crisis, we must develop long term solutions that are environmentally necessary and then, through economic incentives, make them politically feasible" (WWF 1998d, 1).

Facing depleted fish stocks and rising demand for ecoproducts from consumers, Unilever approached the WWF in 1993 about setting up a sustainable fisheries certification system (Wilson 1999). The world's largest public relations firm, Burson-Marsteller, had advised Unilever "that instead of pursuing discussions on sustainable fisheries with Greenpeace, it should develop a partnership with the more 'conservative' WWF" (IPS/GIN 2001).

In February 1996 Unilever and the WWF announced the creation of a joint venture called the Marine Stewardship Council, designed to create a global system of sustainable fisheries. The MSC would "provide powerful economic incentives for sustainable well-managed fishing" (WWF 1996a, 1) and thereby "halt a catastrophic decline in the world's fish stocks by harnessing consumer power" (Llunggren 1996). The goal of the MSC was to link market incentives to consumer preferences through a sustainable fisheries certification and ecolabeling program. It was an outgrowth of WWF's Endangered Seas Campaign, begun in 1994, and was modeled after the WWF's Forest Stewardship Council (FSC), established in 1993.[1] Fisheries that meet MSC standards are eligible for certification by independent certifying bodies, and the MSC encouraged seafood companies to buy their fish products from only these certified sources.

1. Created in 1993, the Forest Stewardship Council is an international association of diverse stakeholder groups committed to using ecolabeling to promote responsible management of the world's forests through its network of national initiatives in more than forty-one countries. Members include representatives from environmental groups, the timber industry and forestry profession, indigenous people's organizations, corporations, community forestry groups, and forest product certification organizations. The FSC accredits independent third-party companies to certify forest managers and producers of forest products to FSC standards. Since its inception, more than 82 million hectares in more than eighty-two countries have been FSC certified (FSC 2003a and 2003b).

At the time of the initiative the WWF was the world's largest private, non-profit conservation organization, with 4.7 million supporters and a global network of twenty-six national organizations, twenty-two program offices, five associates, and thirty-five hundred employees worldwide (WWF 1997b). In 1997 the WWF invested $223 million in conservation programs and support services in a hundred countries. Total income for fiscal 1997 was about $323 million. The Anglo-Dutch firm Unilever was the world's largest buyer of frozen fish and the manufacturer of the world's best-known frozen fish products, with brands such as Iglo, Birds Eye, and Gorton's. In 1997 Unilever had a 25 percent share of the European and U.S. frozen fish market as well as major fishmeal and fish oil enterprises (Smelly 1996). Unilever marketed more than a thousand brands through its three hundred subsidiary companies, had operations in eighty-eight countries, employed about 270,000 people, and generated sales of about $50 billion in 1997 (Unilever 1998; WWF 1998a). Unilever announced that it planned to have all of its fish products certified by the MSC by 2005.

While the WWF and Unilever may have had different motives, their shared objective was to ensure the long-term viability of global fish populations. According to Michael Sutton, director of the WWF's Endangered Seas Campaign (WWF 1996c), "the history of fisheries management is one of spectacular failures. By working together with progressive seafood companies, we can harness consumer power in support of conservation and make it easier for governments to act." Caroline Whitfield, international manager of Unilever's Fish Innovation Center, concurred, adding, "Two of our core principles are that sustainable business is good business, and that we work in partnership to meet our goals. This initiative, on behalf of millions of consumers, is entirely consistent with these principles" (MSC 1998b). When the joint initiative was announced, Sutton maintained that "the market is becoming more important in economic issues. There are limits to regulation and the market has to start trying to solve this problem rather than contributing to it" (Llunggren 1996). Sutton and Whitfield concluded, "An important characteristic of the MSC will be its independence from both the environmental community and the industry. Finding a way to harness market forces and consumer power in appropriate ways to help resolve the crisis in marine fisheries may not be the only arrow in the quiver of marine conservation, but it could well be a powerful one" (ibid.).

The WWF and Unilever retained the international consulting firm Coopers and Lybrand to develop an organizational blueprint and implementation plan for the MSC. Coopers and Lybrand interviewed various fisheries stake-

holders and conducted detailed studies of certifying organizations to evaluate the various successes and failures in such ventures. A search was then
undertaken for a senior project manager and board chairperson. Funding for
the MSC was obtained from private foundations. The World Bank and the
United Nations Development Program indicated their preliminary interest in
the initiative and a fundraising drive was launched to raise startup money
for the MSC (ibid.).

Coopers and Lybrand assembled a team of consultants with expertise in
ecolabeling certification and knowledge of the commercial fishing industry.
They held meetings with experts representing marine fisheries stakeholders.
On the basis of these consultations the MSC team prepared a set of principles
for sustainable fishing, drawing on existing standards in international agreements such as the FAO code of conduct for responsible fisheries. The draft
principles were circulated to a broad spectrum of fisheries stakeholders. The
MSC team then sponsored a series of regional, national, and international
conferences and workshops in order to refine and strengthen the principles
and develop a process of international implementation. After a meeting with
the World Bank's environment division, the bank announced that it was considering enacting a "market transformation initiative" based on the MSC
(Llunggren 1996).

In January 1997 the MSC team announced the appointment of its first
project manager, Carl-Christian Schmidt (Aquatic Network 1997). Schmidt
had fourteen years of experience with the Organization for Economic Cooperation and Development (OECD) and served as its principal administrator responsible for global fisheries issues. Before joining the OECD, Schmidt served
as an administrator with the Royal Danish Ministry of Fisheries in Copenha-
gen, where his principal responsibilities were the commercial aspects of Europe's common fisheries policy and bilateral relations with major export
markets for Danish fish and fish products.

The MSC was formally established in London in February 1997 as an independent, not-for-profit, nongovernmental body. Its mission statement reads
in part: "Marine Stewardship Council's aim is to work for sustainable marine
fisheries by promoting responsible, environmentally appropriate, socially
beneficial and economically viable fisheries practices, while maintaining the
biodiversity, productivity and ecological processes of the marine environment" (MSC 1998a).

In April 1997 the UK firm Sainsbury's became the first food retailer to
announce its support for the MSC. Schmidt commented that Sainsbury's support was a signal to consumers that the retail trade was taking seriously the

growing concerns about the condition of fish stocks. It sent a clear message, he said, that the industry wanted to act responsibly to reverse overfishing and move toward more sustainable fisheries (WWF 1997a).

In March 1998 the Right Honorable John Gummer, MP, former UK secretary of state for the environment and minister of agriculture, fisheries, and food, accepted the position of MSC chairman. "By harnessing the power of commerce in favor of sustainable fisheries," Gummer said, "the MSC can complement the existing regulatory regimes and safeguard both ocean ecosystems and people's livelihoods" (WWF 1998c; Wilson 1999).

In late 1997 the MSC launched a "letter-of-support" campaign to garner widespread support for the initiative. By early 1998 several organizations had signed on. The National Audubon Society signed a letter, and their director of the group's Living Oceans Programme, Dr. Carl Sifina, stated, "The MSC has the potential of significantly altering worldwide fishing practices in favour of more sustainable, less destructive fisheries" (WWF 1998b). After an MSC-sponsored regional workshop in Canberra, Australia, three major Asia-based seafood processors and distributors signed on. Following a similar workshop in Aberdeen, UK, Safeway and Tesco joined Sainsbury's in endorsing the MSC. These companies, the three largest food retailers in the UK, had a significant market share on the European continent as well (WWF 1998b). WWF praised these corporate leaders for recognizing that sound environmental practices are good business and for proactively seeking market-based solutions to solve complex environmental problems instead of waiting for government regulation (PR Newswire 1998). Further support came from James D. Wolfensohn, president of the World Bank. "We recognize the major significance and enormous potential of the Council," said Wolfensohn, "and would seek to support the utilization of market forces in this sector in as many ways as resources will currently permit" (WWF 1998b). Furthermore, the MSC had the potential ability to complement ISO 14000 by certifying sustainable harvesting practices prior to value-added processing (Sproul 1998). By early 1998 the number of supporting organizations exceeded sixty (MSC 1998c). In April the Boston-based chains of Legal Sea Foods and Shaw's supermarkets, the latter with 127 stores in New England, were the first two U.S. firms to sign an agreement pledging to buy only MSC-certified fish (Kilborn and Carden 1999). Legal Seafoods president and chairman Roger Berkowitz stated that he was eager to display the MSC ecolabel because, as he put it, "sustainable seafood protects my future" (Prewitt 1999, 3).

In June 1998 the MSC launched its "fisheries certifiers accreditation scheme" (MSC 1998d). This initiative enabled the MSC to verify the competence of independent certifiers who assessed fisheries' specific practices against the MSC standards. Products from fisheries certified by MSC-accredited certifiers would then be eligible for the MSC logo. In early 2000, after three years of consultation with leaders from academia, industry, government, and NGOs, the MSC presented its "principles and criteria for sustainable fishing" (MSC 2000). The three conditions of certification were (1) that a fishery had to be conducted in a manner that would not lead to overfishing or depletion of the exploited populations, and, for those populations that were already depleted, the fishery had to be operated in a manner that demonstrably led to their recovery; (2) that fishing operations allowed for the maintenance of the structure, productivity, function, and diversity of the ecosystem (including habitat and associated dependent and ecologically related species) on which the fishery depended; and (3) that the fishery was subject to an effective management system that respected local, national, and international laws and standards and incorporated institutional and operational frameworks that required that use of the resources be responsible and sustainable.

The MSC fishery certification program consisted of four key components: (1) the MSC developed and maintained an international standard for sustainable fisheries; (2) fisheries could apply to be certified according to the MSC standard; (3) if a fishery was certified as meeting the MSC standard, the individual companies that sold that fishery's products had to obtain a chain-of-custody certificate; and (4) companies that wanted to use the MSC label had enter into a logo-licensing agreement with the MSC (Humphreys and Tarica 2000).

Early Controversies over the MSC: Questions of Legitimacy and Feasibility

The MSC generated a considerable amount of discussion regarding the pros and cons of the program. Mark Ritchie, executive director of the Institute for Agriculture and Trade Policy, remarked, "While there is controversy surrounding this initiative due to the major involvement of one global corporation, Unilever, in the overall control and design, rather than a broad group of stakeholders as are involved in the Forest Stewardship Council, nonetheless this is an important initiative" (Ritchie 1998). The journal *Samudra* of the International Collective in Support of Fishworkers published several articles on the controversial aspects of the MSC. One supportive editorial commented that "when Unilever and other major seafood companies make commitments to buy their fish products only from well-managed and MSC-certified fisheries, the fishing industry will be compelled to modify its current practices. Governments, laws and treaties aside, the market itself will begin to determine the means for fish production" (*Samudra* 1996c, 2).

Cooper also spoke in support of the MSC. She took issue with Neis's conclusions (see below), which saw the MSC as the death knell for traditional fisheries and a system of disenfranchisement for women who participated in local fisheries and fish markets. Cooper argued that the overfishing that has occurred over the past fifty years has already destroyed many fishing communities. Contrary to its critics, she felt that the MSC was taking into account social and economic factors, as well as environmental and biological ones, in its deliberations over the certification process. The MSC should not be seen as a panacea for the worldwide fisheries crisis, however, but rather as a "more direct way of promoting sustainability in fisheries through market forces, so that women, men, and children may rely on healthy supplies of fish in the future" (Cooper 1997, 1). Cooper did not believe that the MSC would replace or circumvent existing democratic institutions.

One concern about the MSC had to do with questions of equity. According to one observer, the agreement between the "powerful TNC and the famous international environmental organization" seemed to have ignored the welfare of the fisherpeople, in that the expansion of the European market, with a bias in favor of industrial fisheries, has been the "major factor in the price slump which has affected the welfare of fishermen" (*Samudra* 1996e, 5). Through initiatives such as the MSC, environmental and corporate organizations would have a dominant influence on both prices and market access. And the MSC's alleged independence and representation of all stakeholders notwithstanding, some parties would have more weight than others. Faced with well-organized media campaigns, fishermen would find it more and more difficult to get their viewpoints across as envirocorporate agendas took precedence over the social aspects of sustainable resource management (*Samudra* 1996e).

Another concern was preserving the diversity of fishing traditions around the world; how would the MSC accomplish this? Some critics thought that the introduction of new ecoconditions on markets would benefit only well-off consumers in Europe, Japan, and the United States. Consumers and TNCs in those countries might be imposing their definition of a responsible fishery on developing countries. The promotion of ecofriendly fish imports to developed countries whose food requirements had already been met, and the simultaneous neglect of less developed countries' needs, hardly exemplified the principles of sustainable development, critics charged (*Samudra* 1996e).

Critics also questioned whether a program created by an industrial fishing company could really resolve the crisis of depleted fish stocks. According to a Canadian newspaper editorial, the call for "codes of conduct" and sustainable fishing practices were but a "green mantle" adopted by those who were directly responsible for the fisheries crisis in the first place, a transparent attempt to "deflect public rage at what has already occurred, while serving to maintain the perpetrators in the future fishery." The author of this editorial also doubted that the MSC would consider the co-option of indigenous fishing grounds by industrial fleets as part of the certification process. Furthermore, "the people at Unilever and WWF selling the 'new hope,' will look on governments with disdain and label the public sector as venal, while happily embracing markets as replacing the democratic institutions as the key determinant in our society" (*Samudra* 1996b, 9).

Another critic, this one from the global South, voiced concerns about an initiative that placed all its faith in the "magic of the market." While in democratic institutions each person has one vote, this is not the case in market-dominated systems, especially in the Third World, where the history of extreme economic inequality had undermined "blind faith" in the "almighty market's ability to correct all economic and environmental ills" (*Samudra* 1996d, 13). Global southerners understood that depleted fish stocks were the result of First World industrial fishing techniques in Third World waters. Moreover, because Unilever, one of the world's largest fish buyers, would retain quasi-monopoly control over a large segment of the market, many small-scale commercial ventures that did not fit into the MSC certification process would very possibly be left out of the value-added ecolabeling program. And since fish are an important export of many Third World countries, their governments were unlikely to openly support the MSC.

The probable negative impact of the MSC on fishery-dependent women of the North was also noted. The MSC was yet another initiative in fisheries management that failed to consider the potential impact on women. Because poor women "have few votes in the marketplace," they would experience increased marginalization under MSC. Not only would their direct access to local fisheries continue to decline, but they would also be reduced to purchasing "non-sustainably caught fish." Vertically integrated food conglomerates were increasingly the primary consumers and producers of fish products, and they had the most power in the marketplace. Barbara Neis (1997, 2) saw the MSC's market focus as "the equivalent of a death sentence for fisheries and communities that depend on them." In short, thanks to general distrust of Unilever, many fishing communities in both the North and South expressed skepticism about the promise of the MSC (*Samudra* 1996a, 16).

Following an MSC workshop in London in early 1997, held to address such concerns, Brian O'Riordan charged that the MSC had no clear plan for addressing social issues in developing countries and expressed the fear that the MSC would develop its principles and policies in the North and then administer them in the South. At the workshop, MSC manager Schmidt commented that "ecolabeling is a neo-liberal tool, and the MSC is going down that path" (O'Riordan 1997, 1). O'Riordan noted that many global southerners did not share the northern neoliberal agenda on which the MSC was based. Instead, these people felt that the North should be reforming its patterns of consumption and its own behavior rather than letting consumerism drive the agenda.

Additional concerns were raised by Lee J. Weddig, executive vice president of the National Fisheries Institute. In addressing the European Seafood Exhibition in Brussels in April 1997, Weddig expressed dissatisfaction with three aspects of the MSC. First, its core method was ecolabeling, yet previous experiments with labeling, such as dolphin-safe tuna and turtle-safe shrimp, had not been favorable to the fishing industry. Second, the MSC might turn out to be little more than a public relations exercise seeking to impose First World methods on the Third World. The major fish production countries were in the South, yet the MSC workshops had all been held in the North; wasn't the MSC just another form of northern "elitism or leftover colonialism," designed to force the global South to manage its resources in a way that would benefit the North? Weddig's third concern centered on what he saw as a fundamental flaw in the MSC concept. Using the example of the United States, he argued that the use of fishery resources was strictly regulated by law, and that the system of government balanced the needs of competing groups. While the underlying principle of U.S. fishery law was sustainability, the system allowed dissenters to advance their positions, and sometimes they even got Congress or the courts to change the laws. The U.S. system enabled a multiplicity of interests to participate in making policy and addressed a variety of positions and needs. Speaking for the fishing industry, Weddig concluded that the MSC concept would "supersede the flexibility needed to accommodate the needs of all aspects of our society. It attempts to torque the system to a one dimensional agenda" (Weddig 1997).

Others shared Weddig's concerns. At a meeting in June 1998 the MSC initiative suffered a setback at a meeting of the FAO Sub-Committee on Fish Trade, when a Norwegian minister argued that ecolabeling was an issue for fisheries authorities, not NGOs like the MSC. The countries represented at the meeting agreed that an ecolabeling program might constitute "a threat towards free-trade in fish and fish products, especially as it may cause discrimination towards fish exports from developing and/or transition economies" (Walz 1998, 13). Sidney Holt, a marine biologist from the Independent World Commission on the Oceans captured the skepticism of many MSC critics. "I read many of the publications for the fishing industries," he said. "For every sentence that may be published about . . . conservation, there will be a page or more about the building of more, bigger and more powerful boats, the construction of bigger nets. . . . Making profits now or soon is the name of the real game" (Schoon 1998).

The First Certified Fisheries: MSC Success and Criticism

In March 2000 the MSC announced the certification of the first two fisheries to bear its "Fish Forever" ecolabel: the Thames River herring driftnet fishery and the western Australia rock lobster fishery (Chubb 2000). The Thames River estuary herring fishery near Essex, England, was a small fishery that had used special nets for more than one hundred years to strain out immature fish and catch only adult herrings. Local fishers saw certification as a boon that would stabilize prices over the length of the fishing season. The western Australia rock lobster fishery had the longest management plan of any fishery in Australia and was the most valuable single-species fishery in Australia, representing about 20 percent of the total value of Australia's fisheries (Humphreys and Tarica 2000). Its export earnings amounted to roughly $300 million annually, and it employed about two thousand people directly and another six thousand indirectly (*The Australian* 2000).

When the certification of these two enterprises was announced, WWF and Unilever representatives were quick to express enthusiasm. "The MSC's new eco-label creates real market incentives for healthy fisheries," said Scott Burns, director of WWF's endangered species campaign. "For the first time, fishers can be recognized for managing their fisheries in a responsible way, and consumers will be able to purchase seafood that they know comes from sustainable sources." Unilever chairman Antony Burgmans commented, "I congratulate the Marine Stewardship Council in getting the first MSC-certified products on the market. This is a significant step forward in the process of moving toward sustainable fishing, and I am certain other fisheries will follow the example" (Chubb 2000).

Six months later the Alaskan salmon fishery was the first U.S. fishery to be certified by the MSC (Humphreys and Tarica 2000; Jung 2000). When Alaska became a state in 1959, the salmon fishery was in trouble owing to a long history of overfishing. To counter this trend, provisions were included in the Alaska state constitution that required the salmon habitat to be conserved and protected. Since that time the state has focused on rebuilding its five native salmon species. In 2000 Alaskan salmon accounted for more than 95 percent of the entire U.S. salmon harvest (ADF&G 2000). The MSC certification team wrote, "Alaska's management of its commercial salmon fisheries provides an excellent example of a strict effort controlled fishery with day to day adaptive management" (Chaffee 2000).

In April 2001 the British Columbia (B.C.) salmon industry announced that it too was pursuing MSC certification, stating that it was "do-or-die time for their industry" after the MSC had "awarded an eco-certification label to their biggest rivals on world markets." Citing the trend in forestry whereby environmentalists have successfully lobbied major retailers like Home Depot to sell ecofriendly lumber, B.C. fisherman announced their intention to follow a similar path. They noted that Prince Charles supported the MSC, which was staffed with "political heavyweights" from around the world. "It's much like the pressure the environmentalists have put on the logging companies. It's going to put pressure on us here," said Bob Rezansoff, a salmon boat operator and chairman of the Pacific Salmon Harvesters Association (Simpson 2001a). But there was also fear and uncertainty about the B.C. salmon fishery's ability to meet the MSC standards.

These fears were realized in May 2001, when the Sierra Club of B.C. announced that it would oppose the MSC certification. Thousands of jobs in the B.C. salmon industry were potentially threatened by the Sierra Club's stand, because Alaska, B.C.'s largest competitor, had already been certified and had thus secured both price and marketing advantages in the international market. The Alaskan salmon fishery is about ten times larger than that of the B.C. While Unilever had been a major buyer of B.C. wild salmon, the firm had committed to buying and selling only MSC-certified fish products by 2005. Without certification from the "powerful new" MSC, the European price for a can of "B.C. sockeye salmon could be discounted to the value of a comparably sized tin of cat food," according to a Vancouver newspaper. Sierra Club conservation chair Vikki Husband noted that the Sierra Club had also questioned Alaska's certification and the MSC's credibility, however, and that the Alaskan government had refused to release the detailed study that established that fishery's entitlement to carry the MSC stamp. "Any eco-certification of B.C.'s salmon fisheries undertaken according to the kind of performance criteria the Marine Stewardship Council accepted for Alaska," said Husband, "would be an act bordering on consumer fraud" (Simpson 2001b).

In late March the MSC announced that more than a hundred major seafood buyers, including Whole Foods Market, the largest organic/natural food chain in the United States, had pledged to buy seafood only from MSC-certified sources (Pryor-Nolan 2000). Margaret Wittenberg, vice president of governmental and public relations for Whole Foods, lauded the new relationship as a way to ensure that the company would have fish to sell in the long run while simultaneously maintaining their ecological commitments (Habitat Media 2000). Wittenberg added that the MSC ecolabel provided Whole Foods with a reliable way to meet the increasing demands of ecoconscious consumers who want to know the specifics of how the food they buy is produced. In June 2001 Whole Foods became the first U.S. retailer to carry MSC-labeled Alaskan salmon (*Anchorage Daily News* 2001). The Alaska Seafood Marketing Institute (ASMI) reported that seventeen Alaskan salmon processors had completed the "chain-of-custody" certification and thus were able to use the ecolabel on their fish. To support the sale of MSC-certified salmon, Whole Foods held a nationwide promotion in collaboration with the ASMI and MSC called "Fish for our Future" and featuring wild Alaskan salmon. Karen Tarica, U.S. communications director for the MSC, praised the Whole Foods campaign as an "example for the retail industry to take action and reward fisheries that follow sustainable seafood management practices." Steve Parks, national seafood coordinator for Whole Foods, added, "We applaud the certification program backed by the MSC as it gives our customers the buying power to influence the management of fisheries as well as the confidence that purchasing MSC label-bearing products will not contribute to over fishing or the harming of marine ecosystems" (*Total Health* 2001, 1–2).

The New Zealand Hoki Fishery Controversy

In March 2001 the New Zealand hoki fishery became the fourth fishery to be certified by the MSC. Hoki fish is sold by several New Zealand seafood companies that collectively own the Hoki Fishery Management Company, a cooperative established to improve the management of the fishery. Upon MSC certification Hoki Company chairman Ross Tocker commented that he was excited about the announcement and the new business opportunities it had created. According to Tocker, "The New Zealand fishing industry has been committed to sustainable management of its resources for more than two decades, and invests heavily in research and management. Recognition by the MSC of our sustainable management system is also enabling us to generate substantial new business. The contract with Unilever, a major international foods company, is another strong indication that it is a good business strategy. We look forward to signing more contracts." Unilever chairman Antony Burgmans also applauded the certification of the hoki fishery. "This is a very important step for the MSC and for sustainable fishing," said Burgmans. "And for Unilever, even though New Zealand hoki represents only a relatively small portion of our total international fish supply, this is a significant step forward in meeting our objective of buying from sustainable sources by 2005" (Unilever 2001).

New Zealand hoki is the second fish with the MSC logo to be sold by Unilever. Hoki is used in Europe as a whitefish replacement for depleted cod in fish and chips and other products. Alaskan salmon with the MSC logo was launched in Switzerland in late 2000. Burgmans added that he expected it to take "some time" before Unilever was able to source significantly higher volumes of certified sustainable fish. "That reflects the challenges we face in achieving sustainable fisheries around the world," he said. "We need support from all stakeholders, including governments internationally, to achieve these goals" (Unilever 2001).

The MSC certification of the hoki fishery was quickly criticized by New Zealand's leading environmental group, the Royal Forest and Bird Protection Society. The group argued that the huge nets used to catch the hoki also catch large numbers of seals and seabirds and therefore cannot be considered a sustainable way of fishing. Barry Weeber, Forest and Bird senior researcher, maintained that the hoki fishery was "responsible for more than 5,600 seal deaths in the trawl nets between 1989 and 1998" (IPS/GIN 2001). The trawl nets can have an opening the size of a football field and be as long as a fourteen-story building is high. The seals and birds get caught in them near the surface as the nets are deployed and retrieved. Weeber also challenged the MSC certification on the grounds that the hoki fishery was actually divided into eastern and western fisheries and that the eastern fishery was at high risk for collapse within the next few years. If the eastern fishery collapsed and fishing moved to the western area, seal deaths would continue to increase. The hoki fishery also captured an estimated eleven hundred seabirds per year, 80 percent of which died (ECES 2001). About 60 percent of the affected birds were albatross, of which two species were listed as "vulnerable threatened species" by the International Union for the Conservation of Nature (IUCN).

The Protection Society of the IUCN pointed out that there were major information gaps on the ecological impact of the fishery in the certification report produced by the Netherlands-based SGS product and process certification. For example, the report stated that the "medium to long term impacts of hoki fishing on the ecosystem and habitats are not well understood at this time." Despite this lack of information, SGS had approved certification of the fishery on the grounds that "minor corrective actions" were being taken. MSC communications director Louisa Barnett defended the certification by invoking the "precautionary principle."[2] "The MSC standard has incorporated the idea of the precautionary principle," stated Barnett. "The precautionary approach is recognized worldwide as a prudent way of dealing with scientific uncertainty, and this applies to fisheries management." The Protection Society announced that it would appeal the MSC decision to certify the New Zealand hoki fishery as sustainable (IPS/GIN 2001).

Other New Zealand environmentalists disputed the MSC's claim to be taking the precautionary approach seriously. "Many of the problems like seal deaths we have identified were also noted in the certification report itself, but the report suggests that these are minor issues," said Cath Wallace, spokesperson on marine issues for the Environment and Conservation Organizations. "The announcement that the hoki fishery is to be certified is a serious blow to the integrity of the MSC certification scheme. The MSC seems to have been desperate to get a portfolio of fish so that the scheme can get underway." Wallace expressed concern that by certifying the hoki fishery the MSC was "sending a message that it will tolerate high levels of environmental damage and animal deaths," and that such a message could mislead consumers about the real impact of their purchases. "This is a disappointing loss of an opportunity to send reliable message to consumers. Consumers will be offended by the MSC trying to give a green tick to a fishery with major environmental and animal welfare problems," Wallace said (IPS/GIN 2001).

In December 2002 the MSC announced that the independent dispute panel made up of "eminent scientists" formed to evaluate the Royal Forest and Bird Protection Society complaint had decided to uphold the certification of the New Zealand hoki fishery. The panel found that while the certification body had not "fully implemented a precautionary approach" when evaluating

2. The precautionary principle refers to the norm that requires that no new action be taken if its consequences are uncertain and/or not adequately documented as safe.

some aspects of the fishery, still, because the Hoki Fishery Management Company had agreed to implement "a robust corrective action plan," it would be "inappropriate to withdraw certification at this time." As a result of the dispute, the MSC altered its fishery certification methodology to include a formal objection process and "extensive stakeholder consultation" prior to a fishery certification to ensure that "stakeholders would have the opportunity to raise concerns in advance of any decision being made" (MSC 2002).

The Royal Forest and Bird Protection Society reported that it was stunned that the MSC had denied the appeal and upheld certification despite acknowledging that the fishery did not meet sustainability criteria. "The Hoki fishery is one of New Zealand's most destructive fisheries and it is impossible to see how it might be regarded as sustainable," said Barry Weeber. He noted that the appeal decision stated that it could be years before it would be known whether the fishery was sustainable. During that time the killing of a thousand fur seals and about that many albatross and petrels per year would continue. "I think a lot of people in Europe who buy fish-fingers made of hoki would be shocked at how low the environmental standards are for their 'sustainably fished' dinner," said Weeber (ECBC 2002, 1).

The Growing Crisis over MSC Legitimacy

The target market for certified seafood is the same, prime market all retailers are chasing—urban, upscale, health-conscious, and willing to pay a small premium for a product portrayed as environmentally friendly.
—Jim Humphreys, North American director for the MSC (Simpson 2001a)

The conservation community really thinks the idea behind the MSC is a good idea, that you have a label that you can put on at the grocery store, restaurant, whatever, so consumers can decide the right thing to buy, but that label has to be backed up by a very credible certification scheme.
—Mark Spalding, senior programs manager for the Alaska Oceans Program (Bauman 2004, 1)

Fish consumption has risen rapidly in recent years as a result of consumers' increasing preference for healthy food. Sainsbury's of England, the largest fishmonger in Britain and an early cooperator with the MSC, tripled its sales of fish between 1997 and 2007. Fishmongers and chefs report that customers have become increasingly concerned that they not eat a species to extinction. Tina English, spokesperson for Livebait, one of the largest fish restaurant chains in Britain, said, "Our customers are questioning us about where our fish comes from, and whether they are sustainable—and they didn't do that 12 months ago." When the MSC certified New Zealand hoki in 2001, sales increased by 1,300 percent as people switched from eating threatened North Sea cod (Browne 2002).

While the MSC started out by approving small, politically uncontroversial fisheries such as the Thames herring fishery and the western Australian rock lobster fishery, the certification of the New Zealand hoki fishery proved to be much more controversial (McColl 2003). In May 2003 the MSC came under increasing criticism from environmentalists for being a "cover for industrial fishing methods that kill seals and seabirds, damage the seabed, and empty the seas of scarce fish stocks." "People have a right to assume when they see the MSC label on a fish, these kinds of things are not happening," said Gary Leape, head of marine conservation of the U.S.-based National Environmental Trust. "Right now they can't." Leape condemned the certification of the New Zealand hoki fishery for killing approximately a thousand seals and six hundred endangered albatross each year. MSC chief executive Brendan May countered that the MSC and the hoki fishing companies had agreed to a timetable to improve the situation. "In any case, it's a better option than North Sea cod," May contended (Pearce 2003). Leape warned that unless the MSC cleaned up its act, green groups from Greenpeace to the Sierra Club might withdraw their support for the labels. May again defended the practice of certifying fishing companies that promise to improve their methods, rather than waiting until they had made the improvements. He said that the green groups' "desire for a perfect system was undermining pragmatic efforts to improve fishing practices" (Pearce 2003).

In 2003 hoki buyers in Europe began complaining about the quality of the whitefish used for fish and chips and other products. In response, Unilever began looking to Alaskan factory-shipped pollock as an alternative source of whitefish (Foss 2003). Both Unilever and McDonald's were looking for reliable supplies of "sustainable whitefish." On November 21, 2003, the MSC announced that, after a two-and-a-half-year scientific review and extensive stakeholder consultation, the Scientific Certification Systems (SCS) had recommended that the Gulf of Alaska Pollack Fishery be certified (MSC 2003). The certification document was to be posted on the MSC Web site for a public comment period of thirty days. After that time the SCS would consider the comments and make a final determination regarding certification, to be followed by a twenty-one-day period during which organizations opposed to certification could file objections. Only when the objection period was completed would the final decision be made.

The hoki controversy and the news of the nascent certification of the Gulf of Alaska Pollack Fishery prompted environmentalists to question the independence of the MSC and the sustainability of the hoki fishery once again. They maintained that the recent campaign by Unilever to get European consumers to replace cod with hoki was a cynical attempt to improve Unilever's profits "not only at the expense of the beleaguered UK fish catching industry but also the consumers who are being enticed to buy so-called sustainable fish [that] in reality is poor quality and from one of the most destructive of New Zealand fisheries" (McColl 2003). As the hoki quality became an issue for European consumers, Unilever turned to the pollock fishery as its source of whitefish. MSC critics asserted that, because no application for certification had ever been turned down or revoked, it was far from clear what might happen if its standards were not met. The MSC had to "raise its game if the pursuit of the sustainable fishing business is not to become a complete sham," one critic wrote (*New Scientist* 2003). Environmentalists were also quick to criticize possible certification of the pollock fishery because of the negative impact on Stellar sea lions (Welch 2003).

In early 2004 the MSC came under increased criticism as two drafts of independent evaluations reports became public. The Bridgespan Group (Searle, Colbey, and Milway 2004) and Wildhavens (Highleyman, Amos, and Cauley 2004) reports expressed strong support for the MSC's goal of using market incentives to develop sustainable fisheries but also concluded that the MSC was an "enterprise at risk" because it still lacked credibility with one of its "key stakeholder groups: the international environmental community" (Leape and Sutton 2004, 2). The reports concluded that the MSC had not achieved its "conservation promise," and that several recommended reforms were necessary. The most important of these reforms centered on (1) the quality-of-life assessment and certification processes, (2) follow-up measures to assure that the corrective actions required by the certifier were being met, and (3) issues of MSC governance and leadership. The reports suggested that the MSC remove the word "sustainable" from its claims and instead indicate that it was certifying well-managed fisheries that employed best-management practices. More clear-cut metrics regarding both principles and criteria and corrective measures to ensure environmental quality were needed. The reports suggested that the MSC should also specify that eight of its fifteen board members were chosen by the Stakeholder Council, "giving special consideration to ensure a balance of economic, environmental, and social interests" (ibid., 3).

In May 2004 the Royal Forest and Bird Protection Society renewed its objection to MSC certification of the New Zealand hoki fishery (RFBPS 2004). The society reported that the most recent New Zealand Ministry of Fisheries

stock assessment reports indicated that most of the hoki fishery was unsustainable and that fishing pressure needed to be cut by half to prevent the
fishery's collapse. It noted that the situation clearly violated the MSC's first
principle, which required that a fishery be conducted in a way that did not
lead to overfishing or depletion of exploited populations. The society again
pointed to the annual killing of thousands of protected seals and seabirds as
further evidence that the fishery should lose its accreditation.

Later in 2004 the MSC faced increased criticism from several environmental
groups for its certification of the Bering Sea and Gulf of Alaska pollock fisheries, which accounted for about a third of all seafood landings in the United
States (Pemberton 2004). The groups argued that the certifying party had
ignored significant recent drops in Stellar sea lion populations and pollock
populations, especially in the Gulf of Alaska. While the MSC had found numerous deficiencies in both fisheries, none was deemed severe enough to deny
certification. In response to the concerns of the environmental groups, MSC
certification of the Gulf of Alaska pollock fishery was put on hold in October
(Bauman 2004). The MSC office in London announced that it would convene
an independent panel to review the objections. Mark Spalding, senior programs manager for the Alaska Oceans Program, praised the decision. "Everyone was very, very surprised that, given the size of the fishery, the
importance of the fishery, the importance of the credibility of the process of
certification, the MSC did not pull together an independent panel for the
complete [pollock] fishery," said Spalding. In 2005 the Alaska Oceans Program announced that owing to the slow pace of MSC reforms suggested in
the Wildhavens and Bridgespan studies, it would "no longer participate in
certification efforts" until it was convinced that the MSC "certification system
provides conservation benefits to the ecosystem and rewards fisheries that
are truly sustainable" (AOP 2005, 2).

In April 2004 the South African Cape hake fishery was the first African
fishery to be awarded MSC certification (MSC 2004b; WWF 2004). Hake was by
far the most valuable fish resource in South Africa, accounting for 50 percent
of the fisheries sector. Trawl fisheries made up 90 percent of the hake fishery, with the majority of the catch coming from the deep-water fishery and
the remainder from an inshore fishery. The main export market for this hake
was Europe, followed by the United States. A study of the MSC certification
of the South African Cape hake fishery sponsored by Tralac (Trade Law Centre
for Southern Africa) noted that Unilever pursued certification as a source of
whitefish for "fish and chips" in response to the loss of confidence in the
qualify of the product from the New Zealand hoki fishery. The report con-

cluded that the case illustrated that "ecolabeling is sought in the context of competitive pressures, political economies, and specific interpretations, not simply on the basis of value-free science or systemic management alone." More specifically, Stefano Ponte pointed out that although the hake fishery certification was supposed to be done in the context of "impartial readings" of conservation and competition, in reality it was one of the tools employed "against the redistribution of the fish quotas from 'white-owned companies' to the possible benefit of 'black-owned companies.'" Ponte concluded that the evidence of the case supported the contention that fisheries in developing countries, especially small ones, "have been marginalised by the MSC system" (Ponte 2006, 1). Steinberg (1999) reached a similar conclusion, casting the MSC as a "club good" approach to fisheries management that often excluded smaller fisheries in favor of larger and more efficient ones.

The MSC Responds: New Initiatives and Participation

In the November 2004 MSC quarterly newsletter *Fish 4 Thought,* incoming chief executive Rupert Howes recognized the "desperate need" for a "positive and sustainable" solution to the crisis of the capture fisheries, and avowed that the "MSC environmental standard provides such a solution" (MSC 2004a). He noted that with the recent certification of the Bering Sea and Aleutian Island's (BSAI) pollock fishery, the world's largest whitefish fishery, a total of eleven fisheries had been MSC certified worldwide. The MSC ecolabel was on 220 products in twenty-two countries. Howes reported that MSC priorities included getting more certified product to market, implementing a range of recommendations from two independent evaluations of the MSC aimed at improving credibility, and securing and diversifying the MSC's funding base and financial sustainability.

The same issue of *Fish 4 Thought* noted that the initial certification for the BSAI pollock fishery had been issued in June 2004, at which time any organization opposed to the recommendation for certification had twenty-one days to file an objection. An objection was lodged by the Trustees of Alaska on behalf of the Alaska Oceans Program, Greenpeace International, the National Environmental Trust, and Oceana. The MSC board of trustees reviewed the objection and decided that it fell outside the guidelines for objections and that therefore an objections panel would not be convened for the BSAI pollock fishery, which was formally certified in September 2004. At the same time, an initial certification was approved for the Gulf of Alaska pollock fishery. The same organizations filed an objection. In this case the MSC trustees decided to convene and investigate the objection (MSC 2004a).

In 2005 the first three MSC fisheries (Thames herring, western Australia rock lobster, and Alaska salmon) applied for recertification. MSC's Rupert Howes commented, "It's clear that there is a strong business case for fisheries to seek MSC certification, whatever their size and location. The renewed commitment of these pioneering fisheries is not philanthropic; it tells us that MSC certification adds value and that sustainable management practices help competitive success" (MSC 2005a). The MSC announced that the Patagonia scallop fishery, the first scallop fishery and the first fishery in Argentina, was to be assessed. The MSC also announced two new initiatives and an update to its chain-of-custody certification program. First, a new Stakeholder Council steering group was established to create better linkages between the MSC Stakeholder Council, the Technical Advisory Board, and the MSC trustees. Second, the MSC Program for Developing World Fisheries had started a new project called "guidelines for assessment of small-scale and data-deficient fisheries," designed to come up with a way to assess fisheries that operate sustainably but lack access to detailed scientific data. Regarding the chain-of-custody certification program, the original methodology developed in 2000, which allowed the tracing of all MSC-labeled products to a certified fishery, was revised to make the link from "boat to plate" more accessible to retailers and restaurants in the hopes of expanding market outlets (ibid.).

In June 2005 the MSC announced that it had completed its first agreement, a memorandum of understanding, with a nation-state, Vietnam, to encourage certification and explore opportunities to work together over a three-year period (MSC 2005b). The initial focus would be two preassessment pilot projects in the Ben Tre clam fishery and the Phu Quoc anchovy fishery. Howes said he hoped that other governments would engage in similar arrangements. The MSC also announced that the Gulf of Alaska pollock fishery had received its MSC certification in March and that four new fisheries (Maryland striped bass and Oregon pink shrimp in the United States and Yorkshire lobster and sea bass in the United Kingdom) had entered the full assessment stage. Two fisheries in Venezuela (crab and sardine) declared that they intended to seek preassessment, and the New Zealand hoki fishery had applied for its certification renewal. These activities brought the total number of MSC-certified fisheries to twelve, with 251 products in twenty-four countries. After the news that the Gulf of Alaska pollock fishery had been certified, the fish company Iglo announced that "all of its fish fingers sold in Germany would be MSC-labeled by May 2005" (ibid.). In November 2005 the MSC reported that the mackerel, herring, and Dover sole fisheries in Hastings, UK, had been awarded certification (MSC 2005c). It also noted that it had embarked on a "significant research project" to help identify environmental improvements resulting from sustainable management practices and that a leading Malaysian food-processing company, GoldenFresh, was the first company in Southeast Asia to receive the chain-of-custody certification.

In early 2006 several of the world's major food retailers announced their increased commitment to selling MSC-certified fish products (MSC 2006a). Wal-Mart reported that it would sell only MSC-certified fish and seafood products in North America within three to five years. Metro (the world's third-largest food retailer), Deutsche See (Germany's leading seafood supplier), and Compass (a global food service company) all announced increased use of MSC-labeled products. The MSC announced that three new fisheries (Japanese flathead flounder and snow crab, Norwegian saithe, and western U.S. albacore tuna) had entered the full assessment stage of certification. In January the Pacific cod freezer longline fishery became the first cod fishery to receive MSC certification. MSC-certified fisheries now totaled fifteen, with twenty fisheries in full assessment and dozens more in the preassessment stage. This included "over 32% of the global prime white fish catch and 42% of the wild salmon catch" (MSC 2006a).

The MSC's board of trustees announced that the MSC would make two significant changes by the end of June and would then be "wholly consistent" with FAO guidelines for ecolabeling of fish and fish products from marine capture fisheries. First, the decision to accredit or deaccredit a certification body would be made by an external independent organization. Second, decisions relating to complaints and appeals would also be fully independent of the MSC. With these changes, the MSC would be fully in line with FAO guidelines, "including third party independent assessment, a robust standard, science based, and an open and transparent stakeholder process" (MSC 2006a).

In July 2006 the MSC reported that early research on the environmental benefits of the MSC revealed a "provisional" positive relationship. An analysis of ten fisheries found eighty-nine instances of positive environmental benefits. While the MSC lauded this as a major accomplishment, it stated that a "substantial amount of work is still required to fully understand the triggers and levers that create change in the context of a certification programme" (MSC 2006b). In order to amass more "hard evidence," the MSC announced that it was investing heavily in two core projects. The environmental benefits project related to environmental impacts, and the quality and consistency project, would clarify the intent of criteria for principles 1, 2, and 3. The MSC

Stakeholder Council, including several new members, had held face-to-face meetings in London to discuss the recent initiatives and changes to meet FAO requirements. As part of its developing world program, the MSC organized two ecolabeling workshops, one in Ghana and one in Gambia, to explore opportunities to increase participation from African fisheries. Two fisheries (Cornish handline mackerel and Burry Inlet cockle in the United Kingdom) announced their intentions to seek reassessment. The New Zealand hoki fishery reassessment had been challenged again by environmental groups. Several new fisheries (Australian mackerel icefish, U.S. North Pacific halibut, North Sea herring, and U.S. North Pacific sablefish) also achieved MSC certification. MSC-certified products are now being processed in Japan and China, and new chain-of-custody certificates have been issued to several companies. These activities brought the total number of MSC-certified fisheries to nineteen, offering 387 products in twenty-six countries (MSC 2006b).

In November 2006 the MSC announced that it was the only organization fully consistent with FAO guidelines on fishery and fish product ecolabeling. It also reported $236,661,285 in MSC-labeled product sales in fiscal year 2005–6—a 76 percent increase in retail value over the previous year. In October the United States (with ninety-three product lines) overtook Switzerland (seventy-five product lines) as the leading seller of MSC-certified products. In the United States these products included fresh halibut filets at Whole Foods, prepackaged surimi at Wal-Mart, and premium wild Alaskan salmon burgers at Trident. "That's a great achievement for all the companies that have worked to move the American market forward," said Jim Humphreys, director of MSC's Americas regional office (MSC 2006c).

Regarding the certification progress, the south Georgian Patagonia toothfish fishery was certified. The Patagonia toothfish, also known as the Chilean sea bass, has been the focus of a "take a pass on the Chilean seabass" campaign in response to overfishing. This product is currently being sold at Whole Foods Markets with an information leaflet describing the traceability to this particular MSC-certified fishery. The Lake Hjalmaren pikeperch fishery in southern Sweden achieved certification. Three other fisheries entered full assessment (Canadian northern prawn, Gulf of St. Lawrence northern shrimp, and Gulf of California sardine in Mexico). An independent objections panel chairman was appointed to oversee the continued objection to the recertification of New Zealand hoki. At the end of 2006 twenty-one fisheries had been certified, nineteen were in full assessment, and about thirty others were in the confidential preassessment stage (MSC 2006c).

Analysis and Discussion

The MSC is part of a "strange bedfellows" trend of partnerships between environmental organizations and TNCs that produces a new form of regulation, displacing state regulation. Environmental organizations hope that direct collaboration with corporations enhance environmental sustainability, and corporations are eager to increase consumer demand by providing products that are ecologically sound. The MSC is a prime example of what Buttel (1992, 11) calls "a green NGO occupying the regulatory spaces vacated by failures of the nation-state system." With the support of a major TNC and a major environmental organization, the MSC worked to join environmentalism and free trade within an NGO format that bypassed national governments. Do such partnerships represent a substantive alternative to the crisis of the regulatory dimension of the state, or are they public relations gimmicks that do not really address environmental issues and consumer demand, what some critics have called "corporate greenwash"? (See Karliner 1997; Wilson 1999.)

The Forest Stewardship Council provides some historical context for this question. The FSC, formed with the support of the World Wildlife Fund, antedates the MSC. Like the MSC, it was created in response to the perceived failure of governmental bodies to create a labeling system that would protect the global forests. Although the FSC is structured as a membership organization, unlike the MSC's board of directors framework, it too experienced substantial challenges to its legitimacy. Greenpeace and the Friends of the Earth left the FSC early, charging that it gave corporate interests too much power to define certification criteria (Humphreys 1996). Indeed, after further conflict in 1996, the influence of corporate interests actually increased (Steinberg 1999).

The case of the MSC does in fact provide evidence that TNCs—in this case Unilever—can co-opt their detractors and persuade them to embrace their agenda and vision. TNCs have shown that they can establish a socially legitimate system of standards that enhances capital accumulation while at the same time giving the appearance of environmental sustainability and social responsibility. The procorporate component of the MSC is clear. It is funded by private foundations, staffed by previous members of the OECD and Western governments, and supported by the World Bank, which considers it a model for other market transformation initiatives. In this view, the MSC is an agent that rationalizes and restructures both developing and developed nations' economies by incorporating them into TNC-dominated global investment and consumption circuits, while appeasing critics with an environmentally friendly façade. Through the use of numerous private contractors that meet MSC certification standards for sustainable fisheries, the MSC centralizes the ecolabeling process that links individual fisherpeople, whether industrial or craft based, to fishery TNCs that market "green" products to environmentally conscious consumers.

Moreover, the MSC moves the crisis of the global fisheries away from the political venue of individual nation-states. Through a process of de facto deregulation of nation-states—laws, treaties, and policies regarding fisheries issues—the MSC re-regulates the coordination of the global fisheries away from public venues and into TNC-dominated private arenas. It can also be argued that although the MSC was challenged on many fronts, careful planning secured its initial success. When challenged about the lack of participation by local groups in the certification process, the original MSC objection process appeared to be more formal than substantive, a practice that closely resembles the TNC-dominated regulation of CAFOS discussed in Chapter 6. Clearly, while globalization appears to be a contested and open-ended process, more often than not the winners are on the side of TNCs and their supporters. Because of its emphasis on the strict corporate control of the process, this interpretation is compatible with the "corporate domination" thesis.

An alternative interpretation views the development of the MSC as a contested process in which TNCs and environmentalists, consumers and local fishermen, attempt to create a new form of statelike regulation—i.e., NGOs—to stabilize global socioeconomic development that protects their interests. Unilever wants to stabilize and legitimize its business practices by resolving (at least temporarily) the historical antagonism between capitalist accumulation and environmental protection through a "neutral" NGO-based joint venture. Similarly, frustrated by the inability of nation-states to resolve the global fisheries crisis, and already possessing a model of green forestry in the Forest Stewardship Council, the WWF and other groups look to the MSC as a replicable model of sustainable stewardship. The events of the case demonstrate that Unilever and other corporate groups support the current status of the MSC and view it as a desirable solution to the issue of industry regulation. Opposition groups do not necessarily criticize the objective of the MSC, but they oppose the actual evolution of the regulatory process, which they see as favoring corporate interests. In effect, the agenda and parameters of the MSC were challenged on several grounds. The case reveals that the MSC was born in controversy based on the concerns of fisherpeople. These groups charged the MSC with elitism and questioned whether it would include the artisan fisheries in its certification scheme or cater only to large global fisheries dominated by industrial fleets. With limited access to the MSC ecolabel, the small-scale fisheries would be left to sell "dirty fish" by default. These groups expressed their distrust in solutions that put blind faith in the market and privileged northern consumers and corporations over southern producers and consumers. As illustrated by the story of the hoki and pollock fisheries, certification procedures were criticized by consumers, environmental groups, and producers alike. Their goal was to establish a system of regulation and control that protects the interests of noncorporate groups and addresses the negative consequences of fishing practices. In response to these criticisms, expressed most clearly in the two independent assessments, the MSC enacted several reforms designed to increase its legitimacy. Broadening representation in the Stakeholder Council, creating the independent objections process to meet FAO standards, and the "developing country initiative" all attempted to quiet critics while expanding the program. Owing to the open and contested nature of the relationship among the major groups involved in the MSC, this position is compatible with the "contradictory dimension of globalization" thesis.

While both of the interpretations discussed above are plausible, nether is superior to the other. It is certainly clear that the rosy view of NGO supporters stands in stark contrast to the concerns and protest of opponents. Similarly, the assertion that NGOs are an alternative to the regulatory and legitimacy crises of the state is backed up by the actions of supporters and detractors alike. Both groups worked to shape the MSC in ways that addressed their views of the situation. The point is that the establishment of the MSC is a problematic solution to the regulatory withdrawal of the state (see Steinberg 1999). It is problematic because the MSC has not provided a system of regulation and control that simultaneously satisfies the interests of corporations and the demands of other social groups. It has not been able both to expand production and consumption and to legitimize that expansion to the broader society. The mounting opposition to the MSC illustrates the limits of NGOs in creating legitimacy for TNCS.

9

CHALLENGING THE GLOBALIZATION PROJECT:
THE COLLAPSE OF THE MULTILATERAL AGREEMENT ON INVESTMENT

We are writing the constitution of a single global economy. . . . The question is where—
not whether—work on trade and investment should take place.
—Renato Ruggerio, director-general of the World Trade Organization, October 1996 (FOE 1997a)

Through the case of the Multilateral Agreement on Investment (MAI), this
chapter further explores the issue of the role of NGOS in globalization. This
case probes the issues of global business governance in a context marked
by the regulatory crisis of the nation-state, and the role that NGOS play in
supporting, and resisting, globalization. The Organization for Economic Cooperation and Development (OECD) created the MAI to provide a global system
for regulating foreign direct investment and thereby supporting global capital accumulation. It was designed to enhance the freedom of movement of
global capital and provide a "set of rights" for TNCS in their dealings with host
countries. Renato Ruggerio of the WTO describes the MAI as an early attempt
to write part of the "constitution for the single global economy." The MAI
was quickly criticized as a "corporate bill of rights" and was challenged by a
broad-based coalition made up of NGOS and developing countries. Developing
countries saw the MAI as an attack on their sovereignty, while NGOS maintained that the MAI was an illegitimate attack on democracy and the sovereignty of nation-states that would result in a "race to the bottom" in
environmental and labor protection. The combination of internal conflict
among OECD countries and mounting challenges from outside NGOS and developing countries led to the abandonment of the OECD-sponsored initiative. The
"corporate bill of rights" agenda resurfaced quickly, however, this time as
the Multilateral Investment Agreement (MIA) under the auspices of the WTO.

Again a combination of antiglobalization NGOs and developing countries emerged to oppose the MIA. This time, a central tenet of the opposition was the negative impact of northern agricultural subsidies on the socioeconomic development of the global South.

This case demonstrates that attempts at global governance of investment regulations in support of global capital accumulation created a legitimation crisis and gave rise to an organized antiglobalization movement. More specifically, it illustrates four points. First, the MAI is a form of global governance advanced by supporters of the globalization project. Second, the OECD's attempt at global governance was resisted at a variety of levels and in a number of venues. Third, NGOs played a dominant role in representing the interests of subordinate groups in opposition to the globalization project. Finally, while the globalization of economy and society is proceeding, the shape and form of the process is contested terrain, and the outcome is still uncertain.

The Development of the Multilateral Agreement on Investment (MAI): Regulations for Global Capital Accumulation

In May 1995 the OECD announced that the time was ripe for negotiating the Multilateral Agreement on Investment (OECD 1995). The OECD is an international intergovernmental organization with twenty-nine member countries from North America, Europe, and the Asia-Pacific area. As a group, OECD countries produce more than half of the world's goods and services, and its members include most of the world's largest economies. The OECD comprises nations that are home to 95 percent of the five hundred largest TNCs (Hiatt 1998). The OECD's overall goal is to boost prosperity by "helping to knit a web of compatible policies and practices across countries that are part of an ever more globalized world" (Witherell 1997). According to William Witherell, director of financial, fiscal, and enterprise affairs of the OECD, the MAI was to "provide a 'level playing field' for international investors regarding FDI with rules that are 'legally enforceable'" and allow "recourse to international arbitration to settle disputes" (Witherell 1996a).

According to the OECD, the MAI was needed to regulate foreign direct investment (FDI), which increased for the third straight year in 1995 to about US$264 billion. The United Nations Conference on Trade and Development (UNCTAD) reported that in 1996 there were about forty thousand multinationals worldwide with about 270,000 foreign affiliates (Stroh 1996). Many large firms view overseas investment through FDI as necessary for getting established in previously unpenetrated markets. Although non-OECD investments were rising rapidly, in 1995 most inflows and outflows were between OECD countries (85 and 65 percent, respectively) (Witherell 1996b). The 1995 inflows of FDI into OECD countries advanced by about 50 percent, while outflows grew by 40 percent. In 1995 developing countries received between 35 and 40 percent of worldwide FDI, up from 21 percent in 1990 (Durbin and Vallianatos 1997). The growing awareness of the need to invest abroad was simultaneously matched by a fierce competition among host countries to attract firms. Investment rules in the mid-1990s were covered by a patchwork of regional treaties, such as NAFTA and about a thousand bilateral treaties. There was "a consensus that some over-riding common document need[ed] to be created" (Stroh 1996). According to Witherell (1997), the MAI fit the bill. It would respond to the rapid growth in FDI spurred by widespread liberalization and increasing competition for investment capital.

The avowed purpose of the MAI was to build on previous agreements between member countries such as the EU and NAFTA by codifying the best aspects of such agreements into a binding resolution that would regularize investment relations between firms and countries—primarily OECD countries but also non-OECD countries. The MAI was intended to "lock in" the benefits of the liberalization of investments that had occurred over the previous few years and to "roll back" measures that still discriminated against foreign investors (Witherell 1996a). According to the OECD, FDI investors still faced investment barriers and discriminatory treatment by host nations. The MAI would provide a stable and comprehensive framework of global investment that would strengthen the multilateral trading regime. It would also set "clear, consistent, and transparent" rules on the liberalization of capital and investor protection and would provide mechanisms for settling disputes.

The MAI was open to all OECD members and the European Union, and to accession by non-OECD countries. It was designed to be a freestanding treaty; although it was negotiated within the OECD, it would not be an OECD instrument (Witherell 1996a). When finalized, the MAI would serve as a benchmark by which potential investors could judge the openness and legal security offered by countries as investment locations (OECD 1995). In other words, by signing on to the MAI, developing countries could gain a certificate of respectability and credibility that would help them attract FDI. Successful conclusion of the MAI would mean that much of the world's investment flows would be covered by a comprehensive framework of international rules (Witherell 1996a).

In September 1995 a negotiating group of OECD member countries and the EU announced that by May 1997 the framework for the world's first global investment organization would be in place (Jebb 1996). Closed negotiations took place every six weeks in Paris, France. The MAI's first chairman was Franciscus (Franz) Engering, director-general for foreign economic relations at the Dutch Ministry of Economic Affairs. The MAI had two vice chairmen, one each from the United States and Japan. The three main objectives of the MAI were protection for investments, liberalization of markets, and a dispute-settlement process (OECD 1995).

In March 1996 the MAI organized a meeting in Hong Kong that for the first time included non-OECD members. Representatives of Argentina, Brazil, Chile, Hong Kong, Korea, Malaysia, Singapore, Taiwan, Thailand, China, India, and Indonesia were invited to discuss how the liberalization of FDI might affect their countries. The MAI held a similar meeting in Istanbul, Turkey, primarily with countries formerly aligned with the Soviet Union (*Corporate Location* 1996). In May 1996 the MAI negotiating group announced that the initiative was "on course" (Witherell 1996a).

Shortly after MAI negotiations began, some countries suggested that such talks should be held in the WTO because the OECD was perceived to represent only the interests of its members, all of them from rich countries (Jebb 1996). Critics of the MAI maintained that the 121-member WTO included measures similar to the MAI initiative and was run by many of the countries being courted by the MAI (Witherell 1996b). The OECD stressed that the MAI should "operate harmoniously" with the WTO and was designed to be compatible with and complement the WTO (Witherell 1996a). By late 1996 there were more calls to bring the MAI under the aegis of the WTO, so that the negotiations would be more multilateral (Stroh 1996).

In March 1997 the OECD reported that it would need more time to work out specific differences between the negotiating countries. The main contention was that the United States and European Union continued to differ regarding proposed "cultural exemptions" that would protect the movie and publishing industries from foreign competition and ownership (PCPP 1997). France, Belgium, Spain, Australia, and Canada expressed strong concerns about protecting their cultural heritage. The United States adamantly opposed such exemptions. Canada and the EU also expressed concern that the U.S. Helms-Burton anti-Cuba law and the Iran-Libya Sanctions Act ran counter to the principles of the MAI (Morrison 1997). OECD officials set May 1998 as the new target date for completion; at that time the MAI would be presented to individual oecd countries for approval (pcpp 1997). After the oecd counties ratified the mai, non-oecd nations would be invited to join.

Opposition to the "Corporate Bill of Rights": The Legitimacy Crisis Builds

This treaty takes the strongest provisions of gatt, NAFTA and bilateral trade agreements and expands them in a way that is revolutionary. This is on the largest scale that these rights for corporations have been applied. mai is an unbalanced agreement that gives rights to corporations and at the same time burdens governments with new obligations to investors. It ties the hands of governments to choose their own social and economic policies.
—Chantell Taylor, Public Citizen, Inc. (Bleifuss 1997)

The mai's features and effects are so shocking that the non-governmental organizations launched a global anti-mai campaign.
—Martin Khor, director of Third World Network (Khor 1998a)

Although the eu had originally proposed that a global investment treaty to regulate fdi be developed as the centerpiece of the new wto, the United States feared that opposition from developing countries could water down any favorable consensus that might be reached, so the United States backed the oecd-sponsored mai (Clarke 1997). India and Malaysia led the developing countries in opposition to investment agreement talks in the wto (Elliott and Denny 1998). Business and industry groups represented by the U.S. Council for International Business and other lobbies convinced the office of the U.S. trade representative and the State Department to initiate mai negotiations in the oecd. Industry groups had an ongoing role in crafting the agreement and were regularly briefed by U.S. negotiators (Durbin 1997). Discussion of the mai at the oecd aimed to protect the foreign investments of tncs like oil companies Shell and bp from unfair treatment and the expropriation of their assets by national governments (Atkinson 1998). As opponents saw it, the United States decided that the best way to get an investment treaty that realized its primary objective—protecting U.S. investors abroad—was to negotiate through the "rich nations' club," the oecd (Clarke 1997).

In 1996 the mai began to attract more criticism. First, French filmmakers demanded a "cultural exemption" to protect their industry from penetration by Hollywood (*European Report* 1996). Then representatives of the developing world argued that their countries needed the ability to be selective and set conditions on fdi and the actions of tncs, "if developing countries are to get larger social benefits" (Raghavan 1996). In December Indonesia announced that it rejected the mai, arguing that under the mai it would not be able to decide on the kinds of investment it wanted to pursue (Xinhua News 1996). Detractors in the global South, as noted above, feared that the MAI would "accelerate an economic and environmental 'race to the bottom' as countries felt new pressure to compete for increasingly mobile investment capital by lowering wages and environmental safeguards" (Africa News Service 1997). As more developing countries expressed their fear that the MAI would undermine their sovereignty, calls to move the negotiations to the WTO or UNCTAD increased (Asia Pulse 1997b; Durbin and Vallianatos 1997). Furthermore, representatives from the developing world called for a study that would spell out the implications of the MAI for the economies of developing countries (Asia Pulse 1997a). These early controversies took place both within the OCED and between it and the developing countries.

In January 1997 MAI negotiations took place in closed meetings in Paris, but the Council of Canadians obtained a draft of the "secret" investment agreement and posted it on the Internet. As more information about the MAI became available, criticism grew. Friends of the Earth (FOE) attacked the initiative, saying that the proponents of free trade and globalization had turned to foreign investment as their next target for liberalization and deregulation. They warned that the MAI would open up all sectors of countries' economies to FDI, deny nations the right to differentiate between local and foreign companies, ban performance requirements related to wages, environmental compliance, and hiring locally, and allow TNCs to challenge countries' laws directly through its binding dispute-settlement process (Bleifuss 1997; FOE 1997b). For example, the foreign treatment provision would grant "most favored nation" status to each member country and would thereby prevent governments from imposing sanctions on countries that abused human rights. Performance requirements that mandated a certain amount of domestic content, the use of local labor, or technology transfer would be banned, as would environmental protection measures. An American study commissioned by the Western Governors Association indicated that the MAI would undermine numerous state laws (WGA 1997).

A major concern of MAI critics was the issue of expropriation. The MAI expanded the definition of expropriation to include "regulatory takings" and "creeping expropriation." The dispute-resolution process was based on NAFTA and allowed both corporate and individual investors to sue sovereign nations for any failure to follow MAI rules that caused loss or damage to their investment. In the past, international agreements had allowed only countries to sue countries. The MAI did not include provisions allowing governments to sue corporations or to counter anticompetitive business practices such as price-fixing (Bleifuss 1997). Critics argued that the absence of these provisions would have a "chilling effect" on environmental, health, and labor legislation. "Essentially, the MAI is an investors' rights agreement designed to remove obstacles to the increasing globalization of the world economy," said researcher Cheryl Bishop (1998). According to FOE spokespersons, the winners would be the TNCS, and the losers would "be the public, the environment and any hopes for sustainable and equitable development" (Durbin and Vallianatos 1997).

FOE also argued that the MAI would pressure developing nations to agree to a regulated system of global trade in which they had no input (FOE 1997b). Such nations would be more penetrable and could be held accountable for infractions of MAI rules. Opposition groups charged that the MAI had developed its framework with "little or no public or congressional input" on the wide range of concerns surrounding increased international capital mobility; issues such as environmental sustainability, labor rights, and financial stability, they claimed, had been essentially ignored. The MAI gave corporations new rights but contained no mechanisms to hold them accountable for such issues in the host countries. Furthermore, once governments entered into the MAI they were bound to irrevocable twenty-year terms. According to FOE (1997b), the MAI guaranteed unrestricted capital mobility, "the right of big companies and financial institutions to go where they want, leave on their own terms, and therefore play one country against another for the most favorable 'climate' for investment, leading to a downward spiral of labor and environmental standards." Martin Khor, director of the Third World Network, was "highly critical of an investment agreement whereby the developing countries were not included in the negotiations but were 'expected to sign on'" (Khor 1998a). In March 1998 the secretary-general of the World Council of Churches, the Reverend Dr. Konrad Raiser, alerted his member churches to the dangers of the MAI and to the lack of participation on the part of the global South and transition countries (WCC 1998).

Environmental concerns were also paramount. In February 1997 the Sierra Club, the National Wildlife Federation, the World Wildlife Fund, and six other environmental organizations called for a one-year postponement of the MAI. They maintained that it contained mechanisms that were much more lenient than NAFTA and could force countries to roll back environmental and labor protections. They called for enforceable requirements that would prevent the weakening of laws and guarantees that the MAI would not be used to ride roughshod over legitimate environmental concerns. Finally, they demanded that the MAI's dispute-resolution process be opened up to the public and to environmental experts (Pope 1997).

By late 1997 opposition to the MAI had grown to include church groups, environmentalists, and state governments in the United States, as well as developing countries and NGOs in both developed and developing countries. Opponents from Canada argued that the MAI was an attempt to establish a corporate bill of rights and freedoms that would greatly increase the power of TNCs over Canada's future (Clarke 1997). Maude Barlow of the Council of Canadians called the MAI "NAFTA on steroids" (Berton 1998). She felt so strongly about the MAI's threat of "global corporate rule" that she wrote a book about it called *MAI and the Threat to Canadian Sovereignty*. Canadian opponents offered as proof the case of Ethyl Corporation of Richmond, Virginia, the first NAFTA-based attempt to assert treaty rights. In April 1997 the Canadian government passed legislation that banned the use of MMT, a controversial gasoline additive linked to negative health and environmental effects (Abramson 1997; Hiatt 1998). Ethyl Corporation, a major producer of MMT with a plant in Sarnia, Ontario, fought back with a NAFTA investment claim against Ottawa totaling $251 million. The company charged that Ottawa was violating its right, under NAFTA, to immediate compensation for legislation that hindered its operations. Ethyl claimed that the ban on MMT would reduce the value of its plant, hurt future sales, and damage its reputation (Khor 1998a). In July 1998 the Canadian government dropped its ban on MMT and agreed to pay Ethyl Corporation $13 million (Canadian) for legal costs and lost profits (Weisbrot 1998).

The MAI included NAFTA-type FDI-protection provisions that allowed corporations to sue governments for expropriations that violated the investment agreement (Abramson 1997; Khor 1998a). The Canadian government's capitulation to Ethyl Corporation provided opponents of the MAI with the "proof" they needed. Their critique sharpened as the MAI came under increasing attack on numerous fronts. As Don E. McAllister of the Canadian Center for Biodiversity put it at the time, "an immense swing in the balance of global power is taking place. The MAI threatens to turn over powers held by democratically elected governments and their citizens to international corporations" (Hiatt 1998). George Monbiot, one of the UK's leading environmental activists, criticized the British government for supporting the MAI and thereby "signing away our sovereignty" (Monbiot 1997). Robert Strumberg, a professor of law at Georgetown University Law Center, argued that "the MAI would operate as a virtual amendment to the United States Constitution" (Bishop 1998). In testimony before the Sub-Committee on International Affairs of the House of Commons Standing Committee on Foreign Affairs and International Trade in Ottawa, Ontario, Paul Hellyer, author of *The Evil Empire: Globalization's Darker Side,* provided a more analytical view of the MAI:

> The Hungarian-born American financier George Soros is not alone when he warns that unfettered capitalism is replacing fascism and communism as the greatest threat to open societies. This is exactly what is happening. We are spawning a world where the managers of industry and money, and shareholders in their enterprises, get the lion's share of the world's wealth and where the rest get little, if anything. It is an empire where the division of wealth becomes increasingly unequal and ordinary citizens count for nothing at all because it won't matter whom they elect. The real power will lie in the hands of the unelected, unaccountable bureaucrats and autocrats. (Hellyer 1997, 3)

In October 1997, in response to the growing criticism, the OECD invited NGOs to the negotiating table. More than 150 NGOs representing seventy countries met in Paris and presented a "joint consensus statement" to the OECD that included a list of demands that would make the MAI more inclusive of rights for nations, labor, and the environment and hold TNCs more accountable for their actions. "We put the OECD on notice," said Henry Holmes of Sustainable Alternatives to the Global Economy (Bishop 1998). This meeting was the catalyst for the creation of an international coalition against the MAI. Following the meeting, organizations from various African nations started an electronic networking system, the hundred-thousand-member citizen group Council of Canadians pressed for more media coverage of the dangers of the MAI, and the labor movement in France announced that it was committed to defeating it.

In the United States the Alliance for Democracy made fighting the MAI its first priority. To educate U.S. citizens about the threat presented by the MAI, the Preamble Center for Public Policy sponsored debates between supporters and opponents in twenty U.S. cities. Public Citizen, Inc., launched a campaign against the treaty in twenty-five states and joined organizations from twenty-three countries in an international coalition against the MAI (Bleifuss 1997). By early 1998 citizens' groups were holding demonstrations on the steps of the Capitol building and organizing "national call-in days" to members of Congress. The MAI also came under attack on the floor of the U.S. Congress (Bishop 1998). A group of environmental organizations sent a letter of opposition to the Clinton administration (Khor 1998b). Major U.S. cities declared themselves "MAI-free zones" (Taylor 1998).

Opposition was especially fervent in Canada, thanks mostly to the Council of Canadians. By February 1998 British Columbia, Prince Edward Island, and the Yukon Territory had passed resolutions against the MAI (*London Free Press* 1998). In March the Council of Canadians, in coalition with some five hundred organizations, set up information stations across Canada to educate people about the MAI (Cheadle 1998). By July five provinces had declared themselves "MAI-free zones" (Taylor 1998). Maude Barlow, who coined the slogan "NAFTA on steroids," was a prominent organizer and member of the council.

The anti-MAI coalition held an "international week of action" the week before the February OECD meetings that were to determine whether the MAI could be completed by the May deadline (Khor 1998b; Reuters 1998). A Swiss NGO official commented that "all hell has broken loose in some European Union member countries, with a combination of street protests, NGO critiques, outraged parliaments and inter-agency fights within governments on key issues" (Khor 1998b). Tens of thousands of protestors took to the streets in France, forcing the French government to renegotiate the treaty (Taylor 1998). In the Netherlands activists occupied the entrance to the office of MAI chairman Franz Engering at The Hague. In London several NGOs organized a demonstration in front of the Department of Trade and Industry. In a letter to the *Guardian,* Right Livelihood Award winner Jakob von Uexkull warned, "Transnational corporations are already more powerful than many nations states. To describe them as victims of discrimination needing more protection is another example of Orwellian Newspeak of global corporate rule. A democracy which abdicates the right to favour its citizens over foreign corporations will soon lose its public legitimacy, with potentially disastrous consequences" (Khor 1998b). NGO actions also took place in Finland, Sweden, Australia, and France.

Von Uexkull captured the essence of the growing crisis facing the OCED as it attempted to conclude the negotiations on the MAI. In a statement endorsed by 565 environmental, development, labor, consumer, church, and women's organizations from sixty-seven countries, the anti-MAI coalition called on the OECD to suspend the negotiations because it did not "respect the rights of countries" to control foreign direct investment (Khor 1998b). Thanks in part to the actions of this coalition, many countries asked for more exemptions from the treaty's provisions for specific social and economic sectors. This avalanche of requests decreased the likelihood that the MAI would be completed by the May 1998 deadline.

The Six-Month Delay: OECD Member Discontent and the Crisis of Legitimacy

The November 1997 citizens victory stopping the so-called "fast track" authority to expand NAFTA, and the MAI's missed April signing date, show our actions are beginning to create a political space for new rules for the global economy that will serve the public interest, not only narrow corporate interests.
—Chantell Taylor, Public Citizen, Inc. (Taylor 1998)

Just before the February meeting in Paris at which the MAI was to be finalized, U.S. trade representative Charlene Barshefsky announced that the United States would not support the MAI "at this time" because it was "unbalanced and prejudicial to US interests" (Dunne 1998). The United States was especially dismayed that OECD member countries in the European Union continued to seek "broad exemptions" from the agreement, which, in the view of the United States, would defeat the original purpose. The United States was also upset that New Zealand wanted special exemptions for the Maori people. Within the United States, agencies were split over the MAI; the State Department wanted to continue negotiations and the U.S. Trade Office opposed them. Other OECD members were angry because the United States refused to eliminate the Helms-Burton Act sanctions against Cuba and companies doing business with Cuba. This "major shift" in U.S. policy toward the MAI was attributed to rising opposition to the MAI from the NGO coalition of trade unionists and environmentalists, on the left, and the opponents of free trade, led by Pat Buchanan, on the right, who had successfully defeated "fast-track authority" in 1997 and opposed U.S. support for the IMF (Atkinson 1998; *Los Angeles Times* 1998). After the defeat of fast-track authority the Clinton administration was reluctant to bring a "hot potato" like the MAI before Congress just before midterm elections. Even though the State Department and Trade Office were at odds, the Clinton administration was still being pressured by U.S. corporations and the International Business Council to finalize the MAI "within the coming year" (Clarke and Barlow 1998, 8).

French prime minister Lionel Jospin announced at the OECD meeting that "France would not sign unless it was allowed to continue giving home-grown films, television programmes, books and 'creators' subsidies and privileges" (Herbert 1998). Jospin claimed that this demand was a "legitimate defense" against the ever-increasing influence of Hollywood on French film and television. In early March members of the European Parliament voted over-whelmingly in favor of a resolution calling for the MAI to be negotiated in a more democratic forum than the OECD and for social, developmental, and environmental reviews of its content (Elliott and Denny 1998). Even with these setbacks, OECD officials announced that they would "intensify their efforts" to finalize the MAI by the May deadline.

In late March, however, the OECD reported that there was no chance that the MAI would meet the May deadline, as eleventh-hour negotiations had "failed to overcome deep divisions" between the United States and the Euro-pean Union. Anti-MAI coalition forces welcomed the news and called for more public dialogue on the impact of treaty. Nick Mabey of the World Wildlife Fund said the announcement effectively quashed "any excuse by govern-ments to avoid democratic debate and ensure that an open environmental assessment of the MAI is undertaken." Alan Simpson, chairman of a UK labor group, added, "This may wake up the trade union movement in Britain and the political system here to the dangers of the MAI that only the NGOs seem willing to acknowledge" (Elliott and Denny 1998). Expressing her delight with the announcement, Jessica Woodroffe, head of campaigns for the Third World lobbying organization World Development Movement, said, "This shows what a misconceived project it is. The negotiators must be very weary by now, dealing with conflicts on dozens of different fronts, from labour rights to cultural diversity." Ruth Mayne, a policy analyst of Oxfam, con-cluded that "a new approach is needed, based on broad consultation and including the developing countries from the outset." Sol Picciotto, a profes-sor of law at Lancaster University, said the MAI was the "last gasp of a neo-liberal agenda" that sought to promote market integration without address-ing the real issue of regulation (Atkinson 1998). The anti-MAI coalition con-tinued to build broad-based support and momentum into the spring of 1998.

On the last day of MAI talks in April, the OECD announced that it would shelve the negotiations for six months in order to provide time for further assessments and consultations (AP Online 1998b). OECD countries, it said, should consult with "interested parties of their societies" and conduct open public debate on the implications of globalization. Charles Arden-Clark, head of the WWF's International's Trade and Investment Unit, suggested that the "MAI should be placed before the OECD's newly formed Sustainable Develop-ment Steering Group," where a "sustainability impact assessment" should be undertaken (M2PressWIRE 1998). While celebrating the announcement of the delay, MAI critics also noted that the six-month delay would be used to "begin a public relations offensive to create public support for the MAI," and that opponents needed to remain vigilant in their counteractions (Mattern 1998).

At the April meeting of the OECD, the issue of where global investment talks should be held arose again, but no decision was made to change the location from the OECD to the WTO, as some countries had requested. Conservative commentators suggested that maybe the OECD was not in fact the best place for global investment talks, for it included only two Asian countries and one Latin American nation (Coyle 1998). The director-general of the WTO, Renato Ruggerio, stated that the WTO was assessing whether it might start its own investment talks and include developing countries. At the Singapore meeting in 1996 the WTO had considered the issue of global investment regulations (Battye 1996).

From the perspective of the critics, the six-month period in which OECD members were supposed to "seek broader participation" through "consultation and assessment" with civil society and commit to a more "transparent negotiating process" was a failure. Several countries carried out no impact assessments or consultations. Of those that did organize public sessions, open discussion of the potential impact of MAI was limited. In France, the only country in which the government created a commission to study the issue, the conclusion was that "the MAI should be drastically overhauled or abandoned" (CEO 1998).

During the six-month delay, the campaign against the MAI stepped up its efforts significantly. MAI opposition groups sprang up in Turkey, Denmark, Norway, Italy, and Austria. In most other OECD countries, NGOs opposed to the MAI held demonstrations, letter-writing campaigns, call-ins, and public debates, published books and brochures, and mounted speaking tours to raise public awareness. These activities peaked in the "international week of action" held September 21–28 and in various activities in October. Numerous trade unions, environmental organizations, consumer groups, and international NGOs such as Oxfam, the Globalization Observatory, and Third World Network took part (*European Report* 1998b).

The surge in opposition was fueled by events that highlighted the "flawed fundamentals" of the MAI. The Canadian government's yielding to Ethyl Corporation's demands regarding the ban on MMT was a concrete example of the power NAFTA gave TNCs to gain redress for expropriations and use the dispute-settlement process to protect their investments. The global financial crisis that started in east Asia in 1997 and spread to Latin America and Russia also illuminated the high social and economic costs of market deregulation. Critics asserted that if the MAI had been in place, it would have locked in the "financial casino economy" of "speculative financial flows (hot money)" and prohibited the kind of national safeguards needed to avert such crises and to address them when they happened (CEO 1998). These factors both increased the resolve of the anti-MAI coalition and caused more countries, both OECD members and other nations, to question the merits of the MAI in particular and globalization in general.

During the six-month delay the anti-MAI coalition also monitored and opposed attempts to pursue the MAI model through other international venues such as the Free Trade Agreement of the Americas (FTAA), the Lome Convention, the New Transatlantic Marketplace/Transatlantic Economic Partnership, the Asia-Pacific Economic Cooperation forum (APEC), the IMF, and the WTO. Opponents argued that the problem was not just the flawed provisions of the MAI but the "underlying agenda of high-speed, full-scale investment liberalization" that was accelerating "the ecological crisis and social exclusion worldwide" (CEO 1998). Moving the MAI to the WTO would not solve the problem. Democratic governments, clearly, had to be able to regulate investors and investments if sustainable development and social justice were to be achieved.

The MAI Abandoned: Global Events, Member Intransigence, and the Anti-MAI Coalition

The week before the MAI talks were scheduled to resume in October, France announced that it was withdrawing from the negotiations. Prime Minister Jospin stated that the agreement as currently structured was "not open to reform" and "threatened the sovereignty of states, which are asked to commit themselves in an irreversible manner" (Iskander 1998). Jospin said that the United States had not changed its position regarding cultural exemptions for the French film industry, nor would it lift its sanctions against countries that did business with Cuba, Iran, and Libya. Jospin expressed the preference of the French government that new talks on global investment should be held under the auspices of the WTO. The trade minister of Canada, Sergio Marchi, said in response that although the MAI initiative was at the "end of the road," a realistic time frame for a global investment agreement was five years, and he hoped the negotiations would begin anew in the WTO. He said that Canada would have an easier time getting the cultural protections it desired at the 138-member WTO than at the twenty-nine-member OECD, made up of the world's richest countries (Lawton 1998).

The oECD responded that the October meeting would proceed without France and would focus on possible approaches for future action. oECD representative Rainer Geiger said that in light of the financial crises rocking many countries, the talks were critical "to restore confidence in markets" (Burns 1998). On the eve of the meeting, the United States announced that it "could not yet endorse" the proposed MAI but would continue talks on improving the accord (de Jonquieres 1998b). Alan Larson, U.S. assistant secretary of state, said that the current version did not deal adequately with environmental and labor standards and needed more public support. MAI critics maintained that the real reason the United States was backing away from the MAI was that it realized that the dispute-resolution process could be used against it, as it had been used against Canada in the case of Ethyl Corporation (*Financial Times* 1998).

Larson also commented that the MAI could help solve Asia's economic crisis and that abandoning it "would not be a good sign" (de Jonquieres 1998b). He concluded that the United States felt that the oECD was still the best venue in which to hold investment treaty talks and did not share the EU's and other countries' desire to move the talks to the WTO. oECD secretary-general Donald Johnston also defended keeping the MAI in the oECD, saying that oECD members and nonmembers that joined the negotiations accounted for 92 percent of the global FDI outflows and 73 percent of the inflows (*European Report* 1998a). In 1998 global FDI totaled about $8 trillion per year and was growing at a rate of $350 billion annually (Gerwitz 1998).

The day after Johnston's statement, the oECD announced that it was "retreating" from plans to conclude the MAI negotiations (de Jonquieres 1998a). A week later Britain's trade minister, Brian Wilson, one of the MAI's strongest supporters, announced that the UK had withdrawn its support for the MAI as well (Denny and Atkinson 1998). He too endorsed the option of moving the global investment talks to the WTO. In response to growing calls to develop the multilateral investment agreement under the auspices of the WTO, the United States declared that if the treaty could not be reached in the twenty-nine-member oECD, "it would not be reached at the WTO, which has more than 100 members." In November Australia announced that it too had dropped out of the MAI negotiations (Selinger 1998). The same month several developing countries, including India, announced that they opposed the resumption of MAI talks within the WTO because such an agreement would "lock in countries into accepting terms which may not be suitable for their own . . . level of development" (Asia Pulse 1998).

Finally, in December, the oECD announced that it had "indefinitely suspended" talks on the MAI. Business groups expressed disappointment at the news and pledged to keep pushing for international investment rules in some form. "There's still a need out there to have agreed-upon rules governing investment overseas," said William Workman, international vice president for the U.S. Chamber of Commerce (Selinger 1998). As anti-MAI coalition forces celebrated their victory, they were quick to point out that the "MAI agenda is not dead" and that its principles were "still being pushed forward" in such forums as the WTO, the FTAA, the IMF, and APEC. Margaret Strand-Rangnes, facilitator for the MAI-NOT listserve that had used the Internet to coordinate the anti-MAI coalition, urged coalition members to keep working so that the "MAI agenda gets buried once and for all" (Strand-Rangnes 1998).

The Resurrection: The Multilateral Investment Agreement (MIA) in the WTO

We stand at the very beginning of a whole new phase of internationalism. We are living through a time of deep and rapid transition towards a very different world. This year . . . we have the occasion to send a positive message about the reality of the global transition, but also about the unprecedented opportunities this offers, an opportunity to reaffirm our political will to move towards a better system of global governance . . . shaping the institutions of an increasingly borderless economy.
—Renato Ruggerio, director-general of the WTO, at the May 1998 WTO meetings in Geneva, Switzerland (Madeley 1999)

The WTO has become the means by which corporations force governments to open their borders to the crudest forms of exploitation.
—George Monbiot, UK environmentalist (1999)

Although the MAI had been the center of attention for antiglobalization ac-tivists for some time, the WTO was beginning to attract increasing criticism, especially in the developing world. The WTO was created during the Uruguay Round of the General Agreement on Tariffs and Trade (GATT) in January 1995 for the purpose of reducing barriers to trade worldwide (Madeley 1999). The WTO, successor of the GATT, forms the "trade arm" of the triad of global eco-nomic institutions—the other two are the World Bank and the IMF—created at Bretton Woods, New Hampshire, after World War II to regulate global socio-economic development (Kraker and Dawkins 1999). Whereas the GATT was voluntary and contained no enforcement mechanisms, membership in the WTO entails formal responsibilities to reduce trade barriers and a binding dis-pute-resolution mechanism. By 1999 the WTO had 134 member countries, about one hundred of which fell into the category of "developing country" (*European Report* 1999e).

The wto quickly became a target of antiglobalization forces. At its May 1998 meeting in Geneva, Switzerland, ten thousand people gathered outside the un building to protest the negative effects of globalization (Madeley 1999). Critics charged that the wto's vision was "global governance" based on free trade at the expense of national sovereignty and democracy—the same criticisms used against the mai.

Although the mai had died at the oecd in 1994, the eu spurred a new initiative to negotiate the agreement in the wto, focusing the attention of antiglobalization activists on that organization (Kraker and Dawkins 1999). India again took the lead in representing a minority of developing countries, including Pakistan, Egypt, Malaysia, China, Cuba, and others that opposed the initiative, and once more called for an analysis of the impact of a global trading system on development (Asia Pulse 1999; Borosage 1999). Environmentalists added their voice to the opposition. The wwf's Michael Insausti remarked, "wwf supports international regulations on investment, but does not believe the wto is the right organisation to determine these rules" (Reuters 1999). Insausti added that before global investment regulations could be negotiated, an "over-arching international framework" on environmental protection needed to be established in the un Commission on Sustainable Development.

In May 1999 representatives of the eu announced that a central focus of the wto Millennium Round, to be held in Seattle, Washington, should be the "reinforcement of a multilateral trade system" (*European Report* 1999d). They added that the new round would make a special effort to address environmental concerns, include developing countries in the negotiations, and promote dialogue with civil society on the benefits of multilateral investment regulations (*European Report* 1999b). The United States promptly added its support to the Millennium Round negotiations. British prime minister Tony Blair called for a "new Bretton Woods" agreement to stabilize the global financial crisis, a crisis that detractors maintained had "called into question the promise of globalization" (Borosage 1999, 23).

The wwf quickly announced that it would help lead a coalition of ngos to protest the Millennium Round (*European Report* 1999d). As the date of the Seattle meeting neared, some twelve hundred ngos signed a declaration of "international civil society" that opposed the expansion of the wto's power. The coalition called on governments to "review and rectify the deficiencies of a system which has contributed to the concentration of wealth in the hands of the rich few, increasing poverty for the majority of the world's population, and unsustainable patterns of production and consumption" (*Eu-*

ropean Report 1999a, 3). In Seattle tens of thousands of antiglobalization activists held demonstrations and blocked traffic, making it difficult for negotiators to attend the meetings. Seattle police used teargas and rubber bullets to subdue the "riotous" crowds in what became known as the "battle in Seattle" (*European Report* 1999c). While the protesters did disrupt the meetings, the more important conflict unfolded within the WTO, as member countries tried to resolve their multiple disagreements, ranging from hormone-treated beef, to turtle-excluder devices, to intellectual property rights, to agricultural subsidies (Hornblower et al. 1999). The Seattle meetings were taken up with these and other issues, and the hopes for new global investment regulations were not realized.

While global investment regulations were not a prominent feature of the next WTO meeting, held in Doha, Qatar, in November 2001, member countries decided to pursue the issue after the WTO meeting in Cancun, scheduled for September 2003, if an "explicit consensus" could be reached by WTO member countries (KWNS 2002). In Doha developing countries came under intense pressure from the EU and other countries to agree to set up the "modalities" for negotiations on a "multilateral investment agreement" (MIA) at Cancun, to help "kick start the economy" in the aftermath of the September 11 terrorist attacks on the United States (WDM/FOE 2003).

In the lead-up to the Cancun meeting in September 2003, antiglobalization NGOS released studies criticizing the MIA. The World Development Movement and the Friends of the Earth report, entitled "Investment and the WTO: Busting the Myths," concluded that the MIA would "primarily benefit a small number of large transnational corporations who will get greater 'right to roam' around the global economy with no additional responsibilities" (WDM/FOE 2003). The group denounced WTO claims supported by the EU, Canada, and Japan that the MIA would be "good for sustainable development" and called for NGOS and developing countries to continue to resist efforts to create the MIA in the WTO (Lobe 2003). ActionAid, an NGO that works with local communities in more than thirty countries, published a position paper challenging the notion that the value of FDI in developing countries could be taken for granted (Hilary 2003). It presented several cases illustrating how FDI had had severe negative effects on the poor and called for the EU to drop its insistence on passing the MIA in the WTO. Other critics agreed that the "MIA's one-size-fits-all strategy is ill-conceived because WTO members are at different stages of development." This, they said, is why previous attempts at global investment regulations (such as the MAI) had failed, and why recent "mini-ministerial" meetings in Seattle and Qatar had failed and should not be on the agenda for Cancun (Singh 2003). India again affirmed its opposition to MIA negotiations in the WTO (Luce, de Jonquieres, and Williams 2003). The agenda to create the MIA in the WTO was also opposed by Brazil, Indonesia, the Philippines, Egypt, Venezuela, Malaysia, Thailand, Cuba, Jamaica, and the forty-nine least-developed countries in the world (Suri 2003). Antiglobalization activists called for mass demonstrations in Cancun to "underline the global opposition to corporate-centered trade and investment rules" (Investment Watch 2003).

The Cancun meeting opened with marked polarization between the world's richest nations—the United States, the members of the European Union, and Japan—and a newly formed bloc of developing countries led by Brazil, India, China, Argentina, and South Africa called the Group of 22 (G22) (Cevallos 2003; Thornton 2003). On the final day of talks, the negotiations collapsed. No consensus was reached on the major topics of agricultural subsidies and the Singapore issues of trade and investment, trade and competition policy, transparency in government procurement, and trade facilitation (WTO 2003). The chairman of the meetings, Mexican foreign minister Luis Derbez, said that it made no sense to continue the discussions, because the positions were irreconcilable. A member of the Brazilian delegation commented that "huge discrepancies between the rich and poor countries, and among developing countries, persisted to the end" (Cevallos 2003).

Agriculture was the key variable (Schott 2003). The immediate impetus behind the G22 was the need to create a "counterweight" to EU and U.S. protectionist farm policies (Capdevila 2003). G22 countries argued that northern agricultural subsidies prevented southern exports that could support socioeconomic development. While the United States and the EU had promised to reduce their farm subsidies in the past, their "words were not matched with action" (Nimbupani 2003, 3). China joined the G22 in a strategic effort to push for deeper cuts in farm subsidies. Brazil and several African countries targeted U.S. cotton subsidies. The G22 and supporting NGOs demanded concessions on farm subsidies from the EU and United States before the talks could move forward (Schott 2003).

Activists hailed the collapse of the Cancun talks as the greatest triumph for anti-WTO forces since Seattle, asserting that it "marked the emergence of a permanent new power bloc of once-powerless nations defending the rights of millions of small farmers" (Hayden 2003). "This is a triumph of reason, a triumph of the poor countries and civil society, because we could not allow the rich countries to once again impose their views and their pressure," said Albert Villareal, head of FOE's international trade campaign. Phil Bloomer of

Oxfam said that "Cancun failed due to the power and cohesion of the developing countries" (Cevallos 2003). Thanks to "tough negotiating" by the G22, the world's two most powerful economic blocs had "been prevented from riding roughshod over the 100-plus countries that make up the developing world." Celso Amorim, foreign minister of Brazil, concluded that the G22 had "reshuffled the cards" by creating a powerful counterweight to Washington and Brussels and had thereby "changed the entire dynamics of world politics" (Thornton 2003).

Analysis and Discussion

We opened this book by arguing that the globalization project is an overt attempt to revive capital accumulation. By the 1970s a variety of social movements had secured protection and benefits through the civil rights, labor rights, and environmental protection movements. The success of these movements increased the cost of doing business in highly developed economies and brought an end to Fordist stability (Harvey 1989). The resulting accumulation crisis was addressed through globalization, which was designed to minimize or reverse the successes of social-democratic movements in First World economies and thereby increase capital accumulation while reasserting the domination of the ruling class (Harvey 2005; Robinson 2004). At the economic level, the components of the globalization project center on increased flexibility and the hypermobility of capital (Harvey 1989; Lipietz 1992). Its major effects have been capital flight to less regulated countries, decentralization of production in multiple locations, informalization of labor through the use of nonunion and part-time workforces, and global sourcing carried out by transnational corporations (Bonanno and Constance 1996). These components reorganized both developed and developing national economies, as TNCs played country against country in their search for what Porter (1990) calls the best "competitive advantages." At the national political level, in response to this strategy, nation-states deregulated and privatized their economies so as to be creditworthy and attract FDI, engaging in what globalization critics call the "race to the bottom." At the supranational level, regional coalitions such as the EU and NAFTA took on an increased role in socioeconomic governance via "free trade agreements" (Harvey 2006; Friedland 1991). Similarly, at the global level nascent forms of governance such as the WTO have emerged to establish ground rules for the "constitution for the global economy."

It can be argued that the OECD-sponsored MAI was an attempt on the part of the advanced countries and their neoliberal political regimes to formalize and firm up some of the key rules of the globalization project, advancing what MAI opponents called a "corporate bill of rights." The political, economic, and bureaucratic elites that make up what Sklair (2001) and Robinson (2004) call the "transnational capitalist class" made an effort through the OECD to "lock in" the benefits of investment regime liberalization based on the free movement of capital, and to roll back measures that discriminated against foreign TNCS. In other words, through the MAI, the OECD tried to create a global system to regulate FDI and thereby create a more stable global business environment. In this attempt at global governance, the MAI was to emulate the accumulation role historically played by the nation-state—but at the supranational level, under the aegis of the OECD. With the MAI's demise, the MIA became the vehicle for furthering global governance. WTO director-general Renato Ruggerio commented that the question was "not whether" but "where" the new constitution for the global economy would be written.

The MAI story also demonstrates that as the globalization project proceeds, redefining the role nation-states perform in coordinating socioeconomic development, NGOS have emerged as powerful actors to fill some of the space vacated by nation-states. In this case—unlike the case of the Marine Stewardship Council (Chapter 8)—NGOS have supported the interests of subordinate groups and challenged the legitimacy of the globalization project. While environmental organizations like Friends of the Earth and populist organizations like the Council of Canadians were early critics of the MAI, the anti-MAI coalition grew quickly to include hundreds of environmental, consumer, labor, religious, developing country, and indigenous people's organizations. The anti-MAI actions of these NGOS were coordinated through the Internet via the MAI-NOT listserv. After the death of the MAI, the coalition turned its attention to other perceived threats, such as the FTAA and the MIA. The success of the NGO-based antiglobalization movement in the MAI case supports the view of those who see NGOS as providing valuable avenues for democratic action in the face of the declining power of nation-states.

A point often made in this book is that the globalization project is met with ongoing resistance. It can be argued that the MAI failed because it lacked legitimacy at several levels. Once the text of the MAI was posted on the Internet, the anti-MAI coalition grew into a formidable opposition movement. It consistently depicted the MAI as an illegitimate form of socioeconomic development that threatened the sovereignty of nation-states. The Canadian government's capitulation to the Ethyl Corporation was a huge red flag for antiglobalization activists, portending as it did the ever increasing powers of transnational corporations under globalization. A second prong of attack came from developing countries that saw the MAI as another form of northern imperialism that would undermine their sovereignty and socioeconomic well-being. The creation of the G22 before the WTO Cancun talks formalized the South's opposition to the globalization project.

The effectiveness of the anti-MAI coalition notwithstanding, it is likely that the deciding factor in the demise of the MAI was the inability of the dominant OECD members, the United States and European Union, to agree on the MAI parameters. The anti-MAI coalition evolved into the antiglobalization coalition that continues to challenge attempts to write the constitution for the global economy in the form of the WTO-based MIA. Under the MIA/WTO format, agricultural subsidies in the North rose to prominence as a crucial factor for the opposition.

The MAI story provides valuable insights into the contested terrain of the globalization project. In 2000 an MAI observer noted that the failure of the MAI and fast-track authority in the United States, coupled with substantial opposition to the WTO worldwide, "adds up to a breakdown of what was known as the "Washington consensus, the world view pushed aggressively by the US Treasury, the IMF, and the World Bank in the early 1990s" (Engardio and Belton 2000). That consensus held that all countries should open all sectors of their economies to trade, FDI, and short-term capital "as quickly as possible." The promise was that the transition would be painful but in the long run prosperity would be the result—a kind of Schumpeterian *creative destruction*. The broad-based coalition against the MAI in particular and globalization in general was indeed successful in slowing the progress of what Alan Greenspan calls the "unforgiving capitalist process" of wealth creation. But the globalization project reasserted itself, as the U.S. Congress granted fast-track authority to the Bush administration (Phillips 2002) and the MAI was resurrected as the MIA under the auspices of the WTO. The antiglobalization movement's disruption of the WTO talks in Seattle and Cancun, and the creation of the G22, can be seen as successful attempts on the part of subordinate groups to bring about a "more caring" form of global capitalism—but global capitalism it is, just the same.

While the MAI case does support the "corporate domination" thesis, it provides stronger evidence in support of the "contradictory dimension of globalization" thesis. This chapter, like others in this volume, highlights the contested character of the globalization project, as supporters and opponents battle over the regulation of the nascent global economy. The story of the MAI also reveals that the supporters of globalization are often at odds over the particulars of global regulation. Maybe the bickering of the rich nations, combined with the efforts of the G22 and antiglobalization forces, really can "change the entire dynamic of world politics." In our view, the evidence suggests that the outcome of the battle over globalization is uncertain, as the two sides continue to fight it out.

CONCLUSION

The cases discussed in this book provide abundant evidence of the power that TNCs enjoy under globalization. In the stories of Ferruzzi, ADM, Maxxam, and other companies, we saw that TNCs exercise a great deal of control over nation-states and those who resist them. TNCs' ability to source globally for the most convenient conditions of production places nations and regions in fierce competition as they open their territories, deregulate their economies, and provide incentives to please corporations and attract investments. Entities that resist this model are disengaged from global circuits in favor of other, more "willing" regions and communities. Thomas Friedman (2000) and like-minded apologists for globalization define this "golden straightjacket" of globalization as the fundamental condition of socioeconomic expansion. The stories presented in this volume point to different conclusions. While a few groups do benefit from globalization, socioeconomic decay, the increased polarization of rich and poor, environmental degradation, and the undermining of democratic forms of government emerge as the most common consequences of globalization.

Contrary to some of the most radical interpretations of the power of TNCs (i.e., Ohmae 1995; Sklair 2001), our stories also indicate that TNCs' power is *not without limits*—because resistance movements affect the scope and extent of corporate actions, and because resistance materializes even in cases where TNCs achieve their objectives. While stories such as those of hog and chicken CAFOs in Texas show that corporations profit handsomely from the aggressive opening of local economies and from deregulation, they also show that communities will fight back when their quality of life is affected.

There is another reason why the power of TNCs is not unlimited. In their endless pursuit of expanding profits, TNCs must sell ever-increasing quantities of the commodities they produce. At the same time, as consumers become aware of the methods of production, they exercise their power to choose certain products while rejecting others. Although the proportional number of such informed, highly conscious consumers remains relatively small worldwide, in certain markets their choices have forced TNCs to reconsider their strategies and in some cases even modify their agendas. It is possible that this trend will accelerate in the future.

The stories summarized in this volume also suggest that TNCs maintain a contradictory relationship with nation-states. Although they attempt to bypass governmental laws and regulations and pressure governments to back corporate agendas, TNCs also need government assistance, both in the business of making money and in attempting to justify their profit margins to various segments of society. In essence, TNCs' ability to circumvent state laws works only partially in their favor. To the degree that corporations are able to get around existing laws, they pay the price that those same governments are limited in their capacity to mediate social and economic resistance and intervene in favor of TNCs. Transnational social relations thus expand the powers of TNCs but also make them less able to rely on established forms of social, economic, and political assistance historically granted by nation-states.

The loss of state power is part of a broader crisis of the nation-state, the most relevant aspect of which is its reduced ability to legitimize globalized social relations. The nation-state, in other words, is required to justify phenomena that are increasingly outside its sphere of control. This *crisis of legitimation* provides possibilities, however, for democratizing the state, for it exposes the great disparities between global economic expansion and social well-being. The crisis of the nation-state is also a crisis of democracy, for government inability to regulate global economic actions diminishes citizens' ability to participate in decision making. Nor is the state simply a passive spectator of the consequences of corporate action. As several of the stories in this volume show, the state actively establishes conditions that promote corporate strategies. The crisis of democracy, therefore, is a consequence of the interaction between state and corporate actors.

The issue of democracy has been central in globalization research. As we argue below, despite TNCs' enhanced powers, the contradictions experienced by TNCs and the nation-state open the possibility for a new democratic turn, one that could reverse the antidemocratic, economically polarizing trend of globalization. The following section summarizes the development of that trend, as Fordist democracy was displaced by neoliberalism.

The Crisis of Democracy

Fordist or State-Based Liberal Democracy

By the beginning of the twentieth century the growth of large corporations and the concentration of economic power made the classical liberal idea of self-regulating markets increasingly inadequate as a description of mature capitalism (Dewey 1935/1963). In the classical liberal tradition, the efficient functioning of the market assumed the exclusive presence of small operators. Their limited size did not allow them to affect market outcomes, which were determined by the aggregate working of all economic activities. The development of oligopolies and monopolies undermined this arrangement and made it obsolete. Through the concentration of resources, corporations were able to increase control over market outcomes and enhance their competitive position. Larger size created barriers to market entry and made assumptions about mobility of capital within sectors and the idea of a level playing field untenable (Gordon 1996; Reich 1991). In addition, the expansion of capitalism greatly exacerbated socioeconomic inequality and instability (Antonio and Bonanno 1996). While economic growth continued, the first third of the twentieth century was characterized by a series of economic crisis that culminated in the Great Depression of the 1930s. Faced with mounting crises, classical liberal views of democracy came under attack.

Critiques came from multiple sources. At the level of economic theory, Keynesians argued that market failure was an inevitable feature of capitalism. Growth and stability could thus be achieved only through state intervention designed to stimulate the economy and prevent the unwanted consequences of capital expansion (Keynes 1935). At the level of social philosophy, pragmatists and idealists attacked the classical liberal laissez-faire position. Pragmatists like John Dewey viewed laissez-faire economics as a doctrine that failed to perceive the connection between theory and historical events. Dewey argued that the concept of laissez-faire persisted even once the historical conditions that favored it had ceased to exist. Accordingly, he also favored state intervention (Dewey 1935/1963, 49). Hegelian idealists like L. T. Hobhouse (1979) attacked the classical liberal assumption that freedom could be won by eliminating external constraints. Hobhouse pointed out that lifting external constraints did not lead to substantive freedom for all people. He contended that people who lacked sufficient economic, cultural, and social resources were not free to participate in a democratic society. State intervention was thus necessary to ameliorate social and economic inequality.

The economic crises of the first part of the twentieth century, and the criticism they provoked, generated new forms of state intervention. Franklin Roosevelt's New Deal represented the most systematic implementation of the idea of state-regulated market capitalism. In the United States and other areas of the developed world, state intervention successfully fused capital accumulation with social legitimation. State regulation of the economic and social spheres generated a new system in which democracy was defined in terms of free market forces but also public welfare (Antonio and Bonanno 1996).

The stabilizing force of state regulation ameliorated class inequality and fostered the development of democracies anchored by large and predominantly satisfied middle classes (Rostow 1960). Talcott Parsons (1971), among others, observed that a large and powerful middle class is one of the most important conditions for a stable democratic society (Antonio and Bonanno 2000 and 1996). Parsons and others argued that post–World War II democracy had superseded once and for all the premodern hierarchies of achievement, merit, and efficiency on which social organization had been based. The resulting "collegial" pattern of professional authority replaced coercive "line authority" and the military system of command. Consequently, social scientists claimed that compulsory organization had been superseded by the voluntary cooperation of experts. In this view, U.S. democracy based on the combination of state intervention and market capitalism constituted a qualitatively new "postindustrial" system that brought the economic cycle under control, universalized abundance, and, most important, eliminated the tension between capitalism and democracy (Parsons 1971).

Although it greatly exaggerated the equality and inclusiveness of this new form of democracy, this vision of "classless," "pluralist," "meritocratic" postindustrial society encompassed the broadening of equal opportunity and ideological and institutional changes that made new substantive rights an important part of the reproduction and legitimation of capitalist production. Democracy based on state intervention seemed a promising departure from the depression, fascism, and war that had characterized the preceding two decades. To be sure, in this Fordist era the state emerged largely as a class state (Poulantzas 1978; Miliband 1969; O'Connor 1974). Its legitimizing role complemented forms of intervention that assisted capital accumulation domestically and internationally, but it also gave subordinate classes the opportunity for social, political, and economic advancement. Those who sought to enhance substantive democracy saw state intervention as regressive in that it reproduced class domination; but it also allowed broader social and economic integration and tempered the undesirable consequences of capitalism, and in this sense was progressive (Antonio and Bonanno 1996). The Fordist state thus became the partner of both capital mobility and expansion and the progressive movements that saw its regulatory function as a tool to be employed in the struggles for a more just and equitable society.

The crisis of the Fordist period opened the way for the emergence of globalization, greater corporate power, and the crisis of the nation-state as a form of government. The crisis of the interventionist Fordist state involved attacks by "free market" advocates on its attempts to make capitalism more democratic. These so-called free market advocates continued to seek state support for capital accumulation but called for reduced, rather than enhanced, state regulation. Deregulation, tax abatements for the wealthy and corporations, social conservatism, and lower wages became the province of the state (Gordon 1996; Harvey 2005; Mishel and Bernstein 1993; Mishel, Bernstein, and Schmitt 1999). Orchestrated calls for decreased state intervention came primarily from neoliberal and postmodernist sources (e.g., Bauman 1992 and 1993; Friedman 1962/1982; Fukuyama 1992; Harvey 2006; Lyotard 1984).

Neoliberal Democracy

At the theoretical level, the neoliberal attack on state intervention rested on the assumption that market relations take primacy over other spheres of human activity. Political freedom, neoliberals argue, is subordinate to economic freedom, which they see as "an end in itself" and the most basic condition for the development of a democratic society (Friedman 1962/1982, 8–9; 1977, 10–11). Milton Friedman—arguably the most notable proponent of neoliberal social theory—contends that "the kind of economic organization that provides economic freedom directly, namely, competitive capitalism, also promotes political freedom" (1962/1982, 9).

According to neoliberals, laissez-faire economics, in which the market is left alone to regulate itself, is far superior to state intervention, which only retards economic growth and thus diminishes the corresponding political and social benefits. For Adam Smith, John Stuart Mill, and other classical liberals, the market was only a means to achieve the betterment of society. According to neoliberals, the free market is *always* superior to a state-regulated market. In their view, state intervention is in fact the primary source of economic inefficiency, social problems, and cultural disintegration (ibid., 38–39). Friedman saw the Great Depression as the result of the U.S. government's mismanagement of monetary policies, and postwar economic downturns as the consequence of the overwhelming growth of state intervention in, and regulation of, the economy. He and like-minded theorists consider state intervention for the purpose of ameliorating inequality as the problem, and self-help, eliminating social programs, and reliance on market mechanisms as the solution.

In populist-sounding pronouncements about competitive individualism, neoliberals treat poverty and economic inequality as unalterable natural conditions that arise from inherited differences in individual abilities and inborn differences in individual character and morality. Moreover, they hold that the elimination of special protections and programs for the poor, racial and ethnic minorities, gays, and women makes for a more just society (ibid., 108–18). Most important, and in a marked departure from classical liberalism's call for compassion and care for the disenfranchised, Friedman and other neoliberals reject efforts to reduce class disparities and increase the opportunities for upward economic mobility that promises the hope for more meaningful citizenship. They argue that ceasing these misguided efforts actually promotes economic flexibility and tax savings and thus supports the "middle class." They call for a "two-thirds society" that revives opportunity for the middle class and increases control over marginalized people.

Neoliberal individualism embraces liberty without a sense of the importance of equality for maintaining the overall interdependence on which the specialized division of labor depends. This ideology of globalization is more individualistic than classical economic and social theories, which stressed the division of labor and at least the idea of economic cooperation and interdependence. By contrast, neoliberalism transforms the firm into a projection of the supposedly entrepreneurial ego of the CEO; employees, when they are considered at all, are viewed as individual psyches to be approached in terms of human relations strategies. Consistent with the vision of repressive rigidities, neoliberals see social interdependence and public institutions as coercive and even totalitarian concepts. Financial and occupational status is viewed as an outcome of individual attributes, skills, and motivation. And class is by nature a more abstract and less visible "social" phenomenon, easily conflated with race, ethnicity, or other group characteristics. In its most extreme form, neoliberal theory, with its emphasis on individualism, denies the reality of class. Neoliberals deny that class is a collective phenomenon that provides potential for group formation; they see this claim as a reflection of the resentment of unsuccessful individuals, which progressive liberal or leftist forces manipulate for their own political interest. Neoliberals equate justice with liberty, explaining away the contradiction between formal and substantive freedom. They see social equality as a leveling ideology inherently opposed to genuine individuality, real liberty, and meaningful democracy.

By the beginning of the twenty-first century, neoliberal policies dominated the political scene of many advanced and developing countries. In the United States and Europe, neoliberal attacks on "big government" were key factors in the dramatic reduction of unemployment and the prolonged economic expansion of the 1990s (Harvey 2006; Stiglitz 2003). Driven by soaring financial markets, reduced state social spending, tax cuts to benefit the wealthy and corporations, and unprecedented deregulation, U.S., European, and later Japanese and other Asian economies grew rapidly. But this economic growth was accompanied by, and in part based on, the undermining of job security and a huge increase in part-time and low-wage jobs. Most of the jobs created in the last two decades of the twentieth century were of this kind, as secure and well-paid positions evaporated and unstable, marginal, and precarious employment opportunities emerged in new global labor market (Coates 2000; Cox 1997; Gilpin 2000; Gordon 1996; Harvey 2005; Held et al. 1999; Mishel, Bernstein, and Schmitt 1999). By the turn of the century, however, the economy had entered a period of crisis that demonstrated the limits of the neoliberal-inspired growth of the '90s. As employment increased, the costs of education, health, and other social services, as well as of oil and other energy sources, also increased sharply, thereby diminishing the living conditions of the middle and lower classes. These trends were even more severe in developing countries, where neoliberal policies translated into overt class polarization and a downward compression of the middle class, social instability, crime, and the subordination of government policies to the directives of international financial organizations (Greider 1997b; Llambí 1994). Interestingly, the economic downturn of the early years of the new century was accompanied by renewed calls for less state intervention, broader neoliberal policies, and increased reliance on market mechanisms.

The heralded emasculation of the intrusive "welfare" state translated into enhanced opportunities for TNCs to operate in the global arena with many fewer imposed limits and an increased disregard for the socioeconomic well-being of less powerful social groups, communities, and democratic institutions. Neoliberals justify this situation by pointing to what they call the untenable consequences of progressive liberal policies and their supporters' clumsy attempts to achieve equalitarian goals. They also argue that the current form of neoliberal democracy is superior to discredited socialist and Marxist-inspired political arrangements, and that there is no evidence that future conditions will be better than this market-guided democracy (e.g., Fukuyama 1992, 51, 221). They see the crisis of the interventionist state as a positive outcome. Indeed, efforts to eliminate barriers to the full participation of citizens in democratic self-governance and to emancipate oppressed communities are considered a source of social instability. According to this view, today's type of democracy is a model for future societies.

Postmodern Calls for a New Democracy

The neoliberal advocates of the unregulated market have found an ally in theorists of postmodernism. Though postmodernism is a fragmented school of thought, it refers in general to those who denounce the repressive dimensions of modern social arrangements and institutions—including the nation-state—and advocate new kinds of opportunities for democracy (Bauman 1998 and 1993; Lyotard 1984). Echoing neoliberal pronouncements about the oppressive nature of state regulation, postmodernists view Fordist society, the interventionist nation-state, and traditional organizations of the Left—unions, socialist and other radical political groups and parties—as primary sources of sociopolitical oppression, cultural homogenization, environmental degradation, and social problems (Ashley 1997; Bell 1996; Smart 1992). Their attack is particularly pointed when it comes to social democratic policies that, they argue, were responsible for the growth of the repressive state (Lyotard 1984). The classical liberal ideals of individuality and freedom, they contend, have been co-opted by repressive institutions that, in the name of progress and emancipation, forced individuals and groups to conform to ideals imposed from the top down. Membership in Fordist society meant becoming a "client" of the state and pledging allegiance to an imposed set of values and behavior. Diversity, identity, alternative lifestyles, and freedom were repressed by conformism, homogenization, planned action, and class politics. Pro-capital and status quo modernization projects, on the one hand, and the "organized opposition" of the radical and Marxian Left, on the other, became the two poles of a system of total domination. Lyotard, for instance, argues that Marxism and Keynesianism worked together to create a technocratic system of control (1984, 12–13, 27–41).

These claims converged with neoliberal calls for deregulated markets and society, and above all for a noninterventionist state. Postmodernists interpreted state actions aimed at diminishing the undesirable consequences of capitalism as oppressive welfare paternalism that in fact supports big capital and repressive, technically engineered social relations. In this context, post-

Berlin Wall, free market globalization became the source of renewed optimism about the future.

To be sure, postmodernism cannot simply be equated with neoliberalism. A number of authors who stress the importance of postmodernist theory also acknowledge that the postmodernist sensibility is incompatible with the negative consequences that the end of Fordism, the growth of transnational capital, and the crisis of the nation-state have engendered (Beck 1997, 1995, 1992; Giddens 2000, 1994, 1990; Beck, Giddens, and Lash 1994). Zygmunt Bauman, for instance, recognizes the social and economic polarization that characterizes the new global society. But he also contends that the Fordist interventionist state and its distributive policies have exhausted their emancipatory roles and that state-centered modern projects should be abandoned. Indeed, he sees in the triumph of market-based globalization the real emancipatory movement of the era. In his view, the growth of society and democracy are ultimately anchored to the support for further commodification of social relations, unrestricted capitalism, and an end to the quest for universal social justice.

Other writers share Bauman's view of the interventionist state, but unlike Bauman they have not abandoned hope for social justice and equality. Among them are advocates of "reflexive modernization" (Beck 1995 and 1992; Giddens 2000, 1994, 1990; Beck, Giddens, and Lash 1994), who stress that the modern project of individualization—the full emancipation of individuals—never fully realized within social institutions such as the state, the family, and political parties, dictates individuals' actions. This "simple modernization" (Giddens 1994, 42) reached its highest point during Fordism, when society produced enough goods that it legitimized its existence through its ability to distribute them to all social groups and classes. Beck (1992, 13) argues that today's society distributes not goods but global risks like environmental degradation, nuclear disaster, and economic and social decay that cannot be controlled by modern institutions such as the nation-state. With globalization we have entered a period of accelerated individualization that provides us with the potential for freer social arrangements. Giddens views these enhanced opportunities in terms of "life politics"— individuals' enhanced ability to choose lifestyles once dictated by nature or tradition—contextualized in "dialogic democracy," or the rejection of solutions fashioned by top-down power in favor of dialogue-based alternatives (1994). Similarly, the crisis of the Fordist nation-state "might favor the proliferation of local and regional states which could more effectively respond to the wishes of its citizens, a much more localist and pluralist democracy" (Lash and Urry 1994, 325).

Democracy Between the Death of Fordism and the Market

The rosy picture painted by neoliberals and postmodernists alike turns a blind eye to the mounting socioeconomic problems facing subordinate groups across the globe (Antonio 2000; Jameson 1994; Eagleton 1996). The crisis of the Fordist state can hardly be equated with emancipatory possibilities for the majority of the world's inhabitants. Similarly, calls for the strengthening of social relations based on the free market ignore the long-standing objection that the free market itself creates inequality. This has been one of the key points of the Marxian critiques of capitalist democracy and of the debate over how best to create and preserve democratic institutions. Indeed, while Marx shared Adam Smith's and other classical liberals' belief that the expansion of the market created wealth, he saw the result as increasing economic, social, and political exploitation of the working class (Marx 1947). His insistence on the inherited nature of capitalism's crises was accompanied by an equally strong critique of the supposed equality of market relations and the democratic nature of capitalism (Marx 1967).

The wealth of theoretical positions within the Marxian tradition contributed to the creation of a powerful school of modern thought, but one riven by deep divisions. In particular, Marx's insistence on the scientific nature of materialism (1955) meant a deterministic view of the evolution of both capitalism and emancipatory strategies. Marx's scientific determinism was such that it eventually led to the development of political programs emphasizing rigid top-down organization, massive and forced industrialization, and elitist and bureaucratic social and political hierarchies (Antonio 1984; McNall 1984, 484). Stalinism and the Chinese "Cultural Revolution" are perhaps the most emblematic twentieth-century manifestations of this type of Marxism.

Responses to these developments—but also to competing structuralist versions of Marxism (e.g., Althusser and Balibar 1979)—came from several directions. In particular, critical theory emerged as an alternative to the deterministic and oppressive forms of Marxism that characterized Soviet communism and Marxist-Leninist positions (e.g., Adorno 1973; Marcuse 1979; Habermas 1975). Predating postmodernist critiques of capitalism's homogenizing force, critical theorists attacked both monopoly capital and state-centered communism by stressing their totalizing and repressive sides. Departing from mechanistic readings of emancipatory processes, they viewed the contradictions internal to capitalism as "possibilities" for the development of alternative strategies that nevertheless depended on favorable historical conditions. The latter were understood in terms of human actions and class struggle rather than mechanistic contradictions inherent in the economic sphere (Jay 1973; Kellner 1981). In these accounts, tools employed by supporters of monopoly capital to strengthen domination—i.e., cultural institutions and the media—could be employed to mobilize resistance and develop emancipatory discourses (Kellner 1981). The pro-capital, homogenizing role played by the state in advanced capitalism, they maintained, was accompanied by emancipatory possibilities like those embodied in the welfare state, the concept of equal opportunity, and emancipatory social policies (Offe 1996).

The importance of this view of the state is particularly relevant vis-à-vis the behavior of TNCs illustrated in the stories of globalization outlined in this volume. As we have seen, these stories demonstrate that TNCs need state assistance. It is one of the fundamental features of globalization that TNCs attempt to avoid state regulation that limits their freedom of action (i.e., their profits), while demanding government support when it comes to advancing their interests. Neoliberal free market rhetoric notwithstanding, TNCs require state intervention if they are to acquire social legitimacy and maximize their profits. Exponents of both postmodernism and neoliberalism neglect to acknowledge fully TNCs' contradictory demands for increased state intervention on their behalf and decreased intervention on behalf of their opponents and others at a social and economic disadvantage.

The stories contained in this book support the conclusion that the end of Fordism involved the deregulation of areas once characterized by state regulation (e.g., Bonanno et al. 1994; Bonanno and Constance 1996; Cerny 1991; Dicken 1998; Lash and Urry 1994; Marsden 1997 and 1994). But deregulation did not mean simply the absence of regulation. It meant new rules that reconfigured social relations, a process that has often taken one of two forms. First, it meant the commodification of social relations. The reduction of state welfare benefits and social services are a case in point: benefits and services that were once provided by the state are now left to the workings of the market. Second, the rules governing socioeconomic actions have been reorganized and in some cases eliminated. The restructuring of the CAFO permits illustrated in Chapter 6 is an example, as is the creative Marine Stewardship Council initiative discussed in Chapter 8. Arguably, however, the most relevant example of a coordinated attempt to eliminate or reorganize the rules governing global socioeconomic relations is presented in Chapter 9, on the MAI/MIA proposals for a "corporate bill of rights" and the associated expansion of the role of the World Trade Organization. The WTO has in fact regulated the global economy by placing paramount importance on the idea of free trade. Accordingly, domestic laws concerning the protection of labor and the environment, and the quality of production and consumption processes, have been revised on the grounds that they limit "free" trade. This de facto curbing of democratically established rules and regulations has, moreover, been accomplished by an organization whose secretive actions are shielded from public scrutiny and control. Much of the protest against the WTO focuses on its undemocratic nature. Regardless of the forms that deregulation has taken, the result has been that large segments of the population have lost legal protections, while TNCs have benefited handsomely from decreased state regulation of the economic arena.

Neoliberal charges that state intervention is ineffective and inefficient ignore the reality that it has contributed substantially to the well-being of subordinate classes, particularly given that the market, left to its own devices, does not do so. Indeed, the state is a complex and fragmented organism, and its ineffectiveness and inefficiency are in part the result of the very forces demanding that it relinquish its regulatory function (e.g., Offe 1996, 63–64). The point is that the ineffectiveness and inefficiency of the state are social products and as such are not inherently attached to state action. They are the outcome of the interaction of, and struggles between, social groups. Accordingly, state action can tend toward democracy, but it can also be oriented in the opposite direction.

The Possibility of Democracy

One of the key assumptions of this book is that the expansion of TNCs and their increased power over the state are socially created. They are the result of the actions of corporate agents who interacted with subordinated groups and their struggles around the world. The end of the Fordist period and its equilibrium marked this shift, as the worldwide dominance of the neoliberal position and the crisis of the nation-state signaled the onset of the new global era. The postmodernists' theories about emancipation from state oppression notwithstanding, the new era is marked by rising socioeconomic polarization and diminished hopes that social welfare can redress economic imbalance in any meaningful way. The once assumed unity between economic expansion and social betterment has been fractured. The modern Fordist tenet that with economic expansion "all boats will rise" has been replaced by Bauman's vision that increased socioeconomic polarization and injustice are the price we pay for a freer society. Bauman and like-minded thinkers' view notwithstanding, the search for universal social justice and civic participation has not been exhausted.

The Subjects of Emancipatory Actions

Talcott Parsons saw the post–World War II era as the culmination of the modernization process, a period in which the parallel growth of the economy and the improvement of social arrangements would make for continuous stability and development. For Parsons and other social thinkers, the postwar era would fulfill the expectations of classical social theorists who saw in the science-guided expansion of the economy and society the engines to achieve human prosperity. Even Marx—his sharp critique of capitalism aside—believed that the expansion of the forces of production would lead dialectically to social and economic justice. Parsons, however, saw the evolution of society in harmonious terms and failed to recognize the relevance of subordinate groups' opposition and their struggles in the generation of Fordist equilibrium. In the United States and other advanced societies, Fordism was characterized by the strength of organizations of the historical Left, those based on labor militancy in particular, and their ability to establish *avenues*—that is, codified collective actions—to challenge dominant groups. These free spaces depended on the subordinate groups' capacity to mobilize and use powerful instruments of protest that became codified in the laws and culture of numerous nation-states. The long postwar social peace, based in no small part on an accord between capital and labor, signaled the strength of the Left under Fordism. That strength assumed additional historical relevance in light of the transformation of domestic capital into multinational capital, a transformation completed during the Fordist era. The emergence of a multinational bourgeoisie, multinational corporations, and state agents and agencies that operated in favor of multinational capital characterized this side of Fordism.

The struggle between multinational capital and its opponents defined the period's politics, its relative equilibrium, and, above all, its contradictions. Fordist inclusionary pronouncements and outcomes never transcended the dominant class's search for strategies to counter subordinate groups' power and remedy its consequences. This search came to fruition with the emergence of the globalized economy. Globalization, by altering established practices of capital accumulation and social legitimation, allowed transnational capital to reduce subordinate groups' power and their access to Fordist eman-

cipatory avenues. One of the consequences was that the Left faced new difficulties in mobilizing its traditional constituencies and responding to new
corporate strategies. More important, leftist organizations lost credibility
and power, which prevented them from countering the socioeconomic polarization that increasingly dominated late twentieth-century society (Coates
2000; Gray 1998; Greider 1997a; Lash and Urry 1994; Mishel and Bernstein
1993; Strobel 1993; Walker 1997; Western 1995). The neoliberal argument for
greater market freedom and a reduced welfare state, and the crisis of the
Left, undermined the historical agenda of the Left and led to growing class
inequality. Paradoxically, under globalization, socioeconomic polarization
increased at the same time that the issue of class disappeared from social,
political, and economic debate (Antonio and Bonanno 1996; Beck 1995;
Eagleton 1996; Rieff 1993).

Framed as a matter of international competition for direct investments,
TNCs' hypermobility pitted distant and different labor markets, resources, and
regions against one another. As we have documented in the previous chapters, this development reflected TNCs' ability to search for more convenient
factors of production, a result primarily of the weakening of resistance from
opposing social movements and political organizations. Furthermore, this
new organization of production entailed the fragmentation of labor in terms
of both its physical integrity (through decentralized production processes)
and its political unity (through the crisis of unionization) (Bluestone and
Harrison 1982; Gordon, Edwards, and Reich 1982; Harvey 1989; Lipietz
1992). Simultaneously, the opening of global markets required communities
to adopt new strategies in order to remain economically viable. The most
common of these were the discounting of the price of local natural resources,
infrastructure, and social services, corporate tax abatements, and other procorporate political measures, all of them financed largely by public resources.
The stories of economic incentives and global sourcing in the poultry and
hog industries provided in Chapters 5 and 6 illustrate how these incentives
work in the global era.

Because labor- and class-based movements historically have identified
production as the primary site of exploitation and the arena in which to
concentrate struggle, their defeat confirms that globalization has bestowed
great advantages on TNCs at the *production level*. Indeed, the Left's most
important gains have come from its ability to organize and find strength
in factories, agricultural fields, and the other places of production. Once
production was decentralized and spread across distant areas and in dispersed subunits, once labor pools were matched with faraway counterparts,

and once workers' sense of solidarity and cooperation was severely diminished by downsizing and transnational competition, it became clear that labor and its class ideology had lost most of their power.

At the same time the nation-state became increasingly, though not totally, unable to act as a counterpart to the economic and social demands of subordinated groups. The state's decreased capacity to control TNCs and a broad array of negative consequences of capitalism—unemployment, underemployment, social and environmental degradation, and so on—sharply curtailed the effectiveness of subordinate groups' claims against global capital. The state became much less able to direct the socioeconomic development of needy groups and regions. The management of community development, employment opportunities, and regional planning became increasing difficult for state agencies, as they lacked the instruments to establish sufficient control over such projects (Bonanno and Bradley 1994; Buttel and McMichael 1994).

The crisis of the Left, its diminishing inability to mobilize social forces, coupled with TNCs' new powers at the production level, have crippled labor's historical oppositional capacity. Certainly this situation also reflects broader changes in the production sphere and in civil society more broadly. The tertiarization of economic activities in advanced societies, the automation and computerization of labor, sharp increases in productivity, and other factors all contributed to the radical weakening of the labor movement and class-based political organizations (Coates 2000; Harvey 2006; Money 1992; Regini 1992).

Contrary to postmodernist and neoliberal pronouncements, the historical crisis of class- and labor-based movements does not necessarily mean that these organizations have exhausted their oppositional and emancipatory role. The point is that despite the importance of class in today's society, and the still relevant role played by organizations of the historical Left, emancipatory actions centered on labor and class-based movements are increasingly problematic.[1]

1. We would like to make clear that these struggles are still very important. In the general area of agriculture and food, two of these struggles exemplify our point. The first is the Zapatista movement in Chiapas, Mexico, and the second is the land reform movement in Brazil. These two class-based struggles are direct attacks on the consequences of expanded globalized capitalist relations; their importance lies in their ability to mobilize subordinate groups and organize them in emancipatory struggles. The key task is to avoid becoming isolated in these struggles and preventing them from becoming exclusively "local." While the environmental movement has been able to generate awareness of and opposition to the cutting down of the rainforest, the labor movement has not been able to "transnationalize" the struggle of Brazilian landless peasants who are displaced by the same forces that threaten the

The situation is different for other contemporary social movements. Numerous works (e.g., Bauman 1998; Beck, Giddens, and Lash 1994; Giddens 2000 and 1994; Melucci 1996) stress the role that new social movements have played in the democratization of society. Great emphasis has been placed on the contributions that the feminist movement, the civil rights movement, and, to a greater extent, the environmental movement have made to the establishment of democratic spaces. Indeed, the cases presented in this book show that these movements often mount serious resistance to dominant forces.

The environmental movement in particular has been heralded as a force that could bring about new, more equitable and sustainable social arrangements and be the catalyst for uniting opposition to global capitalism (e.g., Beck 1992 and 1995; Buttel 1994; Dreiling 1997; Melucci 1996; Obach 1999; Schnaiberg 1980). As documented in Chapter 7, environmentalists' attack on established patterns of socioeconomic development and its local support contributed to the growth of new sensitivities that now represent important components of contemporary society. Indeed, the new social movements' emphasis on culture as the primary arena for emancipatory struggle has revived and reinvigorated—but also has transformed—critical issues that in the past the Left was unable to elevate to broadly shared social concerns.

To be sure, the environmental movement—like other new social movements—is far from being unified. Its fragmentation and its plurality of theoretical outlooks have been widely documented (e.g., Benton 1996; Merchant 1997; Mingione 1993; Shabecoff 1993). Additionally, splits within the movement have sometimes led to serious conflicts between various factions. The splitting of the "environmentalist coalition" over the Panama declaration, addressed in Chapter 2, and the World Wildlife Fund/Unilever joint venture in creating the Marine Stewardship Council, the subject of Chapter 8, illustrate this fact. Moreover, critics question this movement's ability to counter its opponents effectively, charging that it is a new form of politics that fails to address socioeconomic inequality and thus has limited ability to unite progressive forces. The environmental movement's split over "dolphin-safe" tuna, with grassroots organizations in their sandals on one side, and mainstream organizations in their suits on the other, captures the picture of

---

tropical environment. Indeed, the Left in the global North has been largely indifferent to the struggle of the *sem terra*. Similarly, popular reports on the situation in Chiapas frame it as a Mexican problem. Labor and class-based organizations have not made the connection between the conditions that motivated the Zapatista rebellion and the transnationalization of socioeconomic relations for the purpose of developing broad-based support in the developed world.

environmentalism as a new bureaucratically organized elite of pseudo-leftist professionals (Piccone 1995).

The question of the emancipatory power of the environmental movement aside, its impact on the culture and practices of today's society is significant (Beck 1997; Giddens 2000; Gray 1998; Harvey 2005). Core items of the environmental agenda—protection of natural resources, sustainability, ecological equilibrium—have made their way firmly into contemporary mainstream discourse. As Beck (1995, 6) puts it, the environmental movement's "topics and issues have become established: all political groups have inscribed them on their banners." We saw this in the case of the hog industry in Texas and in the story of the Marine Stewardship Council. In both cases TNCs tried to gain social legitimacy by stressing their environmental responsibility; political campaigns nowadays likewise include environmental issues in their agendas.[2] Even environmentally destructive practices, like rampant consumerism, have adopted environmentalist language and, to some degree, goals, reflecting the extent to which the environmental ethic has become part of everyday consciousness, as we saw in Chapters 2 and 8, on the "dolphin-safe" and MSC ecolabels. "After more than a quarter century of activism," as one study observes, "the environment is firmly ensconced as both a national and international priority" (Yergin and Stanislaw 1998, 385).

The importance of the environmental and other new social movements (e.g., Allen 1993; Faber 1998b; Kaplan 1997; Mellor 1997; Van Esterik 1999) creates *historical possibilities* for the development of emancipatory struggles under globalization. We mean by this that conditions are favorable for struggles that find their objectives in the new social issues and their subjects in new social movement groups. More important, advocates of alternative forms of production and consumption not only denounce TNCs but propose a new way of looking at the world, one that transcends the focus on ever greater accumulation and consumption. The heightened public consciousness that these new social movements have engendered creates a favorable climate for new forms of democracy and civic participation.

Some scholars see new consumption patterns, born of this heightened consciousness, as fruitful avenues for bringing TNCs to heel. The growing demand for environmentally sound and healthier food items has affected the production, distribution, and consumption of food among a certain class of

---

2. Lash, Szerszynski, and Wynne (1996, 19) write on this issue: "By the late 1980s in most industrial societies environmentalism has been adopted as an 'official' agenda of big business, government and international institutions such as the OECD and the EU."

consumers. These consumers' economic power has forced TNCs to be attentive to their demands. Even when the U.S. law was changed to allow the importation of "dolphin-death" tuna, the Big 3 tuna companies announced that they would continue to only sell "dolphin-safe" tuna. Bauman (1992) goes so far as to argue that consumption-substituted labor is the primary social site where identity and behavior are formed. Fredric Jameson, by contrast, questions the emancipatory scope of consumption, citing TNCs' hegemonic power and their ability to transform new and augmented consumption into novel markets that expand sales and corporate power (see also Eagleton 1996; Rieff 1993).[3] While this objection captures some of the limits of the new social movements, it overlooks the impact that environmental and other emerging sensitivities have had in the creation of new patterns of consumption.

Kim Humphery (1998) describes food consumption as a potential arena for the empowerment of individuals and the development of cultural alternatives and political resistance. He rejects the view that consumers are simply instruments of corporate power and sees them as actors who can create new patterns of consumption that transcend the intentions of producers, however subject they may still be to the power of TNCs. Consumers are not merely passive recipients of corporate messages and objectives, Humphery insists; they form a group that historically has empowered itself in contemporary society. Similarly, Tim Lang stresses the emerging power of the "food movement," which, despite setbacks, "has been successful in questioning the New Right logic of laissez-faire and deregulating" (Lang 1999, 175; see also Gabriel and Lang 1995; Miller 1995).

Lash and Urry (1994, 296–98) demonstrate that contemporary social arrangements translate into expanded consumerism, as individuals augment their ability to consume. This expanded consumption, however, entails a departure from long-standing quantity-based models. Today's consumers, they argue, tend to stress quality rather than quantity of consumption. Consumers, in other words, are much more thoughtful about how the food they consume is produced. This "reflexivity" about the conditions of consumption becomes an emancipatory process, they continue, which remains a condition for the creation of free spaces in society. Their notion of aesthetics captures the emergence of consumption patterns centered on meanings established through a critique of conventional methods of growing food. The point is

---

3. Similarly, in a recent study of hog production for alternative consumers in Iowa, Mark Gray (2000) argues that producers have little knowledge of the motivations, lifestyles, and consumption patterns of their clients. They consider this "informed consumption" a niche market to be exploited.

that this new sensibility, born of the environmental and other new social movements, offers a historical possibility for the democratization of social relations.

Sites of Emancipatory Action: The State

The concept of historical possibilities recognizes that possibilities do not automatically translate into reality. As we have acknowledged, the environmental movement is fractured, and the skepticism of its critics is not without merit. The success of TNCs in donning "green garb" must certainly temper our optimism about the emancipatory possibilities of the movement. The nature and strength of progressive action depend on specific historical circumstances. The success of the new social movements depends on the extent to which they can unite a broad-based constituency and exploit their opponents' weakness. Whether, if, and how well progressive movements can accomplish these goals remains to be seen. What can be established, though, is the identification of social sites where the conditions for emancipatory struggles can mature. These are sites in which dominant groups can be contested and democratic spaces established.

As we have seen throughout this volume, TNCs and the state maintain a contradictory relationship while displaying internal contradictions. Accordingly, the extent to which the state can assist TNCs is limited, just as the power of TNCs is limited. These limits mean that ever-increasing capital accumulation, and ever-increasing TNC power, are neither automatic nor guaranteed but remain contested. The conditions for democratizing both the state and TNCs exist.

The possibilities for democratizing the state have their roots in the state's contradictory tasks of fostering capital accumulation, on the one hand, and maintaining social legitimation, on the other. Under Fordism, the interventionist state successfully balanced pro-accumulation measures with inclusionary social policies. The crisis of Fordism signaled the end of this equilibrium, as mounting economic, social, and political costs accompanied state intervention. Under globalization, the contradiction between capital accumulation and social legitimation is starker. It has been contained, however, through economic growth fueled by neoliberal economic policies and the concomitant reduction of state intervention. Despite its "success," this equilibrium is threatened by the antidemocratic dimension of the new state apparatus. The post-Fordist state claims to offer both economic growth and democratic protections, a claim that is increasingly hard to sustain under globalization.

The issue of social legitimation for international bodies like the wto, imf, NAFTA, and the un is different. Unlike nation-states, transnational governing bodies are largely shielded from direct public participation in decision-making processes, which sharply diminishes their need for public or democratic legitimacy. Indeed, they function primarily through the executive actions of elite bureaucracies with only remote—and in some cases nonexistent—links to the constituencies they are supposed to represent. The wto, for example—perhaps the most important economic regulatory agency at the global level—has virtually no connection with the citizens of member countries. Even the European Union falls into this category. Despite its heralded democratic dimension and some important progressive postures that it maintained in a number of situations,[4] its legislative and executive powers are detached from its elected bodies.[5] To date, the directly elected European Parliament maintains only advisory rather than legislative powers (see Bonanno 1993). Murray Low (1997) argues that because such transnational bodies are insulated from public pressure by design, their democratization is a contradiction in terms. The result is that transnational governing organizations can foster capital accumulation without having to worry about the legitimacy of their actions with respect to subordinate groups. This worry is left to the nation-state, which is faced with the task of legitimizing events that do not necessarily involve popular participation. In other words, because the nation-state remains the site where citizens and government interact politically, the state is charged with carrying out processes of social legitimation whose roots derive from events that it can hardly control. The often debated "revolt" of local and regional groups against their national governments can be explained in these terms. Several instances of such "revolts" were seen in the story of the mai in Chapter 9.

The self-contradictory position of the nation-state is magnified by the fact that it is fragmented: subordinate groups control some of its parts. Be-

4. This is certainly the case of the agricultural and food sector, where, over the years, the eu has adopted much more socially oriented postures and policies that depart significantly from the more market-oriented policies of U.S. administrations (Bonanno 1993; Miele 1998; Raynolds and Murray 1998).

5. In a recent editorial on the situation of the European Union, Roger Cohen (1999) writes, "There is a growing perception that the [eu] commissioners, who are appointed by national governments and oversee a bureaucracy of 17,000 people, have enjoyed powers inadequately balanced by democratic oversight." Cohen quotes French diplomat and expert in European affairs Jean-Marie Guehenno as saying, "Europeans have discovered that there is now real power in Brussels, and they are saying they want more democratic control, more transparency, and more rigor." These are all indications of the shape taken by emerging transnational state forms.

cause of this fragmentation, the class nature of the nation-state does not automatically translate into its total subordination to the interests of dominant groups. Indeed, this situation makes the nation-state the site of resistance to dominant groups' designs, as the opposition of subordinate groups complicates the state's legitimizing role.

It is important to stress that this situation does not translate automatically into an overt crisis of legitimation. The economic expansion of the last decade, TNCs' success in co-opting opposition, and the failure of alternative projects like socialism have greatly contributed to the legitimation of the status quo. But the contradiction at the heart of the nation-state's identity remains, and the ability of dominant groups to manage it is not necessarily a given. Indeed, the actions of subordinate groups do threaten the precarious connection between the expansion of current forms of globalization and claims about enhanced democracy and freedom. The antiglobalization movement examined in Chapter 9 challenged the globalization project as an illegitimate form of socioeconomic development that eroded the sovereignty of nation-states and suppressed democratic action on the part of subordinate groups. Similarly, Chapter 6 revealed that while the local social movement group ACCORD successfully challenged Texas's attempt to eliminate the public hearing process regarding CAFO permits, this success was temporary, for the global hog industry mobilized state support to counter ACCORD's resistance.

Spaces of Emancipatory Action: TNCs, Circulation, and the Realization of Capital

TNCS encounter obstacles in their effort to accumulate capital in the form of social movements, segments of the nation-state, and other TNCs. They are also exposed to a set of contradictory relations, including their position vis-à-vis the nation-state and their own internal conflicts. These conditions open up spaces where resistance can be translated into TNCs' democratization, as subordinate groups can force TNCs to behave more democratically. Indeed, one dimension of TNCs' interaction with society points to the emergence of a possible site for the democratization of TNCs: TNCs are vulnerable to actions directed at affecting the process of *circulation of commodities* and the related phenomenon of *realization of capital*. Specifically, TNCs are vulnerable to new forms of consumption born of social movements; the transformation of commodities into money is one locus of this weakness. This is because commodity circulation is one of the primary aspects of the overall process of capital accumulation. For economic growth and equilibrium to occur, money must be transformed into commodities, which in turn must be transformed back into money. Since the classical period economists have recognized that all commodities must be sold; that is, they must be transformed into money if economic equilibrium is to be achieved. Classical economists identified a second dimension of this process—namely, that money must be invested in the next economic cycle to ensure continuous economic growth. Indeed, the velocity with which the money-commodity-money transformation occurs qualifies the rate of expansion of the economy, as it allows a faster reinvestment of capital (capital accumulation). In his classical formulation, Adam Smith maintained that the equilibrium between items produced and items sold would be achieved through the free operation of the market.

More recent economic doctrines, such as Keynesianism, acknowledge the difficulties that free market equilibrium entails and contemplate the possibility of state intervention. For Keynes, the transformation of commodities into money is maintained through state regulation and control of markets. In *Capital,* Marx explains that realization of capital means that production must be "realized," that is, it must be transformed into money (i.e., sold) if capitalist accumulation is to continue. For Marx, the inherent paradox, or contradiction, of realization is that capitalist production mandates the creation of surplus value, that is, value created by the labor of workers, which is expropriated by the capitalist class (profit). Because the value produced (more or less the equivalent of commodity prices) is always greater than the value (wages) received by workers, workers cannot afford to consume what they produce. This results in a crisis, either of overproduction or of underconsumption. Some Marxists acknowledge factors that delay the realization crisis, among them the expansion of consumption fueled by financial strategies (credit) and cultural models (consumerism) (Mandel 1976; Marcuse 1964; O'Connor 1988; Sweezy 1942).

Realization of capital requires that obstacles to the transformation of money into commodities and back into money be removed. Yet, as both classical and contemporary theories recognize,[6] the manner in which commodi-

---

6. Marx describes this condition in these terms: "The division of labor converts the product of labor into a commodity, and thereby makes necessary its conversion into money. At the same time, it makes it a matter of chance whether this transubstantiation succeeds or not" (Marx 1967, 203). Keynes writes of the inadequacy of models that contemplate the automatic translation of commodities into money. He is therefore careful to highlight the danger of underconsumption as the socially grounded phenomenon in which production cannot be sold, i.e., transformed into money. Underconsumption, along with its opposite, overproduction, were the subjects of intense debate during the course of the second half of the twentieth century. James O'Connor (1988) has stressed that the crisis of realization—or the first contradiction of capital—is accompanied by a second fundamental contradiction: that capitalism undermines the reproduction of the conditions necessary for production. For O'Connor, the second contradiction of capitalism is the outcome of the environmental crisis triggered by capitalist growth. In this case, the deterioration of environmental conditions causes capitalist

ties are transformed into money is historically determined, that is, it depends on socioeconomic conditions that allow for equilibrium between production and consumption. The ability of TNCs to realize profits depends on the processes and markets through which their commodities are produced and exchanged. Under globalization these conditions involve, primarily, equilibrium between TNCs' hypermobile global production and stable communities of consumers who can effectively contribute to the process of capital realization. Under current historical conditions, this equilibrium is affected by the socioeconomic polarization that increasingly marginalizes significant segments of the world population,[7] and by the type of consumption that characterizes contemporary social arrangements (e.g., Gray 1998; Hammond 1998; United Nations 1999).

---

underproduction, or the inability of capitalism to maintain adequate conditions for the expansion of the forces of production.

7. UN data indicate that the gap between rich and poor has widened drastically in the past two decades and continues to grow. These data show that economic globalization is fueling a "dangerous" polarization between a small group of the super rich and the overwhelming majority of the world's population, which subsists in an impoverished state. From 1995 to 2001 alone, the two hundred wealthiest people in the world doubled their fortunes to more than $1 trillion, while the number of people subsisting on only $1 a day has remained constant at 1.3 billion. In the early 1970s, the wealthiest fifth of the world's population was thirty times richer than the poorest fifth. By 1990 this ratio had grown to 60:1, and at the end of the twentieth century it stood at 74:1 (United Nations 2002). In addition, from 1980 to 2001 the average personal income in developing regions as a percentage of the average individual income in the United States diminished significantly (Sutcliffe 2004). The average income in Latin America was 36 percent of the U.S. average in 1980 but only 26 percent in 2001. Similarly, the average income in African countries was 10 percent of the U.S. average in 1980 but had fallen to 6 percent in 2001. In the entire global South, the average per capita income dropped from 16 percent of the U.S. average in 1980 to 14 percent in 2001.

Notable attempts have been made to show that economic inequality worldwide actually diminished in the last two decades of the twentieth century. One of the best known of these attempts is an article by Glenn Firebaugh and Brian Goesling (2004) arguing that global income distribution is now more equal than it was in the early 1980s. This reduction is mainly the result of average income growth in the two most populous countries of Asia: China and India. Firebaugh and Goesling maintain that this is the outcome of industrialization in these countries, which in turn is the result of globalization. They propose therefore that we can reduce income inequality by promoting globalization. While this argument may be superficially appealing, it has been sharply criticized on several grounds. Wade (2004) argues that Firebaugh and Goesling artificially inflate income in developing countries by pricing services in those countries at the same level that prevails in the United States. A second objection challenges Firebaugh and Goesling's assumption that inequality has remained static in China and India, when in fact income and wealth inequality have been rising over the period considered (see Arrighi, Silver, and Brewer 2003; Davies 2005). Furthermore, by using the average income of whole countries, Firebaugh and Goesling gloss over possible differences in the distribution of material welfare of individuals or households. A third objection takes issue with the notion that industrialization in the South generates accelerated growth. While it seems likely that additional waves of industrialization will have diminishing returns, it remains unclear whether the type of industrialization experienced in the global South—i.e., global

As we have pointed out above, a new type of socially and environmentally sensitive consumption—which Lash and Urry (1994) call "reflexive consumption" and Humphery (1998) says empowers consumers and pushes them toward cultural subversion and political resistance—is relevant here. Socially conscious consumers pay particular attention to the ways in which products are produced. Products made in sweatshops, made by children, produced in ways that exploit workers and damage the environment, products that involve unspeakable cruelty and waste of animals, that harm communities and destroy cultural enclaves—products that involve these factors and others are increasingly shunned by those who can afford to seek alternative forms of consumption and "vote with their pocketbooks" for products that are healthier, environmentally sound, and produced by workers who are paid a fair wage for their labor. This type of consumption embodies a critique of TNCs' quantity-based mass production over quality and equity. Consumption of this nature holds out hope for enhanced forms of democracy and community. Because TNCs need to realize profits, emancipated consumers can demand that they make quality products using ethically acceptable forms of production. By exploiting this corporate vulnerability, socially conscious consumers can demand accountability where governments have ceded that power.

A Final Comment

The possibilities for establishing democratic spaces must be balanced against the fact that TNCs retain significant power, including the power of shaping consumption. Even as consumers escape the "logic of capitalist production," Jameson and like-minded thinkers remind us that new and potentially emancipatory forms of consumption can be exploited as new ways to make a profit. Moreover, successful exploitation of TNCs' weaknesses depends on the strength of anticorporate movements that seldom are unified and rarely are armed with a coherent vision for breaking decisively with patterns of global capital accumulation. Yet globalization's contradictions remain. The expansion of TNCs has been based on the breaking of Fordist arrangements and the transnationalization of social relations. While production and consumption have increased to the benefit of the upper and middle classes, the gap between rich and poor has widened. Both within and between the North and

---

sourcing for the least expensive labor and other costs of production—is conducive to sustained growth.

the South, social and economic inequality has grown radically. Even worse, in today's neoliberal climate, this inequality is now largely viewed more as inevitable than as pathological. The exclusion of subordinate groups and regions from economic expansion is mirrored by more vicious forms of exploitation, as production is outsourced to less costly parts of the world, where capital-friendly conditions prevail. This situation calls into question sustainability on every level. How much longer can the hypermobility of capital and global sourcing define the expansion of the economy without triggering a global crisis? How much longer can global economic growth be based on the rampant and unchecked exploitation of natural resources? These are some of the questions left unanswered by proponents of the current form of globalization.

Globalization emerged amid promises of enhanced economic well-being and individual freedom. Economic growth, although significant, is geographically and socially circumscribed, and can be justified in its current form only through the formula of the "two-thirds society" and other neoliberal concepts. While the combination of soaring financial markets and technological breakthroughs may seduce the upper and middle classes of the global North and the ruling elites of the South, it condemns growing segments of the world to poverty and exploitation and blames them for their alleged inability to take advantage of the abundant new opportunities of the global "free" market. The neoliberal postures of international bodies like the WTO and IMF offer limited alternatives to this pattern. Indeed, they propose its continuation through the further increase of capital circulation, an end to regulations that protect labor and the environment, and the restructuring of economic policies in the impoverished global South.

The promise of enhanced freedom appears equally difficult to keep. Reflexive modernization theorists heralded globalization as an era of renewed individual freedom. But they also acknowledged that the globalization project lacks the institutional instruments to reduce inequality and promote popular participation in democratic decision making. The crisis of the nation-state and the "covert" nature of the operations of transnational bodies like the WTO and IMF clash with the concept and practice of democratic popular participation in public life. Protests against secretive, elitist, and pro-corporate organizations like the MAI and WTO suggest the difficulties globalization faces in the early twenty-first century. Democracy can be won only if the opponents of globalization can unite to exploit its contradictions, identify fruitful avenues of resistance, and expose globalization's enchanting but often empty promises.

REFERENCES

Abernathy, Tom. 2000. Interview by authors, May 5.

Abramson, Ruth. 1997. "Environment: Paying the Polluters? A New Treaty Could Bring Investors—and Controversy." *Maclean's,* September 1. http://www.elibrary.com/ (accessed November 27, 2002).

ADF&G. (Alaska Department of Fish and Game). 2000. "Commercial Fisheries Statistics." http://www.adf&g.gov/.

ADM (Archer Daniels Midland). 2006. "ADM Investor Relations." http://www.adm world.com/naen/ir/.

Adorno, Theodor W. 1973. *Negative Dialectic.* New York: Seabury Press.

Africa News Service. 1997. "The Multilateral Agreement on Investment: Basic Facts." http://www.elibrary.com/ (accessed September 9, 1997).

Agbiz Tiller. 1996a. "ADM Admits Guilt." AgBiz Archives. http://www.thecalamity-howler.com/tiller/archives/backlog.htm.

———. 1996b. "Plea Deal: Super Make Up to the World." AgBiz Archives. http://www.thecalamityhowler.com/tiller/archives/backlog.htm.

———. 1997."Unraveling the 'Best Documented Corporate Crime in American History.'" Agbiz Archives. http://www.thecalamityhowler.com/tiller/archives/april97/topstory.html.

Aglietta, Michel. 1979. *A Theory of Capitalist Regulation.* London: New Left Books.

Akard, Patrick J. 1992. "Corporate Mobilization and Political Power: The Transformation of US Economic Policy in the 1970s." *American Sociological Review* 57: 597–615.

Allen, Patricia, ed. 1993. *Food for the Future: Conditions and Contradictions of Sustainability.* New York: John Wiley and Sons.

Allen, Vicki. 1997a. "Senate Votes to Lift U.S. Tuna Embargo." Reuters, July 30. http://www.elibrary.com/ (accessed November 11, 1997).

———. 1997b. "U.S. House Panel Votes to Lift Tuna Embargo." Reuters, April 16. http://www.oceania.org.au/soundnet/apr97/dolsafe2.html (accessed August 5, 1997).

———. 1997c. "White House Rejects Tuna-Dolphin Bill Compromise." Reuters, May 15. http://www.oceania.org.au/soundnet/may97/nocomp.html (accessed August 5, 1997).

Allshouse, Woody. 1997. "CDF Firefighters Speak Out." October 9. http://bari.org/~intexile/CDF-Letter.html (accessed December 16, 1999).

Althusser, Louis, and Etienne Balibar. 1979. *Read Capital.* London: Verso.

Amarillo Globe-News. 1998a. "Seaboard Agrees to Pay $88,200 Fine." February 20.

———. 1998b. "Seaboard Cites Moratorium in Hiring Freeze." February 26.

———. 1999. "Seaboard Catalyst for Hog Fight." August 31.

———. 2000. "Seaboard Agrees to $30,250 in Fines over October Spills." February 18.

Anchorage Daily News. 2001. "Alaska, Inside Alaska Business." June 16.

Andreoli, Marcella. 1994a. "Il Processo." *Panorama,* January 7, 7–15.

———. 1994b. *Processo all'italiana.* Milan: Sperling & Kupfer.

Antonio, Robert J. 1984. "The Origin, Development, and Contemporary Status of Critical Theory." *Sociological Quarterly* 24: 325–51.

———. 2000. "After Postmodernism: Reactionary Tribalism." *American Journal of Sociology* 106 (1): 40–87.

Antonio, Robert J., and Alessandro Bonanno. 1996. "Post-Fordism in the United States: The Poverty of Market-Centered Democracy." *Current Perspectives in Social Theory* 16: 3–32.

———. 2000. "A New Global Capitalism? From 'Americanism and Fordism' to 'Americanization-Globalization.'" *American Studies* 41 (2–3): 33–77.

AOP (Alaska Oceans Program). 2005. "Marine Stewardship Council Watchdog." http://www.alaskaoceans.net/aboutus/msc.htm.

AP Online. 1998a. "Logging Company's License Suspended for Environmental Violations." November 12. http://www.elibrary.com/ (accessed November 19, 2002).

———. 1998b. "OECD Ministers Shelve Investment Talks Until October." April 28. http://www.elibrary.com/ (accessed November 19, 2002).

Aquatic Network. 1997. "Marine Stewardship Council Underscores Commitment to Preserve Global Fisheries." Aquatic Network News, Seacoast Information Services, Inc., January 6. http://www.streetcar.com/aquanet/news/newslist/item1_1a.htm (accessed November 7, 1997).

Arce, Alberto. 1997. "Globalization and Food Objects." *International Journal of Sociology of Agriculture and Food* 6 (1): 77–108.

Arrighi, Giovanni. 1998. "Globalization and the Rise of East Asia: Lessons from the Past, Prospects for the Future." *International Sociology* 13 (1): 59–77.

———. 2005. "Globalization and the World System Perspective." In *Critical Global Studies,* ed. Richard P. Appelbaum and William I. Robinson, 33–44. New York: Routledge.

Arrighi, Giovanni, Beverly Silver, and B. D. Brewer. 2003. "Industrial Convergence, Globalization, and the Persistence of the North-South Divide." *Studies in Comparative International Development* 38 (1): 3–33.

Ashley, David. 1997. *History Without a Subject: The Postmodern Condition.* Boulder: Westview Press.

Asia Pulse. 1997a. "ASEAN Urged to Study Implications of Investment Agreement." February 25. http://www.elibrary.com/ (accessed November 27, 2002).

———. 1997b. "OECD to Have Way on Multilateral Investment Pact: Chamber." February 24. http://www.elibrary.com/ (accessed November 27, 2002).

———. 1998. "Developing Countries Oppose Multilateral Investment pact." November 16. http://www.elibrary.com/ (accessed November 19, 2002).

———. 1999. "India Opposed to Investment Treaty Under WTO." March 22. http://www.elibrary.com/ (accessed November 27, 2002).

Associated Press. 1996. "ADM Agrees to Plead Guilty in Price-Fixing Probe." October 14. http://www2.nando.net.newsroom/ntn/nation/101496/nation1_1414.html (accessed March 4, 1998).

Atkinson, Mark. 1998. "Rich Nations Retreat: Shelving of Global Investment Pact Delights Third World Campaigners." *The Guardian* (London), April 24.

Audubon Society. 1988. "Porpoise Mortality Numbers Skewed." *Audubon Society Magazine* 90 (5): 16.

The Australian. 2000. "Flavour of the Week." June 22.

Axford, Barrie. 1995. *The Global System: Economics, Politics, and Culture.* New York: St. Martin's Press.

Bahner, Benedict. 1995. "ADM, Rhone-Poulenc Join in Amino Acids." *Chemical Marketing Reporter,* August 23, 1.

Balzar, John. 2003. "America's 'Dolphin-Safe' Lie: Easing Regulations on Tuna Fishing Endangers the Ocean Mammal." *Los Angeles Times,* January 5.

Barber, Benjamin. 1995. *Jihad vs. McWorld.* New York: Times Books.

Bari, Judi. 1989. "Timber Wars Part 3: Potential for Organizing." Industrial Workers of the World, October. http://bari.iww.org:80/ iu120/local/Judi-1C.html.

———. 1995. "But What About Jobs?" Industrial Workers of the World, March 5. http://bari.org/iu120/local/Judi6.html.

Barlett, Donald L., and James B. Steele. 1998. "The Empire of the Pigs: A Little Known Company Is a Master at Milking Governments for Welfare." CNN News, November 30. http://www.cnn.com/.

Barnum, Alex. 1996. "Oil Rights, Forests Offered for Headwaters." *SF Gate,* December 12. http://www.sfgate.com/.

———. 1997. "Headwaters Deadline Extended: Government Has Until February to Line Up Cash." *SF Gate,* March 13. http://www.sfgate/.

Barrionuevo, Alexei. 2006. "Boom in Ethanol Reshapes Economy of Heartland." *New York Times,* June 25.

Barry, John, Scott Johnson, Jay Wagner, William Underhill, and Elizabeth Angell. 1999. "Frankenstein Foods?" *Newsweek,* September 13, 33–35.

Baskin, Steve. 2002. "Other Opinion: Seaboard Must Take Care of Resources." *Amarillo Globe-News,* February 13.

Battye, Michael. 1996. "India Declares Victory at WTO Conference." Reuters, December 13. http://www.elibrary.com/ (accessed September 21, 1997).

Bauman, Margaret. 2004. "Eco-label for Pollock Fishery Challenged." *Alaska Journal of Commerce,* October 31. http://www.alaskajournal.com/PalmPilot/stories/103104/loc_20041031029.html (accessed December 19, 2006).

Bauman, Zygmunt. 1992. *Intimations of Postmodernity.* New York: Routledge.

———. 1993. *Postmodern Ethics.* Cambridge, Mass.: Blackwell.

———. 1998. *Globalization: The Human Consequences.* New York: Columbia University Press.

Bean, Carl. 2002. "Hog Farming Interests Would Destroy Region's Water Resources." *Amarillo Globe-News,* May 12.

Beck, Ulrich. 1992. *Risk Society: Towards a New Modernity.* London: Sage Publications.

———. 1995. *Ecological Enlightenment.* Atlantic Highlands, N.J.: Humanities Press.

———. 1997. *The Reinvention of Politics: Rethinking Modernity in the Global Social Order.* Trans. Mark Ritter. Cambridge, UK: Polity Press.

Beck, Ulrich, Anthony Giddens, and Scott Lash. 1994. *Reflexive Modernization: Politics, Tradition, and Aesthetics in the Modern Social Order.* Stanford: Stanford University Press.

Becker, David. 1999. "Postimperialism and Realism in Theories of International Relations." In *Postimperialism and World Politics,* ed. David Becker and Richard Sklar, 37–74. Westport, Conn.: Praeger.

Becker, David, and Richard Sklar, eds. 1999. *Postimperialism and World Politics.* Westport, Conn.: Praeger.

Bell, Daniel. 1996. *The Cultural Contradictions of Capitalism.* Twentieth anniversary ed. New York: Basic Books.

Bellamy Foster, John. 1993. "The Limits of Environmentalism Without Class: Lessons from the Ancient Forest Struggle in the Pacific Northwest." *Capitalism, Nature, Socialism* 4 (1): 11–42.

———. 1998. "The Limits of Environmentalism Without Class: Lessons from the Ancient Forest Struggle in the Pacific Northwest." In *The Struggle of Ecological Democracy,* ed. Daniel Faber, 188–217. New York: Guilford Press.

Bennett, William C., Jr. 1998a. Memorandum No. 3 to Normangee Group. In authors' possession.

———. 1998b. Normangee Group Lawsuit Letter, June 11. In authors' possession.

Benton, Ted. 1996. *The Greening of Marxism.* New York: Guilford Press.

Beria di Argentine, Chiara, and Massimo Mucchetti. 1994. "Ridacci Montedison." *L'Espresso,* June 10, 45–48.

Bernton, Hal. 1994. "Battle for the Deep." *MoJo Wire: Mother Jones Interactive,* January. http://www.mojones.com/mother_jones/JA94/bernton.html.

Berton, Paul. 1998. "Stakes Are High in Trade Agreement." *London Free Press,* January 10.

Bevington, Douglas. 1998. "Earth First! in Northern California: An Interview with Judi Bari." In *The Struggle of Ecological Democracy,* ed. Daniel Faber, 248–71. New York: Guilford Press.

Bianco, Giovanni Cesare. 1988. *Il Gruppo Ferruzzi.* Rome: La Nuova Italia Scientifica.

Bilchik, Gloria Shur. 1996. "A Walk on the Corporate Side." *Trustee,* November 12, 1.

Bishop, Cheryl. 1998. "Multilateral Agreement on Investment (MAI): Corporations as Nation-States." *Z Magazine,* March. http://www.thirdworldtraveler.com/WTO_MAI/MAI_Z.html.

Blaney, Betsy. 2002. "Smell of Money Raises Concerns." *Amarillo Globe-News,* January 5.

Bleifuss, Joel. 1997. "Building the Global Economy: The Multilateral Agreement on Investment (MIA)." *In These Times,* January. http://thirdworldtraveler.com/WTO_MAI/GlobEconMai_ITT.html (accessed December 29, 2003).

Bluestone, Barry, and Bennett Harrison. 1982. *The Deindustrialization of America: Plant Closing, Community Abandonment, and the Dismantling of Basic Industry.* New York: Basic Books.

Blum, Ronald. 1995. "Hearing Called on NAFTA Broken Promises." *Oakland Post,* November 29.

Boer, Nicholas. 2001. "Troubled Waters for Fish Supply." Knight-Ridder/Tribune News Service, May 15. http://elibrary.bigchalk.com/ (accessed August 6, 2003).

Boggs, Carl. 1986. *Social Movements and Political Power: Emerging Forms of Radicalism in the West.* Philadelphia: Temple University Press.

———. 2000. *The End of Politics: Corporate Power and the Decline of the Public Sphere.* New York: Guilford Press.

Bonanno, Alessandro. 1993. "Agro-Food Sector and the Transnational State: The Case of the EC." *Political Geography* 12 (4): 341–60.

Bonanno, Alessandro, and Karen Bradley. 1994. "Spatial Relations in the Global Socio-Economic System and the Implications for Development." In *Agricultural Restructuring and Rural Change in Europe,* ed. David Syms and Anton J.

Jansen, 49–64. Wageningen, Netherlands: Agricultural University of Wageningen Press.

Bonanno, Alessandro, Lawrence Busch, William H. Friedland, Lourdes Gouveia, and Enzo Mingione, eds. 1994. *From Columbus to ConAgra: The Globalization of Agriculture and Food.* Lawrence: University Press of Kansas.

Bonanno, Alessandro, and Douglas H. Constance. 1996. *Caught in the Net: The Global Tuna Industry, Environmentalism, and the State.* Lawrence: University Press of Kansas.

———. 2000. "Mega Hog Farms in the Texas Panhandle Region: Corporate Actions and Local Resistance." *Research in Social Movements, Conflicts and Change* 22: 83–110.

Borosage, Robert L. 1999. "The Global Turning." *The Nation,* July 19, 22–25.

Bovard, James. 1995. "Archer Daniels Midland: A Case Study in Corporate Welfare." Cato Institute Policy Analysis no. 241, September 26. http://www.cato.org. pubs.pas/pa-241.html (accessed January 16, 2007).

Bowles, Samuel, and Herbert Gintis. 1982. "The Crisis of Liberal Democratic Capitalism: The Case of the United States." *Politics and Society* 11: 52–92.

Bradsher, Keith. "U.S. Told to Bar Tuna over Dolphin Killings." *New York Times,* January 15.

Brandow, G. E. 1969. "Market Power and Its Sources in the Food Industry." *American Journal of Agricultural Economics* 51 (1): 1–12.

Brass, Tom. 2000. *Peasants, Populism, and Postmodernism: The Return of the Agrarian Myth.* London: Frank Cass.

Breimyer, Harold F. 1965. *Individual Freedom and the Economic Organization of Agriculture.* Urbana: University of Illinois Press.

Brooke, James. 1992a. "America—Environmental Dictator?" *New York Times,* May 3.

———. 1992b. "10 Nations Reach Accord on Saving Dolphins." *New York Times,* May 12.

Brooks, Charles R. 1980. "Structure and Performance of the U.S. Broiler Industry." In *Farm Structure,* report of the U.S. Senate Committee on Agriculture, Nutrition and Forestry, 196–215. Washington, D.C.: U.S. Government Printing Office.

Brower, Kenneth. 1989. "The Destruction of Dolphins: In Spite of Laws Intended to Protect Them, Federal Indifference and Cruel Fishing Methods Once Again Endanger Dolphins." *Atlantic* magazine, July, 35–58.

Brown, Laurie Ezzell. 1998. "House Environmental Committee Tours CAFOS in Ochiltree County." *Canadian Record,* April 23, 8–9.

Brown, Robert H. 1995a. "Sanderson Farm Building Poultry Complex." *Feedstuffs* 67 (22): 7.

———. 1995b. "Sanderson Farms Expanding with Southwest Complex." *Feedstuffs* 67 (10): 9.

Browne, Anthony. 2002. "Ban Cod and Eat More Coley, Say Campaigners." *Times* (London), December 28.

Bruggers, James. 1999. "San Francisco–Area Animal Groups Sue over Dolphin-Safe Tuna Label." Knight Ridder/Tribune Business News, August 19.

Bryce, Robert. 1997. "Fencing Out Factory Farms." *Progressive Populist,* November. http://www.populist.com/97.11.bryce.html.

Burleson, Andy. 2002. "Apathy Leaves Us High and Dry." *Amarillo Globe-News,* June 15.

Burns, Christopher. 1998. "Investment Talks to Resume Despite French No-Show."

AP Online, October 16. http://www.elibrary.com/ (accessed November 19, 2002).

Busch, Lawrence. 1994. "The State of Agricultural Science and the Agricultural Science of the State." In *From Columbus to ConAgra: The Globalization of Agriculture and Food,* ed. Alessandro Bonanno et al., 69–84. Lawrence: University Press of Kansas.

Buttel, Frederick. H. 1992. "Environmentalization: Origins, Processes, and Implications for Rural Social Change." *Rural Sociology* 57 (1): 1–27.

———. 1994. "Agricultural Change, Rural Society, and the State in the Late Twentieth Century: Some Theoretical Observations." In *Agricultural Restructuring and Rural Change in Europe,* ed. David Syms and Anton J. Jansen, 13–31. Wageningen: Agricultural University of Wageningen Press.

———. 1996. "Environmental and Resource Sociology." *Rural Sociology* 61 (1): 56–76.

Buttel, Frederick H., Charles Geisler, and Irving Wiswall. 1984. *Labor and the Environment.* Westport, Conn.: Greenwood Press.

Buttel, Frederick H., and Philip McMichael. 1994. "Reconsidering the Explanandum and Scope of Development Studies: Toward a Comparative Sociology of State-Economy Relations." In *Rethinking Social Development: Theory, Research, and Practice,* ed. David Booth, 42–61. Harlow, UK: Longman.

Capdevila, Gustavo. 2003. "G22 Warmup to Post-Cancun Talks." Asia Times Online, October 4. http://www.atimes.com/atimes/Global_Economy/EJ04Dj01.html.

Capitol Hill Press. 1999. "Statement by US Senator Dianne Feinstein on Finalizing an Agreement to Preserve the Headwaters Forest." March 2, 10–11. http://www.elibrary.com/ (accessed November 7, 1999).

CAPP (Citizens Against Poultry Pollution). 2000a. Monthly Newsletter, March 23.

———. 2000b. Monthly Newsletter, September 27.

———. 2000c. Monthly Newsletter, November 11.

Carnoy, Martin. 1984. *The State and Political Theory.* Princeton: Princeton University Press.

Carter-Long, Lawrence. 1997. "Senate Tuna-Dolphin Deal Mired in Controversy." IGC Headlines, July 28. http://www.igc.org/igc/en/hl/9708041930/hl6.html (accessed November 23, 1997).

Cartwright, Kay. 1999. "Open Meeting a Sham." *Amarillo Globe-News,* May 15.

Castells, Manuel. 1995. *The Rise of the Network Society.* Oxford: Blackwell.

CEO (Corporate Europe Observatory). 1998. "MAI: Reality of Six Months of Consultation and Assessment." MAI-NOT Listserv, October 15. In authors' possession.

Cerny, Philip 1991. "The Limits of Deregulation: Transnational Interpenetration and Policy Change." *European Journal of Political Research* 19: 173–96.

Cevallos, Diego. 1997. "Fisheries: Mexico Dissatisfied with End of U.S. Tuna Embargo." Inter-Press Service, English News Wire, August 2. http://www.elibrary.com/ (accessed November 23, 1997).

———. 2003. "WTO-Cancun: Future Uncertain After Collapse of Talks." Inter-Press Service Agency, September 14. http://www.ipsnews.net/ (accessed January 12, 2004).

Chaffee, Chet. 2000. "Summary Report on Certification of Commercial Salmon Fisheries in Alaska." Marine Stewardship Council. http://www.msc.org/ (accessed December 8, 2000).

Chandler, Alfred D. 1977. *The Visible Hand: The Managerial Revolution in American Business.* Cambridge: Belknap Press of Harvard University Press.

Chandler, Chip. 1998a. "Group Says Pro-Pig View Is Hogwash." *Amarillo Globe-News,* May 27.

———. 1998b. "Opposing Sides Base Arguments on Different Figures." *Amarillo Globe-News,* May 27.

Chase-Dunn, Christopher. 1998. *Global Formation: Structure of the World-Economy.* Lanham, Md.: Rowman & Littlefield.

Cheadle, Bruce. 1998. "Activists Protest Accord on MAI." *London Free Press,* March 20.

Chism, Dave, and Bob Cramer. 1997. "Democracy Is Not a Spectator Sport (Part 1)." Industrial Workers of the World, November 27. http://bari.iww.org:80/~in texile/Fortson1.html.

Christian Science Monitor. 1999. "The Net Effect of Mexico's Fishy Business: Mexico's President-Elect, Vicente Fox, Faces Many Trading Irritants with US When He Takes Office Friday." November 27.

Chubb, Lucy. 2000. "London-Based Marine Council Gives New Label to Sustainable Fisheries." Environmental News Network, Knight-Ridder/Tribune Business News, March 11. http://elibrary.bigchalk.com/ (accessed August 8, 2003).

Cintron, Ivan. 1993a. "International Lysine Production Increases." *Chemical Marketing Reporter,* August 13, 10.

———. 1993b. "Lysine Prices Nosedive Due to Fierce Competition." *Chemical Marketing Reporter,* May 10, 1.

———.1996. "Lysine Price-Fixing Charges Yield $20M in Fines." *Chemical Marketing Reporter,* September 2, 1.

Cirino Pomicino, Paolo. 1993. "Testimony to the Trial of Sergio Cusani." *Il Processo Cusani,* RAI TV, Milan, Italy, December.

Clarke, Tony. 1997. "MAI-Day! The Corporate Rule Treaty." http://www.policy alternatives.ca/mai.html (accessed February 25, 1998).

Clarke, Tony, and Maude Barlow. 1998. "Super NAFTA." *The Nation,* July 6, 7–8.

Clifford, Frank. 1999. "Last-Minute Deal Reached on Headwaters." *SF Gate,* March 3. http://www.elibrary.com/ (accessed November 7, 1999).

CMC (Center for Marine Conservation). 1996. "Save Dolphins from Being Killed." February 25. http://www.cmc-ocean.org/321_save.html (accessed October 8, 1997).

Coastal Post. 1996. "Help Save the Redwoods." September 27. http://www.coastal post.com/96/11/12.html (accessed September 27, 1998).

Coates, David. 2000. *Models of Capitalism: Growth and Stagnation in the Modern Era.* Cambridge, UK: Polity Press.

Cohen, Roger. 1999. "Deep Malaise Plays Role in EU Leadership Disbanding." *Houston Chronicle,* March 17.

Colaprico, Piero. 1994a. "Cusani, di Pietro prova l'affondo." *La Repubblica* (Milan), February 22.

———. 1994b. "In aereo da Forli un miliardo al PCI." *La Repubblica* (Milan), February 3.

———. 1994c. "Signor Ladro, bastava dire si . . ." *La Repubblica* (Milan), April 24.

Colaprico, Piero, and Stefano Rossi. 1993. "Cusani Torna Libero." *La Repubblica* (Milan), December 24.

Connor, John. 1998. "Lysine: A Case Study in International Price-Fixing." *Choices* (3d qtr.): 13–19.

Conovan, Margaret. 1981. *Populism.* New York: Harcourt Brace Jovanovich.

Consarino, Barbara. 1993. "Gardini parló dopo l'arresto di Greganti." *La Gazzetta del Sud,* December 23, 25.

———. 1994. "Per l'amor di Dio, si o no? E bossi urla si." *La Gazzetta del Sud,* January 6, 22.

Constance, Douglas H., and Alessandro Bonanno. 1999a. "CAFO Controversy in the Texas Panhandle Region: The Environmental Crisis of Hog Production." *Culture and Agriculture* 21 (1): 14–25.

———. 1999b. "Contested Terrain of the Global Fisheries: 'Dolphin-Safe' Tuna, the Panama Declaration, and the Marine Stewardship Council." *Rural Sociology* 64 (4): 597–623.

———. 2000. "Regulating the Global Fisheries: The World Wildlife Fund, Unilever, and the Marine Stewardship Council." *Agriculture and Human Values* 17 (2): 125–39.

Constance, Douglas H., and William D. Heffernan. 1991. "The Global Poultry Agro-Food Complex." *International Journal of Sociology of Agriculture and Food* 1 (1): 126–42.

Constance, Douglas H., Alessandro Bonanno, and William D. Heffernan. 1995. "Global Contested Terrain: The Case of the Tuna-Dolphin Controversy." *Agriculture and Human Values* 12 (3): 19–33.

Constance, Douglas H., Anna M. Kleiner, and J. Sanford Rikoon. 2003. "The Contested Terrain of Swine Production: De-Regulation and Re-Regulation of Corporate Farming Laws in Missouri." In *Fighting for the Farm: Rural America Transformed,* ed. Jane Adams, 75–89. Philadelphia: University of Pennsylvania Press.

ContiGroup. 1998. "ContAgriIndustries." http://www.contingroup.com/contiagri .html (accessed January 15, 1999).

Cooper, Laura. 1997. "Don't Be Harsh on the MSC." *Samudra,* report no. 18, July. http://www.gmt2000.co.uk/apoints/icfs/english/samudra/issue_18/content .htm (accessed November 7, 1997).

Corporate Location. 1996. "Global Framework Looks at Developing World." May–June, 7.

Cousteau, Jean-Michel. 1996. "Cousteau Letter to President Clinton." Jean-Michel Cousteau Institute, July 3. http://www.marianne.com/cousteau.html.

Cowell, Alan. 1993. "Ex-Premier Denies Role in Italian Bribe Scandal." *New York Times,* December 18.

Cox, Kevin R., ed. 1997. *Spaces of Globalization.* New York: Guilford Press.

Coyle, Diane. 1998. "Deadlock on Global Investment Accord." *The Independent* (London), April 28.

Crane, David. 1998. "Let's Develop Humane Global Investing." *Toronto Star,* April 11.

Craxi, Bettino.1993. "Testimony to the Trial of Sergio Cusani." *Il Processo Cusani,* RAI TV, Milan, Italy, December.

CRP (Center for Responsive Politics). 2007. "Archer Daniels Midland: Donor Profiles." http://www.opensecrets.org/orgs/summary.asp?ID = D000000132.

Current Science. 2003. "Scientists Say Government Suppressed Research." Vol. 88 (14): 12.

Curry, Matt. 1998a. "Legislator Skeptical of 'Firsthand' Look." *Amarillo Globe-News,* May 29.

———. 1998b. "Seaboard Farms to Visit Panhandle." *Amarillo Globe-News,* February 24.

———. 1998c. "Some See Big Hogs as New Frontier." *Amarillo Globe-News,* May 26.

Dallas Morning News. 1997. "Needed Grade School May Ride Piggyback on Town's Deal with Hog Giant." December 15.

Danley, John R. 1994. *The Role of Modern Corporations in a Free Society.* Notre Dame: University of Notre Dame Press.

Davies, Jim. 2005. "Personal Assets from a Global Perspective." *Wider Angle* 2: 6–7.

Davis, Andrew. 1988. "Caught in the Tuna Nets: The Slaughter of Dolphins." *The Nation,* November 14, 486.

Davis, Bob. 1992. "U.S., Mexico, Venezuela Set Accord on Tuna." *Wall Street Journal,* March 20.

Davis, John E. 1980. "Capitalist Agricultural Development and the Exploitation of the Propertied Laborer." In *The Rural Sociology of Advanced Societies,* ed. Frederick H. Buttel and Howard Newby, 133–54. Montclair, N.J.: Allenheld, Osmun, and Co.

Davis, Robyn L. 2001a. "Economy Gets Pullout Blame, Seaboard Says." *St. Joseph (MO) News-Press Online,* March 15. http://www.stjoenews-press.com/print .asp.031501.shtml (accessed November 12, 2003).

———. 2001b. "Seaboard Bails Out." *St. Joseph (MO) News-Press Online,* March 14. http://www.stjoenews-press.com/print.asp.031401.shtml (accessed November 12, 2003).

———. 2001c. "Seaboard Study Complete; Suggestions Submitted." *St. Joseph (MO) News-Press Online,* January 3. http://www.stjoenews-press.com/print.asp .010301.shtml (accessed November 12, 2003).

———. 2001d. "Seaboard Wins Role in Suit." *St. Joseph (MO) News-Press Online,* February 1. http://www.stjoenews-press.com/print.asp.020101.shtml (accessed November 12, 2003).

———. 2001e. "Zoning Board Denies Permit to Build Plant." *St. Joseph (MO) News-Press Online,* January 10. http://www.stjoenews-press.com/print.asp.011001 .shtml (accessed November 12, 2003).

Dean, Andre. 2000. Interview by authors, May 8.

Deardorff, Julie. 2003. "U.S. Loosens Definition of Dolphin-Safe Tuna." *Chicago Tribune,* January 1.

Decatur Herald and Review. 1998. "Whitacre Recants Story About FBI Agent." March 4. http://www.herald-review.com/0/whitacre0304–8.html (accessed March 10, 1998).

Defenders of Wildlife. 1997. "Congress Comes Closer to Dismantling Dolphin-Safe Tuna Standards." May 8. http://www.defenders.org/pr050896.html (accessed May 27, 1997).

De Jonquieres, Guy. 1998a. "Retreat over OECD Pact on Investment." *Financial Times,* October 21, 4.

———. 1998b. "US Cool About Investment Pact." *Financial Times,* October 20, 7.

Denny, Charlotte, and Mark Atkinson. 1998. "Britain Drops Support for MAI." *The Guardian* (London), October 30.

Derichsweiler, Mark. 1998. "Oklahoma's CAFO Laws Tightened." Oklahoma Sierra Club 3 (summer). http://oklahoma.sierraclub.org/cafo/cafocomments3.html (accessed October 31, 2003).

De Toma, Bartolomeo. 1993. "Testimony to the Trial of Sergio Cusani." *Il Processo Cusani,* RAI TV, Milan, Italy, December.

Dewey, John. 1935/1963. *Liberalism and Social Action.* New York: Capricorn Books.

Dewey, Scott. 1998. "Working for the Environment: Organized Labor and the Origins of Environmentalism in the United States, 1948–1970." *Environmental History* 1: 45–63.

Dicken, Peter. 1998. *Global Shift*. New York: Guilford Press.

Dixon, Jane. 1999. "A Cultural Economy Model for Studying Food Systems." *Agriculture and Human Values* 16 (2): 151–60.

Drabenstott, Mark. 1998. "This Little Piggy Went to Market: Will the New Pork Industry Call Heartland Home?" *Federal Reserve Bank of Kansas Economic Review* (3d qtr.): 79.

Drake, Sandra. 1998. "CAFO 'Public Hearing' in Perryton a Farce." *Amarillo Globe-News,* May 11.

Drake, Wendy. 2001. "Baby Dolphin-Safe?" *Environment* 43 (6): 7.

Dregger, Leila. 1997. "Dolphins Need Panama Declaration, Congress Told." *SoundNet,* April 9. http://www.oceania.org.au/soundnet/apr97/panama.html (accessed August 5, 1997).

Dreiling, Michael. 1997. "Remapping North American Environmentalism: Contending Visions and Divergent Practices in the Fight over NAFTA." *Capitalism, Nature, Socialism* 8 (4): 65–98.

———. 1998. "From Margin to Center: Environmental Justice and Social Unionism as Sites for Intermovement Solidarity." *Race, Gender and Class* 6 (1): 51–69.

Dumont, Clayton W. 1996. "The Demise of Community and Ecology in the Pacific Northwest: Historical Roots of the Ancient Forest Conflict." *Sociological Perspectives* 39 (2): 277–300.

Dunne, Nancy. 1998. "US Shies Away from Multilateral Accord." *Financial Times,* February 14. http://www.hartford-hwp.com/archives/25/042.html (accessed December 29, 2003).

Dunning, John. 1981. *International Production and Multinational Enterprise*. London: Allen and Unwin.

———. 1988. "The Eclectic Paradigm of International Production: A Restatement and Some Possible Extensions." *Journal of International Business Studies* 19 (1): 1–31.

———. 1989. *Explaining International Production*. London: Unwin Hyman.

———. 1991. "The Eclectic Paradigm in International Production: A Personal Perspective." In *The Nature of the Transnational Firm,* ed. Christos Pitelis and Roger Sugden, 116–36. London: Routledge.

———. 1993. *The Globalization of Business*. New York: Routledge.

Durbin, Andrea. 1997. "Ten Reasons to be Concerned About the Multilateral Agreement on Investment." Friends of the Earth, November 25. http://www.hartford-hwp.com/archives/25/037.html (accessed December 29, 2003).

Durbin, Andrea, and Mark Vallianatos. 1997. "Transnational Corporate Bill of Rights—Negotiations for a Multilateral Agreement on Investment (MAI)." Global Policy Forum, April. http://www.globalpolicy.org/socecon/bwi-wto/mai1.htm (accessed December 29, 2003).

Durkheim, Emile. 1984. *The Division of Labor in Society*. New York: Free Press.

Eagleton, Terry. 1996. *The Illusion of Postmodernism*. Cambridge, Mass.: Blackwell.

Earth First! 1997. "The History of Saving Headwaters." September 16. http://www.enviroweb.org/headwaters-ef/about/headwaters_history.html.

Easterling, E. E., Cutis H. Braschler, and John A. Kuehn. 1985. "The South's Comparative Advantage in Broiler Production, Processing, and Distribution." Paper presented at the annual meeting of the Southern Agricultural Economics Association, Biloxi, Mississippi, February.

ECBC (European Cetacean Bycatch Campaign). 2002. "MSC Hoki Appeal Shows Fishery Should Never Have Been Certified." December 16. http://www.eurobc.org/page526.html (accessed November 19, 2003).

ECES (Earth Crash Earth Spirit). 2001. "Marine Stewardship Council Accredits New Zealand Hoki Fishery as 'Sustainable' Despite Fact It Kills Threatened Albatrosses, Drowns Over 1,000 Seals Each Year, Damages Sea Floor with Huge Trawling Nets." March 20. http://eces.org.articles.static/98506800072188.shtml (accessed November 19, 2003).

The Economist. 1991. "Divine Porpoise." October 5.

EDF (Environmental Defense Fund). 1996. "New Efforts Could Strengthen Protection for Dolphins." *Environmental Defense Fund Letter* 27 (January). http://www.edf.org/pubs/EDF-Letter/1996/Jan/m_dolphins.html (accessed September 11, 1997).

Edwards, Cliff. 1996. "ADM Informant Indicted, Stops His Cooperation." *Lexington (KY) Herald-Leader,* September 12.

Egelko, Bob. 2000. "U.S. Appeals Court Reviews Dolphin-Safe Tuna Standards: Clinton Administration Wants to Relax Limits." *San Francisco Chronicle,* December 12.

———. 2003a. "Activists Sue over Relaxed Tuna-Label Rules." *San Francisco Chronicle,* January 3.

———. 2003b. "'Dolphin-Safe' Labeling Will Stand for Now; Judge Blocks Relaxation of Standard." *San Francisco Chronicle,* April 11.

———. 2003c. "U.S. Backs Off on Relaxed Rules on Tuna; Activists Announce Pact That Leaves in Place 'Dolphin-Safe' Standard." *San Francisco Chronicle,* January 8.

Eichenwald, Kurt. 2000. *The Informant: A True Story.* Portland, Ore.: Broadway Books.

EII (Earth Island Institute).1995. "Do You Trust 'Dolphin-Safe' Tuna? Rebuttal," February 13. http://www.earthisland.org/ei/immp/gprebut.html (accessed September 11, 1997).

———. 1996. "Scientists Speak Out Against Dolphin Death Act: Lapses in Congressional Testimony Cited." June 12. http://www.earthisland.org/ei/immp/scientist.html (accessed May 22, 1997).

———. 1997a. "Earth Island Institute Calls for Boycott of Kroger Tuna." July 31. http://www.igc.apc.org/ei/immp/KrogerAA.html (accessed November 10, 1997).

———. 1997b. "The Tuna/Dolphin Compromise in Congress." July 31. http://www.igc.apc.org/ei/immp/tunadolphinpressrelease.html (accessed November 10, 1997).

Elliott, Larry, and Charlotte Denny. 1998. "Finance: Globalisers Run into the Buffers; The Multinationals' Trade Initiative Is in Trouble." *The Guardian* (London), March 24.

Ellison, Katherine. 1991. "U.S. Quest for Dolphin-Safe Tuna Hurts Mexican Fisherman." *Journal of Commerce and Commercial,* October 28, 5A.

Engardio, Pete, and Catherien Belton. 2000. "Global Capitalism." *Business Week,* November 6, 72.

EPIC (Environmental Protection Information Center). 1998. "Summary of EPIC Forestry Lawsuits." January. http://www.igc.org/epic/pages/litigation summaryf.html (accessed October 3, 1998).

European Report. 1996. "Film Makers Demand Cultural Exemption." January 5.

———. 1998a. "EU/OECD: Negotiators Press on With Investment Pact Talks." October 24. http://www.elibrary.com/ (accessed November 27, 2002).

———. 1998b. "NGOs Against Multilateral Investment Pact Stage Summit." September 30. http://www.elibrary.com/ (accessed November 19, 2002).

———. 1999a. "EU/WTO: Chaos Reigns as Seattle Ministerial Looms." November 27. http://www.elibrary.com/ (accessed November 27, 2002).

———. 1999b. "EU/WTO: Commission to Confirm Seattle Ministerial Meeting." July 7. http://www.elibrary.com/ (accessed November 19, 2002).

———. 1999c. "EU/WTO: Seattle Delegated Grind Through Painful Agenda." December 4. http://www.elibrary.com/ (accessed November 27, 2002).

———. 1999d. "EU/WTO: Trade Ministers Edge Towards Seattle Strategy." May 13. http://www.elibrary.com/ (accessed November 27, 2002).

———. 1999e. "EU/WTO: Trade Ministers Ponder WTO Ministerial Strategy." May 8. http://www.elibrary.com/ (accessed November 27, 2002).

Evans, Peter. 1995. *Embedded Autonomy: States and Industrial Transformation.* Princeton: Princeton University Press.

EverGreen. 1997. "Entrepreneurs at Work." September 12. http://ag.arizona.edu/olas/nuc/eg/eg-3/ADM.html (accessed March 10, 1998).

Faber, Daniel. 1998a. "The Political Ecology of American Capitalism: New Challenges for the Environmental Justice Movement." In *The Struggle of Ecological Democracy,* ed. Daniel Faber, 27–59. New York: Guilford Press.

———, ed. 1998b. *The Struggle for Ecological Democracy.* New York: Guilford Press.

FAO (UN Food and Agriculture Organization). 1997. *The State of World Fisheries and Aquaculture: 1996.* http://www.fao.org/DOCREP/003/W3265E/w3265e00.htm.

Fazzo, Luca. 1994. "L'ultimo atto d'accusa: Democrazia venduta." *La Repubblica* (Milan), December 7.

Featherstone, Michael, ed. 1990. *Global Culture: Nationalism, Globalization, and Modernity.* London: Sage Publications.

Feedstuffs. 1995. "1995 Reference Issue." July 19, 21.

Felando, August. 1995. "Declaration of Panama Signed: Twelve-Nation, Five-Environmental-Group Accord Could Bring Sense to 'Dolphin-Safe' Labeling." *Fisherman's News,* November. http://www.canfisco.com/dolphins.html (accessed May 22, 1997).

Financial Times. 1998. "A Case of MAI Culpa." October 20.

Fink, Deborah. 1986. *Open Country, Iowa: Rural Women, Tradition, and Change.* Albany: State University of New York Press.

Fiore, Faye. 1995. "Activists Alarmed by Bid to Reverse Dolphin-Safety Law." *Los Angeles Times,* September 9.

Firebaugh, Glenn, and Brian Goesling. 2004. "Accounting for the Recent Decline in Global Income Inequality." *American Journal of Sociology* 110 (2): 283–312.

Floyd, Jesse M. 1987. "U.S. Tuna Import Regulations." In *The Development of the Tuna Industry in the Pacific Islands Region: An Analysis of Options,* ed. David J. Doulman, 81–90. Honolulu: East-West Center.

FOE (Friends of the Earth). 1997a. "MAI Shell Game." http://www.globalpolicy.org/socecon/bwi-wto/maimaish.htm.

————. 1997b. "The oecd Multinational Agreement on Investment (mai)." February 19. http://www.foe.org/orgs/foe/ga/factmai.html (accessed February 7, 1998).

Foss, John. 2003. "Unilever Eyes msc Alaskan Polack, to Bail on msc NZ Hoki." Sustainfish, May 30. http://csf.colorado.edu/bioregional/2003/msg00033.html (accessed November 19, 2003).

Fox News. 1996. "adm Executives Indicted For Price-Fixing." December 3. http://www.foxnews.com/front/120396/adm.srr (accessed March 9, 1998).

Frazier, Joseph. 1996. "Mexico Fishermen Blame Tuna Troubles on 'Dolphin-Safe' Rules." *Los Angeles Times,* July 21.

Freese, Betsy. 1998. "Pork Powerhouses: 1998." *Successful Farming,* October. http://www.agriculture.com.sfonline/sf/1998/October/pork_powerhouse/chart.ht ml (accessed November 11, 2003).

————. 1999a. "Packing Down the Industry." *Successful Farming,* October. http://www.agriculture.com.sfonline/sf/1999/October/9910pork.htm (accessed June 5, 2000).

————. 1999b. "Pork Powerhouses: 1999." *Successful Farming,* October. http://www.agriculture.com.sfonline/sf/1999/October/9910porkchart.htm (accessed June 5, 2000).

Friedland, William H. 1991. "The Transnationalization of Agricultural Production: Palimpsest of the Transnational State." *International Journal of Sociology of Agriculture and Food* 1: 48–58.

————. 1994a. "Fordism, Post-Fordism, Mass Production, and Flexible Specialization: Whatever Is Going On in the World." Paper presented at the seminar "Restructuring the Food System: Global Processes and National Responses," Center for Rural Research, University of Trondheim, Trondheim, Norway, May 17–18.

————. 1994b. "The New Globalization: The Case of Fresh Produce." In *From Columbus to ConAgra: The Globalization and Agriculture and Food,* ed. Alessandro Bonanno et al., 210–31. Lawrence: University Press of Kansas.

————. 1995. "Globalization, Fordism, Postfordism, Agricultural Exceptionalism: The Need for Conceptual Clarity." Paper presented at the workshop "The Political Economy of the Agro-Food System in Advanced Industrial Countries," University of California, Berkeley, September 5–8.

Friedman, Milton. 1962/1982. *Capitalism and Freedom.* Chicago: University of Chicago Press.

————. 1977. *Friedman on Galbraith, and on Curing the British Disease.* Vancouver, BC: Fraser Institute.

Friedman, Thomas L. 2000. *The Lexus and the Olive Tree.* New York: Anchor Books.

Friedmann, Harriet. 1990. "Family Wheat Farmers and Third World Diets: A Paradoxical Relationship Between Unwaged and Waged Labor." In *Work Without Wages,* ed. Jane L. Collins and Martha E. Gimenez, 193–213. New York: State University of New York Press.

Friedmann, Harriet, and Philip McMichael. 1989. "Agriculture and the State System: The Rise and Decline of National Agricultures, 1870 to the Present." *Sociologia Ruralis* 29 (2): 93–117.

Fritz, Gary. 1985. "Heritage in the Balance." Industrial Workers of the World, November 17. http://bari.org/iu120/local/Heritage.html (accessed December 13, 1999).

Frontline. 1997. "So You Want to Buy a President?" Public Broadcasting System. http://www.Pbs.Org/wgbh/pages/frontline/president/players/andreas .html.

Frost, Greg. 1998. "Critics Call California's Redwoods Plan 'Extortion.'" *SF Gate,* September 1.

FSC (Forest Stewardship Council). 2003a. "What Is FSC? About FSC." http://www .fsc.org/en/about/.

————. 2003b. "What Is FSC? Governance." http://www.fsc.org/en/about/gover nance/.

Fukuyama, Francis. 1992. *The End of History and the Last Man.* New York: Free Press.

Gabriel, Yiannis, and Tim Lang. 1995. *The Unmanageable Consumer.* London: Sage Publications.

Garofano, Giuseppe. 1993. "Testimony to the Trial of Sergio Cusani." *Il Processo Cusani,* RAI TV, Milan, Italy, December.

George, Ricky. 2000. "Sierra Files Suit Against Seaboard." *Amarillo Globe-News,* June 9.

Gereffi, Gary. 1994. "The Organization of Buyer-Driven Global Commodity Chains: How U.S. Retailers Shape Overseas Production Networks." In *Commodity Chains and Global Capitalism,* ed. Gary Gereffi and Miguel Korzeniewicz, 95– 122. Westport, Conn.: Praeger.

Gereffi, Gary, and Miguel Korzeniewicz, eds. 1994. *Commodity Chains and Global Capitalism.* Westport, Conn.: Praeger.

Gereffi, Gary, David Spener, and Jennifer Bair, eds. 2002. *Free Trade and Uneven Development: The North American Apparel Industry After NAFTA.* Philadelphia: Temple University Press.

Gerwitz, Carl. 1998. "OECD Steps Up Efforts on Investment Accord." *International Herald Tribune,* February 18.

Giddens, Anthony. 1990. *The Consequences of Modernity.* Stanford: Stanford University Press.

————. 1994. *Beyond Left and Right.* Stanford: Stanford University Press.

————. 2000. *Runaway World: How Globalization Is Reshaping Our Lives:* New York: Routledge.

Gilpin, Robert. 2000. *The Challenge of Global Capitalism: The World Economy in the 21st Century.* Princeton: Princeton University Press.

Godges, John. 1988. "Dolphins Hit Rough Seas Again." *Sierra* magazine, May–June, 24–26.

Goldberg, Donald. 1994. "GATT Tuna/Dolphin II: Environmental Protection Continues to Clash with Free Trade." Center for International Law, June, no. 2. http:// www.igc.apc.org/ciel/issue2b.html (accessed September 2, 1999).

Goldfield, Michael. 1987. *The Decline of Organized Labor in the United States.* Chicago: University of Chicago Press.

Gordon, David. 1996. *Fat and Mean: The Corporate Squeeze of Working Americans and the Myth of Managerial "Downsizing."* New York: Free Press.

Gordon, David, Richard Edwards, and Michael Reich. 1982. *Segmented Work, Divided Workers.* Cambridge: Cambridge University Press.

Gordon, Robert. 1998. "Shell No! OCAW and the Labor-Environmental Alliance." *Environmental History* 3: 460–88.

Gordy, J. Frank. 1974. "Broilers." In *American Poultry History: 1823–1973,* ed. O. A. Hanke, 371–443. Madison, Wisc.: American Printing and Publishing, Inc.

Gottlieb, Robert. 1993. *Forcing the Spring.* Washington, D.C.: Island Press.

Gramsci, Antonio. 1973. *Quaderni dal carcere: Note sul Macchiavelli.* Rome: Editori Riuniti.

Gray, John. 1998. *False Dawn: The Delusions of Global Capitalism.* New York: New Press.

Gray, Mark. 2000. "Iowa Farmers and California Yuppies: Niche Pork Producers' Concepts of Their Customers." Paper presented at international conference "The Role of Culture of the Agriculture of the 21st Century," San Antonio, Texas, February 25–26.

Graziani, Augusto, ed. 1979. *L'economia italiana dal 1945 ad oggi.* Bologna: Il Mulino.

Greenpeace. 1996. "Testimony of Clifton Curtis on Behalf of Greenpeace Before the Subcommittee on Fisheries, Wildlife and Oceans of the U.S. House of Representatives Committee on Resources on Tuna/Dolphin-Related Issues as Addressed in H.R. 2823 and H.R. 2856." February 19. http://www.greenpeace.org/~usa/campaigns/biodiversity/tunatest.html (accessed October 2, 1997).

Greenwald, John. 1996. "Business: Tightening the Net, Three Feed Companies Cop Pleas in a US Price-Fixing Case That Could Soon Snare Mighty ADM." *Time* magazine, international ed., September 9.

Greider, William. 1997a. *One World Ready or Not: The Manic Logic of Global Capitalism.* New York: Simon and Schuster.

———. 1997b. "Why the Global Economy Needs Worker Rights." *WorkingUSA,* May–June, 32–44.

Grotti, Alberto. 1994. "Testimony to the Trial of Sergio Cusani." *Il Processo Cusani,* RAI TV, Milan, Italy, December.

Guatelli, Arturo. 1994. "Idina: Raul non si é ucciso." *Il Corriere Della Sera* (Milan), July 21, 15.

Guebert, Alan. 2002. "After 13 Years, Lawsuit on 1989 CBOT Soybean Crash Begins." *FoodRoutes* 16, September 20. http://www.foodroutes.org/fwissue_print.jsp?item=23 (accessed March 10, 2007).

Guillen, Mauro F. 2001. "Is Globalization Civilizing, Destructive, or Feeble? A Critique of Five Key Debates in the Social Science Literature." *Annual Review of Sociology* 27: 235–60.

Gumbel, Andrew. 1998. "Fear Among the Redwoods." *The Independent* (London), November 4.

Habermas, Jürgen. 1975. *Legitimation Crisis.* Boston: Beacon Press.

———. 2002. The European Nation-State and the Pressure of Globalization. In *Global Justice and Transnational Politics,* ed. Pablo de Greiff and Kieran Cronin, 217–34. Cambridge: MIT Press.

Habitat Media. 2000. "Interview Transcript—Margaret Wittenberg." http://www.habitatmedia.org/tran-wittenberg.html (accessed November 19, 2003).

Hagerbaumer, Jean. 2001. Interview by authors, October 6.

———. 2007. Interview by authors, January 23.

Hall, John. 1996. "Dr. John Hall's Letter to President Clinton." Earth Island Institute, May 24. http://www.earthisland.org/elf.immp/jhall.html (accessed May 27, 1997).

Hammond, Allen. 1998. *Which World? Scenarios for the 21st Century: Global Destinies, Regional Choices.* Washington, D.C.: Island Press.

Handley, Paul. 1989. "Unicord's Big Catch." *Far East Economic Review* 145 (September 7): 108–9.

———. 1991a. "Off the Hook." *Far East Economic Review* 151 (May 23): 48–49.

———. 1991b. "Row of Canneries." *Far East Economic Review* 151 (May 23): 50.

Harman, Bill. 1999. Personal communication to authors, Houston, Texas, June 6.

Harper, Scott. 1999. "Rule Revised for Tuna Fishing Encirclement Will Be Allowed with Oversight to Help Protect Dolphins." *Virginian Pilot,* May 18.

Harrison, Bennett, and Barry Bluestone. 1988. *The Great U-Turn: Corporate Restructuring and the Polarizing of America.* New York: Basic Books.

Harvey, David. 1989. *The Condition of Postmodernity.* Oxford: Basil Blackwell.

———. 2000. *Spaces of Hope.* Berkeley and Los Angeles: University of California Press.

———. 2005. *A Brief History of Neoliberalism.* New York: Oxford University Press.

———. 2006. *Spaces of Global Capitalism.* London: Verso.

Hatfield, Susan. 2001. "Hatfield: Some Neighborly Advice Before Panhandle Pigs Out." *Amarillo Globe-News,* December 15.

Hayden, Tom. 2003. "Cancun Files: As Empire Falls, Protesters Celebrate." Alternet.org, September 14. http://www.alternet.org/story.html?storyID = 16777 (accessed January 12, 2004).

Haydon, Louis. 2002a. Letter to Governor Rick Perry, June 27. In authors' possession.

———. 2002b. "Hog Waste System Update." *Pampa (TX) News,* December 8.

———. 2002c. "Letter to the Editor: A Forecast for the Future." *Pampa (TX) News,* December 8.

Heartland. 1998. Heartland home page. http://www.lysine.com/Plant/eddyv.htm (accessed February 7, 1998).

Hebert, H. Josef. 1997a. "Dolphin Safe Tuna?" *SoundNet,* April 16. http://www.oceania.org.au/soundnet/apr97/dolsafe.html (accessed August 5, 1997).

———. 1997b. "Dolphin-Tuna? *SoundNet,* May 21. http://www.oceania.org.au/soundnet/may97/tunabill.html (accessed August 5, 1997).

Heffernan, William D. 1972. "Sociological Dimensions of Agricultural Structures in the United States." *Sociologia Ruralis* 12 (2): 481–99.

———. 1984. "Constraints in the Poultry Industry." In *Research in Rural Sociology and Development,* ed. Harry K. Schwartzweller, 237–60. Greenwich, Conn.: JAI Press.

———. 1990. "The Internationalization of the Broiler Industry." Paper Presented at the World Congress of the International Sociological Association, July 9–13, Madrid, Spain.

———. 1999a. "Agriculture and Monopoly Capital." *Monthly Review* 50 (3): 46–59.

———. 1999b. "Societal Concerns Raised by CAFOs." North Carolina Department of Environment and Natural Resources. http://www.p2pays.org/ref/21/20524/ManureMgmt/85.html#TOP.

———. 2000. "Concentration of Ownership in Agriculture." In *Hungry for Profit: The Agribusiness Threat to Farmers, Food, and the Environment,* ed. Fred Magdoff, Jeremy B. Foster, and Frederick H. Buttel, 61–76. New York: Monthly Review Press.

Heffernan, William D., and Douglas H. Constance. 1994. "Transnational Corporations and the Globalization of the Food System." In *From Columbus to ConAgra: The Globalization of Agriculture and Food,* ed. Alessandro Bonanno et al., 29–51. Lawrence: University Press of Kansas.

Held, David, Anthony McGrew, David Goldblatt, and Jonathan Perraton. 1999. *Global Transformations, Politics, Economics, and Culture.* Stanford: Stanford University Press.

Hellyer, Paul. 1997. "The Multilateral Agreement on Investment." Notes for an address to the Sub-committee on International Affairs: Trade Disputes and Investment of the House of Commons Standing Committee on Foreign Affairs and International Trade, Ottawa, Ontario, Canada, November 25. http://www.hartford-hwp.com/archives/25/047.html (accessed December 29, 2003).

Hendrickson, Mary, and William D. Heffernan. 2002. "Multi-National Concentrated Food Processing and Marketing Systems and the Farm Crisis." Paper presented at the annual meeting of the American Association for the Advancement of Science Symposium, Boston, Massachusetts, February 14.

Henkoff, Ronald. 1995a. "ADM Takes the Justice Department for a Spin." *Fortune* magazine, November 27, 35.

———. 1995b. "Checks, Lies, and Videotape." *Fortune* magazine, October 30, 109–16.

———. 1995c. "My Life as a Corporate Mole for the FBI." *Fortune* magazine, September 4, 52–56, 66–68.

———. 1996. "The ADM Tale Gets Even Stranger." *Fortune* magazine, May 13, 113–16, 118.

———. 1997. "Betrayal." *Fortune* magazine, February 3, 82–91.

Herbert, Susannah. 1998. "International: French Film-Makers Say Accord Will Ruin European Cinema." *Daily Telegraph* (London), February 17.

Herrick, Samuel F., Jr., and Steven J. Koplin. 1986. "U.S. Tuna Trade Summary, 1984." *Marine Fisheries Review* 48 (3): 28–37.

Hiatt, Fred. 1998. "MAI: Foreign Affairs in Annapolis." *Washington Post,* March 30.

Highleyman, Scott, Amy Mathews Amos, and Hank Cauley. 2004. "Wildhavens: An Independent Assessment of the Marine Stewardship Council." Draft report prepared for the Homeland Foundation, Oak Foundation, and the Pew Charitable Trusts, January 15. http://www.alaskaoceans.net/aboutus/documents/WildhavensMSC.pdf.

Hilary, John. 2003. "Unlimited Companies: The Developmental Impacts of an Investment Agreement in the WTO." ActionAid, June. http://www.actionaid.org.uk/doc_lib/_1_unlimited_companies.pdf.

Hill, Julia Butterfly. 2000. Personal communication with authors, Houston, Texas, May 15.

Hirst, Paul, and Grahame Thompson. 1996. *Globalization in Question.* Cambridge: Polity Press.

Hobhouse, L. T. 1979. *Liberalism.* New York: Oxford University Press.

Holland, Kerry L. 1991. "Exploitation on Porpoise: The Use of Purse Seine Nets by Commercial Tuna Fisherman in the Eastern Tropical Pacific Ocean." *Syracuse Journal of International Law and Commerce* 17: 241.

Holloway, John. 1993. "Global Capital and the National State." *Capital and Class* 52 (summer): 23–49.

Hornblower, Margot, Hannah Beech, Steven Frank, and James L. Graff. 1999. "The Battle in Seattle: Never Mind the Riots; the Real Threat to the WTO's Free Trade Agenda Lies in Discord Among Member Nations." *Time* magazine, international ed., December 13, 22–23.

Houston Chronicle. 1998. "ADM Trial Jury Finds Three Guilty: One Blew Whistle on Price-Fixing." September 19.

Howard, John. 1999. "Government Takes Over Logging Plan For Headwaters." *SF Gate,* January 6. http://www.elibrary.com/ (accessed November 7, 1999).

Howell, David. 1995a. "Lucky Pluck: B-CS Still in Hunt for Chicken Plant." *Bryan/College Station (TX) Eagle,* February 23.

———. 1995b. "Mississippi Plant Looking at Brazos Valley." *Bryan/College Station (TX) Eagle,* February 17.

Hudgins, Linda Lucas. 1987. "The Development of the Tuna Industry in Mexico: 1976–1986." In *The Development of the Tuna Industry in the Pacific Islands Region: An Analysis of Options,* ed. David J. Doulman, 153–68. Honolulu: East-West Center.

Hudgins, Linda Lucas, and Linda Fernandez. 1987. "A Summary of International Business Operations in the Global Tuna Market." In *The Development of the Tuna Industry in the Pacific Islands Region: An Analysis of Options,* ed. David J. Doulman, 289–302. Honolulu: East-West Center.

Humphery, Kim. 1998. *Shelf Life: Supermarkets and the Changing Cultures of Consumption.* Cambridge: Cambridge University Press.

Humphreys, David. 1996. *Forest Politics: The Evolution of International Cooperation.* London: Earthscan.

Humphreys, Jim, and Karen Tarica. 2000. "Sustainable Salmon: Marine Stewardship Council's Eco-Labeling Program." Endangered Species Update, Marine Stewardship Council, November 1. http://www.elibrary.bigchalk.com/ (accessed August 8, 2003).

Illinois News. 1997. "Former FBI Informant Enters Innocent Plea." January 30. http://www.thonline.com/th/news/013097/Illinois/44618.htm (accessed February 7, 1997).

Industry Group 99. 1998. "Headwaters Forest Documents Released for Public Comment, Public Hearings Scheduled." *SF Gate,* October 2. http://www.elibrary.com/ (accessed November 7, 1999).

Infolatina. 2001a. "CIAT Says Mexico Has Obligation to Dolphin Safety Program." August 17. htttp://www.elibrary.com/ (accessed June 28, 2002).

———. 2001b. "Mexican Fishing Industry Urges Retaliation over U.S. Tuna Ban." July 25. http://www.elibrary.com/ (accessed June 28, 2002).

———. 2001c. "Mexican Scientists to Participate in Crucial U.S. Dolphin Study." December 1. http://www.elibrary.com/ (accessed June 28, 2002).

———. 2001d. "Mexico and United States to Continue Tuna Talks." December 3. http://www.elibrary.com/ (accessed June 28, 2002).

———. 2001e. "Mexico Threatens to Take United States to WTO over Tuna Exports." August 10. http://www.elibrary.com/ (accessed June 28, 2002).

———. 2001f. "Tuna Fleet Stops Compliance with Dolphin Treaty Inspectors." August 8. http://www.elibrary.com/ (accessed June 28, 2002).

———. 2001g. "U.S.-Mexico Tuna Talks Remain Unscheduled." September 14. http://www.elibrary.com/ (accessed June 28, 2002).

———. 2001h. "U.S. Tuna Ruling Will Not Protect Dolphins: Mexican Official." July 25. http://www.elibrary.com/ (accessed June 28, 2002).

———.2002a. "Derbez Warns of 210% Retaliatory Corn-Syrup Tariff." March 21. http://www.elibrary.com/ (accessed June 28, 2002).

———. 2002b. "Mexican Tuna Reappears in U.S. Market." March 27. http://www.elibrary.com/ (accessed June 28, 2002).

———.2002c. "Tuna Production Surpluses May Be Sent to U.S. in Sept.–Oct." April 19. http://www.elibrary.com/ (accessed June 28, 2002).

Investment Watch. 2003. "Corporate Conquistadors of Cancun: The EU Offensive for WTO-Investment Negotiations." July. http://www.globalpolicy.org/socecon/bwi-wto/wto/2003/07corporate.htm (accessed December 29, 2003).

IPS/GIN (Inter-Press Service/Global Information Network). 2001. "New Zealand Sustainable Fishery in Troubled Waters." Inter-Press Service, English News Wire, March 20. http://www.elibrary.bigchalk.com/ (accessed August 6, 2003).

Iskander, Samer. 1998. "France Quits Investment Accord Talks: Multilateral Agreement Jospin Says 'Not Open to Reform' and Sovereignty Threatened." *Financial Times,* October 15.

Iversen, Robert T. B. 1987. "U.S. Tuna Processors." In *The Development of the Tuna Industry in the Pacific Islands Region: An Analysis of Options,* ed. David J. Doulman, 271–88. Honolulu: East-West Center.

Jameson, Fredric. 1984. "Postmodernism or the Cultural Logic of Late Capitalism." *New Left Review* 46: 53–92.

———. 1994. *Postmodernism or the Cultural Logic of Late Capitalism.* Durham: Duke University Press.

Japan Economic Institute. 1991. "Japan-U.S. Business Report No. 249," April, p. 2. http://www.gwjapan.com/ftp/pub/business/jeibus/bus.11-91.tex.html.

Jay, Martin. 1973. *The Dialectical Imagination.* Boston: Little, Brown.

Jebb, Fiona. 1996. "Money Talks." *Corporate Location,* January–February, 20–21.

Jenkins, Ron. 2000. "Sierra Club Suing Over Dorman Facility." *Amarillo Globe-News,* February 25.

Jereski, Laura, and Randall Smith. 1996. "Hog-Tied Wall Street Merchant Banking Firm Wallowing in Pig Farm Losses." *St. Louis Post-Dispatch,* May 23.

Johnson, Sandra. 1998. Letter to attendees of November 23 poultry meeting, December 23. In authors' possession.

Joseph, James. 1986. *Recent Developments in the Fishery for Tropical Tunas in the Eastern Pacific Ocean.* La Jolla, Calif.: Inter-American Tropical Tuna Commission.

Joseph, James, and Joseph W. Greenough. 1979. *International Management of Tuna, Porpoise, and Billfish.* Seattle: University of Washington Press.

Jung, Carolyn. 2000. "American Humane Association, U.S. Agriculture Department Announce New Label." Knight-Ridder/Tribune Business News, September 20. http://elibrary.bigchalk.com/ (accessed August 6, 2003).

Kaplan, Temma. 1997. *Crazy for Democracy: Women in Grassroots Movements.* New York: Routledge.

Karliner, Joshua. 1997. *The Corporate Planet: Ecology and Politics in the Age of Globalization.* San Francisco: Sierra Club Books.

Kay, Jane. 1995. "Part Five—The Future." *SF Gate,* December 21. http://www.sfgate.com/special/redwoods/part5.htm (accessed December 19, 1998).

———. 1997. "Redwoods Swap Now a Cash Deal." *SF Gate,* March 15. http://www.sfgate.com/ (accessed January 29, 1999).

Kay, Janet. 2002. "Tuna Fishing Still Harming Dolphins: Long-Awaited Study Sees 'Little Evidence of Recovery' So Far." *San Francisco Chronicle,* December 5.

———. 2003. "Groups Protest Rules Change on 'Dolphin-Safe' Label." *San Francisco Chronicle,* February 12.

KCSA (Kerr Center for Sustainable Agriculture). 2000. *The Impact of Recruiting Vertically Integrated Hog Production.* Poteau, Okla.: North Central Regional Center for Rural Development.

Kelley, Matt. 1996. "Archer Daniels Midland Sues FBI Mole for $30 Million." Associated Press, November 22. http://sddt.com/files/librarywire/96wire . . . nes/09_96/DN96_09_20/far.html (accessed April 9, 1998).

Kellner, Douglas. 1981. "Network Television and American Society." *Theory and Society* 10: 265–77.

———. 2002. "Theorizing Globalization." *Sociological Theory* 20 (3): 285–305.

Keynes, John Maynard. 1935. *The General Theory of Employment, Interest, and Money*. New York: Harcourt Brace Jovanovich.

Khor, Martin. 1998a. "The MAI—Insult Plus Injury to Developing Nations." Third World Network Features, March 4. http://www.hartford-hwp.com/archives/25/039.html.

———. 1998b. "NGOS Mount Protests Against MAI." Third World Network Features, April. http://globalpolicy.org/socecon/bwi-wto/maingosm.htm.

Kilborn, Robert, and Lance Carden. 1999. "USA." *Christian Science Monitor,* April 22.

Kinsella. 1996. "Lysine Settlement or the Lysine Purchaser Indirect Class Action Settlement." http://wx3.kinsella.com/lysine/notice.html (accessed February 26, 1998).

Kitching, Gavin. 2001. *Seeking Social Justice Through Globalization: Escaping a Nationalist Perspective*. University Park: Pennsylvania State University Press.

Kluger, Jeffrey. 1999. "Food Fight." *Time* magazine, September 13, 43–44.

Kneene, Brewster. 1995. *Invisible Giant: Cargill and Its Transnational Strategies*. London: Pluto Press.

———. 1998. "ADM 'Fixed Again.'" *Ram's Horn* 160 (June): 5.

Knight, Danielle. 1998. "Environment: Greens Split over Dolphin Protection Agreement." Inter-Press Service, English News Wire, February 16.

Kraker, Daniel, and Kristin Dawkins. 1999. "The Continuing Threat from Trade Negotiations." *Dollars and Sense,* March 1, 22–25, 36.

Kramer, Jane. 1994. "Dirty Hands." *New Yorker,* March 28, 70–81.

Kraul, Chris. 1990. "US Fisherman Fear Decision May Be Final Blow." *Los Angeles Times,* April 14.

———. 2000. "Mexico Caught Off Guard in U.S. Ruling Covering Dolphin-Safe Tuna." *Los Angeles Times,* May 10.

Krebs, A. V. 2000. "Supermarkup to the World: ADM Racks Up Another $45 Million in Fines." *Agribusiness Examiner* 78, June 14. http://www.electricarrow.com/CARP/agbiz/78.htm.

———. 2001a. "Dan Glickman: Life After USDA Joins ADM Friendly Law Firm." *Agribusiness Examiner* 105, February 23. http://www.mindfully.org/Reform/Glickman-After-USDA.htm (accessed January 16, 2007).

———. 2001b. "USDA Defends ADM Plea Agreement." *Progressive Populist,* January 12. http://www.populist.com/01.12.krebs.html (accessed January 16, 2007).

———. 2002. "The ADM Way—To Insure That ADM's Business Is Conducted with the Utmost Integrity." *Agribusiness Examiner* 143, February 20. http://www.lectricarrow.com/carp/agbiz/143.htm (accessed January 16, 2007).

Krinsky, Maria. 1998. "Winging It: Sanderson Farms Chicken Operation Prepares to Lift Off." *Bryan/College Station (TX) Eagle,* September 2.

Kronman, Mick. 1991. "Fishing Morally Correct Tuna." *Journal of Commerce and Commercial,* November 27, 8A.

KWNS (Kyoto World News Service). 2002. "WTO Japan Investment." October 17. http://www.elibrary.com/ (accessed November 27, 2002).

Lambert, Chip. 1995. "Chicken Plant Deal Spreads its Wings." *Bryan/College Station (TX) Eagle,* December 15, A1.

Lang, Tim. 1999. "The Complexity of Globalization: The UK as a Case Study of Tensions Within the Food System and the Challenge to Food Policy." *Agriculture and Human Values* 16 (2): 169–85.

Lantos, Ivan. 1995. "La vedova Gardini si fa suora carmelitana." *Gente* 39 (22): 22–25.

Lash, Scott, Bronislaw Szerszynski, and Brian Wynne, eds. 1996. *Risk, Environment, and Modernity.* London: Sage Publications.

Lash, Scott, and John Urry. 1987. *The End of Organized Capitalism.* Madison: University of Wisconsin Press.

———. 1994. *Economies of Signs and Space.* London: Sage Publications.

Lasley, Floyd A. 1983. *The U.S. Poultry Industry: Changing Economics and Structure.* Agricultural Economics Report no. 502. Washington, D.C.: Economic Research Service/USDA.

Lawton, Valerie. 1998. "Investment Rules Years Off: Marchi." *Toronto Star,* October 16.

LCEG (Leon County Environmental Group) 1998a. Meeting minutes, August 16. In authors' possession.

———. 1998b. Meeting minutes, July 9. In authors' possession.

———. 1999. Monthly Newsletter, Jan. 27. In authors' possession.

Leape, James P., and Michael Sutton. 2004. "Report of Fisheries Certification Review Workshop: Arlie House, Virginia, January 26–28, 2004." David and Lucile Packard Foundation, February 5. http://www.alaskaoceans.net/aboutus/msc.htm.

Ledbetter, Kay. 1997a. "Hog Operations Permits Increase Throughout the Area." *Amarillo Globe-News,* December 11.

———. 1997b. "Proposed Farm Would House 400,000 Hogs." *Amarillo Globe-News,* December 11.

———. 1997c. "Ruling Upsets Feed Operators." *Wall Street Journal,* November 29.

———. 1997d. "Swine Operation Could Give Town Feedmill, School." *Amarillo Globe-News,* December 11.

———. 1997e. "Tax Break Bid For Hog Farm Angers Officials." *Amarillo Globe-News,* February 14.

———. 1999. "CAFO Key Issue Plaguing Meat Industry in Texas." *Amarillo Globe-News,* July 13.

Lee, Steven H. 1998. "The Smell of Money: Battle Rages over Lucrative Farms, Residents Fed Up with Hogs' Odor." *Dallas Morning News,* March 3.

———. 1999. "How Farms Find Home in Texas: But Some Neighbors Raise Health Concerns." *Dallas Morning News,* October 10.

Leone, Roberto. 1994. "Il giorno di penne sporche." *La Repubblica* (Milan), February 25.

Levenstein, Charles, and John Wooding. 1998. "Dying for a Living: Workers, Production, and the Environment." In *The Struggle of Ecological Democracy,* ed. Daniel Faber, 60–80. New York: Guilford Press.

Levin, Myron. 1989. "Dolphin Demise; Foreign Tuna Fishing Fleets Blamed for Most of the Sharp Increase in Killings." *Los Angeles Times,* March 5.

Lieber, James B. 2000. *Rats in the Grain: The Dirty Tricks and Trails of Archer Daniels Midland, the Supermarket to the World.* New York: Four Walls Eight Windows Publishing.

Lilley, Sasha. 2006. "Green Fuel's Dirty Secret." CorpWatch, June 1. http://www
.corpwatch.org/article.php?id = 13646.

Linden, Eugene. 1996. "Chicken of the Sea: A 'Dolphin Safe' Tuna Flap Makes the
U.S. Squirm." *Time* magazine, March 4, 57.

Lipietz, Alan. 1987. *Mirages and Miracles.* London: Verso.

———. 1992. *Towards a New Economic Order: Post-Fordism, Ecology, and Democracy.*
New York: Oxford University Press.

Llambí, Luis. 1994. "Opening Economies and Closing Markets: Latin American Agriculture's Difficult Search for a Place in the Emerging Global Order." In *From
Columbus to ConAgra: The Globalization of Agriculture and Food,* ed. Alessandro Bonanno et al., 184–209. Lawrence: University Press of Kansas.

Llambí, Luis, and Lourdes Gouveia. 1994. "The Restructuring of the Venezuelan
State and State Theory." *International Journal of Sociology of Agriculture and
Food* 4 (1): 64–83.

Llunggren, David. 1996. "Unilever, wwf Unite in Bid to Save Fish Stocks." Reuters,
February 21.

Lobe, Jim. 2003. "ngos Organize Against Proposed wto Investment Agreement."
Global Policy Forum, June 23. http://www.globalpolicy.org/socecon/
bwi-wto/wto/2003/0624ngoinvest.htm.

Logan, Sam. 1995. "Sanderson Farms Breaks Bryan Ground." *Bryan/College Station
(TX) Eagle,* October 2.

London Free Press. 1998. "mai: A Little-Known Threat to Canada." February 11.

Los Angeles Times. 1998. "White Houses Backs Off Global Investment Plan." February
14.

Low, Murray. 1997. "Representation Unbound: Globalization and Democracy." In
Spaces of Globalization, ed. Kevin Cox, 240–80. New York: Guilford Press.

Luce, Edward, Guy de Jonquieres, and Frances Williams. 2003. "India Opposes Talks
on Investment Rules." *Financial Times,* August 27.

Luxner, Larry. 1990. "Puerto Rico Lures Asians to Tuna Business." *Journal of Commerce and Commercial,* April 6, 4A.

Lyotard, Jean-François. 1984. *The Postmodern Condition: A Report on Knowledge.*
Minneapolis: University of Minnesota Press.

M2PressWIRE. 1998. "wwf: oecd Countries Stall Globalization Treaty in Face of Public
Pressure." April 29. http://www.elibrary.com/ (accessed November 27,
2002).

Madeley, John. 1999. "Dodging the Pauper's Custard Pies." *New Statesman,* February
12.

Maggs, John. 1991. "Bush Team Feels Heat over gatt Tuna Ruling." *Journal of Commerce and Commercial,* September 30, 3A.

Magnusson, Paul, Peter Hong, and Patrick Oster. 1992. "Save the Dolphins—or Free
Trade?" *Business Week,* February 17, 130–31.

Mandel, Ernest. 1976. *Introduction to Karl Marx's Capital.* London: New Left Review.

Mann, Susan A., and James M. Dickenson. 1978. "Obstacles to Development of Capitalist Agriculture." *Journal of Peasant Studies* 5 (4): 466–81.

Marbery, Steve. 1994a. "Pork Production 2,000: Fewer Farms Doing More." *Feedstuffs*
66 (9): 1, 30.

———. 1994b. "psf to Acquire National Farms of Texas." *Feedstuffs* 66 (16): 1, 3.

Marcuse, Herbert. 1964. *One-Dimensional Man.* Boston: Beacon Press.

———. 1979. "The Failure of the New Left?" *New German Critique* 18: 3–11.

Marion, Bruce W. 1986. *The Organization and Performance of the U.S. Food System*. Lexington, Conn.: Lexington Books.

Marion, Bruce W., and Henry B. Arthur. 1973. *Dynamic Factors in Vertical Commodity Systems: A Case Study of the Broiler System*. Ohio Agricultural Research and Development Center, Research Bulletin 1065. Wooster, Ohio.

Marquis, Christopher. 2003a. "Rule Weakening Definition of 'Dolphin-Safe' Is Delayed." *New York Times,* January 10.

———. 2003b. "Two Scientists Contend U.S. Suppressed Dolphin-Studies." *New York Times,* January 8.

Marsden, Terry. 1994. "Globalization, the State, and the Environment: Exploring the Limits and Options of the State Activity." *International Journal of Sociology of Agriculture and Food* 4 (1): 139–57.

———. 1997. "Creating the Space for Food: The Distinctiveness of Recent Agrarian Development." In *Globalizing Food,* ed. David Goodman and Michael J. Watts, 273–84. London: Routledge.

———. 2003. *The Condition of Rural Sustainability*. Assen, Netherlands: Royal van Gorcum.

Marsden Terry, and Alberto Arce. 1995. "Constructing Quality: Emerging Food Networks in the Rural Transition." *Environment and Planning A* 27: 1261–79.

Marsden Terry, Josefa Salete Cavalcanti, and José Ferreira Irmao. 1996. "Globalization, Regionalization, and Quality: The Socio-Economic Reconstruction of Food in the San Francisco Valley, Brazil." *International Journal of Sociology of Agriculture and Food* 5 (1): 85–114.

Martin, Glen. "White House Loosens 'Dolphin-Safe' Tuna Rules." *San Francisco Chronicle,* April 30.

Martin, Laura, and Kelly Zering. 1997. "Relationships Between Industrialized Agriculture and Environmental Consequences: The Case of Vertical Coordination in Broilers and Hogs." *Journal of Agricultural and Applied Economics* 29: 45–56.

Martini, Daniele. 1994. "Per far la caritá tutti i mezzi sono buoni." *Panorama* magazine, January 28, 14–15.

Marx, Karl. 1947. *The German Ideology*. Moscow: Progress Publishers.

———. 1955. *The Communist Manifesto*. Moscow: International Publishers.

———. 1963. *Capital*. Vol. 3. New York: Vintage Books.

———. 1967. *Capital*. Vol. 1. New York: Vintage Books.

———. 1973. *Grundrisse: Foundations of the Critique of Political Economy*. New York: Vintage Books.

Mattern, Douglas. 1998. "Democracy or Corporate Rule? OECD Member Countries Negotiate New Accord on Foreign Business Practices." *The Humanist,* July 17, 5.

McCain, John. 1997. "Committee Clears Dolphin Conservation Legislation." Press Release, U.S. Senate Committee on Commerce, Science, and Transportation, June 26. http://www3.senate.gov/ (accessed October 1, 1997).

McCarthy, Coleman. 1996. "'Dolphin-Safe' Claim in Danger." *Washington Post,* July 23.

McColl, Roddy. 2003. "Hoki Sustainabily/Marine Stewardship Council Independence?" Fishkey.com, November 19. http://www.fishkey.com.news2.asp?s = 1078 (accessed November 19, 2003).

McDorman, Ted L. 1995. "Additional Essays on Whales and Man." Revised version of a paper presented for the Symposium on Management of Fisheries and Marine Mammals, Washington, D.C., April 1994. http://www.highnorth/no/Library/Trade/GATT_WTO/pr-in-ma.htm (accessed August 25, 2003).

McLean, Jim. 1998. "Great Bend Vote Reverberates in Statehouse." *Topeka Capital-Journal,* April 4.

McMichael, Philip. 1996. "Globalization: Myths and Realities." *Rural Sociology* 61 (1): 25–55.

———. 2000. "The Power of Food." *Agriculture and Human Values* 17: 21–33.

———. 2002. *Development and Social Change.* Thousand Oaks, Calif.: Pine Forge Press.

McNall, Scott. 1984. "The Marxian Project." *Sociological Quarterly* 25: 473–95.

Mellor, Mary. 1997. *Feminism and Ecology.* New York: New York University Press.

Melucci, Alberto. 1996. *Challenging Codes: Collective Action in the Information Age.* Cambridge: Cambridge University Press.

Memarsadeghi, Sanaz, and Raj Patel. 2003. "Agricultural Restructuring and Concentration in the United States: Who Wins and Who Loses?" Food First Institute for Food and Development Policy, Policy Brief no. 6. http://www.foodfirst .org/node/270.

Mendes, Joshua. 1989. "Corporate Performance: A Raider's Ruckus in the Redwoods." *Fortune* magazine, April 24.

Merchant, Carolyn. 1997. *Ecology.* Atlantic Highlands, N.J.: Humanities Press.

Miele, Mara. 1998. *La commercializaione dei prodotti biologici in Europa.* Florence: ARSIA.

Miele, Mara, and Jonathan Murdoch. 2000. "Fast Food/Slow Food: Resisting Standardization in Food Consumption." Paper presented at the Tenth World Congress of Rural Sociology. Rio de Janeiro, Brazil, August.

Miliband, Ralph. 1969. *The State in Capitalist Societies.* London: Winfield and Nicholson.

Miller, Adam. 1998. "Giant Redwoods Fall to Corporate Raider." February 15. http://www.wavenet.com/~prashkin/redwoods.html (accessed September 27, 1998).

Miller, Dale. 2000. "Straight Talk from Smithfield's Luter." *National Hog Farmer,* May 1.

Miller, Daniel, ed. 1995. *Acknowledging Consumption.* London: Routledge.

Mingione, Enzo. 1993. "Marxism, Ecology, and Political Movements." *Capitalism, Nature, Socialism* 4 (2): 85–92.

Minich, Gary. 1998. "Whitacre Gets 9-Year Sentence." *Decatur (IL) Herald & Review,* March 5.

Mires, Susan. 2001a. "Residents Glad Pork Plant Not Being Built." *St. Joseph (MO) News-Press Online,* March 14. http://www.stjoenews-press.com/print.asp .031401.shtml (accessed November 12, 2003).

———. 2001b. "Residents Target Hogs." *St. Joseph (MO) News-Press Online,* March 19. http://www.stjoenews-press.com/print.asp.031901.shtml (accessed November 12, 2003).

Mishel, Lawrence, and Jared Bernstein. 1993. *The State of Working America, 1992–1993.* Washington, D.C.: Economic Policy Institute.

Mishel, Lawrence, Jared Bernstein, and John Schmitt. 1999. *The State of Working America, 1998–99.* Washington, D.C.: Economic Policy Institute.

Modolo, Gianfranco. 1994a. "Ferfim, manovre ai blocchi." *La Repubblica* (Milan), January 13, 48.

———. 1994b. "Nella vita c'é solo posto per servi ed eroi." *La Repubblica* (Milan), February 19, 5.

Monbiot, George. 1997. "A Charter to Let Loose the Multinationals." *The Guardian* (London), April 15.

———. 1999. "Feeding Mammon: Big Business Will Subjugate Developing Countries at the World Trade Talks—with British Help." *The Guardian* (London), November 30.

Money, Janette. 1992. "The Decentralization of Collective Bargaining in Belgium, France, and the United States." In *Bargaining for Change: Union Politics in North America and Europe,* ed. Michael Golden and John Pontusson, 77–110. Ithaca: Cornell University Press.

Moody, John. 1993. "Death Before Disgrace." *Time* magazine, August 9, 39.

Mooney, Patrick H. 1983. "Toward a Class Analysis of Midwestern Agriculture." *Rural Sociology* 48 (4): 279–91.

Morain, Dan. 1990. "US Told to Ban Tuna Imports." *Los Angeles Times,* August 29.

Morain, Dan, and Max Vanzi. 1998. "California and the West; License to Log Ancient Forests Is Suspended." *Los Angeles Times,* November 11.

Morgan, Kevin, Terry Marsden, and Jonathan Murdoch. 2006. *Worlds of Food: Place, Power and Provenance in the Food Chain.* Oxford: Oxford University Press.

Morris, Jim. 1997. "Pork Barrels and Politics: Residents Not So Wild About Hog Operations." *Houston Chronicle,* November 11.

Morrison, John M. 1998. "The Poultry Industry: A View of the Swine Industry's Future." In *Pigs, Profits, and Rural Communities,* ed. Kendall M. Thu and E. Paul Durrenburger, 145–54. Albany: State University of New York Press.

Morrison, Scott. 1997. "World Trade: US Pressed on Helms-Burton." *Financial Times,* October 20.

MSC (Marine Stewardship Council). 1998a. "Homepage." http://www.msc.org/ homepage.html (accessed November 9, 1998).

———. 1998b. "The Marine Stewardship Council Addresses Marine Fishing Crisis." http://www.msc.org/crisis.html (accessed November 9, 1998).

———. 1998c. "The Marine Stewardship Council Signatories and Supporters." http://www.msc.org/cgi-local/signatories/cgi/sign.pl (accessed November 9, 1998).

———. 1998d. "New Scheme Is a Milestone for Responsible Fishing." June 12. http://www.msc.org/ (accessed November 9, 1998).

———. 2000. "Principles and Criteria for Sustainable Fishing." http://www .msc.org/ (accessed December 8, 2000).

———. 2002. "New Zealand Hoki Dispute Panel Releases Its Findings on Certification of the Fishery to the MSC Standard." http://www.msc.org/html .ni_60.htm (accessed November 19, 2003).

———. 2003. "Draft Report of Possible Certification of Gulf of Alaska Pollack Fishery." http://www.msc.org/html.ni_99.htm (accessed December 28, 2003).

———. 2004a. "Fish 4 Thought." November. http://www.msc.org/ (accessed January 9, 2007).

———. 2004b. "South African Hake." http://eng.msc.org/html.consenty1112 .htm.

———. 2005a. "Fish 4 Thought." March. http://www.msc.org/.

———. 2005b. "Fish 4 Thought." June. http://www.msc.org/.

———. 2005c. "Fish 4 Thought." November. http://www.msc.org/.

———. 2006a. "Fish 4 Thought." March. http://www.msc.org/.

———. 2006b. "Fish 4 Thought." June. http://www.msc.org/.

———. 2006c. "Fish 4 Thought." November. http://www.msc.org/.

Mulvaney, Kieran. 1998. "A Sea of Troubles in the International Year of the Ocean: Are We Reaching the Limits?" *E Magazine,* September 28. http://www.elibrary.com/ (accessed July 8, 1998).

Myers, Frank. 1999. "Economic Globalization and Political Action: The Working Class in Industrialized Democracies." In *Postimperialism and World Politics,* ed. David Becker and Richard Sklar, 125–44. Westport, Conn.: Praeger.

Myrick, Albert C., Jr. 1996. "Myrick's Statement on the Tuna-Dolphin Issue." June. Statement on Physiological Effects on Dolphins Due to Chase and Capture by the Tuna Industry, Submitted to the House Resources Committee and Senate Commerce Committee. http://www.earthisland.org/elf/immp/myrick.html (accessed May 27, 1997).

National Research Council. 1992. *Dolphins and the Tuna Industry.* Washington, D.C.: National Academy Press.

Neis, Barbara L. 1997. "Cut Adrift." *Samudra,* report no. 16, November. http://www.gmt2000.co.uk/apoints/icfs/english/samudra/issue_16/art8.htm (accessed November 7, 1997).

Nelson, Trent. 2001. "Seaboard Worrying Atchison." *St. Joseph (MO) News-Press Online,* March 13. http://www.stjoenews-press.com/print.asp.031301.shtml (accessed November 12, 2003).

Nesmith, Jeff. 2003. "Dolphin-Safe Tuna Ruling Allows Some Deaths." *Atlanta Journal-Constitution,* January 1.

New Scientist. 2003. "Marine Stewardship Council Under Fire: In Deep Trouble." Vol. 178 (May 17): 3. http://www.eurobc.org/NS_vol178_iss2395&p3_p1of3_17may2003page102 5.htm l (accessed November 19, 2003).

New York Post. 2002. "Drug Lords Slaughter Dolphins." April 1.

New York Times. 1989a. "Judge Extends Order That U.S. Protect Dolphin." January 19.

———. 1989b. "U.S. Defends Law on Monitoring Dolphin Killings." August 23.

———. 1990. "Judge Orders Tuna Import Ban over Dolphin Kill." August 30.

———. 1992a. "Pro-Dolphin Accord Made." June 16.

———. 1992b. "U.S. Enforces Tuna Embargo." February 3.

Nimbupani. 2003. "Ramification of the Cancun Ministerial Talks." http://nimbupani.com/2003/10/20/ramifications_of_the_cancun_ministeri a l_talks.php (accessed January 31, 2007).

Nissen, Bruce, ed. 2002. *Unions in a Global Environment: Changing Borders, Organizational Boundaries, and Social Roles.* Armonk, N.Y.: M. E. Sharpe.

Nissimov, Ron. 1999. "Kaiser Aluminum Workers Picket Financier's Home to Promote Strike." *Houston Chronicle,* January 10.

Noah, Timothy. 1994. "Tuna Boycott Is Ruled Illegal by GATT." *Wall Street Journal,* May 23.

Normangee (TX) Star. 1998. "Environmental Group Gets Little Help When Big Guns Show Up for Meeting." October 8.

Novelli, Massimo. 1994. "Enimont Tassa da 342,000 lire." *La Repubblica* (Milan), April 26, 53.

NPPC (National Pork Producers Council). 2003. "US Pork Exports Set Record." February 26. http://www.nppc.org/news/stories/2003/030226exports.html.

Nunez, Eric. 1995. "Dolphin Kills and the Panama Declaration." Associated Press, October 5. http://whales.magna.com.au/NEWS/dk.html (accessed September 3, 1997).

NWF (National Wildlife Federation). 1997. "Dolphin Safe Fishing: Questions and Answers." http://www.nwf.org/nwf.news/dolphin.html (accessed May 27, 1997).

Obach, Brian. 1999. "The Wisconsin Labor-Environmental Network." *Organization and Environment* 12 (1): 45–74.

O'Connor, James. 1974. *The Fiscal Crisis of the State.* New York: St. Martin's Press.

———. 1986. *Accumulation Crisis.* New York: Basil Blackwell.

———. 1988. "Capitalism, Nature, Socialism: A Theoretical Introduction." *Capital, Nature, Socialism* 1 (1): 11–38.

Odessey, Bruce. 1996. "House Passes Bill for Changing Dolphin-Safe Tuna Label." U.S. Information Agency, August 1. http://www.usia.it/wireless/wf960801/96080113.htm (accessed May 22, 1997).

OECD (Organization for Economic Cooperation and Development). 1995. "A Multilateral Agreement on Investment." May. http://www.oecd.org/daf/cmis/mai/mairap95.htm (accessed February 7, 1998)

Offe, Claus. 1985. *Disorganized Capitalism.* Cambridge: MIT Press.

———. 1987. "New Social Movements: Challenging the Boundaries of Institutional Politics." *Social Research* 52: 817–68.

———. 1996. *Modernity and the State: East, West.* Cambridge: MIT Press.

Offe, Claus, and Volker Ronge. 1979. "Theses on the Theory of the State." In *Critical Sociology,* ed. J. W. Freiberg, 345–56. New York: Irvington Press.

Ogden, Stephen E. 1998. Letter to Normangee Group member Calvin Hodde, July 15. In authors' possession.

Ohmae, Kenichi. 1990. *Borderless World: Power and Strategy in the Interlinked Economy.* New York: Harper Business.

———. 1995. *The End of the Nation-State: The Rise of Regional Economies.* New York: Free Press.

Oldani, Tino. 1994. "Troppo comodo sparare su Ccuccia." *Panorama,* May 7, 30–33.

O'Riordan, Brian. 1997. "Second-Best Solution?" *Samudra,* report no. 18, July. http://www.gmt2000.co.uk/apoints/icsf/english/samudra/issue_15/sam18_2.htm (accessed November 7, 1997).

Palmer, Mark J. 1996. "Dolphin Law Has Served Its Purpose; Reform It." *USA Today,* December 27.

Palmer, Mark J., and Laura Seligsohn. 1996. "Congress Tries to Weaken Dolphin Protection Laws." Earth Island Institute, March 10. http://www.paws.org/activists/news/news285.htm (accessed August 5, 1997).

Panhandle Alliance. 2001a. Information Brochure. In authors' possession.

———. 2002b. Newsletter, May 26. In authors' possession.

Parks, Wesley W., Patricia J. Donley, and Samuel F. Herrick Jr. 1990. "U.S. Tuna in Canning, 1987." *Marine Fisheries Review* 52 (1): 14–22.

Parrish, Michael. 1992. "U.S. Approves Pact to Protect Pacific's Dolphins." *Los Angeles Times,* October 9.

Parsons, Talcott. 1971. *The System of Modern Societies.* Englewood Cliffs, N.J.: Prentice-Hall.

Payne, Roger S. 1996. "Dr. Roger S. Payne to Members of Congress." Memo to Members of Congress, February. http://www.earthisland.org/ei/immp/payne.html (accessed May 27, 1997).

PCPP (Preamble Center for Public Policy). 1997. "The Multilateral Agreement on Investment: Timeline of Negotiations." http://www.rtk.net/preamble/mai/maihist.htm (accessed March 3, 1998).

Pearce, Fred. 2003. "Marine Stewardship Council Under Fire: Can Ocean-Friendly Labels Save Dwindling Stocks?" *New Scientist* 178 (May 17): 5. http://www.eurobc.org/NS/vol178_iss2395&p5_p3of3_17may2003page1027.h tml (accessed November 19, 2003).

Pemberton, Mary. 2004. "Environmental Groups Object to Eco-Label for Alaska's Pollock Industry." Associated Press, August 27. http://www.flmnh.ufl.edu/fish/InNews/ecolabel2004.html.

Pergolini, Angelo. 1993. "Nella fossa delle Antille." *Panorama,* December 31, 260–61.

———. 1994 "Mediobanca la doppia verità." *Panorama,* June 11, 196–201.

Pergolini, Angelo, and Maurizio Tortorella. 1994a. "Apriti Lussemburgo!" *Panorama,* January 14, 32–33.

———. 1994b. "Manda il grano a Wa Fo Wang." *Panorama,* January 28, 10–12.

Perry, Rick. 2002. Letter to Dr. Louis Haydon, July 9. In authors' possession.

Peruzzi, Cesare. 1994. "Sono stato distrutto da un branco di ladri." *L'Espresso,* May 6, 20–30.

Pfister, Bonnie. 2003. "Dolphin-Safe Tuna Debate Returns; Mexico Could Benefit from New Rules." *San Antonio Express News,* April 19.

Phillips, Michael M. 2002. "Narrow Victory for Fast-Track Provides Bush No Clear Mandate." *Wall Street Journal,* July 29.

Philpott, Tom. 2005. "Archer-Daniel Midland's Man at USDA." *Bitter Greens Journal,* April 29. http://bittergreensgazette.blogspot.com/2005.04/archer-daniels-midland-man-atu sda_29.html (accessed January 16, 2007).

Phinney, David. 1995. "Boxer Seeks to Preserve Law on 'Dolphin-Safe' Tuna." *Los Angeles Times,* December 10.

Picciotto, Sol. 1991. "The Internationalization of the State." *Capital and Class* 43: 43–63.

Piccone, Paul. 1995. "Postmodern Populism." *Telos* 103: 45–86.

Pilgrim's Pride, Inc. 2005a. "From Humble Beginnings to Industry Leader." http://www.pilgrimspride.com/aboutus/default.aspx (accessed May 20, 2005).

———. 2005b. "Pilgrim's Pride Mexico." http://www.pilgrimspride.com.mx (accessed September 30, 2005).

———. 2005c. "The Pilgrim's Story." http://www.pilgrimspride.com/aboutus/pilgrimsstory.aspx.

Piore, Michael, and Charles Sabel. 1984. *The Second Industrial Divide: Possibilities for Prosperity.* New York: Basic Books.

Pitelis, Chistos. 1991a. "Beyond the Nation-State? The Transnational Firm and the Nation State." *Capital and Class* 43: 131–52.

———. 1991b. *Market and Non-Market Hierarchies.* Oxford: Blackwell.

———. 1993. "Transnationals, International Organization, and Deindustrialization." *Organization Studies* 14 (4): 527–48.

Polanyi, Karl. 1975. *The Great Transformation.* Boston: Beacon Press.

Ponte, Stefano. 2006. "Ecolabels and Fish Trade: Marine Stewardship Council Certification of the South African Hake Industry." Tralac Working Paper no. 9, August. http://www.tralac.org/scripts/content.php?id=5212.

Pope, Carl. 1997. "Forging an Environmentally Responsible Trade Policy." Testimony of Carl Pope, executive director, Sierra Club, before the House Ways and Means Subcommittee on Trade, March 19. http://www.sierraclub.org/trade/pope.html (accessed January 23, 1998).

Porter, Michael. 1990. *The Competitive Advantage of Nations*. New York: Macmillan/Free Press.

———. 1998. *On Competition*. Boston: Harvard Business School Press.

Portland (OR) Union Register. 1997 "California Union Locals Act Against Corporate Piracy." October 24. http://bari.org/iu120/local/UBC-wcɪw.html.

Poulantzas, Nicos. 1978. *State, Power, Socialism*. London: New Left Books.

Prewitt, Milford. 1999. "Seafood Depletion Issue Pits Chefs' Boycotts vs. Opponents' Claims of 'Junk Science.'" *Nation's Restaurant News,* July 26.

PR Newswire. 1998. "wwF Calls on Corporate America to Protect the Planet," August 17. http://elibrary.bigchalk.com/ *(accessed August 6, 2003)*.

———. 1999. "Steelworkers Announce Lawsuit Against California Department of Forestry on Faulty Sustained Yield Plan Included in Headwaters Forest Deal." April 7. http://www.elibrary.com/ (accessed November 7, 1999).

Prudencio, Rodrigo. 1997. "nwF Efforts Lead to New International Dolphin Protection." National Wildlife Federation. http://www.nwf.org/international/beyond/dolph.html (accessed May 22, 1997).

Pryor-Nolan, Patty. 2000. "What's Cooking." *Minneapolis Star Tribune,* March 30.

Pulliam, Liz. 1997. "Getty Trust Official Settles Thrift Regulatory Charges." March 17. http://www.elibrary.com/ (accessed March 7, 2000).

Quinn, Andrew. 2001. "Appeals Court Upholds Limits on 'Dolphin-Safe' Tag." Reuters, July 23.

Raggi, Carlo. 1994. "E ora Berlini parla di spese varie finora soltanto un castello di bugie." *La Gazzetta del Sud,* March 3, 23.

Raghavan, Chakravarathi. 1996. "Development: fdɪ Selectivity, Conditioning Crucial." Inter-Press Service, English News Wire, June 17. http://www.elibrary.com/ (accessed November 27, 2002).

Ramos, Tarso. 1995. "Wise Use in the West: The Case of the Northwest Timber Industry." In *Let the People Judge,* ed. John Echeverria and Raymond Booth Eby, 82–118. Washington, D.C.: Island Press.

Rao, Rajiv, and Cindy Kano. 1996. "adm Watch: The adm Tale Gets Even Stranger." *Fortune* magazine, August 24, 6–10.

Ravelli, Massimo. 1994a. "Cosí Tonino il 'duro' ha detto no al palazzo." *La Repubblica* (Milan), April 22, 2.

———. 1994b. "E quel giorno Bossi mi chiese i soldi." *La Repubblica* (Milan), January 5, 6.

Raynolds, Laura, and Douglas Murray. 1998. "Yes, We Have No Bananas: Re-Regulating Global and Regional Trade." *International Journal of Sociology of Agriculture and Food* 7: 7–44.

Reed, Susan. 1997. "Tension High After Pepper Spray Used on Protesters." CNN Interactive, October 31. http://www.cnn.com/EARTH/9710/31/pepper.spray.update/.

Regini, Marino. 1992. *The Future of Labor Movements*. Newbury Park, Calif.: Sage Publications.

Reich, Robert B. 1991. *The Work of Nations*. New York: Knopf.

Reimund, Dorm A., J. Rod Martin, and Charles V. Moore. 1981. *Structural Change in Agriculture: The Experience for Broilers, Fed Cattle, and Processing Vegetables*.

Technical Bulletin no. 1648. Washington, D.C.: Economic Research Service/ USDA.

Rerrink, Jack. 1993. "Central Soya Crushes On." *Futures,* August 1. http://www .allbusiness.com/specialty-businesses/398619–1.html.

Reuters. 1997a. "Congress Clears Bill to Lift U.S. Tuna Embargo." Reuters Business Report, July 31. http://www.elibrary.com/ (accessed October 15, 1997).

———. 1997b. "Former ADM Executive Indicted on Conspiracy Charges." Reuters Business Report, November 10. http://www.elibrary.com/ (accessed February 27, 1998).

———. 1998. "Groups to Protest International Investment Treaty." February 6. http://www.elibrary.com/ (accessed November 27, 2002).

———. 1999. "Trade Round Must Exclude Investment Deal—WWF." May 10. http:// www.elibrary.com/ (accessed November 19, 2002).

———. 2001. "Mexico Seeks Urgent Talks with U.S. on Tuna Rift." Reuters Business Report, August 16. http://www.elibrary.com/ (accessed June 28, 2002).

RFBPS (Royal Forest and Bird Protection Society). 2004. "Unsustainable Hoki Should Lose Marine Stewardship Council Accreditation." May 23. http://www.forest andbird.org.nz/mediarelease/2004/0523_unsustainablehoki.asp .

Rhodes, V. James. 1995. "The Industrialization of Hog Production." *Review of Agricultural Economics* 17: 107–18.

Rieff, David. 1993. "Multiculturalism's Silent Partner." *Harper's* magazine, August, 62–72.

Ritchie, Mark. 1998. "Purchasing Power: Consumer Choices and Environmental Protection." Pyramid Communications and Creative Insite, April. http://www .explorebd.ord/newsviews /nv_ritchie1.html (accessed November 9, 1998).

Ritzer, George. 1998. *The McDonaldization Thesis.* London: Sage Publications.

———. 2004. *The Globalization of Nothing: Why So Many Make So Much Out of So Little.* Thousand Oaks, Calif.: Pine Forge Press.

Riva, Massimo. 1993. "Il regime finisce in polvere." *La Repubblica* (Milan), December 29, 2.

Robbins, Mary Alice. 1998a. "CAFO Rule Revisions Offered." Morris News Service, February 19. http://www.amarillonet.com/ns-search/stories/021998.html (accessed August 31, 1999).

———. 1998b. "Feds Ousted From Ruling on CAFOS." Morris News Service, September 15. http://www.amarillonet.com/ns-search/stories/091598.html (accessed August 31, 1999).

———. 1998c. "Final Hog Views Made to Regulators." Morris News Service, June 26. http://www.amarillonet.com/ns-search/stories/062698.html (accessed August 31, 1999).

———. 1998d. "Lawyer Tells TNRCC to Protect Drinking Water." Morris News Service, April 8. http://www.amarillonet.com/ns-search/stories/040898.html (accessed August 31, 1999).

———. 1998e. "New Feedlot Rules Adopted." Morris News Service, August 20. http://www.amarillonet.com/ns-search/stories/082098.html (accessed August 31, 1999).

Robertson, Ronald. 1992. *Globalization: Social Theory and Global Culture.* London: Sage Publications.

Robicheaux, Gina. 1999. "Trade Track—Coalition Sues Commerce for Weakening Standards of Dolphin Safe Labels with Big Cannery Backing." *Capital Report,* July 1. http://www.elibrary.com/ (accessed August 28, 2001).

Robinson, Mike. 1999. "ADM Executives Sentenced in Price-Fixing Scheme." *Buffalo (NY) News,* July 10.

Robinson, William I. 1998. "Beyond Nation-State Paradigms: Globalization, Sociology, and the Challenge of Transnational Studies." *Sociological Forum* 13 (4): 561–94.

———. 2001. "Social Theory and Globalization: The Rise of a Transnational State." *Theory and Society* 30 (2): 157–200.

———. 2004. *A Theory of Global Capitalism: Production, Class, and State in a Transnational World.* Baltimore: Johns Hopkins University Press.

Rogers, George B. 1963. "Credit in the Poultry Industry." *Journal of Farm Economics* 45 (2): 409–15.

Ross, Robert J., and Kent C. Trachte. 1990. *Global Capitalism: The New Leviathan.* Albany: State University of New York Press.

Rostow, W. W. 1960. *The Stages of Economic Growth: A Noncommunist Manifesto.* Cambridge: Cambridge University Press.

Roth, Daniel. 1997. "The Ray Croc of Pigsties." *Forbes,* October 13. http://www.forbes.com/forbes/1997/1013/6008115a.html.

Roy, Ewell P. 1972. *Contract Farming and Economic Integration.* Danville, Ill.: Interstate Printers and Publishers.

Rubner, Alex. 1990. *The Might of the Multinationals: The Rise and Fall of the Corporate Legend.* New York: Praeger.

Sabel, Charles. 2004. *Work and Politics.* Cambridge: Cambridge University Press.

Sabel, Charles, and Jonathan Zeitlin, eds. 2002. *World of Possibilities.* Studies in Modern Capitalism. Cambridge: Cambridge University Press.

Sablatura, Bob. 1998. "Redwoods, Not Red Ink, May Have Motivated FDIC Against Hurwitz." *Houston Chronicle,* July 19.

Sachs, Caroline. 1983. *The Invisible Farmers: Women in Agricultural Production.* Boulder, Colo.: Westview Press.

Saitas, Jeffrey A. 1998. Letter to U.S. Senator Kay Bailey Hutchinson, October 1. In authors' possession.

Salia, Saul B., and Virgil J. Norton. 1974. *Tuna: Status, Trends, and Alternative Management Arrangements.* Program of International Studies of Fishery Arrangements, paper no. 6. Washington, D.C.: Resources for the Future.

Salmans, Sandra. 1990. "Labels Go Green." *Marketing and Media Decisions,* January, 84.

Sama, Carlo. 1993. "Testimony to the Trial of Sergio Cusani." *Il Processo Cusani,* RAI TV, Milan, Italy, December.

Samudra. 1996a. "Comment: Going Green about the Gills." Report no. 15, August. http://www.gmt2000.co.uk/apoints/icfs/english/samudra/issue_15/edit.htm (accessed November 7, 1997).

———. 1996b. "The Mantle of 'Going Green.'" Report no. 15, August. http://www.gmt2000.co.uk/apoints/icfs/samudra/issue_15/sam15_2.htm (accessed November 7, 1997).

———. 1996c. "New Hope for Marine Fisheries." Report no. 15, August. http://www.gmt2000.co.uk/apoints/icfs/samudra/issue_15/sam15_1.htm#AR T4 (accessed November 7, 1997).

———. 1996d. "A View from the Third World." Report no. 15, August. http://www.gmt2000.co.uk/apoints/icfs/samudra/issue_15/sam15_2.htm (accessed November 7, 1997).

———. 1996e. "Whose Labels? Whose Benefit?" Report no. 15, August. http://www.gmt2000.co.uk/apoints/icfs/samudra/issue_15/sam15_1.htm#AR T5 (accessed November 7, 1997).

Sandel, Michael J. 1996. *Democracy's Discontent: America in Search of a Public Philosophy.* Cambridge, Mass.: Belknap Press of Harvard University Press.

Sanderson Farms. 1999a. "Sanderson Farms: Building Tradition." 1999 Annual Report.

———. 1999b. "Sanderson Farms: Simply the Best." http://www.sandersonfarms.com/info/where.html (accessed May 18, 1999).

———. 2005. "Welcome to Sanderson Farms." http://www.sandersonfarms.com/home/welcome.html (accessed September 19, 2005).

Sanderson, Steven. 1985. "The Emergence of the 'World Steer': Industrialization and Foreign Domination in Latin American Cattle Production." In *Food, the State, and International Political Economy,* ed. F. L Tullis and W. L. Hollist, 123–48. Lincoln: University Press of Nebraska.

Sassen, Saskia. 1996. *Losing Control? Sovereignty in an Age of Globalization.* New York: Columbia University Press.

———. 1998. *Globalization and Its Discontents.* New York: New Press.

———. 2000. "Territory and Territoriality in the Global Economy." *International Sociology* 15 (2): 372–93.

Satterfield, Theresa. 1996. "Pawns, Victims, or Heroes: The Negotiation of Stigma and the Plight of Oregon's Loggers." *Journal of Social Issues* 52 (1): 71–83.

Schiffman, Susan. 1998. "Livestock Odors: Implications for Human Health and Well-Being." *Journal of Animal Science* 76: 1343–55.

Schnaiberg, Allan. 1980. *The Environment: From Surplus to Scarcity.* New York: Oxford Press.

Schoon, Nicholas. 1998. "Environment: UN Launches Battle to Save the Oceans." *The Independent* (London), January 13.

Schott, Jeffrey J. 2003. "Unlocking the Benefits of World Trade." *The Economist,* U.S. ed, November 1.

Schumpeter, Joseph A. 1962. *Capitalism, Socialism, and Democracy.* New York: Perennial Press.

Scott, David Clark. 1991a. "Mexico Chafes as US Revisits Ban on Tuna Imports Involving Dolphin Kills." *Christian Science Monitor,* February 27.

———. 1991b. "Mexico Wins Battle over US Tuna Ban, But Backs Off to Save Image, Trade Talks." *Christian Science Monitor,* September 27.

Scott, Michael. 1998. "The Tuna-Dolphin Controversy." *Whalewatcher,* August. http://maninnature.com/Fisheries/Tuna/tuna1a.html.

Seaboard Corporation. 2003a. "About Us—Seaboard Corporation." http://www.seaboardcorp.com/aboutus.aspx (accessed October 31, 2003).

———. 2003b. "Pork Division—Seaboard Corporation." http://www.seaboardcorp.com/pork.aspx (accessed November 7, 2003).

Searle, Robert, Susan Colbey, and Katie Smith Milway. 2004. "Moving Eco-Certification Mainstream." Bridgespan Group. http://www.bridgespangroup.org/kno_articles_ecocertification.html.

Seidenstein, Sharon. 1996. "The Junk Bond Boss Meets the Ancient Sequoia." *Dollars and Sense,* September 19.

Selinger, Marc. 1998. "Nations Drop Efforts on Global Investment Deal." *Washington Times,* December 5.

Shabecoff, Philip. 1993. *A Fierce Green Fire: The American Environmental Movement.* New York: Hill and Wang.

Sharecoff, Philip. 1990. "Big Tuna Canners Act to Slow Down Dolphin Killings; 70% of Market Affected; 3 Concerns Will Stop Buying Fish Caught in Nets That Are Trapping Mammals." *New York Times,* April 13.

Shon, Melissa. 1992. "Lysine Price Hits a Low—Producers Feel Pinch." *Chemical Marketing Report,* June 22, 14–15.

Siegmann, Heinrich. 1986. "Discussion: Environmental Policy and Trade Unions in the United States." In *Distributional Conflicts in Environmental Resource Policy,* ed. Allan Schnaiberg, Nicholas Watts, and Klaus Zimmermann, 315–27. Berlin: Gower.

Simpson, Scott. 2001a. "B.C. Salmon Industry Seeks Ecological Certification: Industry's Ability to Meet Global Council's Standards Hangs on Sustainability Question." *Vancouver Sun,* April 26.

———. 2001b. "Sierra Club Threatens Salmon Industry: Ecological Certification to Be Opposed." *Vancouver Sun,* May 1.

Singh, Kavaljit. 2003. "Keep Investment Pacts Off Cancun's Agenda." *Financial Times,* July 7.

Sklair Leslie. 2001. *The Transnational Capitalist Class.* Oxford: Blackwell.

Sklar, Richard. 1976. "Postimperialism: A Class Analysis of Multinational Corporate Expansion." *Comparative Politics* 9 (1): 75–92.

———. 1999. "Postimperialism: Concepts and Implications." In *Postimperialism and World Politics,* ed. David Becker and Richard Sklar, 11–76. Westport, Conn.: Praeger.

Skorneck, Carolyn. 1997. "Senate Votes to Remove Tuna Embargo: Nets Must Be Proven Not to Harm Dolphins." *Denver Rocky Mountain News,* July 31.

Skow, John. 1994. "Redwoods: The Last Stand." *Time* magazine, June 6. http:// www.time.com/time/magazine/article/0,9171,980854,00.html.

———. 1998. "The Redwoods Weep." *Time* magazine, September 28. http://www .gapsucks.org/gwa/history/02-time/.

Skully, David. 1998. "Opposition to Contract Production: Self-Selection, Status, and Stranded Assets." Paper Presented at the annual meeting of the American Agricultural Economics Association, Salt Lake City, Utah, August.

Smart, Barry. 1992. *Modern Conditions, Postmodern Controversies.* London: Routledge.

Smelly. 1996. "wwf and Unilever to Use Market Forces in Bid to Halt Fisheries Decline."   http://dspace.dial.pipex.com/town/parade/hw22/smelly.html (accessed July 15, 1998).

Smith, David A. 2007. "Politics and Globalization: An Introduction." *Research in Political Sociology* 15: 1–23.

Smith, James F., and Chris Kraul. 2001. "The Fox Visit: Joint Vision to Evolve Step by Step, Fox Says." *Los Angeles Times,* September 5.

Smith, Rod. 1995. "Sanderson Farms Expands 114% in First Phase of Growth Strategy." *Feedstuffs* 67 (8): 6.

Smithfield. 1999–2000. "Smithfield Food, Inc." http://www.Smithfield.com/.

Sorkins. 1997. "adm & Company or Archer Daniels Midland & Company." Directory of Business and Government. http://www.sorkins/com/top100 (accessed October 27, 1997).

Sproul, John. 1998. "Sustainable Fisheries Certification and Labeling Protocol."

Ocean98.org. http://www.ocean98.org/ocean98/Sproul.html (accessed July 8, 1998).

Spybey, Toni. 1996. *Globalization and World Society.* Cambridge: Polity Press.

State of Texas, Office of the Governor. 2004. http://www.governor.state.tx.us/priorities/ecodev.

Steinberg, Philip E. 1999. "Fish or Foul: Investigating the Politics of the Marine Stewardship Council." Paper presented at the conference "Marine Environmental Politics in the 21st Century," MacArthur Program on Multilateral Governance, Institute for International Studies, University of California, Berkeley, March 23. http://globetrotter.berkeley.edu/macarthur/marine/participants.html (accessed December 19, 2006).

Stiglitz, Joseph. 2003. *The Roaring Nineties.* New York: W. W. Norton.

Stille, Alexander. 1996. *Excellent Cadavers: The Mafia and the Death of the First Italian Republic.* New York: Pantheon Books.

St. Joseph (MO) Morning Sun. 2000a. "City Fears More Jobs than Workers if Plant Moves In." MorningSun.net, August 29. http://www.morningsun.net/stories/082900/kan_0829000022.shtml (accessed November 11, 2003).

———. 2000b. "Seaboard Eyes Northern Kansas Town." MorningSun.net, August 16. http://www.morningsun.net/stories/081600/kan_0816000018.shtml (accessed November 11, 2003).

———. 2000c. "St. Joseph Being Considered for Meatpacking Plant, Report Says." MorningSun.net, February 29. http://www.morningsun.net/stories/022900/kan_0229000018.shtml (accessed November 11, 2003).

Storm, Rick. 1998. "Hog Plant Interested in 3 Cities." *Amarillo Globe-News,* February 19.

———. 2001. "Officials Mum on Possible Seaboard Plant in Dumas." *Amarillo Globe-News,* December 14.

———. 2002a. "Dumas EDC Draws Some Ire over Seaboard." *Amarillo Globe-News,* January 12.

———. 2002b. "Dumas OKs Sale of Water." *Amarillo Globe-News,* January 22.

———. 2002c. "Dumas to Discuss Water for Hog Plant." *Amarillo Globe-News,* January 17.

———. 2002d. "Moore Resolution May Help Seaboard." *Amarillo Globe-News,* February 2.

———. 2002e. "Seaboard Continues Applying for Permits." *Amarillo Globe-News,* June 20.

———. 2002f. "Seaboard Picks Moore Co. Site for Pork Facility." *Amarillo Globe-News,* February 6.

———. 2002g. "Seaboard Seeks New Hog Permit." *Amarillo Globe-News,* June 8.

———. 2002h. "State OKs Hog Farm Near Pampa." *Amarillo Globe-News,* August 24.

Strand-Rangnes, Margaret. 1998. "MAI in 'Deep Freeze'—the Fight Continues." MAI-NOT Listserv, December 9. In authors' possession.

Strobel, Frederick R. 1993. *Upward Dreams, Downward Mobility.* Lanham, Md.: Rowman and Littlefield.

Stroh, Leslie. 1996. "The Four R's of International Trade." *The Exporter,* November. http://www.exporter.com/sr/xnvsrls.htm (accessed January 23, 1998).

Stroud, Jerri. 1998. "Hog-Producing Giant Created in Missouri: Continental Grain Plans to Buy Standard Farms: Environmentalist Slams Both." *St. Louis Post-Dispatch,* January 9.

Stull, Donald, Michael J. Broadway, and David Griffith, eds. 1995. *Any Way You Cut It: Meat Processing and Small-Town America.* Lawrence: University Press of Kansas.

Suri, Sanjay. 2003. "After Trade, a Mess over Investment." Global Policy Forum, September 5. http://www.globalpolicy.org/socecon/bwi-wto/maimia/2003/0905wtio.htm.

Sutcliffe, Bob. 2004. "World Inequality and Globalization." *Oxford Review of Economic Policy* 20: 1.

Sutton, Michael, and Caroline Whitfield. 1996. "A Powerful Arrow in the Quiver." *Samudra,* report no. 16, November. http://www.gmt2000.co.uk/apoints/icfs/english/samudra/issue_16/art7.htm (accessed November 7, 1997).

Sweezy, Paul. 1942. *The Theory of Capitalist Development.* New York: Oxford University Press.

Szala, Ginger. 1992. "Ferruzzi Finale?" AllBusiness, February 1. http://www.allbusiness.com/specialty-businesses/281652-1.html.

Talley, Tim. 1998. "Oklahoma Hog Farmers Say Bill Would Hurt Industry." *Amarillo Globe-News,* May 27.

Tamburini, Fabio. 1994a. "Ferruzzi una e trina." *La Repubblica* (Milan), January 25, 44.

———. 1994b. "Grazie Don Enrico, suo Raul." *La Repubblica* (Milan), February 24, 47.

———. 1994c. "Inchiesta Ferruzzi entra Mediobanca." *La Repubblica* (Milan), May 19, 48–49.

Taylor, Andrew. 1990. "Canners' 'Dolphin-Safe' Vows Spur Tuna Labeling Bills." *Congressional Quarterly* 48 (20): 1553.

Taylor, Burton. 2001. "Foes Cheer as Elwood Mayor Announces News." *St. Joseph (MO) News-Press Online,* March 14. http://www.stjoenews-press.com/print.asp.031401.shtml (accessed November 12, 2003).

Taylor, Chantell. 1998. "Rage Against the Machine." *Dollars and Sense,* July 17, 10.

Taylor, Mark. 1997. "Here Comes Chicken Big." *Insight,* January, 27–33.

Telicon. 2001. "SB1339—as Finally Passed." http:www//telicon.com/ (accessed May 29, 2001).

Tennesen, Michael. 1989. "No Chicken of the Sea." *National Wildlife* 27 (April–May): 10–13.

Thornton, Philip. 2003. "WTO/Cancun." *The Independent* (London), September 15.

Thu, Kendall. 1996a. "Piggeries and Politics: Rural Development and Iowa's Multibillion Dollar Swine Industry." *Culture and Agriculture* 53: 19–23.

———, ed. 1996b. *Understanding the Impacts of Large-Scale Swine Production.* Ames: Iowa State University Press.

Thu, Kendall, and E. Paul Durrenberger, eds. 1998. *Pigs, Profits, and Rural Communities.* Albany: State University of New York Press.

Thurston, Charles. 1990. "Save-the-Dolphin Drive to Spur Asia Tuna Imports: Some Suppliers Out of Stock." *Journal of Commerce and Commercial,* April 18, 1A.

Time. 1990. "Tuna Without Guilt." April 23, 63.

Tobin, Bernard F., and Henry B. Arthur. 1964. *Dynamics of Adjustment in the Broiler Industry.* Boston: Harvard University Press.

Total Health. 2001. "Fish for Our Future." July 1, 14.

Trachtman, Joel P. 1992. "International Trade—Quantitative Restrictions—National Treatment—Environmental Protection—Application of GATT to U.S. Restrictions on Import of Tuna from Mexico and other Countries." *American Journal of International Law* 1 (January): 142–51.

Trees Foundation. 1997. "The Headwaters Forest Stewardship Plan." October 7. http://www.treesfoundation.org/affiliates/30/pdfs/HFSP.pdf.

TRPP (Texans for Responsible Poultry Production). 1999a. Monthly Newsletter, April 12. In authors' possession.

———. 1999b. Monthly Newsletter, May 2. In authors' possession.

———. 2000. Monthly Newsletter, February 22. In authors' possession.

Tyson Foods, Inc. 2004–5. "2004–2005 Investor Fact Book." http://www.tysonfoods inc.com/.

———. 2005a. "About Tyson International." http://www.tysonfoodsinc.com/international.

———. 2005b. "Tyson Foods, Inc. Announces International Initiatives." http://www.tysonfoodsinc.com/corporate/news/.

Uhlig, Mark A. 1991. "U.S.-Mexico Pact Faces Hurdle on Tuna Fishing." *New York Times,* April 4.

Unilever. 1998. "Press Pack." http://www.unilever.com/public/generic/presspack.doc (accessed July 20, 1999).

———. 2001. "Unilever to Offer Sustainable Fish from New Zealand with MSC Logo." http://www.unilever.com/news/pressreleases/2001/EnglishNews_1797.asp (accessed November 19, 2003).

United Nations. 1999. *Annual Human Development Report.* New York: United Nations.

———. 2002. *Annual Human Development Report.* New York: United Nations.

USDA/NASS (United States Department of Agriculture/National Agricultural Statistics Service). 2002. *Poultry Production and Value 2001 Summary.* http://usda.mannlib.cornell.edu/usda/nass/PoulProdVa//1990s/1992/PoulProd Va-05-00-1992.pdf.

USITC (United States International Trade Commission). 1986. *Competitive Conditions in the U.S. Tuna Industry.* USITC Publication 1912, October. In authors' possession.

———. 1992. *Tuna: Current Issues Affecting the U.S. Industry.* USITC Publication 2547, August. In authors' possession.

US Newswire. 1999a. "Clinton Statement on California's Headwaters Forest." March 2. http://www.elibrary.com/ (accessed November 7, 1999).

———. 1999b. "Final Agreement Reached on Redwoods Transaction." March 2. http://www.elibrary.com/ (accessed November 11, 1999).

Van Esterik, Penny. 1999. "Right to Food, Right to Feed, Right to Be Fed: The Intersection of Women's Rights and the Right to Food." *Agriculture and Human Values* 16 (2): 225–32.

Vansickle, Joe. 2003. "Pork Exports Rise Again." *National Hog Farmer,* March 15. http://nationalhogfarmer.com/ar/farming_pork_exports_rise.

Vickers, Robert J. 1989. "Dolphin Kill Label Sought for Tuna Cans." *Los Angeles Times,* October 5.

Vogeler, Ingolf. 1981. *The Myth of the Family Farm: Agribusiness Dominance in U.S. Agriculture.* Boulder, Colo.: Westview Press.

Wade, Robert H. 2004. "Inequality and Globalization: Comment on Firebaugh and Goesling." Center for Global, International, and Regional Studies, paper CBIRS-2004-10, November 12. http://repositories.cdlib.org/cgirs/CGIRS-2004-10.

Wagner, Naomi. 1997. "We Want the Whole Thing Back!" Industrial Workers of the World, May 16. http://www.iww.org/unions/iu120/local-1/PALCO/NWagner1.shtml.

Walker, Richard A. 1997. "Fields of Dreams, or the Best Game in Town." In *Globalizing Food: Agrarian Questions and Global Restructuring,* ed. David Goodman and Michael J. Watts, 273–84. London: Routledge.

Wallace, Amy. 1991. "Dolphin-Safe Tuna Fishing Is Aim of Bumble Bee Study." *Los Angeles Times,* May 2.

Wallerstein, Immanuel. 2005. "After Development and Globalization, What?" *Social Forces* 83 (3): 1263–78.

Walz, Jane. 1998. "Government-Based Eco-labels: Not MSC." *Global Aquaculture Advocate,* August 1. http://www.gaaliance.org/august98.html (accessed November 9, 1988).

Wastler, Allen R. 1992. "Tuna Importers Struggle to Escape Embargo's Snag." *Journal of Commerce and Commercial,* February 10, 1A.

Waters, Malcolm. 2002. *Globalization.* 2d ed. London: Routledge.

WATT PoultryUSA. 2001. "Nation's Top Broiler Companies." Vol. 2, no. 21: 26D.

Wayburn, Peggy. 1978. "Jobs and the Environment." *Environment* 20 (April): 34–39.

WCC (World Council of Churches). 1998. "WCC Warns Churches of Proposed Multilateral Agreement on Investment." March 19. http://www.globalpolicy.org/socecon/bwi-wto/maiwcc.htm (accessed December 29, 2003).

WDM/FOE (World Development Movement/Friends of the Earth). 2003. "Investment and the WTO: Busting the Myths." June. http://www.foe.co.uk/resource/briefings/invesment_and_the_wto_bu s t.pdf.

Weddig, Lee J. 1997. "The Proposed Marine Stewardship Council—Some Concerns." National Fisheries Institute, April 15. http://www.nfi.org/weddigbrussels.html (accessed November 7, 1997).

Weinberg, Bill. 1997. "California Screaming: Police Torture of Redwood Crusaders Sparks National Outrage; Headwaters Forest Still Hangs in the Balance." The Shadow, November 15. http://www.mediafilter.org/shadow/S43/S43california.html.

Weisbrot, Mark. 1998. "A Corporate Bill of Rights?" Knight-Ridder/Tribune Media Services, September 15. http://www.cepr.net/index.php/op-eds-columns/op-eds-columns/a-corporate-bill-o f-rights/.

Weiss, Kenneth R. 2003a. "Court Blocks Easing of 'Dolphin-Safe' Tuna Labeling Rules." *Los Angeles Times,* April 11.

———. 2003b. "Regulators Hold Off on 'Dolphin-Safe' Tuna Labeling Change." *Los Angeles Times,* January 10.

Welch, Lanie. 2003. "Anchorage Daily News, Alaska Fish Report." *Anchorage Daily News,* May 5.

Wellford, Harrison. 1972. *Sowing the Wind.* New York: Grossman Publishers.

Welsh, Rick. 1996. *The Industrial Reorganization of U.S. Agriculture: An Overview and Background Report.* Policy Studies Report no. 6. Greenbelt, Md.: Henry A. Wallace Institute for Alternative Agriculture.

———. 1997. "Vertical Coordination, Producer Response, and the Locus of Control over Agricultural Production Decisions." *Rural Sociology* 62 (4): 491–507.

Western, Bruce. 1995. "A Comparative Study of Working-Class Disorganization: Union Decline in Eight Advanced Capitalist Countries." *American Sociological Review* 60 (2): 179–201.

WGA (Western Governors' Association). 1997. "Multilateral Agreement on Investment: Potential Effects on State and Local Government." http://www.west gov.org/wga/publicat/maiweb.htm.

Whitley, Chris. 1995. "Sanderson Farms One Step Closer After Council Meeting." *Bryan/College Station (TX) Eagle,* April 3.

Williamson, Michael. 1996a. "Case Study: Dolphin Safe or 'Dolphin Safe' Tuna." Reuters, June 9. http://whate.simmons.edu/archives/whalenet/0186.html (accessed August 5, 1997).

———. 1996b. "Case Study Dolphin Safe II—Dolphin Deadly Bill Advances." U.S. Newswire, June 9. http://whate.simmons.edu/archives/whalenet/0187.html (accessed August 5, 1997).

Wilson, Janet.1999. "Uneasy Partnerships Form over Environmental Issues: Business, Green Groups, Corporations Take a Different Tack." *Los Angeles Times,* July 18.

Witherell, William H. 1996a. "An Agreement on Investment." OECD Observer 202 (October–November): 6–9.

———. 1996b. "OECD's Multilateral Agreement on Investment and Its Work on Trade and Competition Policy." Remarks for Overseas Development Council Conference "Shaping the Trading System for Global Growth and Employment," Washington, D.C., November 12.

———. 1997. "Developing International Rules for Foreign Investment. OECD's Multilateral Agreement on Investment." *Business Economics* 32 (1): 38–43.

World Stewardship Institute. 1997. "What Is the Debt for Nature Swap?" February 28. http://www.ecostewards.org/hu/hdfn.html (accessed September 19, 1998).

Wright Analysis. 2000. "Nippon Meat Packers, Inc." http://profiles.wisi.com /profiles/scripts/corpinfo.asp?/cusip = C39293490.htm (accessed June 6, 2000).

WTO (World Trade Organization). 2003. "Day 5: Conference Ends Without Consensus." September 14. http://www.wto.org/english/thewto_e/minist_e/min03_3e/ min03_14sept _e .htm (accessed January 12, 2004).

WWF (World Wildlife Fund). 1996a. "Moving Market in Favor of Fish." WWF News. http://www.wwf-uk.org/news/news1.htm (accessed November 22, 1997).

———. 1996b. "Worldwide Interest in MSC Grows Rapidly." http://www.panda.org/ endangeredseas/msc/vol2news/page2.html (accessed July 8, 1998).

———. 1996c. "The WWF Endangered Seas Campaign." http://www.wwf-uk.org/ species/marine/fish6.html (accessed November 7, 1997).

———. 1997a. "Sainsbury's Is First Retailer to Register Support for Marine Stewardship Council." http://www.panda.org/endangeredseas/pressrelease9.html (accessed July 8, 1998).

———. 1997b. WWF Annual Report.

———. 1998a. "Consumers Have a Role to Play in Halting the Fishing Crisis." http://www.worldwildlife.org/500day/actionkit/msc.htm (accessed November 9, 1998).

———. 1998b. "Fishery Stakeholders Endorse MSC." http://www.panda.org/endan geredseas/msc/vol3news/page1.html (accessed July 8, 1998).

———. 1998c. "John Gummer Appointed Chairman of Marine Stewardship Council." http://www-uk.org/news/news58.html (accessed July 8, 1998).

———. 1998d. "WWF and the Marine Stewardship Council: New Hope for World Fisheries." http://www.panda.org/wwfintlink/news/press/news_177fl.htm (accessed November 9, 1998).

———. 2004. "Success Stories: South African Hake Becomes First African MSC-Certified Fishery." http://www.panda.org/how_ you_ can-help/successes/index .cfm?uNewsID = 13149 (accessed January 9, 2007).

WWIM (Who's Who in Meat). 2000. "Seaboard Farms Finds Site for New Hog Plant." August 31. http://www.spcnetwork.com/mii/20000/000879.htm (accessed November 11, 2003).

Xinhua News. 1996. "Indonesia Rejects Multilateral Agreement on Investment." December 3. http://www.elibary.com/ (accessed September 21, 1997).

Yergin, Daniel, and Joseph Stanislaw. 1998. *Commanding Heights: The Battle Between Government and the Marketplace That Is Remaking the Modern World.* New York: Simon and Schuster.

Young, Nancy. 2002a. "NPD Gets Nod for Swine Facility." *Pampa (TX) News,* June 4.

———. 2002b. "Pig Farm Comments Slow TNRCC." *Pampa (TX) News,* April 24.

———. 2002c. "Pig Protest Letters Flood TNRCC Offices." *Pampa (TX) News,* July 4.

Young, Nina M. 1996. "Protecting Dolphins and the Ocean Ecosystem." Statement before the Subcommittee on Oceans and Fisheries of the Senate Committee on Commerce, Science, and Transportation, April 30. http://www.edf.org.pubs/ Filings/96.04.03.a_tuna.dolphin.htm (accessed September 25, 1997).

Zurlo, Stafano. 1994. "Processo Cusani, Istruzione per l'uso." *L'Europeo,* January 19, 26–31.

INDEX

Rural Studies Series

Clare Hinrichs, General Editor